D1006319

LINEAR ORDER

AMSTERDAM STUDIES IN THE THEORY AND HISTORY OF LINGUISTIC SCIENCE

E. F. KONRAD KOERNER, *General Editor*

Series IV – CURRENT ISSUES IN LINGUISTIC THEORY

Advisory Editorial Board

Volume 7

Jürgen M. Meisel & Martin D. Pam (eds.)

Linear Order and Generative Theory

LINEAR ORDER AND
GENERATIVE THEORY

edited by

Jürgen M. Meisel & Martin D. Pam

Gesamthochschule Wuppertal

JOHN BENJAMINS NORTH AMERICA, INC.
One Buttonwood Square - 202
Philadelphia, PA 19130

DISTRIBUTOR

AMSTERDAM / JOHN BENJAMINS B. V.

1979

TABLE OF CONTENTS

PREFACE

The term "word order studies" designates an area of syntax which has become an increasingly central theme in linguistic research. Since, in at least a narrow sense, syntax *is* the study of how meaningful elements are put together to form sentences, a preoccupation with word order would seem inherent in any syntactic study. However, the focus implied by "word order studies" is anything but trivial, going as it does to the heart of two vital areas of linguistic theory: language universals, and the form of linguistic models. The first area has a long tradition, its roots going back to the first modern attempts at language typology in the early nineteenth century. The current surge of interest, translating typological categories into the interest in language universals stimulated by the generative-transformational model, goes back to Greenberg (1963). His pioneering article has served as the point of departure for most of the work in the area of synchronic universals, and his continuing work has provided the inspiration for the study of diachronic universals. Greenberg's work has not only been taken up by those working in the field of descriptive linguistics, it has profoundly influenced the work of the generative-transformational school of linguistics. This is evident in the frequent use of Greenberg's criteria in the postulation of underlying word order. Further questions are: is there a universal underlying word order, is underlying word order linear, what kinds of movement rules are there?

A recent collection of papers on word order (Li, ed., *Word Order and Word Order Change*) presents a variety of views on individual aspects of word order. The present collection of papers offers the reader an oppor-

tunity to examine some of the more recent ideas in this broad area, con-
centrating on some of the more controversial issues within the generative-
transformational model.

The first paper, by Nigel Vincent, is a general review of word order
studies. After explaining such basic theoretical distinctions as the difference between real versus descriptive order and of iconic versus symbolic order, he goes on to summarize the treatment of word order in the major variants of the generative-transformational schools, i.e. Standard
Theory, Case Grammar and Relational Grammar. The treatment of word order
in typological studies is also considered.

The next five papers form, in a sense, the core of the volume. The
discussion of word order within the generative-transformational model is
a reflection of the particular problems which linear order presents for
this model. In models which simply categorize rather than relate disparate
sets of surface facts, a listing of all occurring orders exhausts the syntactic description of the language concerned. In generative-transformational grammar, however, the problems are two-fold:

(i)   First, sentences which have the same "meaning" but different
      orders of constituents have to be formally related.
(ii) Second, the concept of an "underlying structure" as distinct
      from a "surface structure" presents a problem when surface
      structures with different orders have to be related -- that
      of choosing an underlying order. Is it to be one of the occurr-
      ing orders (and if so, which one?), or perhaps some non-occurr-
      ing order? Concepts of linguistic metatheory often complicate
      the problem of reconciling the model with the data.

With the exception of the contribution by Paul Werth, the papers in
this section concentrate on demonstrating that the Chomskyan assumption of
a uniquely ordered underlying structure is not supported either by logical argumentation or empirical data. But whereas Hudson and Sanders favor
a base which is not linearily ordered, Peterson postulates a multi-ordered

base - that is, a base in which all theoretically possible linear orders are generated. For Werth the problem of where to assign linear order is subordinated to that of which discourse-conditioned factors underlie the application of the standard movement rules of transformational grammar.

The next two contributions allow the reader to compare the word order processes in two very closely related Germanic languages, namely German and Yiddish.

Characteristic for both of these papers is the importance they assign to the role of discourse factors in the determination of linear order at the level of the individual sentence. The paper by Beatrice Hall is particularly welcome as a contribution to the study of a well-known but nevertheless little -explored Germanic language.

The volume concludes with a contribution by A. v. Stechow, who addresses himself to the problem of German word order in a theoretical framework different from that of the other authors. This approach, which ultimately derives from the work of Richard Montague, is increasingly developing as a viable competitor to the generative-transformational model. Since this paper is in German, the author has provided an extensive summary in English.

Compiling a reader of this size requires the cooperation of, and diligent effort on the part of, many people. We would like, in the first instance, to thank the publisher, John Benjamins B.V.,for undertaking the project and for the patience he has shown during the years that this work was in progress. We are especially grateful to E.F.K. Koerner for his constant encouragement and his assistance with the technical aspects of the preparation of the manuscript. Undoubtedly the most difficult and not always pleasant task was the actual typing of the manuscript. In performing this onerous duty the following people have earned our gratitude: Dorothea Alberts, Christel Arränz, Sabine Faust and Stephan Zimmer. Thank you all for a difficult job well done!

J.M.M. & M.D.P.

WORD ORDER AND
GRAMMATICAL THEORY

NIGEL VINCENT

It is a trivial, perhaps the most trivial, observation we
can make about the utterances of a language that the various units which
go to make up those utterances emerge from the speaker's mouth in a certain order. One might suspect that this state of affairs simply reflects
the fact that language use occurs in real time, and that the order of
elements is therefore in a rather uninteresting sense a necessary property of human language, just as it is of all physical activities.
Further inspection of the languages of the world reveals, however, that
the situation is a good deal more complicated than this, and that the
ordering properties of natural languages provide a classic instance of
making a virtue of a necessity.[1]

If the order of elements in natural languages was indeed a matter
of temporal necessity, then changing that order should make no appre-
ciable difference to the meaning. Thus, XYZ should be synonymous with
ZYX, XZY, etc. The nearest approximation to this is to be found in the

---

[1] For some clear and helpful remarks on the importance of the inherent
linearity of time to the design of language, see Chafe (1970: Ch.2,3).

so-called 'free word order' languages. For example, Dixon (1972: 59)
writes of Dyirbal, an aboriginal Australian language:

> syntactic relations are marked by case inflections and not
> by word order; word order is remarkably free. ... It should
> be borne in mind that in almost all cases the words could
> be arranged in ANY order. (Emphasis his)

He does note, however, that there is a statistically preferred order
which might be regarded as basic. More generally, one or both of two
possibilities seem to hold for most, if not all, languages. Either there
are strict constraints on the possible sequences of constituents - XYZ
is grammatical but, for example, *ZXY is not: hence in English the
contrasting grammaticality of *Henry hates Martians* versus *Henry Martians
hates*. Or a change in order provokes a change in meaning. This change
in meaning may either relate to the nuclear propositional content -
Martians hate Henry describes a different state of the world from *Henry
hates Martians* - or to a variety of 'pragmatic' differences, as in the
contrast between *Henry hates Martians* and the topicalized version
Martians, Henry hates. In what follows, the assumption will be that no
languages completely ignore the dimension of word order in achieving the
complex mapping between meanings (taking this term in its broadest
sense) and physically realized utterances. If it should turn out that
there are languages where order of elements is exclusively constrained
by the exigencies of linear time, then the grammars of those languages
will contain a random scrambling rule, and nothing further need be said.
The rest of this paper is devoted to a survey of the ways in which the
linear properties of natural languages are handled by a number of
grammatical theories. It should be added immediately that the study does
not pretend to a comprehensive coverage of all linguistic theories that
have ever been proposed. Nor does it limit itself to those which have
evinced a particular interest in the role and functioning of word order.
For example, we shall have virtually nothing to say, except in passing,
about the important work in the Prague-school mould of writers such as
Firbas, Sgall, etc. Equally, the reader will find little mention of
Halliday and his theory of systemic grammar, or more recent developments

from that tradition such as Hudson's (1976) Daughter Dependency Grammar. This is not because we seek in any way to denigrate these scholars or their work, but simply because the present goal is a narrower one. The theories which come up for consideration here are all developments from what is broadly called Generative Grammar, with the possible exception of Montague Grammar, which is included partly because, due to the work of Partee and others, this approach is showing signs of a profitable cross-fertilization with the generative tradition, and partly because the rigorous formalism of the model makes certain points of theoretical interest especially clear.

Before proceeding, then, we must first treat two issues of principle which will have to be taken into account by any theory, namely the question of real versus descriptive order, and second the distinction between iconic and symbolic factors affecting linearization.

(i)   *Real v. descriptive order*

Palmer (1964:146) distinguishes between *sequence* which 'is of observable speech events', and *order* 'of the linguist's constructs'. In similar vein, Tesnière (1965:19 ff) recognizes 'l'ordre structural' and 'l'ordre linéaire'. This distinction between order of elements inherent in the data and orderings imposed for descriptive convenience by the analyst is an important one and must be kept in mind. The problem is transposed, and complicated, by the post-Chomskyan recognition of underlying and surface levels of grammatical structure, but it still remains, and, in order to see its full ramifications, we must briefly examine the number of levels of representation recognized within a grammar and the nature of the ordering at each level. Essentially, four levels have come up for consideration in recent discussions of syntax and semantics:

       a) a level of cognitive or thought structure;
       b) a level of semantic structure, usually characterized
          in terms of predicates and arguments or cases;
       c) a level of syntactic deep structure;
       d) a level of surface syntactic structure.

Of these, (a) and (b) may be taken together, as they are in different ways by both generative semanticists and advocates of the strongest form

of the Sapir-Whorf hypothesis, according to whether a universal set of
cognitive units and structures are taken as defining a universal semantic
base, or whether language-particular semantic configurations are seen
as reflecting cultural differences in cognition. A third alternative is
to separate these two levels as suggested by Langacker (1976), following
here, among others, Hjelmslev and Lamb. In any event, it is clear that
the utilization of ordered statements at these levels is a matter of
descriptive convenience rather than empirical necessity. Thus, a representation of the semantic structures of our example sentence *Henry hates
Martians* in the form (HATE, Henry, Martians) exploits the mathematical
notion of ordered sets to permit the determination of the semantic roles
of the participants, but these roles could equally well be indicated by
case indices associated with the members of an unordered set, viz.
(HATE, Henry$_{Agentive}$, Martians$_{Objective}$) without any gain or loss in
descriptive adequacy.

One signal attempt to make questions of underlying semantic order
susceptible to emirical testing is McCawley's celebrated paper 'English
as a VSO language' (1970). Here it is argued that the function-argument
order which provides a convenient basis for the semantic interpretation
is also justified syntactically for English in that it facilitates the
statement of certain independently motivated rules of the language such
as Subject-Raising. Fairly extensive criticism has, however, subsequently
been mounted by various scholars - notably Berman (1974) - against
McCawley's position (for a convenient summary of the arguments see Radford 1977: 8-12). In particular, it has been noted that VSO order significantly complicates the statement of some rules of English (e.g.
Dative Movement) as well as simplifying others (Berman 1974), and second
that McCawley's ends would be served just as well by SOV order as by VSO
(Postal 1974:31). In view of these considerations and the fact that
McCawley now appears to have abandoned the crucial part of his claims
regarding underlying word order (see McCawley 1973:228), we conclude
that there is at present only support for the view that there are distinct notions of and purposes for linearization according to whether the
level of representation is syntactic or semantic. A further question to

which we shall return in the appropriate section below relates to
whether any linear ordering is to be imposed at level (c) - syntactic
deep structure - for those who believe in the existence of such a
beast.

(ii)   *Iconic v. symbolic order*

A helpful distinction when it comes to dealing with the linearization of elements in surface structure is that between *iconic* and
symbolic aspects of word order. Our understanding of the former term
accords with that of Lyons (1977:105), who writes:

> If the relationship is one of form and meaning, and
> the general principle is resemblance of some kind,
> the form may be described as iconic.[2]

Examples of such parallelism, or 'geometric similarity' as Hockett
(1958:577) has it, between form and meaning are regularly found in the
study of word order. As a simple instance we may note the situation where
the temporal sequence of events is reflected in the order of conjuncts
in a conjoined sentence. Thus, *John opened the door and walked into the
hall* differs from *John walked into the hall and opened the door* both in
linguistic and temporal sequence.[3]

Iconicity is also highly relevant in the area of topicalization,
and more generally in those aspects of sentence construction which traditionally come under the heading of rhetoric. Thus, in an important
article, Li and Thompson (1976) note that topics always occur sentence
initially, whereas subjects, for those languages which permit the independent identification of such a constituent, may occur in one of several positions (SVO, VSO, etc.). There is an iconic relation between the
primary role of the topic as establishing the focus of the discourse and
its sentence-initial position. Other essentially iconic notions per-
taining to order which have figured in the recent literature are Hyman's
(1975) concept of 'afterthought' and Hetzron's (1975) 'presentative
movement'.

---

[2] It should be noted that we are using the term *iconic* for a different
range of phenomena from those which concern Enkvist (1976:11) when he
talks of 'iconic cohesion' as a parameter affecting word order.

[3] For further discussion of temporal conjuctions and linearization, see
Halliday & Hasan (1976 : 261 ff).

The importance of the iconic/symbolic distinction to our previous
discussion of the different uses of order at the semantic and syntactic
levels lies in the fact that it is feasible, though of course not necessary, that iconic aspects of ordering may be incorporated directly
into the semantic representation, and thereby provide a counter-example
to our claim that order in semantic structure is purely a matter of descriptive convenience. We may however permit the iconic side of word order
to stand outside of our generalization on the grounds that it either reflects universal constants such as the time dimension which are themselves
outside language, or because it relates to the general features of the
communicative goals which all languages serve.

Another way of treating this same problem lies in the revival of the
traditional notion of 'grammaticalization' (see, for example, Meillet
1912). According to this view, there exist various universal, generally
semantic, parameters, some of which in the course of time come to take on
a particular importance in the structural patterns of a given language
to the extent that their original motivation may be lost. Thus, Li and
Thompson (1976: 484-5) have argued that 'subjects are essentially grammaticalized topics'. The loss of semantic, or whatever, motivation for a
particular pattern in a language would involve a reduction in iconicity,
and an increase in arbitrariness or symbolicity. Lyons (1977:511, note 12)
makes a similar point citing further references, and in Vincent (1978)
we have suggested that more detailed research into the historical os-
cillation between the iconic and arbitrary poles as they affect word
order is a prime necessity. One speculation as to the direction which
such research might take involves the possibility of differential influence of the iconic factors at different levels of grammatical constituency. Thus, in many languages, the order of clauses in sentences
containing subordinating conjunctions (*John left after the party finished*
and *After the party finished, John left*) seems to be freer than the order
of major sentence constituents (subject, object, etc.), which in turn are
freer than the internal parts of those constituents (determiners, pronouns, etc.).

With the foregoing provisos safely made, we can concentrate on the central issue which confronts all theorists and which may be summed up in the question: Is word order predictable? If the answer is no (either universally or for any particular language), then word order will have to be specified as a brute fact about the language or languages under analysis. However, probably the majority of investigators have assumed that word order can be predicted on the basis of other aspects of sentence or discourse structure, though there has been considerable discussion as to what exactly these other aspects are, and how they are to be incorporated into a formal model of language. I think it is possible to identify three major types of information in terms of which attempts have been made to predict word order.[4]

   (a) syntactic relations - i.e. subject, object, etc.

These are the concepts, in their traditional, intuitive but not precisely specified, sense in terms of which Greenberg's (1963) classic typology of word orders was set out, and they have accordingly remained in typological studies ever since, with most such work going on to link the question of grammatical relations to the wider phenomenon of syntactic/ semantic modification. (See section 7 below for further details.) They are also, of course, at the heart of Relational Grammar (q.v., Section 5). Dissatisfaction with the looseness of the traditional definitions has led to several recent attempts to characterize the linguistic parameters associated with subjecthood, etc. For more extended discussion see the contributions to Li (1976), particularly Keenan (1976), and the recent critique of Keenan's position by Johnson (1977).

   (b) semantic relations - i.e. agent, instrument, locative,etc.

   They are various ways of defining these categories, but they are again part of the traditional armoury of grammatical description, and have recently been revived, notably in the framework of Case Grammar (q.v., Section 4), but also for example in Gruber (1976). As an instance

[4] My three-fold division here corresponds very closely to Lyons' (1977: 506) distinction between logical, grammatical and thematic (or psychological) subjects.

of predictions about linearization being made on the basis of semantic
relations, see Schachter's (1977: 295-6) brief discussion of word-order
in some Philippine languages.

(c) discourse relations

This term is here used to cover a wide range of (generally dichotomous pairs of) terms, such as topic v. comment, theme v. rheme, given v.
new, focus v. presupposition, etc. The area is bedevilled by an enormous
amount of terminological confusion and overlap. THEME, for example, is
generally used to refer to the old or given information in a sentence.
However, it has recently been adopted by Jackendoff (1972) and Gruber
(1976) to designate the most neutral *semantic* relation - roughly equivalent to Fillmore's earlier OBJECTIVE. Similarly, Contreras (1976) equates
THEME with GIVEN, and distinguishes it from TOPIC, whereas Antinucci
(1977) defines TOPIC in terms of GIVEN. For some attempt at terminological
disentanglement, see Dahl (1976) and other contributors to the same
volume, and also Contreras (1976: Ch. 1). The latter is also an excellent
example of an extended study of one particular language in which an
attempt is made to predict word order largely on the basis of discourse
notions.

A further problem arises because the preceding tri-partite division
is not a completely watertight one. The historical process of grammaticalization (see above p. 6) can involve transfer from discourse to
syntax, as when topics become subjects (cf. Li and Thompson (1976) and
Vennemann (1974)). Similarly, Keenan's (1976) parameters for the definition
of subject are based variously on factors of all three kinds. Anderson
(1977: Ch. 3) is very helpful on the interpenetration of syntactic and semantic relations. Where possible, we will cope with these discrepancies
by indicating in our review how each theory handles the different types
of information and their interaction. A fourth determinant of order,
which is probably to be regarded as common to all approaches, though
not always explicitly recognized, is the perceptual one. Vennemann
(1974: 339) refers to what he calls Behaghel's First Law, which states:

'Das oberste Gesetz ist dieses, daß das geistig eng
Zusammengehörige auch eng zusammengestellt wird.'

(The most important law is that what belongs together
mentally (semantically) is placed close together syntactically.)

(Translation - TV)

The motivation here seems plainly that processing and semantic retrieval
will in general be facilitated by syntactic grouping which reflects the
semantic grouping - incidentally, another iconic aspect of syntax. However, cases such as the by now notorious centre-embedding phenomena in
English show that this 'law' cannot always be obeyed, and in these instances another principle, also attributed to Behaghel, this time by
Enkvist (1976), supervenes to move perceptually intrusive or 'heavy'
material to the end of the sentence. This possibility, reflected in TGG
by such rules as Extraposition, Heavy NP Shift, Extraposition from NP,
is not widely catered for in most discussions of word order, though it
could presumably be added at no great theoretical cost. Therefore, perceptual factors will not figure greatly in what follows, though they are
of undoubted importance in a global theory of word order. For some further
discussion, see Vincent (1976) and the references cited therein, notably
Kuno (1974).

We now proceed to a model-by-model review of the treatment of word
order within linguistic theory.

1.   Standard Theory (ST)

Since the grammatical models included within this review are
mainly those which grow out of, or are closely linked to, the generative
tradition, it is both fitting and convenient to begin by considering the
way in which word order phenomena are handled in the so-called 'standard
theory' as set out in Chomsky (1965) and a number of associated publications. We immediately hit upon a complication with respect to our previous discussion because of Chomsky's insistence on a level of underlying
structure which is not semantic. Thus debate can arise over deep v. surface order, where the question is in both cases syntactic. This much at
least is clear: that there is no attempt made to predict the basic or
derived order in terms of any other factor. An underlying order is chosen
as basic, and this is encoded directly into the left-right precedence

relations which are defined by the PS-rules. Derived order may vary from
the underlying order to the extent that various transformations can be
motivated to break up underlying constituents and re-position their elements. These mechanisms are too familiar to require further elaboration
here. What, however, we should note are the types of language which pose
problems for this approach. On the one hand, there are 'mixed' word order
languages, such as German, where superficially there is evidence for two
conflicting orders, one of which has to be chosen as basic to meet the
fundamental requirements of the phrase-structure component. Debate may
then arise over which order is to be chosen. Thus, Bach (1962) argues
for German as underlying SOV, with a rule moving the verb to second
position in main clauses. Ross (1970), on the other hand, advocates underlying SVO and a rule to position the verb at the end in subordinate
clauses. It is difficult to avoid the conclusion, however, that debates
such as these are otiose, and an artefact of the frameworks within which
they are conceived.

Problematic, though in a different way, for ST are 'free' word order
languages, if such exist, since once again the formal principles of the
model require what may turn out to be an unnatural decision regarding
underlying order. This is the burden of Staal's (1967) critique, and
similar objections have been raised in Boas (1975) and the various
writings of Sanders (1972, 1975). In the face of these general criticisms,
several variants of ST have been proposed with either unordered base structures (see especially Sanders, 1972, 1975) or multi-ordered ones (Peterson
1971, 1977 and this volume). The viability of these alternatives has recently been reviewed by Bach (1975), who comes to the tentative conclusion that a fixed-order base is to be preferred. Anderson (1977: 72-3)
discusses and rejects Bach's conclusions. The whole question of linear
order and standard theory is extensively examined and exemplified by
Paul Werth in his contribution to the present volume. We need only em-
phasise here the treatment of basic word order as a brute fact, and the
importance of the prior establishment of linear order to the formulation
of many transformations and to Chomsky's (1965) famous 'configurational'
definitions of syntactic relations such as subject and object. The theory

has very little to say on the interaction of word order with semantic
and discourse relations, which are conceived of as belonging to the semantic component (though cf. our discussion of Topicalization in section
2 below), and therefore irrelevant to an 'autonomous' syntax. However,
for a very interesting recent attempt to examine some rules in ST (and
Generative Semantics) from a broader perspective which includes largely
discourse information see Langacker (1974). Otherwise, ST is fairly oblivious of discourse considerations, as might be expected of an essentially sentence as opposed to text-based model of grammar (cf. the remarks of Werth 1977 and this volume).

2.   (Revised) Extended Standard Theory (R)EST

There are a number of recent developments in linguistic theory
proposed by scholars such as Chomsky, Emonds, Bresnan, Jackendoff, etc.
which have come to be known as Extended Standard Theory, and, with the
development of Trace Theory by Chomsky and his associates, Revised Extended Standard Theory. Here is not the place to endeavour to disentangle
the various strands, particularly since word order data does not appear
to be crucial to any of the debates. (R)EST is characterised by an increase
in the importance given to the PS-rules at the expense of a reduction in
the power of the transformational component. A central proposal is
Emonds' (1976) Structure Preserving Constraint, whereby the so-called
'major' transformations are required not to produce derived structures
which could not have been independently generated by the base rules. In
other words, the PS-rules act as a kind of filter constraining the output of the transformations. Since basic word order is defined by the
PS-rules, it follows that, with certain specified exceptions, transformations will not create new word order possibilities. The exceptions
include either such grammatically defined and language particular facts
as the obligatory inversion of Subject and Auxiliary in English, or what
Emonds (1976:9) refers to as 'stylistic' rules.

As an example of the kind of reanalysis (R)EST leads to, let us con-

sider briefly the case of Topicalization.[5] This rule is said to relate
(a) and (b), and applies optionally, in an ST-type model.

> (a) I disapprove of Alphonse.

> (b) Alphonse, I disapprove of.

In Generative Semantics, on the other hand, it would presumably be obligatorily triggered by an appropriate marking on the constituent in
question in semantic representation (compare the proposals for Spanish
in Contreras 1976:82 ff). The derived structure resulting from Topicalization involves Chomsky-adjunction of the topicalized element to the original S-node (cf. Postal 1971:147 and Contreras 1976:83, and Anderson
1977:90 who, citing Gundel 1975, suggests daughter-adjunction). Emonds
(1976:40) proposes that the NP is moved into the initial COMP position,
whereas Chomsky (1977:§0 ff) now argues for the following PS-rules, with
a specific topic position identified for all sentences:

$$\bar{\bar{S}} \rightarrow TOP \quad \bar{S}$$

$$\bar{S} \rightarrow COMP \quad S$$

In either case, the topicalization process has been made to conform to the
word order possibilities defined by the base rules, rather than creating
any new ones.

Increasingly, therefore, as the effects of movement rules such as
Topicalization on linear order are pre-empted in the base, it becomes
clear that cross-linguistic generalizations about word order will have
to be fitted into a universal theory of base rules, though, to my knowledge, this has not yet been attempted. Reconciliation of typological
questions such as those discussed in Section 7 below with proposals of
the sort made by Jackendoff (1977) suggests an interesting and promising
line for future research, though the problems noted for PS-rules in the
remarks on ST in the preceding section still remain.

---

[5] This rule is also known in the literature as Y-Movement. For some discussion, see Postal (1971:142 ff). Werth (1976) argues that there are
distinct processes at work here, but the purposes of our argument are
not thwarted by treating them as a single phenomenon.

3.   Generative Semantics (GS)

For present purposes, the central trait of work in GS is its
monolithic approach to semantics and syntax. Not only are these two domains of language amalgamated into a single component of the grammar, but
no formal differentiation is made between various aspects of meaning.
Where Jackendoff (1972) provides a variety of formal devices - the Thematic
Hierarchy Condition for basic semantic relations; a table of coreference
for pronominalization and related facts; surface structure semantic interpretation for presupposition and focus; etc. - Lakoff (1971: 234-5) unites
all facets of sentence meaning in a single semantic representation:

> Given a syntactic structure $(P_1,\ldots,P_n)$ we define the
> semantic representation SR of a sentence as SR = $(P_1$, PR,
> Top, F,....), where PR is a conjunction of presuppositions,
> Top is an indication of the 'topic' of the sentence, and
> F is the indication of the focus of the sentence. We leave
> open the question of whether there are other elements of
> semantic representation that need to be accounted for.

Although there is not much in the GS literature specifically devoted to
questions of superficial word order, it is clear that with this framework there are the formal means available to make predictions about
linearization on the basis of any of the kinds of factors mentioned in
our preceding discussion (pp.7-8).   Both discourse and semantic relations are present in the underlying structure, and syntactic relations
can be handled configurationally on a cyclic basis, or specified primitively, as in Relational Grammar.

We have already noted the attempt by one of the leading generative
semanticists, McCawley (1970), to motivate syntactically the order which
fits best with their forays into predicate calculus as a notation for
underlying structures. With the failure of these arguments, there is
nothing for it but to recognise that order in SR's is a non-empirical
matter of descriptive convenience. This point is explicitly made in
Parisi & Antinucci (1976: 18-9).

A generative semanticist in spirit, if not in strict practice, is
Wallace Chafe (1970)[6], and he too recognises the irrelevance of linearity
in semantic structure (1970:27-8). It follows, of course, that linear
order must be introduced at some stage in the mapping process between
semantic structure and surface structure. Where GS is not always very explicit regarding the rules whereby this mapping will be achieved, at least
with respect to the kind of general serialization process which concerns
us here, Chafe makes specific proposals building on a distinction between
primary and *secondary linearization*.

> 'Primary linearization involves the linearization of nouns
> and verbs with relation to each other .... Secondary linea-
> rization involves the linearization of the elements within
> each noun and verb - the lexical, derivational and inflec-
> tional units which are present at this stage.' (Chafe 1970:250)

Such a distinction recalls our remarks above (p. 6) concerning the
different nature of linearizing processes at different levels of constituent structure. Chafe's rules are to some extent paralleled by the
Sequence Rules of Hudson (1976: 108-15). Contreras (1976) represents an
attempt to provide an extended analysis along Chafean/GS lines.

4.   Case Grammar (CG)

The heart of CG, as is by now well known, is the representation
of underlying structures as configurations of predicates and associated
cases. The question of deep order therefore evaporates. A linear surface
has still, of course, to be achieved by means of appropriate rules. The
two main exponents of CG, Fillmore and Anderson, differ significantly in
their approach to this problem. Fillmore (1968) follows orthodox TG in
operating with underlying representations conceived in terms of phrase-
structure trees. Rules then operate to move one of the cases, selected
according to a universal hierarchical ranking of possible cases, into subject position (which is by definition initial for English). A set of
'case placement' rules designed to get the constituents of the case repre-

[6] For discussion of Chafe and some of the differences between his approach
and GS, see Langacker's (1972) helpful review.

sentations into the appropriate linear order for the operation of conventional ST-style transformations is worked out in Stockwell, Schachter &
Partee (1973: Ch.2). There are various anomalies in this way of proceeding,
since the rules Fillmore provides apparently convert unordered trees into
ordered ones, or else operate on redundantly ordered initial structures.
Anderson (1971, 1977), by contrast, exploits a dependency formalism with
no implicit or explicit ordering. Fillmore, in recent years, though he has
discussed criticisms and shortcomings of his theory at some length, has
had very little to say on the question of order, and therefore we will
concentrate in what follows on the work of Anderson.

Anderson has devoted considerable attention to problems of word
order and its treatment within the framework of CG. In a recent statement of his views, he writes:

> I am proposing then, to sum up, that 'base structures' are
> unordered, but serialization is introduced cycle-initially
> or pre-cyclically and is invariant throughout the application
> of cyclic rules; and that with respect to these rules of
> serialization languages are either centripetal (i.e. head
> follows modifier - NBV) or centrifugal (i.e. head precedes
> modifier - NBV). (Anderson 1977:74)

The effect of having pre-cyclic, as opposed to post-cyclic linearization
(cf. section 5 on Relational Grammar), is to introduce a constraint which
is in spirit closely akin to Emonds' Structure Preserving Hypothesis - the
underlying word order acts as a condition on the application of syntactic
rules. The difference between Anderson's and Emonds' proposals lies in the
nature of the linearization process itself. Where Emonds regards linear
order as being arbitrarily specified by the PS rules, Anderson (1977:74)
argues that 'Linearization is imposed on the basis of (a) modifier-head
relations and (b) grammatical relations.' For more remarks on the former,
see Section 7 below. The latter term for Anderson includes both semantic
and syntactic relations, the concept of subject, for example, being derived form a neutralization of more fundamental semantic relations. His
view, therefore, is intermediate between Fillmore's original (1968) claims
that the underlying cases and the associated hierarchy are sufficient to

determine subject-position without also having to define an independent
notion of subject[7], and, alternatively, the views of the Relational
Grammarians that subject, object, etc. are to be taken as undefined primitives. Anderson (1977: Ch.3) offers valuable discussion of the difference
between Case and Relational Grammar.

Finally, we should note that discourse-conditioned aspects of order
can be handled within CG by post-cyclic rules, as is also proposed for
Relational Grammar. Alternatively, an EST-style structure-preserving
analysis is also compatible with the model (see Anderson 1977: 89-91).
Fillmore (1968: 57-8) alludes briefly to a distinction between primary
topicalization, equivalent to subjectivalization in his system, and
secondary topicalization. He writes:

> Primary topicalization for English involves position and
> number concord; stylistic changes involving stress-assign-
> ment, late word-order changes, and possibly the 'cleft-
> sentence construction' fall into what might be called
> 'secondary topicalization'.

5. Relational Grammar (RG)

This recent arrival on the linguistic scene takes its inspiration from a course of lectures given by Postal and Perlmutter at the
Linguistic Institute in 1974. These, however, at the date of writing
remain unpublished, but fortunately Pullum (1977) is available as an
exposition of the way facts of word order can be incorporated into such
a model.

Underlying structures in RG take the form of unordered dependency
trees, where the root is a predicate to which are adjoined a number of
nominal dependents bearing primitively specified grammatical relations
(GR's) such as subject, object, indirect object, etc., to that predicate.
These structures then undergo a series of cyclic, relation-changing rules
such as Passive, Raising, etc. A level is definable after all such rules
have applied, generally called 'shallow-structure', and at this point,

---

[7] Fillmore (1977:80) has now accepted the need to recognise subject as a
separate syntactic notion.

in the words of Pullum (1977:250):

> linearization rules assign a basic order to the elements of the
> clause - an order which is ceteris paribus obligatory, the cetera
> being postcyclic rules', after which, '...postcyclic movement rules
> operate to modify the order in ways which may lead to preferred
> or required positioning of constituents that is not attributable
> to linearization.

The postcyclic rules provide the means whereby discourse conditioning
may be incorporated into the eventual order of elements in the syntactic
surface. The basic order, however, is clearly specified in terms of the
syntactic relations which the theory takes as undefined primitives. The
burden of Pullum's paper is to attempt a statement of a universal principle of linearization, based in turn on a universal hierarchy of the
GR's (compare Fillmore's approach to linearization in CG). This principle
is given by Pullum (1977:272) as follows:

> The NP constituents of a clause are linearized in
> their GR hierarchy order, from left to right.

He goes on to comment:

> This (principle - NBV) does not have to be stated in the
> grammar of any particular language. What does have to be
> stated is first, the position of the verb relative to the
> NP's (which is clearly a language-particular matter), and,
> second, any departure from the basic principle which is
> imposed.

The main problem with this approach is to limit the nature of the
permissible 'departures' from the basic principle, since otherwise the
enterprise is reduced to near vacuity. At the time of Greenberg's (1963)
famous survey of word order types it was thought that the only occurring
orders in natural languages in unmarked constructions were SOV, SVO and
VSO, and all these cases can clearly be handled by Pullum's principle
plus a language-particular rule for positioning the verb. Subsequently,
VOS languages such Malagasy, Gilbertese, etc. (see Pullum 1977:254 ff for
a list of other possible candidates and some discussion) were discovered,
thus requiring a special 'departure' permitting the subject to occur in
final position. Derbyshire (1977) has now brought the attention of the
linguistic world to Hixkaryana (and possibly other Carib languages) which

has OVS as a basic order. Thus, the only combination not so far attested
is OSV, and Pullum (personal communication) agrees that any attempt to
state universal principles formulated so as to exclude this single case
would be either impossible or vacuous. In other words, the linearization
rules of RG are irreducibly language-specific, and in this respect do not
differ from the EST proposal to incorporate word order facts into the
PS-rules. The general conclusion therefore seems warranted that syntactic
relations alone are insufficient as a basis for predicting word order
universally.

6. Montague Grammar (MG)

One of the advantages of the persistent concern for formal
rigour which typifies all work in MG is to make very clear the distinction
we have emphasised more than once in this article between semantic and
syntactic order. It is not possible to give a full characterization of
MG here (the interested reader is referred to Partee, 1975, 1976), but
the essential points are as follows. On the syntactic side, MG seeks to
generate pretty well directly the surface structures of English via a
categorial grammar which

> contains two types of rules: the basic lexical rules that
> specify the syntactic category of each primitive element
> ....and the recursive rules that build up the larger phrases.
> Each recursive rule is of the following form:
> (19) *Rule:* If α is of the category C_1 and β is of
> the category C_2, then γ is of the
> category C_3, where $\gamma = F_k (\alpha, \beta)$.
> (Partee 1975:214)

The nature of the function F_k varies, of course, from rule to rule, but
in many cases it is simple concatenation. The word order properties of
English sentences are therefore dealt with in rather brute force fashion
by the syntactic rules, in this respect the system being not unlike the
way in which linear order is encoded directly into the PS-rules in ST
and EST. It should be noted, however, that there is nothing strictly
equivalent to 'deep structure' in MG, nor is it possible to make clearly
the distinction between T-rules and PS-rules.

By general stipulation, for every syntactic rule in MG there is a corresponding translation rule which converts the syntactic representation into a particular formalized language of intensional logic. It is the latter which then becomes the basis for a model-theoretic semantics. In the translation rules there is, for every function F_k in the categorial part, a corresponding function G_k which:

> specifies the particular way in which the interpretations of the parts determine the interpretation of the whole, just as F_k specifies the particular way in which the parts are syntactically combined. (Partee 1975:223)

Thus:

> Syntactic rule S10 combines *slowly* and an intransitive verb phrase like *walk* to give *walk slowly*. The corresponding semantic rule combines their interpretations, *slowly'* and *walk'* to give *slowly' (walk')*.
> (Partee 1975:222)

Here F_k is simple concatenation and G_k is a function-argument structure.[8] The arguments of a predicate may well be more than one, in which case they will form an ordered set, but the ordering is mathematical, not linguistic. In general, then, ordering in the syntactic part is determined by simple inspection of the linear sequence of words and morphemes in the relevant English sentences, while ordering in the intensional logic which forms the basis of the semantic interpretation is established to suit the convenience of that logic. The essential independence of these two notions of ordering could not be more clear.

MG has not yet been sufficiently developed to handle the kind of 'discourse' and 'semantic' relations we have been discussing in previous sections. It should, in all fairness, be pointed out that the initial concern has been for notational rigour as a basis for accurate and precise work on some standard problems of logical semantics. Syntactic naturalness has had to take a back seat, though it is to be hoped that

---

[8] A general way of passing from function-argument representation to linear order has been proposed by Bartsch & Vennemann (1972) in their work on Natural Serialization which is briefly discussed in the next section.

this is only a temporary state of affairs.

7. The Typological Method

Recent typological approaches to word order all draw part, if
not all, of their inspiration from Greenberg's (1963) classic study. In
most of that work, however, the aim was not so much to establish a number
of syntactic/semantic variables which could in turn be used to predict
word order as it was to link word order and other facts about the languages investigated via a series of interacting, implicational generalizations. These implicational relationships were consolidated in subsequent work by Lehmann (1973) and exploited by him in the reconstruction
of the syntax of a dead language (Lehmann 1974). The particular thrust of
Lehmann's work has been along the following lines: first, ignore the position of the subject (always supposing such a constituent can be identified
for the language in question), and then see whether the language has
V(erb) O(bject) or OV order. This is taken as a single instance of a wider
generalization concerning the order of modifier and modified, for the object is regarded as the modifier of the verb, just as an adjective modi-
fies a noun. The languages of the world are seen as dividing into two
classes:

a) modifier precedes the modified or head constituent

b) modifier follows the modified or head constituent

Whether a language falls into class (a) or (b) is usually regarded as an
essentially arbitrary matter, though Vennemann (1974: 358 ff.) suggests
that *ceteris paribus* OV is the ideal order. Hence most typologists must
make an underlying specification of head-modifier order. All other particular facts relating to individual constructions will then follow from
this basic ordering statement.

The common factor which unites the typological approaches is the
need to define the notions of head and modifier. However, in other respects the models adopted may, and do, differ widely. Thus, Anderson (1976)
departs from underlying structures which, as we have already indicated,
are a version of CG using dependency trees. Vennemann (1976) achieves
similar results working from a base which is formulated as a categorial
grammar similar to that used by Montague, while Antinucci (1977) exploits

the predicate-argument system of generative semantics which is developed
in Parisi & Antinucci (1976).

As we have said, the only requirement which unifies these approaches
is that they should avail themselves of a formal notation which permits
the definition of the crucial concept of modification. It is therefore
not surprising that ST has not given rise to typological work, since,
among other things, its formalism for PS rules does not provide naturally
for a definition of heads and modifiers (cf. Robinson 1969, 1970).[9]
Different, on the other hand, is the situation with (R)EST, since one of
the major merits of the $\bar{X}$ Convention used therein is that it does offer
a means to define the relevant notions (cf. Jackendoff 1977:30). To my
knowledge, comparative work in the $\bar{X}$ system - a necessary preliminary
to typological inquiry - has not yet been carried out, but there are signs
that such investigations could have interesting results, since the theory
appears to make different empirical predictions from its competitors.
Thus, on the principle that the X of an $\bar{X}$ is the head of that construction
(see Bresnan 1975, Jackendoff 1977), S will be the head of an $\bar{S}$, i.e.
a sequence of [COMP - S]. Vennemann (1976), on the other hand, is forced
to argue that the COMP is head of such a construction since it follows
the embedded S in a consistently modifier-precedes-head language like
Japanese. Another case where predictions among the various theories differ
concerns the relative position of nouns and adjectives. The standard wisdom is that adjectives precede nouns in OV languages and follow in VO.
English is then treated as a, by no means isolated, exception to this
general rule. A large part of Anderson (1976), however, is devoted to
showing that the adjective in English is in fact the head of an Adj-Noun
construction, and that therefore English is entirely consistent from
a typological point of view.

This last example also raises another, and as yet unsolved, difficulty for the typological method, namely the existence of 'mixed' languages, which exhibit conflicting typological indices in different parts

---

[9] An exception to this is the small literature on the typological implications of Gapping arising out of Ross (1970). See also Maling (1972),
Rosenbaum (1977) and the discussion in Werth (this volume).

of their syntax. Vincent (1976) tackles this situation and its implications for Classical Latin, but the general theoretical difficulty still
remains.

It is perhaps in the diachronic domain that the typological approach
to word order has had its greatest impact, particularly in the work of
Lehmann (1974), Vennemann (1974), and more generally in the contributions
to Li (1975). These scholars share an effort to establish a universally
valid cycle of change, into which attested word order, and associated
typological, shifts can be integrated. Although the details of the individual pathways proposed vary, there is one important common factor,
namely that the movement from one historical stage to the next is mediated
by largely iconic or, as Hyman (1975) calls them, 'natural discourse',
principles. (See also Vincent (1978) for more discussion). Many interesting
prospects for research lie in the reworking of this traditional, though
recently somewhat neglected, view in the light of the more exacting demands
of modern advances in the formal theory of grammar, and it has been our
aim in the present paper to indicate some of these formal ways in which
facts of word order have been incorporated into proposed theories of natural language structure.

IS DEEP STRUCTURE LINEAR?*

GROVER HUDSON

1. INTRODUCTION

The base or phrase structure rules of generative grammars perform "two quite separate functions: they define the system of grammatical relations, and they determine the [linear] ordering of elements of
deep structure" (Chomsky 1965: 123). By the latter function a relationship of linear order (left or right of one another) is established between the morphemes of the first and every subsequent line in a derivation. It is perhaps not obvious that there is no logical necessity for
requiring that both these "quite separate functions" be performed at
once by the phrase structure rules. On the contrary, it is obvious that
since in probably all natural languages at least some morphemes occur in
two or more linear orders relative to one another in surface structure,
some transformational rules will be required which have as part or all
of their function to redetermine the linear ordering of morphemes.

*
An earlier version of this paper appeared in UCLA Papers in Syntax,
No. 2, edited by George Bedell, pp. 51-77, July 1972. The editors of
the present volume would like to thank the Department of Linguistics
at UCLA for their permission to reprint it here. The present version
differs in the addition of Section 6, a few rewordings for clarifica-
tion, the addition of footnotes, and the omission of the last paragraph of the earlier version, which now seems to me to have been at
best unnecessary.

There is therefore a splitting up of the rules which establish linear ordering in the model of generative grammar which requires that deep structure be linear.

It has occasionally been suggested that the phrase structure rules
be limited to performing the categorial function, with the linear ordering function taken over by rules which perform only this function. By
this proposal the structures defined by the phrase structure rules are
conceived of as non-linear. Chomsky (1965: 123-127) briefly discussed
previous proposals along these lines, but dismissed them without substantive counter-argument. J. F. Staal (1967) proposed that such a grammar
was necessary for describing the free word-order phenomenon in Sanskrit,
and also correct on intuitive grounds for universal grammar. Wallace
Chafe (1970) proposed a model of grammar which employs separate linearization rules applying post-transformationally, and Gerald Sanders (1970,
1975a) has argued convincingly that only such a grammar is sufficiently
constrained to be compatible with facts about natural language. The main
purpose of the present paper is to present further evidence that linear
order is absent in deep structure. Three arguments will be presented.

In Section 2 an examination of analyses of the main constituent order of English shows how the requirement that a particular linear order
be established in deep structure leads inevitably to 'paradoxes of analysis': the requirement of linearity forces us to choose some deep order,
but the evidence for one or the other is either contradictory, or non-
existent. Such paradoxes or necessary indeterminacies can never arise if
linear order is only established at the level of post-transformational
structure. The second argument, that of Section 3, is that in its most
general form a transformational rule of a grammar with linear deep structure is reducible to a rule of a grammar with non-linear deep structure.
In other words, at their best grammars with linear deep structure are
notational variants of grammars with non-linear deep structure. This will
be shown through examination of analyses of the main constituent order of
Amharic.

The most important argument that can be given in support of a particular grammar of a language is that it expresses a linguistically sig-

nificant generalization which is unexpressible in other observationally adequate grammars. The purpose of Section 4 will be to show that this is the case for grammars in which linear order is not a characteristic of deep structure, but is instead established by a set of post-transformational rules. These rules are required since this is the earliest level in derivations at which linear order becomes relevant for linguistic description, and also the only level at which information necessary for establishing such order is fully available. Through an examination of dative constructions in English Section 4 will illustrate this higher level of descriptive adequacy attained by a grammar with non-linear deep structure.

2.1. ORDERING PARADOXES IN LINEAR DEEP STRUCTURE

James McCawley (1970) presented an argument that English is in deep structure a VSO language.[1] According to McCawley, English deep structure has the main constituent order VSO, and a "postcyclic" transformation takes the clause-initial verb and puts it in second position. McCawley, indeed, claims that all languages have either VSO or SOV main constituent order in deep structure, and languages that show surface SVO order are always synchronically derived from the former of these by a rule of V-NP inversion. He gave basically two arguments in favor of his analysis of English as a VSO language. The first of these concerned the linear order of logical semantic structure, which he equates with linguistic semantic structure. The second argument purported to show that several English transformational rules may be simplified if deep linear order is VSO.

McCawley says that for most English transformations the linear order of their input is suitably stated as either SVO or VSO. I wish to assume the correctness of this claim, and go on to show that the same is actually true even for those transformations that McCawley claimed are simplified by positing VSO ordered input structures. Hence deep structure (arguments based on the simplicity and generality of transformations) ap-

[1] Let V and O be understood in the general sense, with V including the copula, and O any verb complement.

pears to present no evidence in favor of one or another deep main constituent order. What we do find is that, if we posit and justify a post-
transformational rule which assures SVO ordered surface structures in
English, i.e., a rule which 'corrects' exceptions to SVO order which have
arisen in the course of a derivation, certain simplifications of transformations are achieved, but this is so regardless of what linear order
of main constituents we begin with. First it will be necessary to deal
with the claim that English semantic structure is in VSO order.

2.2. ENGLISH AS A VSO LANGUAGE

McCawley says that first and last positions in a semantic representation are "special", and are therefore reserved for predicates --
as first position is used for predicates in formulas of symbolic logic
(p. 291). He prefaces to this claim the set of sentences (1) intended to
show how logical formulas may effectively serve as semantic representations.

(1)   a. himself
            Only Lyndon pities { b. Lyndon
                                   c. only himself

In question here is not whether semantic representations equal such formulas, but whether there is something necessary about having predicates
in first position in these formulas. Can the suggested semantic representations for (1), given by McCawley as in (2), be rewritten with predicate
second? The formulas of (3) show, not at all surprisingly, that they can.

(2) a. $Only_x(Pity(x, x), Lyndon)$
    b. $Only_x(Pity (x, Lyndon), Lyndon)$
    c. $Only_x(Only_y(Pity (x, y), x), Lyndon)$

(3) a. $((x) Pity (x)) Only_x(Lyndon)$
    b. $((x) Pity (Lyndon)) Only_x(Lyndon)$
    c. $(((x) Pity (y)) Only_y(x)) Only_x(Lyndon)$

First (and last; (2) can obviously be rewritten with predicates last) is
only special in that it is customarily reserved for predicates in such
formulas. The custom leads to a sort of convenience in reading. But we
could learn to read (3) as conveniently as (2).

Yet even when one accepts that the verb is first in English semantic representations, he is still obligated to determine, as McCawley noted,

> whether such semantic representations as (2) are syntactically justified, i.e., the question of whether a dividing line can be found between 'early' transformations, which give evidence of operating on inputs that have predicates at the beginning of clauses, and 'later' transformations, which give evidence of applying to structures with predicate second... (p. 291)

Such determination is necessary since if the rule which applies to universal predicate first semantic structures and puts the verb second in surface SVO languages like English applies before the first transformation, then ordering pre-transformational structure VSO would be completely arbitrary, as SOV order would be completely equivalent, and, besides, the rule could be said to mark the dividing line between the levels of semantics and syntax, the existence of which McCawley and others deny. In order for there to be a basis for deciding that English is a VSO language, and for maintaining the denial of the existence of different levels of semantic and syntactic structure, it is necessary to show that the significance of VSO order is apparent in the transformational component of English grammar.

Therefore McCawley attempts to show that for five cyclic transformations of English "the underlying constituent order makes a significant difference in the complexity of the conditions under which the transformation applies, or its effect" (p. 292). The preferred underlying constituent order in each case is said to be VSO. The five transformations are Passive, *There*-insertion, Subject-raising, Negative-transportation, and Predicate-raising. Either VSO or SVO input he says to make no difference for ten other cyclic transformations.

The Passive rule with an SVO input performs two operations (ignoring the insertion of the grammatical morphemes *be* and *by*): the object goes before the verb, and the subject goes after. The same rule with VSO input has only one operation: the subject NP is moved after the object NP. Then, by the later rule of V-NP inversion which a deep VSO, surface SVO language like English would require, the formerly object NP will be

moved into subject position. Provided V-NP inversion can be independently
justified, this argument is very neat: with deep VSO order the English
Passive rule is rendered a one-operation transformation.

McCawley, attributing the argument to Paul Postal (p. 297), gives
independent justification for the rule of V-NP inversion by identifying
it with the rule of verb-inversion in questions. This rule relates in (4)
(a) to the question (b), and (4c) to the question (d). The same rule will
also relate the string (e) derived by transformation from the VSO ordered
string (e') to the passive sentence (f).

    (4) a. God is alive.

        b. Is God alive?

        c. Power corrupts.

        d. Does power corrupt?

        e. has corrupted men power < e'. has corrupted power men

        f. men have (been) corrupted (by) power

The relationship between these pairs of sentences is that of subject-verb
inversion (where, of course, tense is treated as a verb in the deep structure of sentences like (c)). According to McCawley, however, if English
is a deep VSO language, questions such as (4b) and (d) will result not
from application of V-NP inversion, but from failure to apply the rule.
The rule will apply to give the right result in the derivation of the
passive sentence (4f) from the VSO ordered string (e'). Hence it can be
argued that the rule that gives surface SVO order from deep VSO order is
not something new which the VSO grammar has to add to the transformational rules; the VSO grammar just reverses the role of the old inversion
rule used in question formation.

There-insertion is an argument similar to that concerning the Passive rule, based on the same considerations of operational simplicity.
There-insertion with an NP-V-X (SVO) input requires two parts: it creates
and adds *there* as the first item in the string, and inverts NP and V.
With VSO input only the first of these operations is necessary. *There*,
marked +NP, is inserted after V. Now again the rule of V-NP inversion
will apply to give the right result, putting *there* in subject position.[2]

2 An interesting problem arises concerning the form of *There*-insertion.

Subject-raising, Negative-transportation, and Predicate-raising are
the three remaining transformations which McCawley believes to be significantly simplified by a VSO input. "To formulate any of these three
transformations if they applied to structures that had predicate-second
order would require great ingenuity in the manipulation of symbols."
(p. 295). The larger part of the necessary ingenuity is called on to deal
with Negative-transportation and Predicate-raising, and a smaller part to
handle Subject-raising. Since there is, first, little hard evidence that
the former two transformations exist, and since, besides, a formal statement of their form has never been made by those who believe in their existence, it makes little sense to allow the problems their supposed complexity presents to become an argument for substantial changes in other
parts of the grammar. We can focus attention on the purported difficulty
with Subject-raising in English as an SVO language. McCawley's version of
Subject-raising relates in (5) both (a) to (b), and (c) to (d).

(5) a. John believes his brother is a narc.

b. John believes his brother to be a narc.

c. [Art admires Spiro]seems

d. Art seems to admire Spiro.

That is, it treats both Subject-raising to object (5b<5a), and Subject-
raising to subject (5d<5c) as one rule.

Provided there is a basis for claiming that the same rule is involved in both these cases of subject-raising, this unitary rule is indeed
expressed very nicely under the VSO analysis of English. With VSO ordered
input, in both cases the rule removes the subject NP of the embedded sentence and places it to the immediate left of that sentence. With SVO in-

---

We can insert *there* as the initial element of a VSO string. Then the
environment of V-NP inversion would not be met, assuming this is actually ##V-NP, and *there* would remain in subject position. Alternatively,
[+NP] *there* can be inserted between V and S in the VSO ordered string.
Now V-NP inversion will move it into surface subject position. There
appears to be no good reason for choosing one or the other of these
apparently purely notational variants which the linearity of deep
structure permits.

put, on the other hand, the transformational relationship between the
pairs of sentences seems quite different and the unity, if it exists, is
not expressed at all. Compare Subject-raising to subject in (6b) and
(7b).

(6) a. Subject-raising to object with VSO order

$$\frac{[V \ S \ [V \ S \ O]]}{1 \quad 2 \quad 3 \quad 4} \quad \Rightarrow \quad 1 \ 3 \ 2 \ 4$$

b. Subject-raising to subject with VSO order

$$\frac{[V \ [V \ S \ O]]}{1 \quad 2 \quad 3 \quad 4} \quad \Rightarrow \quad 1 \ 3 \ 2 \ 4$$

(7) a. Subject-raising to object with SVO order

$$\frac{[S \ V \ [\quad S \ V \ O]]}{1 \quad 2 \quad 3 \quad 4} \quad \Rightarrow \quad 1 \ 3 \ 2 \ 4$$

b. Subject-raising to subject with SVO order

$$\frac{[\ [\ S \ V \ O] \ V \ ]}{1 \ 2 \ 3 \quad 4 \quad 5 \ 6} \quad \Rightarrow \quad 1 \ 3 \ 5 \ 2 \ 4 \ 6$$

It seems that a VSO analysis of English gives markedly better results,
by simplifying the statement of the transformation, and in this way,
provided one transformation is involved in both Subject-raising to subject and to object, by making this apparent. With the SVO analysis it
does not seem to be at all the case that one rule is involved. The two
cases of of subject-raising in (7) could only be awkwardly collapsed by
the use of complex bracketing.

However, if it does appear that the VSO analysis is in this case
preferred over the SVO alternative, it is not preferred over a third possibility: SVO order. As seen in (8), the rule of Subject-raising which
combines raising to subject and to object is just as simple, and just as
unitary with an SOV ordered input.

(8) a. Subject-raising to object with SOV order

$$\frac{[S \ [\ S \ O \ V] \ V]}{1 \quad 2 \ 3 \quad 4} \quad \Rightarrow \quad 1 \ 3 \ 2 \ 4$$

b. Subject-raising to subject with SOV order

$$\frac{[\ [\ S \ O \ V] \ V]}{1 \ 2 \ 3 \quad 4} \quad \Rightarrow \quad 1 \ 3 \ 2 \ 4$$

Let us assume that the two cases of subject-raising should be collapsed in a single rule. Then, if it is true that the SVO analysis of

English is inferior to the VSO analysis, it must at the same time be recognized that the VSO analysis has no advantage that it does not share with an SVO analysis. In fact the same is true for the Passive and *There*-insertion arguments. It could easily be shown that SVO input order would make these two transformations just as simple in number and type of operations as VSO input.

Even the purported independent justification of the VSO grammar's rule of V-NP inversion would be an argument neutralized in this case. Whereas V-NP inversion is justified by its use in forming statements from V-NP question order (as in 4a/b, c/d), the late rule required by an SOV analysis of English, a rule which would put the verb second, also has independent justification in sentences like these:

> (9) a. Who is Ed investigating now? (<Who Ed is investigating now?)
>
> b. Ed is investigating someone.
>
> c. Who can you trust? (<Who you can trust?)
>
> d. You can trust someone.

These questions may be analysed as resulting from a transformation the effect of which is to put the verb second in a string of the form, after WH-fronting, NP-NP-(X)-V-Y. The questions of (9a) and (c) would result if we prohibit the rule from applying on the right-most verb in WH-questions. In this way the rule required by an SOV analysis of English deep structure may also be given independent justification. The rule would apply subsequent to the Passive and *There*-insertion rules to give the right results. Surface strings (9f) and (h) result from application of the verb-second rule on the intermediate strings (9e) and (g) which are derived from (e') and (g') by one-operation Passive and *there*-insertion rules, respectively.

> (9) e. men power has corrupted <e'. power men has corrupted
>
> f. Men have (been) corrupted (by) power.
>
> g. there a fly in it is < g'. a fly in it is
>
> h. There is a fly in it.

Such an analysis of questions, passives, and *there*-sentences may seem utterly spurious, but it is not clearly more so than Mc Cawley's

analysis of the same sentences. Shall we therefore argue that English is
an SOV language? Actually the situation is even worse than this for the
VSO analysis, and for the general problem of deciding just what the deep
order of English main constituents is.

2.3. THE EQUIVALENCE OF VSO, SOV, AND SVO ANALYSES OF ENGLISH

Since the simplification of Subject-raising, Passive, and *There*-
insertion is the clearest achievement of the analysis of English as either
a VSO or SOV language, fatal to the arguments is the fact that the same
simplification of these three transformations, even along with the collapsing of the two cases of subject-raising, can readily be obtained not
only with SOV ordered inputs, but with SVO order. This alternative will
also employ the rule which puts the verb in second position. The effect
of this rule is to restore SVO order after one-operation rules of *There*-
insertion, Passive, and Subject-raising have applied. This rule moves the
verb into position to the right of the clause-initial NP.

(10)   [NP X V Y]
          S
          ‾‾1̅ 2̅ 3̅ 4̅   ===> 1 3 2 4

A version of rule (10), recall, is otherwise required in the derivation
of WH -questions like (9a) and (c). Rule (10) applies to the strings resulting from the three transformations in question, which can therefore
be stated as single operation rules applying to SVO ordered inputs.

(11) a. *There*-insertion

           [NP be PP X]
           S _____   [+NP]
           1   2   ===> 1 there 2

           a fly is in it   there a fly is in it
                              by (10): There is a fly in it.

     b. Passive

           [NP V NP X]
           S
           1̅ 2̅ 3̅ 4̅   ===> 1 3 2 4

           power has corrupted men   men power has corrupted
                              by (10): men have (been) corrupted
                                       (by) power.

c. Subject-raising to subject

[[NP X] V]
S S
1 2 3   4   ===>   1 3 2 4

[Art admires Spiro] seems   Art [to admire Spiro] seems

by (10): Art seems to admire Spiro.

d. Subject-raising to object

[NP V [NP X]]
S   S
  1   2 3   4   ===>   1 3 2 4

Sam believes his brother   Sam believes his brother

is a narc   to be a narc.

Rule (10) does not apply.

Notice that in this approach as in McCawley's both cases of Subject raising are raising to the immediate left.[3]

Perhaps the most interesting observation which McCawley made was that ten of the fifteen English transformations which he examined accept with equal facility either VSO or SVO ordered inputs. It is reasonable that this should be so, since transformations typically make no reference to linearity in locating the morphemes which they will affect. Items affected by transformations may be defined by linear position, constituency, and label, but label and constituency alone are enough. This is certainly

---

[3] Postal (1974: 263) says, for reasons unclear to me, that in this analysis subject raising to subject and subject raising to object are not treated as one rule. He says that while in (11) "these have been formulated in such a way as to have the same number of terms and the same elementary transformational operation, they cannot be combined in a single natural rule because of the different positions of the symbols". He agrees with McCawley that under the VSO analysis they are combined, for which he gives the single structural analysis suitable for both cases:

X Verb (NP) [[Verb NP Y]   ]   Z
            NP   S   S NP
 1   2   3   4   5 6   7

The structural analysis for both types of raising from SVO ordered deep structure, which seems to me similar in every significant respect to that above, is:

X (NP V) [[NP V Y]   ]   Z
         NP S   S NP
 1   2   3 4 5   6

true of the typical non-movement transformation, but it is true of movement transformations as well. This is true of the three transformations
just discussed, which McCawley believed to be simplified by VSO input
structure. The fact is that if we allow the linear order of the verb to
be established by a late rule, any English transformation that would
otherwise require this as one operation can be simplified. But if this is
done, depending on what form the late rule which linearizes the verb
takes, these transformations will as readily accept SOV,SVO, or VSO ordered input structure.

   It therefore cannot be argued that the grammar of English is significantly simplified by establishing deep VSO order. The fact that these
transformations remain   fundamentally the same regardless of main constituent order emphasizes the difficulty faced by the linguist who looks
for deep structure evidence to resolve this paradox of analysis.[4] This
may be considered an indication of the actual absence of linear order
in deep structure. Another indication of this is the equivalence of different deep order analyses of main constituent order to an analysis with
non-linear deep structure. This will be seen in the next section through
examination of the problem of the deep order of Amharic constituents.

3.1. THE REDUCIBILITY OF LINEAR TO NON-LINEAR DEEP STRUCTURE[5]

   With rare exceptions the sentences of Amharic have SOV order.
VSO order never occurs. In a 1970 article Emmon Bach presented an ingen-

----

[4]Arthur Schwartz (1972) has tried to resolve certain types of linear order paradoxes by proposing various possibly universal constraints. For
example, if X and Y are sisters occurring in different environments in
both the orders XY and YX, and X is the nucleus of the construction (e.
g. N of NP), it is Y that moves, while X is stationary. Regardless of whether   one finds Schwartz's arguments convincing, it is important to
note that such problems just don't arise if the grammar employs linearization rules. The order is XY in environment A, and YX in not-A, and
until these environments are determined, X and Y are in a non-linear relationship to one another.

[5]This section is an abbreviation of an earlier study: Hudson 1972. Where
Bach's examples are used here I have conformed them to the phonemiciza-
tion commonly used in the literature on Amharic: /ä/ =Bach's /ə/, phonetically [ə]; /ə/=Bach's /ɨ/, [ɨ].

ious argument attempting to show that, nevertheless, Amharic is in deep structure a VSO language, with surface SOV order accomplished by a post-cyclic rule of verb-movement. The intent of this section is to show that whether Amharic is in deep structure an SOV or VSO language is necessarily a moot point. As with English, there appears to be no deep structure evidence regarding the linear order of Amharic main constituents. Indeed, the generalization about Amharic syntax which Bach believed to argue for deep VSO order, when fully understood, is found to make no reference to the linear order of elements in deep structure.

Bach presented several arguments. Four of these may be called 'descriptive,' since they are based on claims of greater simplicity or increased generality in the VSO grammar of Amharic. Two other arguments are 'explanatory,' the first being based on historical considerations, and the second on a proposed criterion of syntactic naturalness. I wish to limit consideration here to the descriptive arguments, since unless these are effective there is no need to seek explanatory criteria in order to justify the VSO analysis of Amharic. In fact the first descriptive argument will receive no attention here, since it relies completely on the theory of 'gapping' proposed by John Ross (1970), a theory which has been shown inadequate in work by Gerald Sanders (1970) and Andreas Koutsoudas (1971). Still, Bach's remaining arguments are persuasive insofar as they show the sufficiency, if not the necessity, of a VSO analysis of Amharic.

3.2. AMHARIC AS A VSO LANGUAGE

Bach's first argument that Amharic is a VSO language begins with two observations: first, possesser-possessed phrases in Amharic are introduced by the prefix *yä*, which is identical to the verb prefix which marks relative clauses; second, such possessive phrases are "presumably derived by reducing relative clauses with 'have' constructions..." (p. 12) Thus (12a) and (12b) are paraphrases:

     (12) a. yä-yohannəs bet
            of-John house 'John's house'
        b. yohannəs yä-allä-w bet
           John that-is-(to)him house 'the house that John has'

We find that the morpheme *yä* is always prefixed to the first word of the genitive phrase, but *yä* is always prefixed to the verb of a relative clause, though the verb is preceded by all other words of that clause (basic main constituent order in independent and dependent clauses being SOV). The following examples will make this clear. The examples of (13) show expansion of a genitive phrase, and those of (14) expansion of a relative clause. Note that with expansion of the genitive phrase *yä* remains in first position, whereas expansion of the relative clause results in the embedding of *yä*.

(13) a. yä-säw bet
        of-man house   'man's house'

     b. yä-rayjəm säw bet
        of-tall man house   'tall man's house'

     c. yä-bät'am räyjəm säw bet
        of-very tall man house   'very tall man's house'

(14) a. yä-allä-w bet
        that-is-(to)him house   'the house that he has'

     b. əssu yä-allä-w bet
        he that-is-(to)him house   'the house that *he* has'

     c. əssu bä-kätämä yä-allä-w bet
        he at-city that-is-(to)him house
        'the house that *he* has in the city'

In deriving relative clauses, therefore, the morpheme *yä* has to be 'lowered' onto the verb from logical position commanding the clause. (Or we could set up *yä* and other conjunctions as sister to the clause main constituents; nothing depends on this. We may accept here Bach's analysis in which *yä* commands the relative clause in deep structure.)

Bach proposes a derivation of the genitive phrase (12a) and the relative clause (12b) from the phrase marker (15), in which the clause of S_2 is in VSO order.

(15)

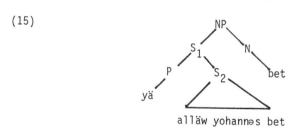

alläw yohannəs bet

The derivation requires identical NP deletion (deleting *bet* under S_2),
"a rule of copula deletion [deleting *alläw*], a rule attaching *yä* to the
next element to the right --call it *yä*-attachment-- and of course, verb-
shift, a rule putting the verb at the end of the clause, applying in
that order." If optional copula deletion is skipped, we derive the relative clause; *yä* will be attached to *alläw* and be moved along by verb-
shift as a prefix on the verb. Bach says that this manner of derivation
from underlying VSO order is superior to derivation from SOV order since
in the latter case we would be "forced to give two rules for *yä*-attach-
ment, one affixing it to a verb at the [right] end of the clause, if
there is one, otherwise to the first element in a noun phrase... What we
miss in this analysis is the generalization that *yä* is attached to the
next lexical element, no matter what it is, and since we have two rules,
we fail to express the identity of the two elements in the two rules."
(p. 13)

Actually, the advantage of a single rule of *yä*-attachment is equally
present in parallel derivations from the SOV ordered phrase marker (16).

(16)

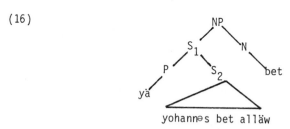

yohannəs bet alläw

In derivation from (16) we order attachment after the rule which the SOV
analysis has in lieu of verb-shift, a rule which can be called preposi-

tion-shift. This rule moves *yä* and positions it before the verb of the
relative clause. To derive the relative clause the transformations apply
in the sequence NP deletion, preposition-shift, and finally *yä*-attach-
ment; to derive the genitive phrase we apply copula deletion before preposition-shift; now the environment of preposition-shift will not be
met and *yä*-attachment attaches *yä* to *yohannəs*. The number of transformations and the apparent complexity of their operations is the same
whether derivation is from (15) or (16). Attachment in either case says:
"Attach *yä* to the next element to the right." The presumed identity of
relative and genetive *yä* is expressed equivalently in the two analyses.

  At this point we have two approaches which are fundamentally different only in deep order of main constituents, VSO or SOV, and in the
element moved by transformation. If we begin with VSO order a rule of
verb-shift is required, and if we begin with SOV order a rule of preposition-shift.

  The second argument that Amharic is a VSO language is said to
"converge on the conclusion that there should be a rule of verb-shift,"
hence VSO deep structure. This argument observes that prepositions other
than genitive *yä* 'of' are prefixed to the first of a series of simple
modifiers which precede their head noun, but in the event that the head
noun is modified by a relative clause, these prepositions are 'attracted'
to the verb of the relative clause, and are prefixed to it. This is illustrated in (17) with the preposition *bä*, 'at'.

  (17) a. yä-yohannəs bet 'John's house' (=12a)
       b. bä-yohannəs bet < bä-yä-yohannəs bet
          at-John house   at-of-John house   'at John's house'
       c. yohannəs yä-allä-w bet 'the house that John has' (=12b)
       d. yohannəs bä-allä-w bet < yohannəs bä-yä-allä-w bet
                                    John at-of-is-(to)him house
                                    'at the house that John has'

Note that the preposition *yä* is deleted when preceded by another preposition. This is the morphologically conditioned relic of an earlier
phonologically conditioned rule (Leslau 1968, §§71, 75; Praetorius 1879:
452). The present-day rule is (18).

(18)   yä

     [PREP] ===> Ø / [PREP] ____

The underlying structure of (17d) with VSO order is (19), and with SOV order (20).

(19)   (20)

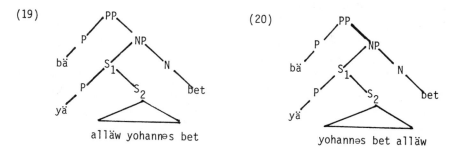

    alläw yohannəs bet   yohannəs bet alläw

According to the argument that Amharic is a VSO language, if we accept deep structures like (19), "we need only assume that the [rule of *yä*-deletion (18)] applies after *yä*-attachment and before verb-shift in order to get examples like [17d]. The preposition will then be shifted along with the verb." On the contrary, if we have SOV ordered deep structures like (20), "once again it would be necessary to split the rule into two cases." (Bach, p. 12) We need a rule which would lower *yä* on the S_1 cycle, and *bä* or other preposition on the higher cycle. *Yä* can be readily lowered to the verb on the S_1 cycle since that verb is the rightmost element in S_1, and *yä* the leftmost. But *bä* must be lowered in a higher cycle and in a more complex environment.

As Bach notes in his third argument, it would be difficult to write a rule of preposition-shift which would apply to both *yä* and *bä*, since the rule which would lower *bä* would have a variable at the right in its environment (represented in (20) by the simple noun *bet* 'house'. The material here is of potentially unbounded length, including all simple modifiers of *bet*.) According to Bach, to make the rule work for both cases we would need a statement of logical quantification, "There is no verb in the variable," and we are properly constrained by standard transformational theory against using such statements in transformations. This problem seems to effectively rule out the SOV analysis of Amharic

since, though the rule of preposition-shift for *bä* in (20) might be com-
plexly written without logical quantification, the problem would remain that the resulting rule would be considerably different from the
rule which lowers *yä*. By having two rules we would fail to express the
generalization which undoubtedly underlies both these cases of preposition lowering.

Another solution available under the SOV analysis and not considered by Bach would be to make attachment and preposition-shift last-
cyclic and left-to-right iterative. Under this approach *bä* first would
attach to *yä*, and *bä-yä* would be lowered together and prefixed to the
verb of the relative clause. (And *yä* would be deleted by (18).) But this
approach would be unsatisfactory due to the absence of precedents for
left-to-right iterative rules in syntax.

With the VSO analysis we are able to achieve a simpler solution.
Verb-shift will have to be last-cyclic, but there would be no need for
any left-to-right iterative rule, and both cases of preposition lowering are handled in the same way. On each cycle attachment takes place:
yä to *alläw*, and then *bä* to *yä-alläw*. When last-cyclic verb-movement
applies *bä-yä* would be carried along with *alläw* to the end of the relative clause. (Again *yä* is deleted by rule (18).)

The simplicity and availability of the VSO analysis, and its clear
superiority to the SOV analysis seems to lead to the conclusion that
Amharic is a VSO language. Bach can bring in his explanatory arguments
to confirm the case for VSO order in deep structure. There is no necessity to examine these explanatory arguments, however, since a careful
study of the phrase makers (19) and (20) will show that a generalization has been missed, and in fact in Amharic as in English there is not
only no deep structure evidence for VSO order, but none for any linear
order at this level at all.

3.3. THE NON-SIGNIFICANCE OF LINEAR ORDER IN PREPOSITION LOWERING

The VSO analysis of Amharic has the advatage of a simple, cyclic rule of preposition-attachment which makes no distinction between
the morphemes which a preposition is attached to: it is always simply

attached to the right. When the preposition stands before a clause, if
the clause is in VSO order the preposition will be attached to the verb
of the clause, and the verb always is shifted in the last cycle to the
opposite end of its clause. But on a careful study of prepositional
phrases such as (17d) we find that preposition embedding in relative
clauses is an even less complex phenomenon than the relatively straightforward VSO analysis makes it seem.

Under either the SOV or VSO analyses a relative clause phrase marker such as (21a) leads to the prefixing of the preposition to the verb
of S_2, whereas a prepositional phrase marker such as (21b) leads instead to the prefixing of the preposition to the sister constituent of
the nucleus, or head noun.

(21) a.   b.

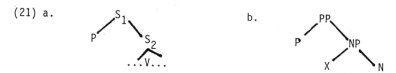

In other words, (21a) should become (22a), and (21b) should become (22b).

(22) a.   b.

By tree-pruning an S node would be lost in (22a). Note that where X in
(21b) is an S, the change (21b> 22b) creates an input for a change of
the sort (21a > 22a). This is the *direct* statement of the observable
generalization about the position of Amharic prepositions. The rule of
verb-movement in the VSO analysis is an only indirect statement of the
same generalization, made possible by the unnecessary positing of
VSO order.

The three-dot notation in (21a) and (22a) is deliberate, for it
expresses the fact that the transformation which relates (21a) to (22a)
may be interpreted to apply without regard to whether linear order of

main constituents in S_2 is VSO or SOV. This order might even be SVO or
OSV. The two transformations which attach prepositions in Amharic may
therefore be expressed in completely non-linear form as follows, where
the commas indicate that no linear relationship is established between the items they seperate.

(23) a. [P, [X, V]]
          S
     1 2   3   4 5   ===>   1 3 2-4 5

     b. [P, [X, N]]
          NP
     1 2 3 4   5   ===>   1 3 2-4 5 (where X may be
                                         and 2-∅ 5 = 2-5)

These two rules will now apply in an intrinsically ordered sequence
to properly derive prepositional phrases with and without relative
clauses. Note that transformations such as these are unambiguously
interpretable despite the unlinearized variables they contain. The
phrase structure rules establish only one sister constituent of a
single type. Thus, barring cases arising from conjunction reduction
(which applies after other transformations: Sanders 1970, and Koutsoudas 1971), there can be only one maximal node V in S, or N in NP.
The A over A principle (cf. Chomsky 1968: 42-43) limits reference of
the rule to a maximal node. Rule (23b) depends on there being only
one sister to N in NP (S or some X < S). I am aware of no reason not
to make this assumption if, again, we except cases of conjunction.

     As illustration take the complex prepositional phrase (24), which
Bach considered to show the necessity for a VSO analysis of Amharic.

(24) a. əne yä-ayyä-hu-t säw bä-allä-w bet
        I that-saw-I-him man at-is-(to)him house
        'at the house that the man that I saw has'

The logical, deep structure of (24) is (25).

(25)

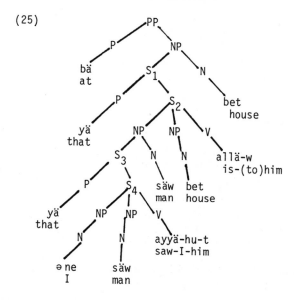

With identical noun deletions this will become (26). (26) has two environments for rule (23a), at S_1 and at S_3, and one environment for rule (23b) directly under PP. After these rules apply we will have (27).

(26)

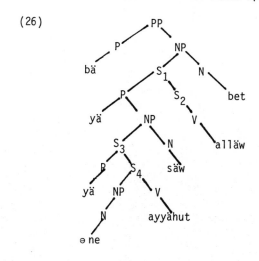

(27)

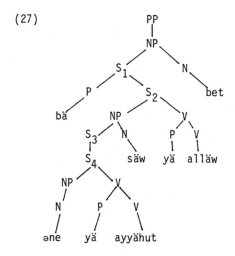

(27) now has a derived input for rule (23a), at S_1, and applying this
rule once again, plus tree-pruning, we will get (28). It will be seen
that this phrase-marker, except for preposition-deletion by rule (18)
(which will delete *yä* / *bä___alläw*), directly underlies the complex
Amharic prepositional phrase in question, (24).

(28)

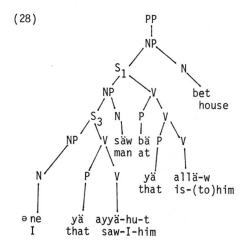

The non-linear rules (23a) and (b) express the same facts about
the position of prepositions in Amharic as are expressed in the parallel rules of attachment and movement under the VSO or SOV analyses.
But since they are expressed in non-linear form, they could be rewritten to apply to either VSO or SOV ordered deep structures. The
generalization which these rules express is therefore no argument for
any particular linear ordering of main constituents. The derivation illustrated in (25)-(28) has been accomplished with SOV order, but any
other order would give the same results.

It bears emphasis, though this is not the main purpose of the present argument, that the non-linear rules (23a) and (b) are not only more
general than the rules of preposition-attachment and movement in the
VSO or SOV analyses insofar as they apply to any linear ordering of the
items they affect, but also in that they are unordered sequentially with
respect to one another. They require not only no statement of one before
the other, but also no specification of cyclic versus last-cyclic application, or left-to-right iteration. They apply when and wherever their
environments are met. It is enough for the present purpose to have seen
that, whether the non-linear solution of the problem of the deep order
of Amharic main constituents is considered to be a more general solution
or not, the opposing solutions with differing linear deep structure are
reducible to the non-linear solution once the actual generalization
about preposition-lowering in Amharic is completely recognized.

The task of Section 4 will be to show how a grammar which employs
post-transformational linearization rules attains a higher   level of
generality than a grammar which establishes linearity in deep structure.
This will be shown through examination of a long-time problem in English
transformational grammar: dative movement.

4.   THE GENERALITY OF GRAMMARS WITH NON-LINEAR DEEP STRUCTURE

Whenever two linear orders of the same underlying elements
occur in a language, and when neither of the orders is of low frequency
of occurrence, transformational grammar has been hard put to decide which
order is basic. There is apparently no case where a linearity paradox of

this sort arises in which an even moderately convincing argument has
been presented for choosing one or the other surface order as the basic,
deep structure order. In the previous section we saw that the power of
standard transformational theory is so great that it even becomes possible to argue for a deep linear order that never has surface realization.
Such a syntactic analysis is an obvious parallel to a phonological analysis which employs absolute neutralization. As with arguments for absolute neutralization in phonology, the argument for such a fully abstract
syntactic analysis is still utterly inconclusive, however, and the result is again a deep structure linearity paradox as in cases where two
or more orders co-occur in surface structure, and one of these is to be
taken as basic.

The problem of the deep linear order of English dative and object
noun phrases is a typical one. It has been recognized since work by
Fillmore (1965), and has recently frustrated Jackendoff and Culicover
(1971: 397) despite their success in solving some problems related to
so-called 'dative movement' in English. The alternation between the
order of dative and object NPs is seen in sentences such as these:

(29) a. Jack sent the Red Cross $10.

b. Jack sent $10 to the Red Cross.

c. ?Jack sent to the Red Cross $10.

d. Jack sent it to the Red Cross.

e. *Jack sent to the Red Cross it.

It is apparent that two factors interact to determine the linear
order of the dative and object NPs: whether the dative NP is realized
with the preposition *to*, and the length and composition of the object
NP. Sentences (a) - (c) illustrate the effect of realizing the dative
with *to*. Sentences (c) - (e) illustrate the effect of the length and
composition of the object NP on linear order. This factor is somewhat
more complex than (c) - (e) indicate. The order of (c) would be more
acceptable, even completely so, if, for example, the object NP were of
greater length, say, as in (29f). The order *to*-dative followed by object
is even preferred if the reverse order leads to ambiguity as is seen in
the pair of sentences (29g) and (h).

(29) f. Jack sent to the Red Cross the $10 that was in the cookie jar.

g. $^?$Jack sent the $10 that was refunded by the insurance company to the Red Cross.

h. Jack sent to the Red Cross the $10 that was refunded by the insurance company.

In a transformational grammar which makes the dative without *to* basic, and also establishes linearity as a function of the base rules, sentences which in the course of derivation get a *to*-dative require a transformation to subsequently put the *to*-phrase after the object. If the *to*-dative position is established as basic and if in the course of derivation we delete *to*, a transformation is necessary to move the dative in the opposite direction. For certain objects, for example a pronoun, unless the *to*-dative is basic, it has to be derived by transformation. This is summarized in (30), where the two-directional arrows indicate that no particular phrase-marker is here considered basic.

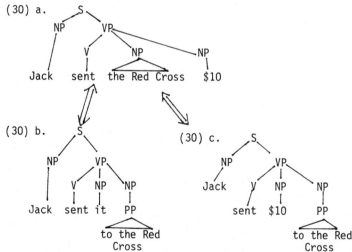

(Nothing hinges on whether there is a VP node. This is just a notational convenience here which permits us to set apart subjects; these, like objects, will have to be marked some way in any theory.)

Now, compare the sentences of (29) with those of (31).

(31) a. *Nixon sent China an envoy.

b. Nixon sent an envoy to China.

c. ?Nixon sent to China an envoy.

d. Nixon sent   him to China.

e. *Nixon sent to China him.

China in these sentences is, of course, not a dative, but an adverbial NP, as shown by the ungrammaticality of (31a). It expresses roughly 'direction'. Note that like the *to*-dative this adverbial phrase preferably follows the object, and also like the *to*-dative is marginally acceptable in the position between the verb and object in a sentence such as (31c). Like the *to*-dative the *to*-adverbial NP is definitely excluded from this position if the object is a pronoun. But, again, the pre-object position becomes preferred as a consequence of the length and composition of the object NP. This last similarity with the *to*-dative is illustrated in sentences (31f)-(h).

(31) f. Nixon sent to China his most trusted advisor, Henry Kissinger.

g. ?Nixon sent a secret envoy who would arrange a summit meeting to China.

h. Nixon sent to China a secret envoy who would arrange a summit meeting.

This similarity between the linear order possibilities in the two sentence paradigms (29) and (31) can hardly be accidental. The fundamental parallel is that if the dative is realized as a *to*-phrase, it typically follows the object, as does the adverbial *to*-phrase. And the *to*-adverbial is apparently subject to the same sorts of surface structure-sensitive constraints that affect the *to*-dative and have to do with the length and composition of the object.

Parallel treatment of the *to*-dative and the *to*-adverbial could be expressed in a number of ways. Preferably, however, the method chosen should through some economy in notation express the nature of the generalization involved: the fact that the linearity of two phrases of different semantic character is sensitive to the same factors.

If the deep structure of a grammar is linear, the rule which would move the dative NP after an object NP if the dative is realized with *to* or (depending on which position is basic for the dative) would leave the dative in this position if it keeps *to* merely replicates the base rule that establishes the position of the *to*-adverbial within the verb phrase. Most would agree that the unmarked position of the *to*-adverbial, as with other adverbial phrases, is after the object, since the cases where it is just after the verb and before the object (examples (31f, h)) are clearly the special cases. Hence the movement transformation that applies to the dative on the basis of whether or not it gets *to* seems in effect to 'refer back' to this phrase structure rule which in a grammar with linear deep structure first establishes the position of the *to*-adverbial.

We could employ a convention of some sort or a notation which will relate the linear ordering function of these two rules in different parts of the grammar. But such devices are only necessary if deep structure is linear. Besides, the (f) and (h) examples of (29) and (31) show that fine surface structure distinctions are critical in the linearization of both the *to*-dative and the *to*-adverbial. (It makes no difference that these distinctions are mostly characteristic of written, rather than spoken, language.) Therefore it is apparent that the full generalization will only be expressible if linearity is finally established for both phrases at the post-transformational, post-lexical insertion level.

In an alternative grammar where deep structure is non-linear, the phrase structure rules establish hierarchical but not linear structure, and linearity is only established by post-transformational rules. In this alternative not only does the necessity not exist for a convention or notation to link up the linearization function of separate rules in different parts of the grammar, but the linearization rule that establishes the linear order of both the dative and the *to*-adverbial is itself a statement of the generalization involved. We should desire as a general principle that the grammar perform identical functions identically.

This principle cannot be followed in the model of grammar in which

linearization is of necessity established at two points in a derivation:
first in the base as one of the functions of the phrase structure rules,
and then in the transformational component as one of the functions of
some transformations. The principle cannot be followed since in such
a grammar the latter function is bound to be at least a partial repetition of the former. The principle can be followed in the model of grammar in which deep structure is non-linear, and which employs post-transformational rules to establish all relationships of linearity between
constituents.

Following are rules which express the basic generalizations which
hold for the linearity of elements of the sort in question. Again the
commas indicate that no relationship of linearity is established for
the items that they separate. The mark ⌢ is used here to show linear
order.

(32) a.   [[OBJ] [DAT] , V]
        VP   NP , NP
              ‾1‾   ‾2‾   3   ===>   3⌢2⌢1

     b.   [NP, to-NP, V]
        VP
           ‾1‾   ‾2‾   3   ===>   3⌢1⌢2

These two linearization rules may be collapsed as (33), without use of
the dative label.

(33)   [[OBJ], <to->NP, V]
         VP NP
            ‾1‾   ‾2‾   3 ===> { <3⌢1⌢2> }
                                 { 3⌢2⌢1 }

Rule (33) is of course generalizable to certain other prepositional
phrases, not just those with *to*.

It is easy to extend this line of reasoning to numerous other
instances in order to show the greater generality of grammars which
employ linearization rules. As shown by Emonds (1970), except for a
limited class of exceptions, transformations are "structure preserving": they do not build structures of a type not also created in
the base. They build structures the linearity characteristics of
which are already specified by ordinary phrase structure rules.

English expletive *there* sentences provide an example.

In Section 2 it was noted that in the typical generative grammar which has deep SVO order, the transformation which yields *there* sentences has to perform two operations: it introduces *there*, and moves the formerly subject NP into post-verb position (*a fly is in it* ==> *there is a fly in it*). In the VSO analysis of English the rule of V-NP inversion gives the right result if the linear ordering step is omitted from the transformation that introduces *there*, treated as an NP, at the right of V. In other grammars with other deep orders proposed in Section 2 different late rules perform the linearizing operation depending on where we choose to insert *there*. Here again we find that whichever form the rule which establishes the linear order of *there* takes, that rule must duplicate the work of the phrase structure rule which makes subjects the first main constituent of the English clause. Thus if the linear ordering function is abstracted from the phrase structure rules and assigned to a post-transformational level in derivations, the rule which at this level puts subject NPs first (regardless of how subject is marked, whether structurally as sister to VP, or by case grammar-type labels) will do the job for both base and transformationally derived subjects including *there*, and at the same time be the unique expression of the correct generalization about the position of the subject NP of English clauses.

It might seem that linearization rules would be prohibitively complex due to the great diversity of the transformationally derived structures with which they will have to deal. Therefore it is important to point out that these rules are no more complex than the phenomena they describe. For example rules (32a) and (b) are suitable for establishing the linear order of the verb phrase of certain kinds of relatively simple sentences; but these rules are no more an over-simplification than the phrase structure rules that in the current model of generative grammar establish only the three named constituents of rules (32a) and (b) as the members of such verb phrases, and as well place them in some order. Also rule (33) is no more an over-simplification than would be any so-called 'dative movement' transformation that acts

on phrase markers of the relatively simple types subsumed in the structural index of (33). But linearization rule (33) performs at once both
the 'movement' function of the transformation, and the linearizing
function of the standard phrase structure rules.[6] The linearization rules
of a generative grammar with a non-linear base will have to accept as
their inputs the outputs of the transformations, and since these same
transformations are present in the model of a grammar with linear deep
structure and no linearization rules, the specification of these structures is not a new, complex problem in a model of grammar with non-
linear deep structure and linearization rules.

    5.   CONCLUSION

        The assumption that linear order is imposed as a characteris-
tic of the deep structure of generative grammar has led to insoluble
paradoxes of analysis. This was exemplified in Section 2 by an examination of James McCawley's claim that English, in spite of the low frequency of main constituent order VSO in surface structure, is a VSO
language in deep structure. We found that while this VSO analysis of
English cannot be rejected on grounds of descriptive adequacy, the state
of syntactic theory is such at present that it nevertheless cannot be
selected over analyses with other theoretically possible orderings of
the same constituents. While this and similar paradoxes may be indicative of the continuing need for an appropriate evaluation measure,
it also clearly suggests as an alternative the irrelevance of the
linear order of elements of deep structure.

        Emmon Bach's argument for Amharic similar to McCawley's for English
was examined in Section 3. Here it was shown that a VSO analysis of the
deep order of Amharic main constituents, while descriptively adequate,

---

[6]Actually, it is a reasonable presumption that it is topicalization
and/or focusing which usually determines the linearization of dative
and object NPs, and this, then, determines the insertion of *to*. A
topicalized dative NP precedes an object, or a focused object follows
a dative. Topicalization and/or focusing is the goal of the typical
movement transformation of English.

is based on a mistaken generalization about Amharic syntax: a rule of verb movement. The transformation which fills the role of verb movement, as well as the role of preposition movement in the SOV analysis of Amharic, and which most directly captures the correct generalization about Amharic syntax is simply oblivious to the deep linear order of the constituents to which it refers. The structural index of this more general transformational rule will as easily accept SOV, VSO, or other theoretically possible main constituent orders. This suggests that it may actually be impossible to present coherent arguments for any particular linear order of elements in deep structure, and is a further indication of the irrelevance of linearity as a characteristic of deep structure.

An argument was presented in Section 4 that non-linear deep structure is a requirement for the most general expression of the linearity characteristics of a language. This was shown through examination of the English dative transformation. The linearizing function of this transformation duplicates the linearizing function of a phrase structure rule. The duplication can be eliminated, and a generalization about the linear order of the dative noun phrase directly expressed by a linearization rule applying post-transformationally. This line of reasoning can be extended to other cases in which transformations in a grammar with linear deep structure perform linearization, since this function will often duplicate the work of the phrase structure rules in such a grammar. In short, full generalizations about the linear order of elements can only be captured at the post-transformational level. Hence the deep structure of generative grammars is non-linear.[7]

The linearization rules are 'post-transformational' in the sense that post-transformational application is thus both necessary and suffi-

[7]An important additional argument for non-linear deep structure is that this imposes the constraint on grammars that transformations be stated in non-linear form, or in other words with such generality that they will apply to structures of whatever linear order. For these and other arguments see Sanders 1970 and 1975a. This article, though written independently of Sanders' work, nevertheless breaks little ground not broken by Sanders.

cient for their full effect. However, until evidence to the contrary can
be presented, it may be best to assume that linearization rules and
other rules are persistent rules, ordered only intrinsically with respect to one another. This approach is superior to saying that the linearization rules apply only after the transformations, since it eliminates the necessity of the definition of the 'post-transformational
level'.[8] Linearization rules ordered only intrinsically would apply in
the earliest line of a derivation (e.g. [NP, VP] → NP^VP), and in every
subsequent line which provides a set of constituents equivalent to the
input of a linearization rule.

But this paper has argued that application of linearization rules
on pre-terminal lines is irrelevant to the subsequent application of
transformations, and even that the use by the transformations of the
information which linearity provides constitutes loss of generality.
Since therefore application of persistent linearization rules on nonterminal strings is vacuous, deep structure is as a practical matter
non-linear.

[8]For other arguments for intrinsically ordered rules and the prohibition of extrinsic order see, for phonology, Vennemann (1971, 1972),
and for syntax Koutsoudas (1972) and Lehmann (1972) and other papers
cited by them.

6.   POSTSCRIPT: ON COUNTER-ARGUMENTS TO NON-LINEAR DEEP STRUCTURE

In a 1975 paper Emmon Bach presented six arguments intended "to undermine the notion that base structures are unordered". These arguments were said to be "facts which seem best explicable on the basis of rules or constraints that are applicable to intermediate structures that differ in their order from surface structures" (Bach 1975: 331). Such facts, if they existed, would indeed be sufficient evidence against the argument of this paper and others in this volume, since the most precise sense of the notion "unordered deep structure" is that expressed in Sanders' Invariant Ordering Constraint, according to which, once any order is determined between two elements in a derivation, that order is fixed (Sanders 1970: 1). (There are no reorderings.) Therefore, I wish here to review Bach's purported evidence, and to give counter-arguments to this.

6.1. METATHESIS.

Metathesis is "the simplest example of reordering", and "surely no one would argue that the underlying phonological representations of formatives are unordered. But if they are ordered and if metathesis is a possible phonological rule, the invariant ordering hypothesis must make the peculiar claim that reorderings are allowed in phonology, ...but disallowed in syntax" (Bach 1975: 332).

Where this argument goes wrong is in the words "surely no one would argue...", for it is quite possible that, indeed, just as there are no syntactic reorderings, there are no phonological reorderings, or synchronic metatheses. If two phonological segments a and b of some morpheme have the order ab in some realizations of the morpheme, and the order ba in others, then there is no necessity for the grammar to declare one or the other as basic in the sense of underlying, and the other derived. If E is all the relevant environments and the order ba occurs in the subset D of E, then the grammar has a rule $a, b \rightarrow ba$ / D; ab otherwise. I can see little significant difference between this formulation and that which Bach has in mind, the traditional formula-

tion in which instead of lexical a, b, we have lexical ab, and a rule
by which $ab \to ba$ / D. The linear temporal-spatial modes in which we
work in expressing such things makes the latter formulation seem simpler,
since we refer to the morpheme as having the lexical form XabY, without
noting that this representation has two parts: (i) constituent analysis
(the morpheme includes a and b), and (ii) linearization (these are in
the order ab). These are also the two parts of a standard phrase structure rule, as has been pointed out by Chomsky (1965: 123). The non-linear
analysis makes both statements explicitly. The significant difference
which does exist between the two formulations is that while the linear
(in this way, concrete) analysis claims that the variable morpheme's
lexical form has a and b in the order ab, a completely speculative and
non-empirical claim, the analysis with non-linear (in this way, abstract) structure underlying variable orders expresses only facts:
the morpheme has a and b in both orders, depending on the environment.

Just as the abstraction underlying the two phonological segments
d and t is the archi-phoneme D, with voicing 'abstracted out', so the
abstraction underlying the two orders ab and ba is reasonably the non-
linear structure [a, b], from which linearity has been abstracted.

True, most morphemes, those with invariable segment order, can be
conveniently and properly expressed in lexical form with order, e.g.
XabY or XbaY, whichever that invariable linear order is. In these cases
the linearization rule is implicit, since order is explicit in the
representation. But in the non-linear analysis, a morpheme which has
variable segment-order will take the form X[a, b]Y, and then a, b
will be linearized by context-sensitive rule.[9] This linearization rule
is paralleled in the traditional analysis by the synchronic metathesis
rule which inverts segments. The following example (from Hudson 1975)
illustrates such description of metathesis.

[9]The brackets are needed since a representation Xa,bY would be wrongly
interpreted as allowing the two possibilities XabY or bYXa. The bracketed
structure X[a, b]Y seems awkward, and is only necessary when we stay
on the horizontal dimension. Preferable would be a representation em-
ploying the vertical dimension, X $\frac{a}{b}$ Y, thus eliminating the need for
brackets.

In Faroese, the sequence *skt* is disallowed; stem-final sequences of *s* and *k* are *ks* before suffix-initial *t*: cf. [baįskωr] 'bitter' masc. sing. vs. [baįkst] neut. sing.; [fɛskωr] 'fresh' masc. sing. vs. [fekst] neut. sing. The spelling rules for these morphemes should leave the linear order of their final segments *k* and *s* unspecified: thus: *bai* [*s, k*] and *fe* [*s, k*]. Now since only the sequence *ks* is possible before *t*, this fact, or rule, must be expressed among the surface phonetic constraints (or morpheme structure conditions) of Faroese, i.e. ~ *skt* (the sequence *skt* is disallowed). In the absense of any applicable deletion or insertion rules, a necessary interpretation of this negative condition is: $s, k \rightarrow ks$ / ___*t*. The alternative *sk* of *s, k* in other environments than before *t* can be considered determined by convention: orders not determined by particular environments occur in non-particular environments.

It is not necessary to point out here-- where my purpose is just to show how the non-linear analysis of metathesis works, and its descriptive equivalence to the traditional, inversion-rule analysis-- that the non-linear analysis is, indeed, superior, insofar as it accomplishes the order *kst* without a metathesis rule, by use of the rule of surface phonetic constraint, which must be present in some form in the traditional analysis in addition to the rule of metathesis or segment-inversion, and which is the explanation of the metathesis in the first place.

6.2. PRONOUNS AND ANTECEDENTS.

The second argument against non-linear deep structure is found by Bach in the sentences (1), (2), (3), and (4), below. We are concerned with the interpretation of these sentences in which *John* and *him* are coreferential, as indicated by the subscript *x*'s.

(1) That Mary loves John$_x$ is obvious to him$_x$.

(2) *It is obvious to him$_x$ that Mary loves John$_x$.

(3) *John$_x$, it's obvious to him$_x$ that Mary loves.

(4) *It's John$_x$ that it's obvious to him$_x$ that Mary loves.

Bach's assumptions are that (3) and (4) are derived from (2), which is derived from (1). Sentence (2) is ungrammatical because in it the re-

quirement that a pronoun may not both precede and command its antecedent is violated. According to Bach the only way to explain the ungrammaticality of (3) and (4) is by reference to (2), an intermediate
(deep) structure with linear, if ungrammatical, characteristics, namely
the precedence of *him* to *John*.

Let me clarify this argument by noting that (2), (3), and (4) are
all good sentences on the interpretation of non-coreferentiality between
him and *John*. This is clear when another proper noun is substituted for
him: cf. *It is obvious to Bill that Mary loves John; John, it's obvious
to Bill that Mary loves; It's John that it's obvious to Bill that Mary
loves.* Thus it does seem that the problem with (2), (3), and (4) is pronominalization.

Obviously, in grammars with non-linear deep structures, pronominalization, since it depends on linear order, or precedence relations, cannot be a deep structure or pre-linear process, but has to be accomplished
in structures after these are linearized. Hence (3) and (4) cannot be
considered derived from (2), but from the non-linear and non-pronominalized structure equivalent to (2), (2'). The capital letters are to emphasize that we are dealing in (2') with not only pre-linear, but pre-
pronominalized structure.[10]

(2') It is obvious to JOHN$_x$ that Mary loves JOHN$_x$

This is transformed into (3'), or (4') by raisings.

(3') JOHN$_x$, it's obvious to JOHN$_x$ that Mary loves JOHN$_x$

(4') It's JOHN$_x$ that it's obvious to JOHN$_x$ that Mary loves
JOHN$_x$

These structures, when linearized, can then be pronominalized (where
pronominalization includes deletion, the extreme case of pronominalization) into perfectly good sentences (3'') and (4''):

[10]Since the non-linearity of sentence 2' is not crucial here, I have for
convenience neglected to express it as a non-linear structure, i.e.:
    It, [is, obvious, [to, John], [that, [Mary, [loves, John]]]]
    Again, the expression of non-linearity is awkward, involving extra
elements, since in the spatial-temporal modes in which we write-talk
about abstract linguistic structures for which there is really no significance for, nor evidence of linearity, we are used to having the
linearity expressed automatically.

(3'') John$_x$, it's obvious to that Mary loves him$_x$.

(4'') It's John$_x$ that it's obvious to that Mary loves him$_x$.

What is wrong, that is, with Bach's sentences (3) and (4) is not that they are derived from the ungrammatical sentence (2), but that pronominalization has been accomplished in them improperly.

Another pair of examples presented by Bach is part of the same argument, sentences (5) and (6):

(5) *Though he$_x$ expects me to be cruel to Harry $_x$, I will still help him$_x$.

(6) *Cruel to Harry$_x$ though he$_x$ expects me to be, I will still help him$_x$.

Sentence (6) is supposed to be derived from (5) by fronting/raising of the phrase *cruel to Harry*. Sentence (5) is ungrammatical since the pronoun *he* (coreferential with Harry) both precedes and commands its antecedent. This underlying ungrammaticality Bach offers as explanation of the asterisk on the derived sentence. Again, a deep linear order is said to explain surface facts. Paradoxical though this notion 'underlying and ungrammatical sentence' is, since it is common in much work on transformational syntax, let us continue to accept it here as a basis for argument.

Now sentence (6) cannot be explained as were those above, as ungrammatical not due to the ungrammatical order of its source, but due to improper pronominalization. However, I think that it really does not need much explanation at all, since it is not ungrammatical. It is unpragmatic. It has a marked order --fronting of *cruel to Harry*-- which is justified or explained by 'cruelness to Harry' having been established as the topic of the discourse in which this sentence is utterable. It is therefore unlikely that the proper noun *Harry* would not be pronominalized when fronted in this topicalized phrase. As evidence for this note that (6) is not all bad in the way that (3) and (4) are; in fact, with repetition and a little imagination sentence (6) begins to sound okay. This difference in status between (6) and (3) and (4) is a fact unexplained by the theory in which the ungrammaticality of these is explained identically.

There are a range of facts having to do with unpragmatic topicalization which require explanation within grammatical theory, for example,
why definite NPs are usually inappropriate in the post-verbal position
of expletive-*there* sentences (**There is the book on the table*; but cf.
Why do you think he's guilty? --Well, there's the way he looks at me.);
why unstressed pronouns are usually inappropriate in the *by*-phrase of
passive sentences (*The airplane was landed by the navigator* vs. *The airplane was landed by him*). It will not do to look for the explanation of
these phenomena in the linear order of underlying sentences.

Furthermore, sentence (6), if in fact it is ill-formed, would not
thereby be counter-evidence to non-linearity in deep structure, since
its ill-formedness would be consistent with the clearest expression of
the non-linear hypothesis, Sanders' Invariant Ordering Constraint. This
will be seen better in the next section, regarding Bach's next argument.

6.3. POSTAL'S GLOBAL CONSTRAINT ON PRONOMINALIZATION

This constraint, argued for by Postal (1972), relies on the
existence of linearity in deep structure. It states that a sentence
would be ill-formed in which (i) a *wh*-word is to the left of its coreferent pronoun, and (ii) that *wh*-word was to the right of its coreferent
pronoun in deep structure. The example given by Bach is (7), coming
from (8):

(7) *To which actress's$_x$ mother did the columnist report
her$_x$ victory?

(8) The columnist reported her$_x$ victory to which actress's$_x$
mother?

Sentence (7) is said to be a violation of the constraint, and "ill-
formed"; the word "ungrammatical" is not used. I mention this, since
many persons find this sentence and others given by Postal as violations
of his constraint to be okay, or at least no worse than, say, clustered
negatives, and extra-embeddings, which are complex, but not ill-formed
in the sense 'ungrammatical'.

But this argument against non-linear deep structure can be handled
by briefly noting that Postal's constraint, if true, is consistent with

the existence of such structure. In grammars with non-linear deep structure pronominalization has to be done after linearity is fixed, and,
following Sander's Invariant Ordering Constraint, no movement can be
allowed subsequently. This says: "If an element A is ordered to the
left of an element B in any line of any derivation there is no line in
that derivation in which A is ordered to the right of B." (Sanders
1970: 1; also in Sanders 1975a and Sanders 1975b) This is more-or-less
what Postal's constraint says, but about just one class of words: *wh*-
words. Sentences (5) and (6), then, are therefore also consistent with
invariant ordering; (6) is supposed to come from (5), by inversion of
cruel to Harry and *though he expects me to be*. Notice how reasonable
it is that such inversions be disallowed. Pronominalization, accomplished in (5), has to have been accomplished in a linearized structure,
and partly for reasons of linearity (*him* both commands and precedes
Harry) has been accomplished ungrammatically. The derivation is properly terminated and rejected at this point. This is just what invariant
ordering requires.

Consider Postal's example *Who did Joan talk about his illness to?*
(16b), a violation of his constraint on moving *wh*-words, whereas *Who
did Joan talk to about his illness?* is not. As Postal says, both can
be said to come from [*Joan talked to who about his illness*]. Clearly it
would be inefficient for the grammar to first move *to who* to the right,
then extract *who* and move it to the left. This is just the sort of unmotivated hypothetical moving around of things which is explicitly disallowed by the Invariant Ordering Constraint. Instead the grammar is
directed to put things where they belong, the first time. A global rule
interpreting the input and output of *wh*-movement treats a symptom of
the problem only. And note that the example above (Postal's 16b) is
difficult to interpret whether coreferentiality between *Who* and *his*
is assumed or not. The problem is the 'stranded' preposition.

Many of the sentences said to violate the constraint on *wh*-word
movement seem all right, if complex, e.g. *The official$_x$, who$_x$ the
policeman who arrested him$_x$ claimed was drunk, was drunk* (Postal's 4c);
Who$_x$ did Mary say his$_x$ mother yelled at? (2a); *The astronaut$_x$ who$_x$ his$_x$*

mother claimed was a psychotic was arrested (9a). The questions, such
as Postal's (2a), above, and (7) are more difficult to interpret for
reasons discussed by Chomsky (1975: 98-100). Others are problematic
for reasons unrelated to the proposed constraint on *wh*-word movement,
such as *Who did Joan talk about his illness to?*, with the stranded
preposition.

Consider *The tigers$_x$, which$_x$ their$_x$ keepers were eaten by, are not
hungry now* (Postal's 4d). This sentence is bad pragmatically. It has
an embedded passive sentence, and the function of the passive, topicalization, doesn't often exist for embedded sentences. Consistency of
topicalization would require either *The tigers, which ate...*, or *The
keepers, which were eaten...* Similarly with the example *Who did Joan
claim his mistress had been visited by?* (14b) --the passive construction (marked order motivated by topicalization) is unmotivated in the
embedded sentence. In terms of linear deep structure this sentence has
to be derived by first moving (*by*) *who* to the right, and then extrac-
ting *who* and moving it to the left. The first step is pragmatically
unmotivated.

Another example starred by Postal is: *An engineer$_x$ who$_x$ Mary
claimed his$_x$ mother refuses to let out after dark arrived* (10a). This
sentence would be a lot better if it didn't have the 'heavy' modifier
on the subject. The subject of a sentence is ordinarily a topic, and
thus unlikely to be appropriate with such extensive modification.
Notice how much better is a sentence, structurally also a violation
of Postal's constraint, when we shorten the relative clause modifier
of the subject and extend the verb phrase focus: *That little boy whom
Mary claims his mother pampers is nevertheless down there in the rain
knocking on our front door!*

There is no contradiction in saying, first, that Postal's constraint is consistent with non-linear deep structure or invariant
ordering, and, second, that the constraint is mistaken. If true, the constraint is consistent; if false, it says nothing one way or the other.

6.4. STRESS FACTS

This argument depends on Bach's acceptance of Bresnan's (1971) analysis of English stress, according to which, he says: "a wide variety of intonational facts...can be explained on the assumption that the stress rules apply within the syntactic cycle. Among other things, her hypothesis accounts for the difference in placement of main stress and high pitch on examples like these":

(15) What has Helen written?

(16) What books has Helen written?

The argument here against non-linear deep structure resides in the fact that Bresnan's analysis "depends crucially on the application of the stress rules to examples like (15) and (16) *before* the interrogative has been shifted to the front of the sentence." That is, stress assignment, which happens in deep structure, is on linearized structure.

This argument against non-linear deep structure totally relies on the claim that stress assignment can be done, at least in general, along the lines of Bresnan's analysis. That is, stress is assigned as a function of syntactic structure. I am satisfied to respond to this argument with simply the counter-claim that this assumption is wrong, and I refer to Bolinger (1972), who presented numerous counter-examples to the stress assignments predicted by Bresnan's analysis, and concluded: "The distribution of sentence accents is not determined by syntactic structure but by semantic and emotional highlighting. Syntax is relevant indirectly in that some structures are more likely to be highlighted than others. But a description along these lines can only be in statistical terms" (Bolinger 1972: 644).

We can take sentences (15) and (16) to illustrate this point. Bresnan's analysis will place main stresses as in these sentences. But what then of sentences (17) and (18), which have the same structure, but different stress?

(17) What has Helen written?

(18) What books has Helen written?

Sentence (17) would be heard when the speaker doubts an assertion that Helen has written something, and sentence (18) is heard in contexts

where *books* is topicalized, and where the emphasis of the question is
'what books?'. One who would maintain Bresnan's analysis might wish to claim
that (17) and (18), unlike (15) and (16), are 'contrastive', or in some
sense special, marked, deserving special treatment. But while this may
be true for (17), it is doubtfully so for (18), which seems just as
probable a sentence as (16). And, with Bolinger, we would question as
adequate a grammar which merely accounts for most of the sentences of
the language, and leaves as exceptions innumerable quite common others.
Again the foundation of the argument against non-linear deep structure
proves faulty.

6.5. CHINESE AS AN SOV LANGUAGE

Chinese has both SOV and SVO main constituent orders, relative clauses both before and after their heads, and, except in relative
clauses, no backward pronominalization (Tai 1973). Tai argued that
Chinese is in deep structure an SOV language, the relative clause is
after its head, and pronominalization is then always forward. Later,
relative clauses will be preposed and SVO orders derived as appropriate. The argument for linear deep structure in all this is supposed to
be a resulting simplification of the pronominalization rule, which
operates only forward.

The rule which, after pronominalization, would invert head nouns
and relative clauses is said to be universal for SOV languages (Bach
1965; Tai 1973: 663). It is important to note that this 'universal rule
of relative clause preposing in SOV languages', as not part of the
grammar of specific languages, does not itself succeed in simplifying
the grammar of Chinese as an SOV language, since Chinese does have some
post-posed clauses (Tai 661-62 and footnote 7). These would have to be
derived by a language-specific blocking of the proposed universal rule.
The argument from Chinese as an SOV language for deep linear order
(Bach's argument; Tai did not consider non-linear alternatives) depends
on the claimed simplification of pronominalization.

Let us compare the relevant parts of the two grammars of Chinese,
that with deep SOV order, and that without deep order.

Deep SOV Order	*No Deep Order*
(i) Pronominalize: always forward;	Linearize main constituents: some SVO orders, otherwise SOV;
(ii) Block in some cases the universal rule of relative clause preposing in SOV languages;	Linearize relative clauses: some postposed, otherwise preposed;
(iii) SOV → SVO in some cases.	Pronominalize: backwards in preposed relative clauses, otherwise forward.

The two analyses seem relatively equivalent, except for the greater complexity of the pronominalization rule in the analysis with deep order, which has to work both forward and backward.

Recall that an advantage that could not be claimed for the SOV analysis of Chinese was elimination of a language-specific rule of relative clause preposing in favor of the universal rule with this effect. Since the language does have some post-posed relatives, this possible advantage is immediately neutralized in Chinese by the necessity to block some applications of the universal rule.

But this sort of advantage, arguing from universals, can be claimed for the analysis in which Chinese deep structure is non-linear. For pronominalization is universally into a relative clause, on whichever side of the head noun it stands. The pronominalization (or deletion) of a noun phrase of a clause when that clause is sister to a coreferential noun phrase is virtually a definition of 'relative clause'. Thus language specific statements of the direction of pronominalization between head nouns and relative clauses ought certainly, if universals do have this 'discount value', to be discounted, and the analysis of Chinese as without deep linear order turns out to be no more complex than that of Chinese as an SOV language.

6.6. ORDER DEPENDENCE OF UNIVERSAL RULES

This last argument by Bach is easy to dispose of since it is based on a misunderstanding on his part about the relationship in grammars without linear deep structures between rules which change

constituency (transformations) and rules which linearize. The argument
is based on an apparent fact, discovered by Kuno (1974), about extraposition rules. "Languages like Japanese, with clause-final complementizers, never seem to allow extraposition, while languages like
Hindi do allow it (both being verb-final languages). In Turkish, it is
just those clauses that have clause-initial complementizers (*ki*) that
can extrapose." (Bach 1975: 336) What Kuno showed was a dependence of
extraposition rules on complementizer position. Clauses with preposed
complementizers can extrapose; clauses with postposed complementizers
cannot.

Bach then says (336) of "grammars with unordered structures and
ordering rules", that "since extraposition affects not just order but
also dominance relations, it must be a regrouping rule ordered before
any order has been defined on the structures." That is, since "extraposition occurs only with structures containing complementizers that will
eventually be preposed, we must constrain this rule to operate only on
clauses containing these items". The rule cannot be constrained to
operate on clauses containing inparticular but *preposed* complementizers.
As Bach says, "Surely, this is turning things on their head."

Surely it would be, if grammars with unordered deep structures
worked this way. Unfortunately for this argument against such grammars,
such a 'separation of levels' requirement has not been suggested.
Sanders' Invariant Ordering Constraint, which Bach specifically refers
to as "the most precise hypothesis about unordered base structures"
(Bach 1975: 330) says, recall (already quoted above, §6.3): "If an element A is ordered to the left of an element B in any line of any derivation, there is no line in that derivation in which A is ordered to
the right of B" (Sanders 1970:1;   also in Sanders 1975a and 1975b:
400).

What this means is that the complementizer can certainly be ordered
before its clause prior to the movement of the clause, with its preposed
complementizer, in extraposition. If the generalization is, indeed, as
Kuno says, it will be properly expressed in the grammar by making extraposition conditional on the presence of the preposed (linearized)

complementizer. Thus extraposition is necessarily and intrinsically ordered after the linearization of the complementizer before its clause.

Bach's sixth argument is useful since it forces us to clarify the meaning of the notion 'non-linear deep structure'. Probably because of the vagueness in the notion 'deep structure' itself, the former term has been often misunderstood. Sanders, whose writing has been characterized by precision and explicitness (and perhaps for that reason not widely enough read), has always avoided the phrase. Still, it is perhaps useful as a general expression of the fact that the formal and abstract sentence relationships ordinarily expressed by transformations (in 'deep structure') are not linear relationships. In Section 5 I wrote, "full generalizations about the linear order of elements can only be captured at the post-transformational level." The analysis of extraposition just discussed either disproves this, or is consistent with it as with the Invariant Ordering Constraint when we interpret the linearization of the complementizer and its clause to mark the "post-transformational" level for that relationship. The wider, higher level of the relationship of the clause, with its complementizer, to the rest of the sentence, can still undergo at least the transformation of extraposition. Simply put, the point about linearity of deep structure is whether transformations change linearity, and the answer to this is that they do not, or at least there is no evidence of this.

There are, however, two further questions about Bach's sixth argument. First, regarding how Kuno's interpretation of the interdependence of extraposition and preposed complementizers is to be expressed, another possibility would be to say that extraposed clauses select complementizers with the characteristic of being linearized before the clause. This means that the selection of a particular complementizer would be tantamount to linearizing it. This seems reasonable, since complementizers are grammatical morphemes with no intrinsic selectability. Selection of grammatical morphemes may ordinarily be dependent on linearization, rather than vice versa.

Second, it may be questioned whether Kuno's functional interpretation of the interdependence of extraposition and complementizer posi-

tion ought to be expressed synchronically. According to Kuno, extraposed clauses need preposed complementizers to prevent confusion in
preception of the clause structure of sentences; stacking of subordinating particles is avoided, and the complementizer in preposed position is able to announce the new clause (Kuno 1974: 126-127; Bach
1975: 336). If the problem of misunderstandings is great this will
explain how the interdependence came about in language evolution via
natural selection, much as humans are generally believed to have evolved
upright stance. Such explanations perhaps need not be built into synchronic grammars since they would not have to be considered available
to language learners in order to control aspects of synchrony. (For
discussion of the issue, see Sampson 1975.) On the other hand, if
preposed complementizers make extrapositions easier to comprehend, they
are reasonably a factor in learning extrapositions, and hence available
for incorporation as a condition on the synchronic extraposition rule.
The differentiation of functional factors which control diachronic
evolution only, and those which contribute to synchronic development
is sure to be an issue for future research.

We have examined Bach's six arguments against non-linearity in
deep structure, and found each of these wanting. Yet linearity is something which the usual model of transformational grammar would have us
believe is present throughout every deep line of every derivation. If
it is, shouldn't there be better evidence of this claim than the six
arguments discussed above?[11]

[11] Occasionally throughout Bach 1975 one finds other arguments against
non-linear deep structure. Since Bach himself did not find any of these
strong enough to include in his section of counter-arguments, I have
not considered it necessary to reply to them here. Anyway, they all
seem to me also faulty. For example, arguments on pp. 323-24, 337-38
are also based on the incorrect requirement that all transformations
precede all linearization rules.
        According to Bach (p.340), not only the argument for Chinese as
an SOV language, but "all analyses of languages in which the underlying order is different from the surface order count as evidence
against invariant ordering..." Among these are Bach's article on
Amharic as a VSO language and McCawley's for English as a VSO language, both of which have been discussed above (first in 1972). It
seems reasonable to suppose that Tai's discussion of Chinese as an

SOV language was chosen as the most defensible of these analyses.
Elsewhere we read that "There is something inherently linear in
language." (p. 338) This is unquestionable, and is expressed in grammars with non-linear deep structure in the linearization rules. But
what is inherently linear in the abstract structure which relates the
two clauses of, say, *When the bell rang, we went out*, and *We went out
when the bell rang*; or that which relates the object NP and prepositional adverb in *He put the ball down* and *He put down the ball?* The
point is: deep structures ought to be considered abstractions *away
from* linearity.

CONSTRAINTS ON CONSTITUENT ORDERING*

GERALD A. SANDERS

1.   Grammars specify symbolic equivalence relations between the empirically-interpretable semantic and phonetic representations of linguistic objects. In all theories of grammar, it is assumed that the terminal phonetic representation of any linguistic object must include, for at least some of its constituents, an explicit specification of their relative linear ordering. This paper will be concerned with the manner in which these ordering specifications are assigned by grammars and with some of the metatheoretical constraints on ordering which are required for the adequate explanation of natural language data.

Possible alternative treatments of ordering are determined by alternative assumptions concerning the derivational predictability, variability, and terminal completeness of the ordering relations that hold between linguistic constituents. Evidence will be presented here to support

*
 An abbreviated version of this paper was presented at the Summer Meeting of the Linguistic Society of America, Urbana, Illinois, July 25, 1969. Further treatments of this topic will be found in Sanders (1969a, 1969b) and in my paper "On the explanation of constituent-order universals" in C.N. Li (ed.), *Word Order and Word Order Change* (Austin: University of Texas Press, 1975). I am indebted to Andreas Koutsoudas for his valuable comments and criticism, and have also benefitted from the discussion of various ordering problems with Emmon Bach, Robert Lefkowitz, Gunter Schaarschmidt, and James Tai. This research was supported in part by a grant under the NSF Science Development Program in Language and Behavior, the University of Texas at Austin. This paper has previously appeared in *Papers in Linguistics* 2, 1970. 460 - 502. We would like to thank Anthony Vanek and Linguistic Research, inc., for allowing us to reprint it here.

the claim that the most general and most revealing grammatical theories
are precisely those which assume that all terminal phonetic elements are
ordered and that all linguistic ordering relations are derivationally
predictable and invariant. This restriction will be seen to follow naturally from the conjunction of the following three universal constraints
on grammatical derivations:

(1) the *Semantic Completeness Constraint*, that all constituents of terminal semantic representations are grouped and
not ordered;

(2) the *Phonetic Completeness Constraint*, that all constituents of terminal phonetic representations are ordered
and not grouped;

(3) the *Invariant Order Constraint*, that if an element *A* precedes an element *B* in any line of a given derivation, then
there is no line in that derivation in which *B* precedes *A*.

These constraints all appear to be independently reasonable and
well-motivated. The two Completeness Constraints could in fact be derived from the general formal definition of an interpretable linguistic
representation as a string of property and relational elements which are
each uniquely interpretable in the same mode.[1] The Invariant Order

---

[1] Something can be a linguistic object only if it has an empirical interpretation in each of   two entirely distinct modes -- one of these
being characterized by observation statements about cognitive states
or events, the other by observation statements about articulatory or
other physical gestures which generate publically-perceptible changes
in the extra-organic universe. At the level of ordinary non-micro-
scopic human observation, which is the only level of interest to the
linguist, these two modes of interpretation clearly share no elements
or relations in common, there being no resemblance whatever between
a cognitive object and a physical one, and no such things, for example,
as a "green nasalization" or a "glottalized hope". For simplicity, it
will be assumed here that all non-cognitive interpretations of linguistic objects are *phonetic* interpretations, specified by observation
statements about the sound-generating configurations of the human articulatory apparatus; none of our conclusions depend on this choice,
however, since all other possible physical interpretations of such objects must also include specifications of distinctive spatial or
temporal ordering relations. It should also be noted that the Completeness Constraints follow from either a strong or a weak version of

Constraint could likewise be viewed simply as a necessary implication of the defining asymmetric, or non-commutativity, axiom for ordering relations.[2] We will be concerned here, however, not with the logical basis and naturalness of these constraints, but rather with their empirical implications and their specific values in motivating and directing the expression of significant explanatory generalizations about natural languages.

    2.   In order to make any real comparison of alternative theories, there must be some single theory or metalanguage to which each of the alternatives can be accurately reduced. The joint reduction of all alternative theories of ordering can be adequately achieved by means of a theory which assumes that there are two and only two distinct relations which may hold between the constituents of linguistic representations, and one and only one schema for rules mapping instances of one relation into instances of the other.

    The two relations we will assume are those which nearly all grammarians have assumed to be jointly necessary for the adequate description of natural languages. These relations are distinctively different both in their formal properties as relations and in their empirical interpretations.

    The first relation is symmetric, or commutative, and has the rough interpretation 'is (cognitively or psychologically) associated with'. We may call this relation *grouping*, or co-constituency, and symbolize it by a comma between bracketed arguments. Thus, for any

the elementary definition of terminality, the former requiring that every element of a terminal representation must be interpretable and interpretable in the same mode, the latter requiring only that every *interpretable* element must be interpretable in the same mode, thereby allowing for the possible occurrence of intermediate, or purely hypothetical, elements in either or both of the terminal representations of an object.

[2] This is strictly true only if the relation that holds between the lines of any given derivation is an equivalence relation, i.e. a binary relation that is symmetric, transitive, and reflexive. I know of no evidence to the contrary, and there actually appear to be a number of very strong arguments for making equivalence an explicit condition for the well-formedness of all derivations. See Sanders (1969b) for detailed discussion.

constituents A and B,

      (1) (A, B) = (B, A)

The second relation that may hold between linguistic constituents is asymmetric, or non-commutative, and has the empirical interpretation 'precedes', or 'is initiated prior to'. This relation, usually known as *ordering*, or linear concatenation, will be symbolized here by an ampersand between arguments. Thus, for any (non-identical) constituents A and B,

      (2) (A & B) ≠ (B & A)

Given the relations of grouping and ordering, we can now formally define an *ordering rule* as any statement of the form

      (3) X (A, B) Y = X (A & B) Y

where X and/or Y may be null and where A and B are both constituents, i.e. bracketed strings that are free of unpaired brackets.[3]

Each ordering rule expresses an empirical generalization about the order of the constituents of some grammatical construction. Thus, for example, rule (4) expresses the generalization that in constructions consisting of a determiner and a noun it is always the case (e.g. in English) that the determiner precedes the noun.

      (4) ((DET), (NOUN)) = ((DET) & (NOUN))

---

[3] Like all other grammatical statements, ordering rules are assumed to express simple equivalence relations between linguistic representations and thus to justify the prediction of groupings from orderings as well as the prediction of orderings from groupings. All of the matters under consideration here, however, are independent of the distinction between equational and non-equational grammar, since the full range of alternative assumptions about ordering is available to all theories of either type. For simplicity of discussion, moreover, we will restrict ourselves here to the context of phonetically-directed derivations, and will thus assume that all relational mappings are from groupings to orderings rather than the reverse; all references to precedences in the application of rules will also refer here to their precedence in phonetically-directed derivations. It should also be noted that ordering rules are defined here in such a way that ordering relations can be assigned only to sister immediate constituents of the same construction. As this restriction has been implicitly observed in most of the conventional statements about ordering, its motivation, naturalness, and explanatory value will not be discussed here independently of the proposed theory of derivational ordering that presupposes it.

Each such rule determines a pair of converse intermodal, or lexical, substitution transformations which justify derivational mapping relations between pairs of phrase-markers which differ only in the nature of the relational element which is associated with a certain specified pair of constituents. Like other rules of grammar, therefore, each ordering rule is empirically justifiable in terms of its specific contributions to the general grammatical mapping function that specifies the proper pairings between the interpretable semantic representations of linguistic objects and their interpretable phonetic representations.

This general system, with its two relations and one inter-relational mapping schema, is sufficient for the reduction of all possible theories of ordering. We are thus able now to discuss the alternative assumptions of these theories in an explicit and notationally uniform manner.

Concerning the *predictability* of ordering relations, there are only three logically-possible alternatives: either no orderings are predictable, or else some are predictable, or else all are predictable. Ordering would be *wholly unpredictable* in some language if and only if, for any (A & B) in its phonetic representations, (A & B) is not in the range of any possible true ordering rule. It goes without saying that there is no natural language which has this property, and even an artificial language of this sort appears to be inconceivable.[4] Ordering would be *partly predictable* in some language if and only if there is at least one (A & B) in its phonetic representations which is in the range of a true ordering rule, and at least one (C & D) which is not in the range of any such rule. Ordering would be *completely predictable*, finally, if and only if *every* (A & B) is in the range of some true ordering rule.

[4] Thus, for any language whose terminal representations are subject to parsing into a finite sequence of constructions with finite constituents, there will be a finite set of possible orderings for the constituents of any given representation, and these will thus be specifiable by a finite set of ordering rules. Moreover, even for a language which consists merely of randomly-ordered and randomly-bracketed strings over any finite or infinite alphabet of symbols, every ordered pair of constituents will still fall within the range of a true ordering rule (X, Y) = (X & Y), where X and Y are unrestricted variables for any constituents.

With the possible exception of some constituents of certain independently exceptional idioms and polysyllabic names, I know of no evidence which might lead one to doubt the claim that ordering is completely predictable in all languages. The possibility of complete prediction has in fact been explicitly demonstrated already, both for invariant-order grammars (by Hockett, 1954) and for variable-order ones (by Chomsky, 1965). However, since it is possible to predict almost anything, given the right assumptions and initial conditions, we will assume here that the only interesting questions about the prediction of ordering relations involve not the *possibility* of prediction, but rather its explanatory *significance*. We will take up these questions shortly.

Given the standard empirical conditions that at least some terminal phonetic elements are ordered and at least some terminal semantic elements are grouped, there are only four possible assumptions about the *completeness* of the relations between constituents of terminal representations, a pair of mutually contradictory assumptions for each terminal mode. Thus phonetic representations must be either completely or partially ordered, and semantic representations either completely or partially grouped, where partial grouping implies partial ordering, of course, and vice versa. For theories which observe neither of the completeness constraints, semantic and phonetic representations are relationally nondistinct, both being strings of elements that are partially ordered and partially grouped. For theories which observe both of these constraints, these two modes of terminal representation are mutually exclusive not only in their constituent property or categorial elements but also in the relations which hold between them.

There appears to be no presently known evidence against either of the two completeness constraints. Moreover, the only possible way of falsifying them would appear to be by demonstrating that some states in the proper cognitive renditions of some sentence are *significantly ordered*, or that some states in its proper articulatory renditions are *significantly simultaneous*. Pending such evidence, therefore, it is necessary to consider both of the completeness principles to be true, since they determine a smaller class of possible grammars than their contradictories and have a much greater capacity to motivate and direct the search for significant generalizations about languages.

Concerning the derivational *variability* of ordering relations, finally, there are only two possible assumptions: Ordering is either invariant in derivations, or else it is variable. The latter assumption allows for the possibility of rules effecting the derivational reordering, or permutation, of constituents; the former precludes any such rules. Since any ordering and subsequent reordering of constituents, as in (5),

(5) (i)   (A, B) = (A & B)

(ii) X (A & B) Y = X (B & A) Y

will always be descriptively equivalent to a pair of simple ordering rules, as in (6),

(6) (i)   X (A, B) Y = X (B & A) Y

(ii) (A, B) = (A & B)

the choice between the contradictory assumptions of variance and invariance can obviously be made only on the basis of the range and generality of the explanations which they respectively determine. On this basis existing evidence appears to consistently favor the assumption of invariance. A small sample of such evidence will be considered in the remaining sections of the present study.

3.   We have roughly delimited the set of possible alternative theories of ordering and have established a general framework for their comparison and empirical evaluation. By translating these alternatives into the common metalanguage of derivational ordering, we have already shown, in effect, that, in terms of ordinary descriptive capacity at least, any fact which can be accounted for by a theory that assumes unpredictable, variable, or incomplete ordering can also be accounted for by a more restricted derivational theory which observes both the completeness and invariance constraints. We turn now to some of the positive evidence suggesting that these constraints are not only possible principles of grammar but also necessary ones.

The Semantic Completeness Constraint implies that all ordering relations are predictable in natural languages. The Phonetic Completeness Constraint implies that some such prediction can be made about every constituent of every terminal phonetic representation.

The Invariant Order Constraint implies simply that all predictions about
ordering must be true -- in other words, that contradictory orderings can
never be assigned to the same structure, and that each ordering rule
must be consistent with all other rules and theorems of the grammar that
includes it. Since the generation of true predictions by consistent theories is the primary goal of any science, these constraints are clearly
superior to their contradictions in their power to motivate and direct
significant research in the science of linguistics. Moreover, for any
given language, each of the completeness and invariance constraints
determines a smaller class of possible grammars than its contradictory,
thereby providing a more precise and more restricted formal characterization of the set of natural languages. It thus seems entirely appropriate to consider each of these principles to be true until proven otherwise. However, even if we ignore their superior restrictive and motivating
power and assume that the burden of proof rests equally on all possible
hypotheses about ordering, it would still be possible to demonstrate the
truth of the completeness and invariance constraints by showing that
there are some facts about languages which can be adequately explained
only by theories which are inconsistent with their contradictories. With
respect to semantic completeness and invariance at least, there appear
to be a number of facts of this sort.

   Thus if, in contradiction to the Semantic Completeness Constraint,
some orderings were unpredictable in natural language, then it would be
possible that some grammar might generate or accept a pair of pre-transformational structures which are related to each other in the manner of
(7a) and (7b).

   (7)   (a) $_S$(NP & PREDICATE)
         (b) $_S$(PREDICATE & NP)

But, although the power of postulating such pairs is available to all
grammars governed by any of the standard models of transformational
grammar, I know of no actual grammar which has ever made use of this
power. In fact, while there are many superficial contrasts in ordering,
such as that illustrated by the Chinese sentences (8a) and (8b),

   (8)   (a)   háizi lái-le   'The child came'

(b)   lái-le háizi   'A child came',

these have invariably been found to be predictable from independently
motivated differences in the properties and groupings of constituents;
and most serious linguists would undoubtedly agree that an adequate explanation of these or any other facts about natural language can never be
achieved on the basis of postulated underlying order contrasts of the
sort illustrated in (7). This strongly suggests that it is a fact about
natural languages that they do not have distinct underlying constructions
which differ *only* in the order of their constituents. If this is true,
then it is a significant fact about language which can *only* be accounted
for by theories which assume the Semantic Completeness Constraint, since
the only reasonable explanation for the universal non-existence of contrasts in underlying order is the universal non-existence of underlying
order.

The primary empirical question about ordering involves the determination of the level or levels of representation with respect to which
ordering relations can be most appropriately predicted. Since ordering
is predictable from the properties of constituents and their grouping
relations, it is logically possible that ordering rules might apply at
any or all levels at which such properties and relations are specified.
For simplicity, though, we will consider the only available choices to
be the mutually-contradictory hypotheses of Deep Ordering and Surface
Ordering. The Deep Ordering Hypothesis asserts that, in phonetically-
directed derivations, ordering relations are assigned prior to the application of all or most of the adjunction, deletion, and regrouping transformations of a grammar, and thus that the latter rules are defined upon
structures which are at least partially ordered. The Surface Ordering
Hypothesis asserts that ordering rules are applied only subsequently to
the application of other transformations, and that the latter are thus
defined on structures that are wholly unordered. The basis for choice
here is quite straightforward, and the relevant evidence is abundant and
varied. The conclusions following from this evidence, moreover, appear
to be consistently the same, namely that the hypothesis of Surface
Ordering is correct and that the hypothesis of Deep Ordering is false.

With respect to order itself, the necessity and sufficiency of the
Surface Order Hypothesis is strongly evidenced by the fact that all significant generalizations about the order of syntactic constituents hold
with respect to the constituents and constituency relations of representations at the level of syntactic surface structure, a level which is
derivationally subsequent to the application of all rules effecting alternations in the content or constituency relations of syntactic constructions. In fact, many true generalizations of this sort have been adequately expressed even in those traditional and structuralist grammars
which recognized no other level of representation than that of surface
structure. Moreover, Hockett's (1954) demonstration of the complete or at
least near-complete predictability of orderings from superficial groupings
appears to have gone wholly unchallenged thus far; nor, it seems, has any
real effort been made to justify any postulation of pre-superficial
ordering, or to show how an observed regularity in superficial ordering
might be explained by any theory that permits such postulations. But, a-
part from all of this, there is even more important evidence which can be
brought to bear on the question of Deep vs. Surface Ordering, evidence
which shows that Surface Ordering is necessary for the expression of
generalizations not only about order but also about many of the other
significant properties and relations of linguistic objects.

In order to falsify the Surface Ordering Hypothesis it would be
necessary merely to show that if some transformation is assumed to depend
on a prior ordering of constituents a more general explanation of some
facts results than if the contrary is assumed. I know of no explicit arguments to this effect[5], and I will attempt to demonstrate shortly that
what would appear to be the strongest implicit one is actually invalid.

[5] It would appear that Chomsky's very brief and inconclusive remarks on
ordering (Chomsky, 1965:123-27) constitute the only explicit effort
that has been made thus far to provide any defense at all for the hypothesis of Deep Ordering. Chomsky says nothing here, however, about the
question of the existence or non-existence of motivated adjunction, deletion, or regrouping transformations that are dependent on a prior
ordering of constituents. Moreover, the two arguments which he does
present in support of a particular version of the Deep Ordering Hypothesis are both invalid -- the first because it depends on a factual

Moreover, with respect to syntax at least, there is an abundance of evidence suggesting that the situation is precisely the reverse of that which would be required for the falsification of Surface Ordering, evidence showing that there is a significant loss in explanatory generalization if transformations are permitted to apply to ordered rather than unordered representations.

One rather simple example should suffice to illustrate what appears to be the general situation here. Thus, consider the fact that in English all superficial subjects are ordered before their superficial verbs -- this being true, of course, *regardless of* the *underlying* properties or constituency relations of the subject. This is a straightforward and extremely general principle of English, and one would expect it to be expressed in one way or another by any adequate grammar of this language. But this simple generalization cannot *possibly* be expressed by any grammar which accepts the assumption of Deep Ordering rather than Surface Ordering.

Thus English has alternations of the active-passive type. If these are accounted for by means of an optional transformation of the conventional sort, then this transformation must, by Deep Ordering hypothesis, apply to a structure that is ordered either like the surface order of the active, or like that of the passive, or like neither of the surface orders. If it is like either of the actual surface orders, though, the generalization that surface subjects precede their verbs will necessarily be lost, since the preverbal order of active and passive subjects will

claim (that all alternate-order paraphrases have determinate derivational precedence relations) which is falsified by data from every known language (e.g. by pairs such as *John and Bill ran* and *Bill and John ran*), the second because it depends on a fact (that no natural language has both free ordering and free grouping of all its superficial constituents) which is simply incapable of differentiating between the hypotheses of Deep and Surface Ordering, both of these being equally consistent with both free- and non-free ordering, and neither having any implications at all with respect to free grouping.

follow in this grammar from *different* sets of rules -- in one case from
a pretransformational ordering rule, in the other from that rule *in
conjunction with* some *re*ordering rule.

Thus the only way that a Deep Order grammar might hope to prevent
such loss of generality with respect to alternation sets of this type
would be by the postulation of a base order for the set which differs
from the surface order of *any* of its members. Thus, for example, the base
order (Verb & Agent & Patient) might be postulated for English, the
passive rule might permute agents and non-agents, and a single reordering
rule permuting the verb and its immediately subsequent nominal could then
be posited and claimed to express at least some sort of approximation of
the generalization that all surface subjects precede their verbs. But any
such treatment would clearly be arbitrary, excessively complex, and
grossly unnatural, since it would require an ad hoc ordering rule and
two ad hoc reordering rules to do exactly the same work that a single
entirely natural surface ordering rule can do. Moreover, any attempt to
extend this approach to accomodate facts about other constructions in the
language would quickly lead to the postulation of pretransformational
structures whose orderings are *wholly unrelated* to those of the surface
structures which are derived from them, with the further result that the
base orders required to preserve generalizations about some alternation
sets will be incompatible with those required to preserve generalizations
about other sets.[6]

It can thus be seen that the Deep Ordering assumption is inherently
inconsistent with the fact that surface subjects precede their verbs in

---

[6] It might conceivably be argued that the given data here could be
accounted for by means of a general "everywhere" condition to the
effect that no line of a derivation is well-formed unless every subject
is ordered before its predicate. However, such a constraint, which
could be justified only in grammars without rules of formation
(cf. Sanders, 1967, 1969b), would clearly appear to be too powerful
here, since there is no independent evidence that order is ever relevant to the well-formedness of linguistic representations at any level
other than the levels of syntactic and phonetic surface structure.

English, a fact which can be adequately explained, it seems, only by theories which incorporate the contradictory assumption that ordering relations are not assigned to verbs and nominals until all rules affecting their constituency relations have already been applied. It is also readily apparent that this will generally be the case for all alternation sets whose members differ as to the order of their constituents, since an appropriately general explanation of their ordering properties will always depend on the prior application of all relevant constituency-differentiating transformations, the latter rules being most simply and most generally expressed as relations between wholly unordered representations.

This dependency relation between ordering rules and other transformations is even more striking in the case of complex sentences, where nominals raised from a subordinate clause are found to be ordered in exactly the same way as the ordinary nominals of simple clauses -- before sister predicates, in English, and after sister verbs. It is not logically necessary that this should be the case, of course, since, in grammars which do not observe the completeness and invariance constraints, it would be quite possible to specify that when a nominal is raised into the subject relation of a superordinate clause it is ordered after its predicate rather than before it, as would be the case for all non-raised subjects. The fact that natural languages of this sort are apparently non-existent thus provides further empirical support for the particular theory of derivational ordering which has been proposed here, since this theory requires that all ordering rules must be applied at a level of representation at which raised and non-raised subjects are completely non-distinct -- the level of syntactic surface structure -- and thereby explains why they are always governed by exactly the same principles of ordering.

For grammars which observe the Invariant Order Constraint, and for any other optimally general Surface Order theory, the principles of Passive Formation and Subject Raising could be formulated as simple regrouping transformations such as (9) and (10), respectively.

$$(9) \quad (N_a, (N_p, V)) = (N_p, (N_a, (V, PASSIVE)))$$

(10) $(V, {}_S(N, (V, X))) = (V, N, {}_S(V, X))$

But as soon as these rules are defined on unordered rather than ordered
structures, it becomes apparent that there is a common principle here of
considerable generality, namely, the principle that a subordinate nominal
may be raised into the construction immediately higher if that construction does not immediately include another nominal. To bring this
principle to bear on alternations of the active-passive type, however,
it is necessary to factor (9) into its constituent processes of Subject
Lowering and Nonsubject Raising, where the latter could then be reduced,
along with (10) to a single general process of nominal raising. But the
dubious assumption of Subject Lowering could also be dispensed with then
if agentive and non-agentive nominals are assumed to be mutually nonsubordinate sisters of their predicates in underlying clause representations. The latter assumption, which has been proposed in Fillmore (1966),
Sanders (1967), and a number of other recent studies, would thus make it
possible for us to dispense completely with any separate rule of Passive
Formation in grammars, the functions of this rule being wholly subsumed
by a much more general rule of Subject Formation, which raises the nominal arguments of all predicates, subject to the appropriate precedence
restrictions on case, person, referentiality, etc. (cf. Postal, 1968;
Sanders, 1967, 1969a.) But this rule itself would then be subject to
further reduction, along with Subject Raising (10), to a single general
rule of Nominal Raising, such as (11), which justifies the simple regrouping of any nominal into an immediately superordinate nominal-free
construction.

(11)[7] $(X, -N, (N, Y)) = (X, -N, N, (Y))$

This rule determines a vast number of distinct alternations in
superficial constituent structure. For each of these various alternants,
then, the correct ordering of its nominal and verbal constituents in
English can be effectively assigned by the single superficial ordering

---

[7] The notation (X, -N) stands for any (possibly null) set of sister constituents such that no constituent of the set is a nominal. Thus, while
X may include subordinate nominals, it may not have any nominal as one
of its immediate constituents.

schema (12), whose constituent subrules provide an explicit expression
of the true generalizations that in this language (i) all non-subject
nominals are ordered after their verbs, and (ii) all other nominal
sisters of verbal expressions (i.e. all subjects) are ordered before
their verbs.

$$(12) \quad (N, V) = \left\{ \begin{array}{l} (V \& N) \\ (N \& V) \end{array} \right/ (N, \underline{\quad}) \right\} \quad \begin{array}{l} (i) \\ (ii) \end{array}$$

The level of explanatory generalization represented by rules (11)
and (12) would clearly appear to be beyond the reach of any possible
theory that incorporates the hypothesis of Deep rather than Surface
Ordering. Thus, while the preceding remarks are obviously not intended
to represent an even partial or projected explanation of nominal constituency alternations in English, they do suffice, it seems, as a demonstration of the power of the Surface Ordering assumption to facilitate
significant simplifications in the rules of grammars, and to motivate
higher levels of explanation not only about ordering but also about a
wide range of other linguistic properties and relations.

Further support for the hypothesis of Surface Ordering is also provided by a number of other types of significant data about languages.
These include, for example, (1) the fact that all traditionally-recog-
nized major grammatical relations are order-independent, including such
relations as dominance, command, scope, agreement, government, attribution,
coordination, and subjecthood; (2) the existence in Deep Order grammars
of partial as well as complete mirror-image relations between many transformational rules, a fact that has been explicitly noted by Bach (1968)
and Langacker (1969); and (3) the obvious irrelevance of order to the
proper specification of semantic and syntactic co-occurrence relations;
and (4) the occurrence in many ordered-domain transformations of constituents which are clearly irrelevant to the generalization expressed
except for the fact that they are superficially ordered *between* certain
relevant terms of the rule's structural description.

In the light of the existing evidence, in fact, it would appear that
the assumption that any major principles of grammar are applicable to
ordered structures has no significant logical or empirical basis at all.
This assumption would actually be defensible, it seems, only if it were

the case either that transformations defined mapping relations only between the *surface structures* of sentences, or else if it were possible to
define *all* grammatical rules on strings which were *only* ordered -- that
is, if linguistic objects had no hierarchical structure. Since the latter
assumption is false, and since the former makes significant higher-level
explanation impossible, the assumption that transformations apply to
ordered rather than unordered strings would appear to be entirely without foundation.

If the Surface Ordering Hypothesis is correct, as appears to be the
case thus far, then this is a fact which itself requires some explanation.
That is, any adequate theory of grammar would be expected to explain *why*,
in the maximally-general grammars of different languages, ordering rules
are always found to be most appropriately applicable at the level of surface structure, and never at any other level. All variable-order grammars
allow for the prediction of ordering relations at *any* point in a derivation, since any ordering that is rendered incorrect by the application
of adjunction, deletion, or regrouping transformations could always be
corrected, or re-predicted, by means of subsequent reordering rules.
These grammars are compatible, therefore, with both the Deep Ordering and
Surface Ordering hypotheses, and their governing metatheory is thus inherently incapable of explaining why the most general explanations of
particular linguistic data are always compatible only with the latter of
these hypotheses.

For grammars which observe the Invariant Order Constraint, on the
other hand, the Deep Ordering Hypothesis is directly falsified by each
occurrence in language of a set of surface structures which are distinctively ordered but otherwise equivalent in their semantic and syntactic properties. Thus, for example, sentences (13a) and (13b),

    (13) (a)   I turned off the light
         (b)   I turned the light off,

suffice to falsify any grammar of English that is consistent with both
the Invariant Order Constraint and the hypothesis of Deep Ordering, since
any such grammar would have to posit distinct base orders and entirely
distinct derivations for these two sentences, and would thus be inca-

pable of providing any principled basis for the characterization of their obvious semantic and syntactic relationship. An invariant-order grammar can thus account for this relationship only by assuming, in contradiction to the Deep Ordering Hypothesis, that the underlying structure of (13a) and (13b) is unordered, that this structure is superficially differentiated by means of an optional unordered-domain Particle Raising rule, such as (14), and that it is only after the application of this regrouping transformation that ordering relations are assigned to all particles and their sister verbs or verb-phrases by a general ordering rule such as (15).[8]

(14) $((V, PRT), X) = ((V, X), PRT)$

(15) $((V, X), PRT) = ((V, X) \& PRT)$

Surface Ordering thus follows necessarily from the conjunction of linguistic data and the Invariant Order Constraint. This invariance principle thus provides a general metatheoretical basis for the consistent selection of Surface rather than Deep Order grammars, and hence can be said to explain why grammars of the former sort are found to have consistently greater explanatory value with respect to the particular data of particular languages.

4.   The three principles of ordering that have been proposed here all play a role in facilitating the expression of true generalizations about the ordering of constituents in languages, and help to motivate and direct the continued search for higher levels of explanation in all areas of grammar. It is clear, though, that the invariance principle has a much wider range of presently-testable implications than the others, and a much greater capacity to restrict the set of possible grammars and the set of possible explanations of particular linguistic data. On the basis of present evidence, moreover, it is also by far the most well-substantiated, I believe, and thus can be most strongly maintained as a

---

[8] Among other things, rule (15) serves to explain why in English -- unlike German, for example -- verbs always precede their particles regardless of whether the particle is superficially raised or not. For further discussion of the extraposition and ordering of particles and nominals, see Sanders (1969b).

necessary universal principle of grammar.

I have discussed the substantiation of the Invariant Order Constraint extensively in a separate paper (1969a), in which I attempted to
test the adequacy of this principle with respect to what I feel are the
strongest possible arguments that might be raised against it. I assumed
there that these arguments would have to involve the existence of one
or the other of the following situations.

The first situation, which depends on the acceptance of rule-specific
conditions on the relative order of application of transformations, would
involve the necessary application of some rule to different orderings
of the same construction at different levels of derivation. More precisely,
this situation would require the existence of certain facts such that
the simplest, most general, and most revealing of their presently-attaina-
ble explanations depends essentially on the assumption that there is some
rule which must apply to ordered representations and which must be applicable to *one* ordering of certain constituents *before* it is applicable to
a *different* ordering of those same constituents, where, moreover, this
rule must be applicable *before* some other motivated rule if it has applied
to the first ordering and *after* that rule if it has applied to the second.

The other hypothetical situation which would demonstrate the necessity of reordering would involve the existence of some motivated general
constraint against the reordering of *some* but *not all* grammatical constituents, the applicability and filtering function of such a *partial
invariance* constraint being dependent, of course, on the existence of
rules which do in fact effect the reordering of some constituents.

I have suggested that there is no evidence of the existence of either
of these situations thus far, and that the Invariant Order Constraint can
thus continue to be appropriately asserted as a true principle of explanatory grammar. Thus, with respect to partial invariance, one finds
that all of the particular selective constraints on reordering that have
been proposed thus far (see especially Ross (1967b) and Postal (1968))
actually depend essentially on the grouping relations between constituents and are apparently only accidentally associated with superficial
differences in their relative order. Since any alternation in the order

of non-coordinate constituents presupposes and is predictable from an
alternation in their superficial constituent structure, it will always
be possible to prevent the derivation of an ungrammatical ordered representation simply by preventing the derivation of the superficially-
grouped representation from which it is derived. The intended explanatory functions of any proposed partial constraint against reordering
can thus always be achieved with equal or greater generality by means
of constraints on the associativity, or derivational regrouping, of constituents.[9] The possibility of such reduction evidently suffices to in-
sure the Invariant Order Constraint against falsification on the basis
of any possible facts about the grammaticality or ungrammaticality of
sentences in any language. Arguments suggesting the necessity of this
reduction, such as those presented in Sanders (1969), would thus be
superfluous here. Instead, I would like to conclude with a brief consideration of the adequacy of the invariance principle with respect to the
facts underlying what I believe to be the strongest known argument for
the existence of the first, or rule-sequence, occasion for reordering;
namely, that presented by J.R. Ross in his seminal paper on "Gapping
and the Order of Constituents" (1967a).

In this paper Ross addresses himself to the explanation of two very
interesting related observations[10] about verbally-reduced coordinations
in natural language.

[9] It is possible that all derivational regroupings may ultimately be reducible to the elementary transformations of identity adjunction and
identity deletion (cf. Sanders, 1969b), and that all apparent constraints on alternations in order or constituent structure will be most
appropriately accounted for by means of general constraints on the deletion of identical elements, constraints which specify the possible
grouping relations which hold between the operant terms of any given
deletion transformation. Some of the particular explanatory values of
the latter assumption are illustrated in Sanders and Tai (1969) with
respect to the treatment of certain facts about coordination, topicalization, dislocation, and relativization in various languages.

[10] These observations, of course, constitute only a very small and quite
arbitrary sample of the relevant facts about coordination in natural
languages. In fact, all of Ross's generalizations about reduced coordinations derived by identical verb deletion are only special cases of
much more general observations which also hold for reductions derived

First, he reports that, while various languages exhibit one or more of
the superficial reduction patterns (16a), (16b), and (16c), it is
apparently the case that no language has reductions of the form (16d).[11]

(16)   (a)   SVO and SO
       (b)   SOV and SO
       (c)   SO and SOV
       (d)   *SO and SVO

(The symbols S, V, and O are used as expository abbreviations here for
the distinctive properties and grouping relations which respectively
identify the class of superficial subjects, the class of superficial
verbs, and the class of superficial objects, prepositional phrases, and
other verbal complements.)

Ross's second observation concerns the co-occurrence of these reduction patterns in particular languages. On this basis, four language-
types are found:[12]

by the deletion of identical objects, subjects, predicates, adverbials,
etc. However, we will not be concerned here with the restricted nature
of Ross's chosen domain of explanation, or with the viability of his
observations and assumptions within the larger and more natural domain
of coordination reduction in general. Our purpose, rather, is simply
to show that even within the smaller domain of verbal reduction, where
Ross's reordering hypotheses are most strongly favored by the restricted
data, the most highly-valued theory is one which includes no postulations of reordering or pretransformational ordering.

[11] The only reported exception to this that I know of is Quechua, in which,
for some dialects at least, all four of the reduction patterns of (16)
are said to be fully grammatical.

[12] There is also a fifth type, of course, consisting of languages such as
Chinese, Hausa, Lebanese Arabic and Thai, in which there are no verbally-
reduced coordinations at all. These languages differ systematically
from those of the other four types in a number of other respects as well,
these differences being explainable, as proposed in Sanders and Tai
(1969), by their observance of a general Immediate Dominance Condition
on identity deletion. Furthermore, if the reported facts about Quechua
are correct, then this language establishes the existence of yet a
sixth distinct type, which differs from the other five by having all
four of the reduction patterns of (16).

(17)   *English-type*:   (SVO and SO)

   Japanese-type: (SO and SOV)

   Russian-type: (SVO and SO)(SO and SOV)(SOV and SO)

   Hindi-type: (SO and SOV)(SOV and SO)

In English and Japanese, the relation between the superficial structures of reduced and unreduced coordinations is quite obvious and direct, left-branching identical constituents being absent from right-branching clauses of a reduction, right-branching constituents being absent from left-branching clauses.[13] To account for this generalization, Ross proposes in effect that the directionality relation itself be incorporated into all grammars as a condition on the applicability of any rules which effect deletions of identical verbs in clause coordinations. Ross's directionally-restricted verbal deletion rule, which he refers to as a "gapping" rule, can also directly account for two of the three reduction patterns of Russian and for one of the two patterns of Hindi, since Russian has both reduced and unreduced coordinations of both the English- and Japanese-types, while one of the Hindi reduction patterns and all of its unreduced clauses are of the Japanese-type. The problem then is to find some way of accounting for the occurrence of the third

---

[13]This directionality relation holds in these languages not only for verbal reductions but also for all other ordinary reduced coordinations as well. This is illustrated , for example, by the following types of well-formed reductions in English:

 (a) (S PRED) (Ø PRED) John sang and J̶o̶h̶n̶ danced
 (b) (S P̶R̶E̶D̶) (S PRED) John s̶a̶n̶g̶ and Bill sang
 (c) (S (VØ)) (S (VO)) I wrapped t̶h̶e̶ p̶a̶c̶k̶a̶g̶e̶ and you tied
            the package
 (d) (DET N) (D̶E̶T̶ N) The king and t̶h̶e̶ queen arrived
 (e) (ADJ N̶) (ADJ N) The young m̶e̶n̶ and old men left

It should be noted, though, that this relation does not hold with respect to anaphoric or deictic reductions, such as those associated with the presence of an overt referential marker such as *too*, *also*, or *even*:

 (f) John can play the piano, and Bill can too
 (g) John didn't sing, and Bill didn't either
 (h) Sweden might go to war, and even Monaco might.

It also does not hold for reduced interrogative coordinations of the A or not-A type:

 (i) Did John sing, or did Bill
 (j) Are you going, or not

reduction-pattern (SOV and SO) in Russian and Hindi without losing the
generalization expressed by the directionality condition on verbal reduction.

To solve this problem, Ross makes a number of additional assumptions[14], the most important being (1) that prior to the applicability
of reduction the clauses of Japanese are orderd SOV and the clauses of
of the other three languages are ordered SVO; (2) that the general rule
of verbal reduction can be applied to these ordered structures, yielding,
in accordance with its assumed directionality restriction, the reductions
(SO and SOV) in Japanese and (SVO and SO) in the other languages;
(3) that there is a reordering rule, optional in Russian, conditionally
obligatory [15] in Hindi, and universally non-reversible, which effects

[14] Serious objections could be raised against each one of these assumptions.
In the context of the present discussion, however, it is fortunately
unnecessary to do this.

[15] That is, objects must be permuted obligatorily at the level of surface
structure in Hindi, but only optionally at levels prior to the application of verbal reduction. Alternatively, the rule of object preposing could be assumed to be unconditionally optional and unordered
with respect to verbal reduction, provided that it is also assumed
that there is a general verb-final well-formedness condition on the
surface clauses of languages of this type. In the context of variable-
order grammar, the latter treatment would appear to be preferable,
since it allows for the differentiation of Ross's four language-types
in terms of only two general principles: object preposing (present in
Russian and Hindi, absent in English and Japanese), and the verb-final
condition (present in Japanese and Hindi, absent in English and Russian).
The basic ordering problems for languages of the Hindi-type are not
explicitly dealt with in Ross's study, and he assumes there that there
are actually two distinct rules which effect preposings of objects
in these languages, one being optional, pre-reductive, and shared by
the Russian-type, the other being obligatory, post-reductive, and
unique to the Hindi-type. Moreover, he also assumes that the first of
these preposings can be subsumed under a more general rule of "Scrambling", which optionally effects a random reordering (and regrouping)
of the major constituents of clauses. However, this Scrambling rule,
which Ross has proposed (1967b) in order to account for certain facts
about languages such as the variety of literary Latin used in the odes
of Horace, is neither empirically nor metatheoretically justifiable,
some of the reasons for this having been noted by Ross himself
(1967b: 43-45).

the permutation of verbs and objects, yielding (SOV and SOV) coordinations and, from the reduction (SVO and SO), the alternant (SOV and SO); and (4) that reduction is again applicable then to the products of this reordering, yielding finally the (SO and SOV) reductions in Russian and Hindi. To account for the presumed universal non-occurrence of the fourth logically-possible reduction (*SO and SVO), Ross must then assume not only that verb-object permutation rules are universally non-reversible but also that such rules can never occur in the grammar of any language which assigns a pre-reduction ordering of SOV to its clauses.[16]

Since Ross's theory of verbal reduction depends essentially on a postulation of derivational reordering, it must be the case then either that the Invariant Order Constraint is false or that there is an alternative explanation of these data whose assumptions are at least equally general and include no postulations of reordering at all. There is at least one such theory, clearly, namely that consisting of the general reduction rule

$$(18)^{17} \quad ((S,(V,O)),(S,(V,O))) = ((S,(V,O)),(S,(O)))$$

[16]Both of these restrictions could be more adequately accounted for simply by assuming that objects can be preposed but never postposed in phonetically-directed derivations, i.e. that the rule (V & O) = (O & V) justifies only (V & O) $\rightarrow$ (O & V) as a phonetically-directed inference, and only (O & V) $\rightarrow$ (V & O) as a semantically-directed one. Actually, this appears to be only a special case of a much more general principle which applies to all superficial alternations in the order of nominal constituents, and which seems capable of also explaining the apparently universal non-occurrence of right topicalizations in natural language. Thus, in the context of variable-order grammar, it appears to be the case that, for any equation of the form (X & N & Y) = (X & Y & N) in the grammar of any language, the left representation can be appropriately derived from the right only in phonetically-directed derivations, and the right can be derived from the left only in semantically-directed derivations. For additional examples of such general principles for the prediction of directions of inference, see Sanders (1969b). The existence of these principles clearly provides one of the strongest possible confirmations of the hypothesis of equational grammar.

[17]This is, of course, only a special case of the general rule of coordinate idempotency, a rule which might perhaps be expressed in the form
    ((W, (X,A)), (Y, (Z,A))) = ((W, (X,A)), (Y, (Z)))
Such a rule would justify the optional reduction of any partially-identical coordination by the deletion of one of its identical constit-

and the following sets of language-specific ordering rules:[18]

(19)   *English:*   (i)   (V, 0)   =   (V & 0)

                      (ii)   (S, 0)   =   (S & 0)

        Japanese: (i)   (V, 0)   =   (0 & V)

                      (ii)   (S, 0)   =   (S & 0)

        Russian: (i)   (-0, 0)   =   (-0 & 0)

                      (ii)   (-V, V)   =   (-V & V)

        Hindi: (i)   (S, 0)   =   (S & 0)

                      (ii)   (V, 0)   =   (0 & V)

This theory requires no special ordering restrictions on coordination reduction and no special coordination restrictions on ordering. This is because the reduction rule applies here only to unordered structures, and because each of the ordering rules applies to sister clauses and sister phrases alike, and to the constituents of ordinary simple sentences as well as to those of reduced and unreduced coordinations. Among other things, therefore, this theory provides a very natural explanation of

uents, subject to the appropriate general constituency and precedence constraints on identity deletion. Some of the products of this deletion transformation will fall within the domains of certain general rules or metarules of associativity, which will justify appropriate regroupings of their constituents. For a detailed discussion of these and other possible principles of coordination reduction, see Tai (1969). With respect to the special case of (17), it should be noted that there is a precedence restriction here to the effect that an identical verb is deletable only if its associated subjects and objects are not identical, i.e. that coordinations must be analyzed with respect to subject and predicate identity before being analyzed with respect to verb identity. This provides further evidence in support of the assumption that verbal reduction is only one of the many intrinsically disjunctive subrules of a single general rule of coordination reduction.

[18] These rules are designed to account for the specific set of sentence types discussed in Ross. For larger domains of explanation these rules would of course be replaced by other ordering rules of a much more general character. With respect to the Russian-type rules in (19), it should be noted that any negative variable of the form (-X) stands for any string which is not analyzable as (X). It should also be recalled that the symbols *S*, *V*, and *0* are used here only as expository abbreviations for the distinctive properties and groupings that characterize superficial subjects, verbs, and verbal complements, respectively.

the fact that the clauses and phrases of a language observe the same ordering restrictions and always appear to be governed by precisely the same set of general ordering rules. This fact, which appears to represent a highly significant generalization about the nature of all natural languages, is clearly beyond the possible descriptive or explanatory capacities of any theory which permits ordering relations to be assigned to constituents before rather than after the application of deletion transformations on coordinate structures.

The general relationship between clause- and phrase-ordering is most readily illustrated here by the case of verb-object ordering in English and Japanese. Thus it can be seen from (17) that a (verbless) *clause* including an object precedes a sister clause including a verb (as in Japanese) precisely when it is also the case in that language that a (verbless) *phrase* including an object precedes a sister phrase including a verb.[19] Similarly, when *some* object constituents *follow* sister verb constituents (as in English), then *all* constructions observe this relation, (0) being ordered after (V), and (S, 0) clauses after (S, (V, 0)) clauses.

To account for the apparent universality of this uniformity relation, as well as for the non-occurrence of the reduction pattern (*SO and SVO) in the language-types under consideration here, I have assumed (Sanders, 1969a) that all ordering rules are governed by a general condition of uniform analysis and across-the-board applicability,[20] a condition which may also be motivated with respect to all other obligatory

[19] In the case of unreduced (and anaphorically-unrelated) clauses, either clause of the coordination can be appropriately analyzed as an object constituent, with the other being appropriately analyzable as a verb constituent. The two possible analyses of any grouped pair of unreduced clauses would thus yield, by the application of rule (i), the two grammatical orderings of these clauses in Japanese.

[20] It is important to note that, while the occurrence of (SO and SVO) reductions in Quechua (cf. notes 11 and 12) would suffice to falsify Ross's theory of ordered reduction, this would *not* falsify the alternative unordered reduction theory that has been proposed here. In fact, all of the principles of the latter theory, including the general principle of uniform analysis, are equally consistent with the occurrence or the non-occurrence of languages like Quechua, the existence of such languages being dependent here solely upon the existence of certain

transformations as well. The principle of uniform analysis is illustrated
by the analysis of a verbally-reduced coordination with respect to the
first ordering rules of English and Japanese (given in (20)), by the three
possible analyses of this structure with respect to the first ordering
rule of Russian (given in (21)), and by its two possible analyses with
respect to the first ordering rule of Hindi (given in (22)):

(20)　　$((S, \underline{(V, \underline{0}))}, \underline{(S, \underline{0})})$

　　　　　　　　　　$\underline{V}$　　　$\underline{0}$

(21)　　$((S, \underline{(V, 0))}, (S, 0))$　　$((S, \underline{(V, 0))}, (S, 0))$

(22)　　$((S, \underline{(V, 0))}, (S, 0))$　　$((S, \underline{(V, 0))}, (S, 0))$

Each of these distinctively analyzed representations will be mapped by
the appropriate first ordering rule for its language-type into a distinct

particular sets of language-specific ordering rules. Thus all of the
reported facts about Quechua can be accounted for simply by adding
to the present theory the assumption that in this language all major
clause constituents are ordered by means of the ordering rule $(X, Y) =$
$(X \& Y)$. This rule will apply to the unordered products of verbal
reduction (18) to yield, in full conformity with the uniform analysis
condition, all four of the ordered reduction patterns of (16), as well
as a large number of the other well-formed clause- and phrase-orderings
of Quechua. Moreover, the operant rule here is, in fact, simply the
universal maximally-unmarked rule of Alternative Ordering, a rule which
assigns a random order to each pair of constituents which remains
unordered subsequent to the application of every one of the more marked,
or more fully specified, ordering rules of any given grammar. Thus a
Quechua-type language would differ from the four types discussed by
Ross simply by its possession of a smaller number of marked rules for
the ordering of clause constituents. The important point here, though,
is that the principles of unordered reduction, and the more general
principles of completeness and invariance are all consistent with all
possible degrees of freedom in the ordering of the constituents of
superficial constructions, and that these principles are capable of
providing highly general explanations of the facts about languages
at any and all levels of the scale of relative freedom.

partially-ordered structure -- in English, for example, the structure ((S, (V & O)) & (S, O)), and in Russian the three structures that are derived from (21) by the ordering of each constituent analyzed as (-O) before a sister constituent analyzed as (O). The second ordering rule for each language-type will then map the appropriate partially-ordered structures into the correct fully-ordered representations of the grammatical verbally-reduced coordinations of that language-type.[21]

All of Ross's data about verbally-reduced coordinations can thus be accounted for by means of a very general and straightforward theory which also accounts for the ordering of constituents in non-coordinate as well as coordinate constructions, and which succeeds in explaining, rather than merely stipulating, the observed directionality relation in coordinate reductions, a relation which follows here as a necessary consequence of the independent principle of identity deletion and the independent general ordering rules of each language. This theory makes no postulations of reordering and is thus completely consistent with the Invariant Order Constraint.

Ross's treatment of verbal reduction appears to achieve the highest level of explanatory generalization that is possible for any theory which assumes that ordering relations are assigned before rather than after the application of deletion transformations. But such theories not only fail to reveal the relationship between clause-ordering and phrase-ordering in various languages, but also are inherently incapable of explaining why there should be any relation at all between deletion and ordering, or in particular why the order of reduced clauses should be any more resticted that that of unreduced ones. Thus it is not only the

---

[21] In one of the three derivations for languages of the Russian-type, the sequential application of rules (i) and (ii) yields a structure in which one pair of constituents is still grouped rather than ordered. However, since all ordering rules are obligatory, and since this grouping satisfies the structural-description of rule (i), this rule will properly apply again here to complete the assignment of correct orderings to all groupings. See Sanders (1969a), where complete derivations are given for each of the sentence-types under consideration here.

case that the given facts about verbal reduction fail to falsify the Invariant Order Constraint, but also that they can be fully accounted for, it seems, *only* by means of theories which are fully *consistent* with this principle.

As in the case of the two completeness constraints, therefore, it would appear that the assumption of Invariant Ordering cannot be falsified by any of the known facts about natural languages, and that it is consistently superior to its contrary or contradictory assumptions in its explanatory powers with respect ot these facts. In the light of the existing evidence, each of the three proposed constraints on constituent ordering would thus appear to be not only a possible universal principle of grammar, but also a necessary one.

CONSTRAINING GRAMMARS THROUGH
PROPER GENERALIZATION:
MULTIPLE ORDER GRAMMAR

THOMAS H. PETERSON

0. INTRODUCTION [1]

In recent years there has been considerable research and discussion in the area of constraining the power of the generative-transformational model of language as set forth by Noam Chomsky in *Aspects
of the Theory of Syntax* (1965). These efforts have been primarily directed at restricting the power of transformational rules, which, when
unconstrained, have been found to produce certain ungrammatical sentences. The common approach to this problem has been to propose

[1] A preliminary and rather truncated version of the theory presented
in this paper appears in Peterson (1971); since that time it has
undergone some revision and considerable expansion. I am indebted
to Lars Andersson, Judi Maxwell, and Jürgen M. Meisel, participants
in my syntax seminar at the University of Massachusetts in the
spring of 1973, for their interest and helpful comments. I would
like to thank Anna Meyer for the German examples in 2; any mistakes
or wrong interpretations of that language are my own. Finally, I am
grateful to my friend and neighbor Gary Segal of the Physics Department at UCLA for many interesting discussions on the nature of
theory building in the physical sciences. The paper as it appears
in this volume is a slightly revised version of the article in
Theoretical Linguistics 4 (1977), 75-127. Both the author and the
editors wish to express their sincere gratitude to the editor and
publisher of *Theoretical Linguistics* for their permission to re-
publish this article.

various general constraints on the operation of transformations or on
the final output of the transformational component and to tack these
constraints onto the model without actually changing the basic nature
of the model itself. Examples of this can be found in Ross (1967),
Chomsky (1964; 1973) and Perlmutter (1971).

Viewing the situation from the perspective of the history of
science, we might pose the following question: are such constraints
really a solution to the problem of the excessive power of the system,
or is the necessity for their imposition merely symptomatic of a fundamental error in the design of the model? Just as the Ptolemaic
astronomers piled on epicycles to accommodate the incorrect predictions
of that system, so today generative grammarians add constraint after
constraint to prevent the ungrammatical sentences predicted by their
model.

In the present paper, we take up the following problem areas of
the *Aspects* theory and its current offshoots, hereafter referred to
as Standard Theory (ST):

   (i)   Constraints on Variables in syntactic rules (Section I)

  (ii)   Word order (Section II):

      (a) the assignment of surface word order

      (b) multiple order assignment: scrambling rules

 (iii)   Universal Grammar (Section III):

      (a) limiting the number of possible base structures

      (b) defining the notion 'possible surface structure'

In the present paper, all of these problems are viewed as being
connected with the way in which linear order is assigned to constituents. In assigning a unique, distinctive order at the deep structure
level, ST is not able to separate the hierarchical (vertical) dimension of P-markers from the linear (horizontal) dimension. (In
Saussurian terminology, we might translate these as 'paradigmatic'
and 'syntagmatic', respectively.) It will be our contention that
transformations change hierarchical structure but they do not directly change linear structure and that transformational environments,

such as those normally covered by variables, are hierarchical in nature. Assignment of distinctive word order is seen as a function of surface structure, the only level at which valid generalization about order can be made.

In place of ST, we offer a revised theory, hereafter referred to as Multiple Order Grammar (MOG), in which distinctive linear order is neutralized at all levels above surface structure. This is accomplished through a fundamental revision of the notion 'P-marker' and, consequently, of transformations. Variables in rule statements and their outside constraints are replaced by 'hierarchical constants', which make up a well-defined notational system that makes positive generalizations about transformational environments. At the level of surface structure, far-reaching generalizations about word order are presented in the form of Phrase Structure Ordering Conditions (PSOC).

1.   ON CONSTRAINING TRANSFORMATIONS
1.1.   THE PROBLEM OF VARIABLES IN STANDARD THEORY

One principal source for the excessive power of ST is transformations which utilize in their structural description (SD) a variable over which some operation such as movement, deletion, or feature change applies. Let us call variables of this type *internal variables*. Following Postal (1971), we will call variables which occupy the leftmost and rightmost positions of the SD and over which no operations occur *end variables*.

Postal goes on to define two types of internal variables: *abbreviatory variables* and *essential variables*. Abbreviatory variables appear in rules whose domain of operation is limited to the bounds of a simplex sentence. Reflexivization is a rule of this type. Thus the examples in (1) are acceptable, but those in (2), where Reflexivization has been applied down into an embedded sentence, are not.

(1) a.   Dick$_i$ has been flagellating himself$_i$.

    b.   John$_i$ addressed a letter to himself$_i$.

(2) a. *John$_i$ said that himself$_i$ likes Mary.

   b. *Bill told Susan$_i$ that George likes herself$_i$.

The ST statement of Reflexivization is given in (3).

(3) X, NP, Y, NP   , Z ⇒
                  [-REFLEXIVE]

    1   2   3   4   5 ⇒

    1   2   3   4
                  [+REFLEXIVE]

   Condition: 2 = 4

Since (3) is a bounded rule, the variable Y is an abbreviatory variable and covers a finite and listable set of contexts: ...Aux V... as in (1a), or ...Aux V NP PREP..., as in (1b). Conceivably, we could replace Y with a disjoint list of the above contexts; but, as Postal has pointed out, to follow this course would be to abandon any attempt to distinguish between relevant and irrelevant elements in rule statements. The important fact about the reflexive rule is that, given two co-referential NPs in the same sentence, the rightmost will be reflexivized; what the elements are that intervene between the two NPs is irrelevant, so long as there is no sentence boundary among them. Therefore a variable must be used to cover these elements, but we must specify that its domain is limited to a simplex sentence.

Essential variables occur in rules whose domain of operation is unbounded, which means that the contexts that they cover are potentially infinite and unlistable. WH-Question is an example of an unbounded rule; it moves a WH-word to the head of a sentence containing the question morpheme Q. In (4a) it has operated in a simplex sentence moving the WH-word from object position and in (4b) it has operated two sentences deep over a considerable amount of intervening material. The ST statement of WH-Question is given in (5).

(4) a. Who did John see Ø?

   b. Who does Mary believe that Bill said that John saw Ø?

(5) X, Q, Y, [+WH] , Z ⇒ 1, 4, 3, Ø, 5
                NP   NP

    1   2   3   4   5

Y in (5) is an essential variable. Unlike the abbreviatory variable of (3), there exists no possibility of replacing it with a list of contexts because there is no limit to the length and variety of strings that it may cover.

It is essential variables which cause the major difficulty for ST. Though they are not restricted with respect to depth, they are restricted in the grammatical contexts which they may cover. For example, WH-Question may move elements out of 'object clauses', as shown in (4), but not out of relative clauses, nominalizations with lexical head nouns, subject clauses, or coordinate structures, as illustrated in (6a,b,c,d) respectively.

(6) a. *What does John like the girl who bought Ø?

    b. *What does John believe the claim that Harry bought Ø?

    c. *Who did that Harry kissed Ø bother John?

    d. *Who did John say that Bill saw Mary and Joe saw Ø?

Therefore, the essential variable Y in WH-Question must be restricted or defined in such a way that it includes potentially unbounded contexts like that in (4) while at the same time excluding those of (6). The same is true of other 'chopping' rules, that is, rules which engage in long distance moving or deletion, such as Relativization, Topicalization, etc.

The most extensive treatment of this subject is John Ross' thesis *Constraints on Variables in Syntax* (1967). Ross responds to the problem by formulating a series of general constraints on chopping rules. These constraints can be summarized as follows: the Complex NP Constraint prohibits chopping out of any clause dominated by an NP with a lexical head noun, as in (6a) or (6b); the Sentential Subject Constraint prohibits chopping from subject clauses, as in (6c); and the Coordinate Structure Constraint prohibits chopping from any member of a coordinate structure, as in (6d). In terms of essential variables like Y in (5), these constraints amount to the following metatheoretic list: an essential variable in a chopping rule may contain no complex NP, sentential subject, or coordinate structure which dominates the item which is to be chopped.

This manner of limiting the power of transformations cannot be faulted on empirical grounds, since, given the unlimited license to formulate constraints, in the face of counterevidence one can either patch up one of the existing constraints or add a new one to the list. For example, Ross' constraints will not block the sentences in (7), where a WH-word has been moved out of an adverbial clause.

(7) a. *Who did Bill say that although Mike saw ∅ in the house,
         he didn't say anything.

    b. *Who did Bill say that he ran away because he saw ∅ in
         the house?

But we cannot conclude from this evidence that Ross' approach does not work; for all one need do is formulate another constraint, call it the Adverbial Clause Constraint, which prohibits movement from adverbial clauses.

Although the imposition of such constraints succeeds in making ST 'work', that is, in producing the correct output, this is not the principal aim of a linguistic theory. It must also make interesting and significant generalizations about grammatical processes in the form of rules. It is on these grounds that we must evaluate the use of internal variables and the consequent necessity of constraints of the type Ross and others have proposed.

1.2. THE VERTICAL NATURE OF SYNTACTIC ENVIRONMENT

In viewing the problem of constraining unbounded rules, suppose we define the contexts out of which items may be moved, rather than those out of which they may not be moved. This amounts to finding the complement of Ross' constraints. As it turns out, the unbounded environments out of which items may be chopped are fewer than those out of which chopping is prohibited. Chopping is permitted from the following three types of clauses: noncomplex-NP sentential objects, as shown in (8); so-called 'extraposed' clauses, as illustrated in (9); and purpose adverbials in postverbal position, as shown in (10).

(8) a. Who does John believe that Harry saw ∅?

    b. What does John want Max to eat ∅?

    c. Who does John object to Helen's dating ∅?

(9) a.   Who is it obvious that Esmiralda likes ∅?

b.   Who would it bother Marvin for Melva to kiss ∅?

(10) a.   Who did Harry go to New York (in order) to interview ∅?

b.   Who did Harry go to New York so (that) he could interview ∅ ?

c.   *Who (in order) to interview ∅ did Harry go to New York.

One thing that all these clauses have in common is that they are postverbal. (Notice that when the adverbial clause of (10a) is fronted, the sentence is ungrammatical, as shown in (10c).) So let us say that they are all constituents of VP; following Rosenbaum (1967) and Emonds (1970), we assume that object clauses with *That* and *For-To* complementizers have the structure shown in (11a), while clauses with *Poss-ing* have that shown in (11b).

(11) a.

We differ from Emonds in that we assume clauses of the type in (11a) to be dominated by NP when appearing as subjects, e.g. '*That Henry has disappeared* is obvious'.

As for postverbal purpose clauses like those in (10a,b), we will not go into their deep structure origins, but will be content with the assertion that they have a derived structure like (11a). Actually, they share many features with S complements: (a) they take the same complementizers, *That* and *For-To*; (b) they undergo obligatory Equi-NP-Deletion when occurring with *For-To*; (c) they optionally undergo *That*-Deletion.

Parenthetically, it should be pointed out that there is one difficulty with assigning the structure in (11a) to both purpose adverbials and to object clauses: the former, as an adverb, may be fronted while the latter may not. We can assume that adverbial clauses carry a feature (+Adverb) in their complementizers and that Adverb Fronting is sensitive to this feature.

We are now in a position to make the following tentative generalization about the hierarchical structure of the unbounded context of chopping rules.

(12) The unbounded context of a chopping rule is limited to any
      sentence or chain of sentences having the form of an 'object
      clause', that is, S dominated by VP or S dominated by NP do-
      minated by VP.

The above positive generalization excludes all the cases covered
by Ross' Sentential Subject Constraint, (6c) for example, as well as
adverbial clauses like those in (7), because these clause types are not
dominated by VP. (There is no conclusive argument demonstrating that
postverbal adverbials like (7b) are or are not in VP; we simply assume
that they are not.) In addition, (12) eliminates the need for the Coordinate Structure Constraint in all cases where the coordinate structure involves conjoined sentences, for example (9d), since any S that is
a member of a coordinate structure will be directly dominated by S and
not by NP. (Coordinate structures involving conjoined NPs will be dealt
with later.)

However, given the NP-S expansion for relative clauses and nominalizations with lexical head-nouns assumed by Ross, the statement in (12)
will not exclude certain instances of the clause types which are subsumed under the Complex-NP Constraint, namely complex-NPs which are dominated by VP. Examples of this type are shown in (6a,b); according to
the NP-S analysis they would have the structure of (13):

(13)

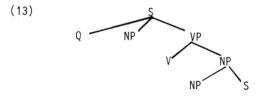

But there is an alternative expansion for NP proposed in the UCLA
Grammar (Stockwell, Schachter, Partee, 1973) called the NOM-S analysis.
It assigns the following structures to the clauses embedded in NP:

(14) a. sentential complements with Poss-ING complementizers

b. nominalizations with lexical head nouns (e.g. *the fact*):

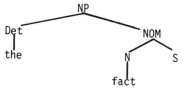

c. relative clauses

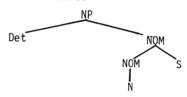

We shall not review here the arguments in favor of the NOM-S analysis over the NP-S proposal; in many respects the two are equivalent. The central point to be noted for this discussion is that in providing a richer structure for NP, the NOM-S expansion sets up two configurationally unique clause types within NP: S dominated by NOM (14b,c) and S dominated by NP (14a). The former delineates Ross' "Complex NP" and the latter comprises object clauses with a Poss-Ing Complementizer. Thus the adoption of the NOM-S expansion for NP makes (12) a valid generalization.

By the criteria of simplicity, unity, and generality, the single positive statement in (12) is preferable to the four negative constraints mentioned above. Yet there remains something unsatisfying about this form of constraining grammatical rules. What we have done is to put a statement detailing what an essential variable *must* contain in place of a series of statements saying what it *may not* contain. But in retaining internal variables, we are still in the position of writing maximally powerful (i.g. general) rules and then restricting them in a separate statement. The need for internal variables and their attendant constraints, whether negative or positive, points up the failure of ST to express in rule form a type of relation which is crucial to the statement and explanation of syntactic processes, namely the hierarchical relations that connect the significant elements of a rule statement.

Although it is recognized that "... grammatical transformations are necessarily 'structure dependent' in that they manipulate substrings only
in terms of their assignment to categories" (Chomsky, 1965: 55), nevertheless transformations in ST analyze and operate on P-markers in terms
of the fixed *horizontal* relations connecting the significant categories
in a rule statement rather than in terms of the hierarchical relations
which link these categories. (In this respect, ST is identical to the
earlier theory of transformations proposed by Harris 1952, 1957.)

1.3. 'ARTIFICIAL ORDER' AND THE STATEMENT OF TRANSFORMATIONS

Artificial order, which is the grouping of categories in deep
structure in some order which never occurs in surface structure, is a
basic and well-established abstractive device of generative grammar in
expressing significant generalizations about syntactic processes. It is
used in conjunction with the transformational component. The justification for positing a given artificial order is that it makes possible or
simplifies some transformational generalization. Perhaps the most elegant example is Chomsky's analysis of the English auxiliary phrase
where he orders the auxiliary affixes in positions in which they never
occur in surface sentences. That order enables him to formulate one
very simple rule, Affix-Hopping, which produces all the various surface
forms of the auxiliary phrase. In a more recent case, McCawley (1970)
argues for a deep structure Verb-Subject-Object order in English. His
principal justification is that the statement of several transformations
will be significantly simplified.

ST assumes that the categories of P-markers have one and only one
linear order at any given stage of a derivation. This means that artificial order must be introduced at the level of deep structure by the
categorial component, for in order to introduce it at intermediate
stages, it would be necessary to add special transformations. In our
revision of ST, we will greatly expand the use of artificial order to
simplify transformational statements by creating a theory in which no
P-marker of a derivation except the final one has a single fixed linear
order of categories.

1.4. MULTIPLE ORDER GRAMMAR AND THE USE OF MULTIORDERED P-MARKERS

Before introducing the above-mentioned revisions, let us list the following basic features of the ST model:

(15) i. *categorial rules* of the type A →B C which produce P-markers;

ii. *P-markers* which have:

   a. labeled nodes, e.g. S, NP, VP, etc.

   b. hierarchical structure, that is, vertical relations such as 'NP of S', 'NP of VP', etc.

   c. fixed linear structure, that is, horizontal relations such as 'NP is to the left of VP' where NP VP ≠ VP NP;

iii. *transformations* (the mapping of P-markers onto P-markers) which through certain elementary operations introduce the following kinds of changes in P-markers:

   a. a change in the constituent-set membership

   b. a change in the linear order of constituents

   c. both (a) and (b);

iv. *surface structure*, which is characterized in a given derivation by the stage at which all transformations of that derivation have been applied.

With regard to the rule properties in (15iii), rules involving simple deletion, addition, and substitution of some elements within a single constituent-set belong to type (a), e.g. AGENT-DELETION (deletion), REFLEXIVIZATION (substitution). Permutation rules, which involve the movement of some item(s) from one position to another, may be of all three types. For example NEG-CONTRACTION, if we consider it to be a rule of encliticization, has the effect of changing constituent-set membership but not linear order, as illustrated in (16).

(16) a. John did not leave. ⇒

   John [do Tns] [NEG] leave

      V   V

   b. John didn't leave.
       John [do Tns NEG] leave.
            V   V

A movement rule which changes linear order but not constituent-set membership, type (b) of (15iii), is the rule which varies the order of prepositional phrases within VP, as illustrated in (17):

   (17) a. Miss Scarlet committed the murder in the lounge with the
           revolver. ...[...PP_1 PP_2...]... ⇒

                     VP   VP

   b. Miss Scarlet committed the murder with the revolver in
      the lounge. ...[...PP_2 PP_1...]...

                 VP   VP

Finally, a movement rule which alters both constituent-set membership and linear order, type (c), is exemplified by PARTICLE-MOVEMENT, where the particle is not only moved from the left to the right of NP, but at the same time it is moved from the constituent-set V into VP. This is shown in (18):

   (18) a. I called up John ⇒
           ...[[verb part] NP]...
           VP V   V VP
   b. I called John up.
      ...[[verb] NP Part]...
      VP V   V   VP

This last type is the commonest sort of movement rule.

From this classification of transformations in ST, we can make the following observation: with the exception of movement rules of the type specified in (15iii) and illustrated in (17), transformations in ST always bring about a change in the membership of some constituent-set. This point is basic to the revision of ST to be presented below. Its validity will make it possible for us to factor out linear order as a distinctive property of P-markers at all levels above surface structure, a process which is necessary in isolating the hierarchical environment of transformations as noted above.

The most obvious way to eliminate linear order from ST at the transformational level is to replace the categorial rules of (15) with ones
which generate unordered constituent-sets, e.g. A→{B, C}. Such a proposal was first put forward by Šaumjan and Soboleva (1963) (cf. Hall
1964 for a review in English) and more recently by Sanders (this volume and 1970) and by Bartsch and Venneman (1972). Speaking in response to
Šaumjan and Soboleva, Chomsky (1965) points out that there is no real
gain in positing a stage of unorderedness, since it is always necessary
to supplement categorial rules which generate unordered constituents
with *two* sets of rules, the first of which must be a set of rules which
assign intrinsic order to each constituent-set and the second of which
must be a set of grammatical transformations of the type originally proposed. In other words, proponents of a nonlinearly ordered base have
failed to show that such a stage is necessary in terms of greater simplicity and generality in the characterization of syntactic processes.
Although Sanders attempts to show a gain in simplicity, it is not clear
how successful he is. For example, with respect to Ross' constraints,
rather than replacing them with a more unified statement, he merely offers a reformulation in hierarchical terms, leaving the constraints intact (Sanders, 1970). However, we should mention that the observation
made above concerning transformations as changes in set membership has
has been made independently by Sanders in the works cited. We are in
accord with his basic critique of ST.

The principal difficulty with eliminating linear order from P-markers by simple substitution of unordered constituent-sets for ordered
ones is that this approach makes crucial use of an undefined primitive
of set theory, the notion 'unordered'. For example, in terms of pairs,
any set with two elements is called a *pair*, or more usually an *unordered
pair*, by comparison to the construct of an *ordered pair* (cf. Halmos,
1960). (In the standard notation for an unordered pair there is no
significance to the order in which the elements are written, i.e.
{a,b} = {b,a}; this is, of course, not the case for ordered pairs, i.e.
<a,b> ≠ <b,a>.) The term 'unordered' as applied to a set {a,b} is in no
way a defined property in the sense that 'ordered' is; rather it is only

gratuitously assigned from the fact that $\{a,b\} \neq <a,b>$ and $\{a,b\} \neq <b,a>$. In other words, 'unordered' means only something that is 'not ordered'. Thus presented with an unordered P-marker, we immediately ask "What is it? What are its formal properties and how are these properties used to a greater advantage than those of an ordered P-marker in a theory of syntax?" There are no clear answers to these questions because we do not really know what 'unordered' means.

In formulating a revision of the notion 'P-marker', we begin by creating a definition for 'unordered set'. (Actually, whether or not one uses this name is immaterial; we will call our creation by another name in applying it to P-markers. What is being said here is that if there is some substantive meaning to the term 'unordered' as applied to sets, this is what we imagine it to be.) First, let us assume that primitive sets, signified by n-tuples of elements enclosed by $\{\ \}$, are neither ordered nor unordered. Second, we assume that ordered sets are defined in terms of Cartesian products, i.e. $<a,b> = \{\{a\}\{a,b\}\} = A \times B$ for $a \in A$ and $b \in B$ (cf. Halmos, 1960:22 ff.). Third, let us propose the following axiom:

(19) *Axiom of Factorials:* for each set A with n members there
exists a collection of sets that contains all the well-or-
dered sets with n members to which A belongs.

This merely specifies the set of all complete orderings for any primitive set. We call this set the factorial set because it has n factorial members; it is symbolized as '!'. (Among its more obvious properties are the following: $\cap !(A) = A$ and $\cup !(A) = \mathcal{P}(A)$.) Given (19), let us say that the unordered set which corresponds to a primitive set A is $!(A)$. In other words, we have chosen to define 'unordered' as 'the collection of all possible orders'.

Now let us apply the above concept in defining the notion 'unordered P-marker'. In speaking of ordered constituent-sets in a P-marker, we substitute the more specialized relation 'concatenated', familiar in linguistic theory, for 'ordered'.First, we propose the following definitions:

(20) a. *'unordered' constituent-set:* let the unordered constituent-
         set which corresponds to a primitive constituent-set A be
         defined as the factorial set (of concatenated constituent-
         sets) of A.

    b. *'unordered' phrase tree:* for any primitive phrase tree T
         with constituents C arranged in hierarchical relations H,
         let the unordered phrase tree which corresponds to T be
         defined as the set of all concatenated phrase trees with
         constituents C arranged in hierarchical relations H.

Hereafter, for 'unordered' we substitute the designation 'multiordered',
since this is more descriptive of the construct we have devised.

Multiordered P-markers are produced in the following way. In place
of the concatenating categorial rules of ST, we assume a set of categorial rules which generate primitive sets of elements, as mentioned above
in connection with the proposal of Šaumjan and Soboleva. A phrase tree
generated by rules of this type, i.e. with nonconcatenated elements,
will be represented schematically as a tree structure with nonangled
branches, as shown in (21a). Immediately following the categorial rules
is a general order-assigning function which assigns to each nonconcatenated phrase tree the set of all possible fully concatenated phrase
trees definable on it. We represent such a collection as a multiordered
phrase tree like that in (21b), which is the multiordered tree that
corresponds to the nonconcatenated tree of (21a).

(21) a.

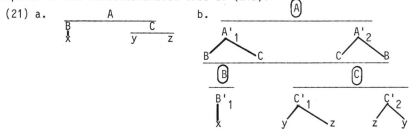

The interpretation of this pair of structures is as follows: for
each nonterminal node A, B,... of (a) there is a corresponding circled
node Ⓐ , Ⓑ ,... in (b) which dominates a set of primed nodes
$A'_1...A'_{m!}$, $B'_1...B'_{n!}$,.... (! = factorial) where m, n,... equals the

number of elements dominated by A, B,... in (a) and where each primed node in the sequences $A_1'...A_{m!}'$, $B_1'...B_{n!}'$,... dominates a fully ordered string of the same elements as its corresponding nonprimed node A, B, ... in (a) and where no member of the sequence $A_1'...A_{m!}'$ dominates the same *ordered* string as any other member, and the same for the sequence $B_1'...B_{n!}'$, and so forth.

If we look at phrase structure trees as mobiles, an ordered tree in ST represents one state of a two-dimensional mobile, while a multi-ordered tree portrays all the states of a two-dimensional mobile.

From the multiordered structure in (21b) different strictly ordered trees of the familiar sort can be derived. Examples of this are shown in (22).

(22) a.

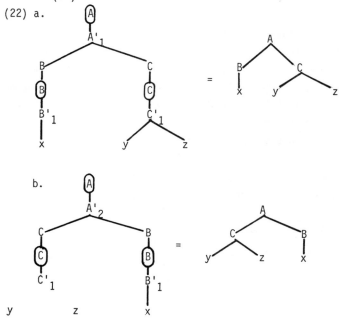

b.

Each of the trees on the left in (22) is derived from (21b) by selecting one primed node from each circled node throughout the tree. By application of a simple redundant node reduction convention the standard ordered tree on the right is achieved. Put another way, (21) can be interpreted as follows: 'the multiordered P-marker (21) is (22a) and (22b) and ...' and so forth through all the possible structure-preserving permutations of the constituents of (21a). For reasons of economy, when representing P-markers in MOG, we will continue to use the familar tree diagrams of ST, but they are to be understood as abbreviations for a pair of structures like that in (21).

Given the revised format for P-markers described above, the definition of transformations will necessarily be altered. In stating the environment of a rule, the SD mentions only those items which are essential to the statement of the rule. This is accomplished by stating the SD in terms of an ordering in which all extraneous items are removed from the path between essential items. In other words, the SDs of transformations will often use 'artificial order' in their statements. On being presented with a multiordered P-marker, i.e. a pair like that in (21), a transformation searches through the multiordered tree until it finds an ordered tree which meets the conditions of its SD. The SC is a mapping of the nonconcatenated tree of a multiordered P-marker, which bears a one-to-one relationship to each ordered tree derivable from its multiordered mate, onto a new nonconcatenated tree which reflects the changes brought about by the rule.

In this new format, transformations effect only changes in constituentset membership; they never *directly* bring about changes in linear order. Thus the operation known as 'permutation' in ST is eliminated, i.e. transformational changes such as (15iiib,c) do not occur. Membership changes are of the following two types: (a) simple addition, deletion, or substitution of elements within a single constituent-set and (b) movement of elements from one constituent set to another. After a transformation has wrought its changes, a new multiordered tree is automatically associated with the new nonconcatenated tree by the general ordering function described above.

To give a concrete example of how transformations in MOG work, let us look at the statement of a simple rule, Particle-Movement. The practice of writing variables as the left- and rightmost members of every SD ('end variables') is abandoned, since in MOG all relevant contexts

are specified in the rule proper; consequently, end variables are simply
assumed, as is the case in phonology. The statement of Particle-Movement in (23) illustrates these points:

(23) PARTICLE MOVEMENT (OPTIONAL)

PART] $_V$ NP $\Rightarrow$ $\emptyset$, 2, 1, 3

1   2   3

(23) is an instruction to move the constituent PART(icle) from the constituent-set V into the constituent-set dominating V, i.e. VP, when that
set contains NP. The NP object is a necessary part of the environment
of the rule, since we want to avoid assigning a dual derived structure
to intransitive verb-plus-particle constructions, e.g. the sentence
'John called up' only has one derived constituent structure where *up*
is sister to *called* under V and not a sister to V under VP. But the
position of the NP is not relevant to the actual change brought about by the
rule because it does not place PART to the left or right of NP, it
merely puts it in the same set. (24) provides a picture of how this
operates in terms of P-markers.

(24) a. SD: b. SC:

It should be mentioned that given this multiordered definition of
P-markers, any statement like (23) always has a mirror image, as shown
in (25):

(25)   NP $_V$[PART $\Rightarrow$ 1, 3, 2, $\emptyset$

1   2   3

This duality of statement is not damaging to the proposal of MOG because it is completely predictable. Since MOG assumes that only ver-

tical relations are significant in transformational statements, (23)
and (25) are completely equivalent. By convention, we will write all
rules with left brackets, as in (25).

Finally, surface linear order is assigned in MOG by Phrase Structure Ordering Conditions (PSOC) which apply to the last multiordered
P-marker of each derivation, that is, the stage at which all transformations have applied. Just how this works will be explained in
Section II.

1.5. ELIMINATING ABBREVIATORY VARIABLES FROM RULE STATEMENTS

Now let us turn to applying the model proposed in the preceding section to the problem of constrained variables, as discussed in
1.1 and 1.2.

Before beginning, we should note certain further assumption about
constituent structure. First, it is assumed that prepositional phrases
are NPs with the structure shown in (26), as suggested in Postal (1971).

(26)

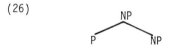

Second, the feature [$\pm$ REFLEXIVE] is present on the NP node that dominates P and NP, just as it is on the NP node that dominates conjoined
NPs in sentences like 'John, Bill, and Harry divided the property
among themselves' where the identical reflexivized NP is the whole
conjoint 'John, Bill, and Harry' and not the individual NPs in the
conjoint. Third, we assume that auxiliary verbs have the structure of
main verbs that take obligatory VP complements. The structure of the
sentence 'Harry has seen Hugo' (after Subject-Promotion) is shown below.

(27)

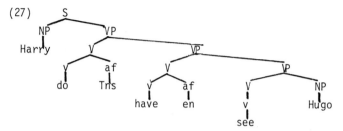

This approach eliminates the node AUX and all the specialized categories contained in it. We will not present justification of this analysis here; a full account is given in Peterson (1974).

   With the above assumptions about constituent structure understood,
the statement of Reflexivization in MOG is given in (28):

   (28) Reflexivization

                                          Conditions: 1 = 3

Note that the internal variable Y of the standard statement, given in
(3), has been replaced by a constant, a VP bracket. The subscript signals a convention used in phonology to enumerate possible sequences of
segments; subscript 1 means 'one or more', 2 means 'two or more', etc.;
superscripts are interpreted as 'not more than ___'; by convention, unmarked brackets are interpreted as 'one and no more than one', i.e.
subscript 1, superscript 1 (cf. Chomsky and Halle, 1968). (28) is an
instruction to reflexivize the lower of two identical NPs within a
sentence, i.e. the one contained in VP. For a sentence such as (1a),
'Dick$_i$ has been flagellating himself$_i$', the order shown in (29) meets
the SD of (28).

(29)

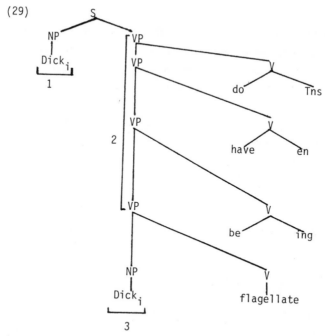

The ordering of (29) removes all verbs from the path between the two identical NPs, since they are irrelevant to the operation of the rule. In the case of (1b), 'John$_i$ addressed a letter to himself$_i$', not only the verb but also the NP 'a letter' would be ordered out of the rule statement to the right.

We should mention that there is one type of reflexive sentence not covered by the statement in (28), namely such sentences as 'Harry talked to Joe$_i$ about himself$_i$' (cf. Postal, 1971), where the two identical NPs are contained in the same VP. This defect can be remedied by a slight amendment to the statement in (30); however, since this would require a good deal of discussion about the constituent structure and the origin of such sentences, we will not take the space to go into it here.

1.6. ELIMINATING ESSENTIAL VARIABLES: THE HIERARCHICAL CONSTANT h

　　　　Having shown how MOG employs artificial order to eliminate
abbreviatory variables, let us now turn to rules with essential variables. In section 1.2., it was demonstrated that by adopting the NOM-S
expansion for NP, the list of negative constraints necessary to constrain essential variables can be replaced by the single positive constraint in (12). Given our theory of P-markers as collections of ordered
P.markers, (12) can be represented in the form of a hierarchical constant and essential variables dispensed with altogether. The phrase
"... S dominated by VP or S dominated by NP dominated by VP" is equi-
valent to the sequence [$_{VP}$ $\left(\begin{array}{c}[\\ _{NP}\end{array}\right)$ [$_S$. Since this same sequence turns up
as an environment in several different rules, we will substitute the
letter h for it in rule statements, as shown below.

　　(30)　h = [$_{VP_1}$ $\left(\begin{array}{c}[\\ _{NP}\end{array}\right)$ [$_S$

The phrase "... any chain ..." of h is represented as h_1, in accord
with the phonological convention mentioned above.

　　　　Using the constant h, we now state a preliminary version of
WH-Question in the MOG format.

　　(31)　　WH-Question (first version)

$$Q \quad]_C \quad (h_1 \quad \not|\ \ [_{VP_1}\ ) \quad [_{NP} \quad +WH]_{NP} \quad \Rightarrow \quad \emptyset,\ 3,\ 2,\ \emptyset$$

$$\underbrace{}_{1} \quad \underbrace{}_{2} \quad \underbrace{}_{3}$$

In appearance, (31) is similar to the familiar ST version, given in (5).
What we have done is to substitute for the essential variable Y an
optional occurrence of the well-defined constant h plus an optional
VP bracket. The VP bracket signifies that the NP of item 3 may be a
subject or an object. In addition, we have added the bracket]$_C$ enclosing Q, where C stands for Complementizer. We assume that the WH word
is attached under C, and appears as a complementizer in surface structure as proposed in Bresnan (1970). Note that the parentheses enclosing

the constants of item 2 are interlocking. This is a convention which
signifies that either one or both must be present. The result is that
with our version of WH-Question only WH words which are main clause
objects or are contained in an object clause are moved; WH words which
are main clause subjects are not moved into complementizer position.
We do this to eliminate counterintuitive surface structures. For
example, according to Bresnan, the sentence 'Who left?' has no surface subject while the sentence 'he left' does. Under our proposal both
sentences will have surface subjects.

Presented below is an ordering for the sentence 'Who does Mary
believe that Bill said that John saw?' that meets the SD of (31). (We
are assuming that Affix-Hopping is postcyclic here.)

(32)

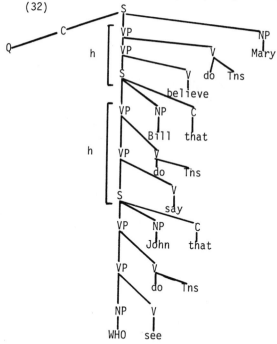

It should be noted that there are two different sequential orders for the brackets in h. In rules where h is dominated by S, as in WH-Question, it represents the sequence in (30); however, in rules where it is dominated by VP, as in Tough-movement (cf. (68) and (70) of 1.10) the brackets have the order $[_{NP} \left([_{S} \right) [_{VP_1}$ because we start counting at a different node.

1.7. STANDARD THEORY CONSTRAINTS ON VARIABLES COVERING THE INTERNAL STRUCTURE OF NP

In addition to the observations on chopping from subordinate clauses, Ross notes certain other constraints on chopping within NP. The principal constraint of this type is known as the Pied Piping Convention, given below.

(33) *The Pied Piping Convention*

Any transformation which is stated in such a way as to effect the reordering of some specified node NP, where this node is preceded and followed by variables in the structural index of the rule, may apply to this NP or to any noncoordinate NP which dominates it, as long as there are no occurrences of any coordinate node, nor of the node S, on the branch connecting the higher node and the specified node.

The phenomenon of Pied Piping is actually quite limited in that it comprises only chains of prepositional phrases embedded in NP. The examples below are taken from Ross, though they have been changed from relative clauses to WH-Questions; (34) is the basic sentence from which the sentences of (35) and (36) are derived by permission of the Pied-Piping Convention.

(34) Q The Government prescribes the height of the lettering on the covers of WH reports.

(35) a. Which reports does the Government prescribe the height of the lettering on the covers of?

b. The covers of which reports does the Government prescribe the height of the lettering on?

c. The lettering on the covers of which reports does the Government prescribe the height of?

(35) d. The height of the lettering on the covers of which reports does the Government prescribe?

(36) a. Of which reports does the Government prescribe the height of the lettering on the covers?

b. On the covers of which reports does the Government prescribe the height of the lettering?

c. Of the lettering on the covers of which reports does the Government prescribe the height?

There is no uniform agreement on the acceptability of the above sentences. For example, Ross (1967: 111) finds sentences of the type in (36), both questions and relatives, to be unacceptable in his 'dialect'; for Postal (1971: 98), sentences of the type in (35d) are unacceptable, but only in questions, not in relatives. For the present, we shall regard all of the above sentences as grammatical. (Indeed, for me they are, though some are rather clumsy and carry the ring of quiz-show English.)

The convention in (33), like those discussed in 1.1., is essentially a negative constraint on an internal variable, as the *except* clause indicates: "... or to any noncoordinate NP ... as long as there are no occurrences of any coordinate node, nor of the node S, on the branch connecting the higher node and the specified node." It attempts to specify the essential hierarchical structure covered by the variable; but, as the above quote shows, it is redundant in that it partially restates the constraints on chopping from subordinate clauses.

Viewed from the perspective of MOG, the Pied-Piping phenomenon is seen as indicating the presence of another hierarchical constant. So let us examine the structure of these prepositional phrase chains for some reoccurring hunk of hierarchical structure. We assume the sentence in (34) to have the structure shown in (37). (Example (37) shown on next page.) The rule of WH-Question may move any one of the numbered NPs in (37). In order that the hierarchical structure of NP_1 may be more easily examined, we present a reordering of it in (38).

(37)

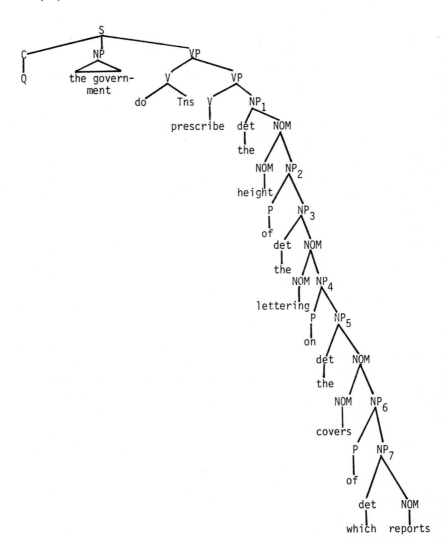

(38)

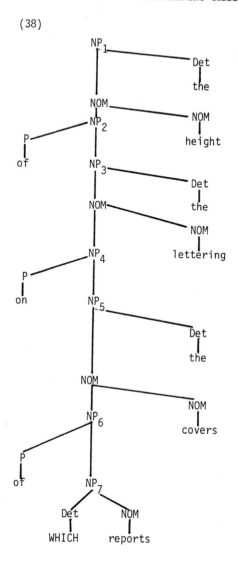

In a left-to-right format (38) appears as the sequence in (39), where
the irrelevant items to the right are not mentioned.

(39)

$$[\quad [\quad [\quad P[\quad [\quad [\quad P[\quad [\quad [\quad P[\quad [\quad [+WH]$$

$$NP_1 \quad NOM \quad NP_2 \quad NP_3 \quad NOM \quad NP_4 \quad NP_5 \quad NOM \quad NP_6 \quad NP_7 \quad Det$$

Notice that the structure which NP_1 dominates is analyzable as a recursive string, as indicated by the reoccurring underlined sequences
in (39).

Given the format of MOG,we are in a position to restate the negative constraint of (33) as the positive and more simple generalization
in (40):

(40) *Revised Pied Piping Convention*
      Any transformation which operates over the constant h and
      which moves an NP containing some specified element may move
      that NP or any NP which dominates it from a sequence of the
      type:

$$\underbrace{[\quad\quad [\quad\quad \left([\atop NP \right) \quad P[}_{1}$$
$$NP \quad\quad NOM \quad\quad\quad NP$$

(We will return to the connection between Pied Piping and the constant h
in section 1.9.) The line with subscript 1 indicates a chain of any
length of the underlined sequence of brackets. The optional brackets in
the above formula allow for application to simple prepositional phrases.
Thus the sentences in (41) are also accounted for by (40).

(41) a. Who did you speak to?
     b. To whom did you speak?

In making a precise generalization about the environments within
NP out of which NP may be moved, the above revision of Pied Piping eliminates the necessity for specifying the environments in which it may
not operate, that is, coordinate NPs and sentential subjects. For exam-

ple, the positive generalization of (40) automatically excludes such
ungrammatical strings as '*Who was John arguing with Bill and?' because the underlying NP 'with Bill and WHO' would have the structure
in (42) and could not, with any ordering, meet the specifications of
the formula in (40).

(42)

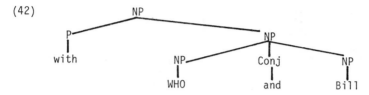

Now let us turn to another constraint proposed by Ross, the Left
Branch Condition, stated in (43):

(43)   *The Left Branch Condition*
       No NP which is the leftmost constituent of a larger NP can
       be reordered out of this NP by a transformational rule.
This constraint is used to prevent the movement of possessive NPs out
of the NP which contains them. It permits the generation of sentences
like (44a), where the uppermost NP which dominates the possessive WH-
word is moved, while preventing sentences like (44b,c), where some
lower NP in the possessive chain has been moved.

(44) a. The man whose friend's brother the police arrested was an
        informer.
     b. *The man whose friend's the police arrested brother was an
        informer.
     c. *The man whose the police arrested friend's brother was an
        informer.

If there is indeed a transformational environment of the sort in
(43) based on linear order, "No NP which is the leftmost constituent...",
then it provides a counterexample to MOG. For since MOG has eliminated
distinctive linear order at the transformational level, it is incapable
of expressing such notions. However, upon closer examination, we see
that the need for stating the constraint in linear terms arises out of
Ross' peculiar analysis of the derived structure of possessive phrases.

He would assign the structure in (45) to the phrase "... the man's
friend's brother ...":

(45)

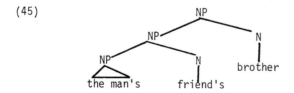

No justification for this analysis is given by Ross. But there is another structure which is more plausible, namely, that prenominal
possessive NPs are dominated by Determiner. This becomes apparent when
we examine the formation of prenominal possessives from postnominal
prepositional phrases. This process involves the replacement of the
article within the determiner of the head NP by the NP of the postnominal prepositional phrase and not the replacement of the entire determiner. We see this most clearly when there is a prearticle present,
as in (46):

    (46) five of the friends of this boy ⇒ five of this boy's friends.
The NP *this boy* has replaced the definite article *the* in the determiner
[[five of] [the]] . From this we infer the structure of (45) to be
the one presented below.

(47)

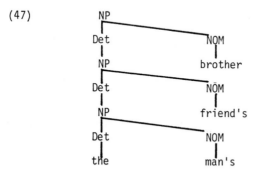

Now it is no longer necessary to rely on a statement involving linear
order to capture the prohibition against movement of possessive NPs;
instead, the constraint can be stated in hierarchical terms, as given
in (48).

(48) *Possessive NP Condition* (Left Branch Condition revised)
      Any transformation which moves an NP containing some speci-
      fied element may move only the topmost NP of any sequence
      of the form   [[[
                      NP   Det   NP
                             ‾‾‾‾‾‾‾‾‾‾
                                 1

1.8. HIERARCHICAL CONSTANTS WITHIN NP: THE NP CONSTANT

In this section, we consider the expression of the two positive
constraints formulated in the previous section as hierarchical constants
and the relationship of the constants to each other. First let us convert the revised Pied Piping Convention of (40) into a rule constant.
This is accomplished in the preliminary formula below, which utilizes
the hierarchical sequence mentioned in (40):

(49) NP Constant (first version)

$$\underset{NP}{i \; [} \; \underset{NP}{i' \; =} \; [\; (\underset{NOM}{[} \; \underset{NP}{[} \;) \; P \; \underset{NP}{[}$$
                                  ‾‾‾‾‾‾‾‾‾‾‾‾‾‾‾‾
                                         0

The NP bracket between i and i' represents the specified NP of a rule such
as WH-Question and may be any of the NPs in the sequence on the right-
hand side of the above formula. The subscript 0 indicates that the recursive part of the sequence may be null, that is, the specified NP may
be simple. An expanded version of WH-Question is given below:

(50) WH-Question (second version)

$$Q \quad] \, (h_1 \, [\, [\,)i \quad [i' \quad [+WH] \Rightarrow \emptyset, 3, 2, \emptyset$$
$$\underset{C}{} \quad \underset{VP_1}{} \quad NP$$
      └─┘└─────────┘└──────────┘
       1   2   3

It is assumed that, by convention, any rule which applies to a labeled
bracket without mentioning its complement bracket applies to the entire
node represented by that bracket. For example, in the above rule, if
the specified NP is not the last (i.e. the lowest) in the sequence specified in (49), then i' will cover some sequence of brackets some of

whose constituents will be ordered to the right of the WH-word. Our convention states that all of the 'unmentioned' constituents of the specified NP are moved as well as the 'mentioned' ones. So the values of i and i' vary in a precise and predictable manner according to the position of the specified NP in the hierarchical chain. (An example is presented in (53).)

Next we take up the Possessive NP Condition of (48). First, note that there is a relationship that holds between Pied Piping and the Possessive NP Condition (Left Branch condition in ST), namely, that any rule which is subject to the former is also subject to the latter and vice versa. Second, both the formula for the NP Constant in (49) and the sequence mentioned in the Possessive NP Condition of (48) contain a single NP bracket dominating a recursive hierarchical sequence.

Keeping these points in mind, we abstract the recursive sequence from the Possessive NP Condition and call it the constant j, as indicated in (51).

$$(51) \qquad j = [\qquad [$$
$$\qquad\qquad\quad \underline{Det \quad NP}$$
$$\qquad\qquad\qquad\quad 0$$

(The subscript 0 permits j to be null.) Then we add j to the NP Constant of (49), as shown in final form below:

$$(52) \qquad NP \text{ Constant (final version)}$$

$$i [i' = [\quad ([\quad [ ) P [\quad j$$
$$\underline{NP \qquad\quad NP \quad NOM \ NP \qquad NP}$$
$$\qquad\qquad\qquad\qquad\qquad 0$$

Thus j is mentioned only as a subpart of the NP Constant, and never independently of it. By making j the rightmost (i.e. the lowest) member of the NP Constant, we assure that the specified NP of any rule containing this constant will lie outside of (that is, will dominate) the sequence covered by j, which is what the Possessive NP Condition (Ross' Left Branch Condition) requires.

(53)

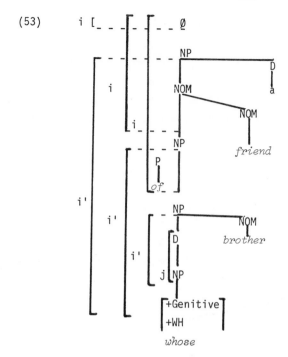

As indicated, there are three possible values of i and i' for this P-marker; these will produce the surface variations for questions shown in (54).

(54) a. A friend of whose brother did the police arrest?
      b. Of whose brother did the police arrest a friend?
      c. Whose brother did the police arrest a friend of?

Sentences like '*Whose did the police arrest the friend of brother?' are automatically prohibited, since the NP dominating the WH-word lies within j and therefore cannot be the specified NP of the NP Constant.

Notice that by arranging j as the lowest member of the NP Constant, we account for an additional set of facts for which ST has, at present, no explanation. In English, it is possible under certain conditions to apply the Possessive Preposing Rule to an NP which contains a prepositional phrase within it, for example 'the hat of *the King of England'* ⇒

'*the King of England's* hat'. Some other examples are given in (55):

(55) a. The police arrested *the president of the Company's* brother.

b. *The owner of our building's* car was destroyed in the fire.

c. *The city of the future's* problems are as yet unknown.

It is probable that these complex possessive phrases have the same structure as regular possessive prepositional phrases, since the Possessive Preposing Rule may apply within them, e.g. 'the King of England' ⇒ 'England's King', 'the President of the Company' ⇒ 'the Company's President', etc.

According to the constituent structure analysis assumed by MOG, the structure of NPs containing preposed prepositional phrases is that given in (56):

(56)

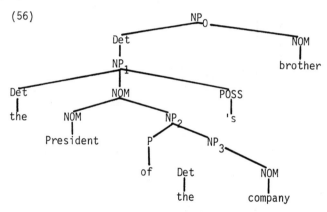

But if we question NP_3, the ungrammatical sentences in (57) result. The (a), (b), (c), and (d) sentences come about from movement of NP_3, NP_2, NP_1, and NP_0, respectively.

(57) a. *Which company did the police arrest the president of's brother?

b. (?)*Of which company did the police arrest the president's brother?

c. *The president of which company's did the police arrest brother?

d. *The president of which company's brother did the police arrest?

Of these sentences, only (57c) is blocked by the Left Branch Condition of ST, since only NP_1 of (56) is "... the leftmost constituent of a larger NP ...". Thus, once again ST is found to be inadequate and must be supplemented further by some as yet unformulated constraint.

On the other hand, MOG need add no such special statement, for in making the positive generalization embodied by the NP Constant, all of the sentences of (57) (and the corresponding relative clause sentences) are automatically blocked. This is because in NPs like (57), the internal structure does not conform to the pattern required by the NP Constant, that is, where j is the lowest member.

Finally, although space does not permit it here, the notational system of hierarchical constants provided by MOG can easily be modified to handle the individual restrictions on movement out of NP noted by Ross and Postal (referred to above in (35) and (36) of 1.7); it can also be extended to account for register and cross language differences in the movement of prepositions, where in questions and relatives of informal English, prepositions are not moved with the WH word, e.g. (41a), while in formal English and in all varieties of such languages as French and German they are obligatorily moved with the WH word, e.g. (41b). ST is not able to handle these phenomena in any systematic fashion.

1.9. THE RELATIONSHIP OF THE NP CONSTANT TO OTHER HIERARCHICAL CONSTANTS

Just as certain relationships hold between the constants within NP, so also there exist certain other relations between the NP Constant and the constants h and [. The link between the NP Constant and h is
$$VP$$
captured by the statement in (58).

> (58) Any rule which contains the NP Constant i___i' must also contain the constant h.

In other words, the NP Constant appears only in unbounded rules and never in bounded rules such as Passive, Subject Raising, etc. as illustrated in (59).

(59) a. The truck hit the fender of John's car. ≁
         *John's car was hit the fender of by the truck.
      b. Bill believes [the president of the company is guilty]. ≁
         *Bill believes the company [the president of to be guilty].

In ST, the relation in (58) has never been explicitly stated. Notice that, by implication, Ross does prevent sentences like those in (59) by inserting the following proviso in the Pied Piping Convention: "Any transformation which is stated in such a way as to effect the reordering of some specified node NP, *where this node is preceded and followed by variables in the structural index of the rule* ..." (my emphasis). Since no bounded chopping rule that applies to NP meets this condition, that is none that we know of, sentences like (59) are blocked.

In the reformulation of the Pied Piping Convention offered in (40), we inserted the phrase "Any transformation which operates over the constant h ..." This not only prevents the sentences in (59), but also explicitly ties Pied Piping to unbounded chopping over sentence boundary. However, once (40) has been converted to the NP Constant i___i', there is no way of showing the relationship between unbounded chopping from NP and unbounded chopping over sentence boundary other than by simply never writing a rule with i___i' which does not also contain h, as indicated by the observation of (58).

Before dealing further with this relation, let us consider some additional facts about Pied Piping discovered by George Horn (1972). He points out that application of the Pied Piping Convention is more limited than hitherto realized in that an NP may not be moved out of a higher NP that functions as a subject; only the entire subject NP may be moved. Thus while the sentences of (60) are acceptable, those in (61), where an NP has been moved out of the subject NP, are not.

(60) a. The back of which sofa is chartreuse?
      b. The car the rear fender of which was damaged by that truck
         belongs to Harry Jones.
      c. The book the last chapter of which was written by George
         is now a best seller.

(61)   a. *Which sofa is the back of chartreuse?

b. *The car which the rear fender of was damaged by that truck belongs to Harry Jones.

c. *The book which the last chapter of was written by George is now a best seller.

The sentences in (61) become acceptable once the NP out of which the lower NP has been moved is made a constituent of the predicate, as in (62).

(62)   a. The car which you damaged the rear fender of belongs to Harry Jones.

b. The book which George wrote the last chapter of is now a best seller.

Working in the framework of ST, Horn suggests that these facts be accounted for by generalizing the Sentential Subject Constraint so that it prohibits movement of any item out of a subject NP. But since MOG has replaced constrained variables with constants, this approach is not available for us. However, the rules of MOG that contain the NP Constant (and this includes at least the following: WH-Question, Relativization, Topicalization, Focus) all contain an optional VP bracket to the left of i signifying that the rule may apply to a subject or an object; see WH-Question in (49), for example. Now if in these rules we include i within the parentheses surrounding the VP bracket, then the above facts described by Horn are automatically provided for. The statement of WH-Question below includes this revision:

(63)   WH-Question (third version)

$$Q \ [\ (h_1 \ )[\ \ i) \ [\ i' \ [+WH] \Rightarrow \ \emptyset, \ 3, \ 2, \ \emptyset$$

$$\underbrace{}_{1} \underbrace{\underbrace{}_{VP_1}}_{2} \underbrace{\underbrace{}_{NP}}_{3}$$

This is tantamount to placing the following condition on i: i is always null unless it is dominated by VP; but since this can be expressed notationally in the rule proper, we need not add it as an outside condition. Thus (63) assures that the specified NP of WH-Question will not be part of some higher NP unless it is a constituent of VP.

There remains the relationship between i___i' and h noted in (58)
at the beginning of this section. How are we to make the mutual occurrence
of these constants and that of [explicit? For it is now the case that
                                VP
the entire sequence to the right of the C bracket in 2 of the SD of (63)
reoccurs in several rules. In order to signify that this group funtions
as an integral unit, we establish this chain as the constant k, in (64).

(64)   k = (h$_1$ $[$ [i)

             VP$_1$

So in all rules, k replaces this sequence. WH-Question, the sample rule
throughout this paper, is given below as an example:

(65)   WH-Question (final version)

       Q] k [i' [+WH] ⇒ Ø, 3, 2, Ø
       ⌊_⌋⌊___⌋ ⌊_____⌋
        1 2   3

(65) is similar to the statement given in (5) of section 1.1., though
the similarity is only superficial. We have replaced the internal
variable Y of (5) and all the attendant conventions and constraints by
certain well-defined constants.

1.10. 'BONDED' h

       In this section, we show how certain other grammatical constants
are fused with h in a relationship called 'bonding' to express environments for movement which contain h but which are more restrictive than
h alone.

       Let us look at the rule of Tough-Movement. That this rule operates
over unbounded contexts is shown by the examples in (66).

(66)   a. It's hard to imagine anyone trying to fix that old car. ⇒
          That old car is hard to imagine anyone trying to fix.

(66)   b. It's difficult to conceive of anyone even wanting to
          attempt to read that book in one night. ⇒
          That book is difficult to conceive of anyone even wanting
          to attempt to read in one night.

However, there is a peculiar restriction on unbounded application of
Tough-Movement: the object clauses down through which it applies must
be *For-to* or *Poss-ing* types. If it applies through a *That* clause, the
resulting surface sentence is unacceptable, as illustrated in (67).

(67)   a. It's hard to imagine anyone trying to claim that Joe
          fixed that old car. ≁
          *That old car is hard to imagine anyone trying to claim
          that Joe fixed ∅.
       b. It's easy to believe that Nixon tried to get Rosemary to
          erase the tapes. ≁
          *The tapes are easy to believe that Nixon tried to get
          Rosemary to erase.

In terms of MOG, the above restriction is phrased as follows: in
Tough-Movement, every h must contain either the *ing* of a *Poss-ing* complementizer or the *to* of a *For-to* complementizer. When a hierarchical
constant is restricted by some other constant in this manner, we term
this relationship 'bonding'. The notational expression of bonding is as
follows. The element or elements which bond the constant are joined to
it by the symbol '+'. (In ST, '+' signifies sister adjunction, a notion
which needs no special designation in MOG because the constituent-set
to which a given element is added by a rule is always specified.) Let
us assume Rosenbaum's (1967) feature representation of complementizers
where *For-to* and *Poss-ing* are both classified as [+C,+D] and   *That* is
classified as [+C,-D]. The rule of Tough-Movement with bonded h appears
below. (In a general treatment of NP movement, this rule is combined with
raising in a single rule of NP-raising - see the following paper in this
volume.)

(68)   Tough-Movement

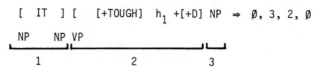

It is assumed that the subscript 1 extends over the entire bonded sequence, that is, $h_1+[+D]$ = $\underline{h+[+D]}$. In effect, this redefines h as in
(68).   1

(68) $h + [+D]$ = $([~)$ [[[+D]   [
                     NP   S   VP VP_1

The partial tree in (70) indicates an ordering for (66a) which meets the above environment.

(70)

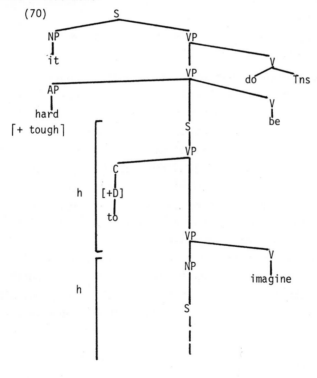

1.11. WHY CONSTANTS ARE PREFERABLE TO VARIABLES WITH CONSTRAINTS

Before passing on to the subject of order assignment, let us
address ourselves briefly to a possible criticism of the approach to
constraining transformations outlined in the preceding pages. Certainly
most people will agree that it is a gain to collapse the four negative
clause constraints of ST discussed in 1.1. into a single positive constraint, as suggested in 1.2. However, some might balk at the creation
of rule constants in place of variables with constraints, throwing out
the familiar barb that, after all, the former is merely a notational
variant of the latter. We would respond to this in the following way.

To begin with, the glib use of the phrase 'notational variant' as
a pejorative epithet is something of an inanity; for it is not the case
that the value of a given theory is automatically diminished by showing
it to be a notational variant of some existing one, since by this line
of reasoning we could arrive at the foolish conclusion that the indis-
pensable mathematical system of vector analysis ought to be discounted
on the grounds that it is merely an alternative expression of Cartesian
coordinates. Leaving aside this general objection, if two theories are
to be declared notational variants of each other, it must be the case
that both are, in fact, theories expressed by reasonably well-defined
notational systems. It is in just this respect that ST is lacking, for
constraints on variables are essentially informal statements about what
sorts of structures may (as in positive constraints) or may not (as in
negative constraints) be covered by variables. There are no well-defined
bounds or content to which ST constraints are confined and therefore
they can be used to say just about anything and often in more than one
way.

On the other hand, the hierarchical constants of MOG constitute a
notational system which is keyed specifically to the well-defined area of
configurational relations of P-markers and this confinement constrains
it to making generalizations about certain discrete reoccurring hunks
(or 'quanta') of such structure. For example, we can think of 'h' as a
basic threshold for unbounded movement out of S; any such movement must
be measured in multiples of this unit. It is the computation of such

contexts in discrete units which provides the limiting factor to transformational statements. It seems quite normal to assume, then, that no
natural language computes unbounded environments over clause boundary
in units greater than one sentence deep; that is, we would not expect
to find a constant such as 'h' with the value [[[[[, etc. There-
$$\text{VP NP S} \quad \text{VP S}$$
fore, rather than containing a notational variant of ST constraints, MOG
presents a notational *expression* of these constraints, something for
which there was previously no clear notation; furthermore, this notation is included as an integral part of the theory of transformational
mechanics. In theoretical science, it must be considered an advance whenever we succeed in capturing in a unified theory facts which were formerly expressible only in statements lying outside the main body of theory.
The importance of notational systems in this endeavor should not be
underestimated. It is for this reason that hierarchical constants are
preferable to variables with outside constraints.

2. ASSIGNING LINEAR ORDER

2.1. SURFACE STRUCTURE CONSTRAINTS: POSITIVE FILTERS

It has been recognized for some time that there exist certain
linguistic phenomena which cannot be properly regulated by the transformational component alone no matter how we try to limit it by constraints
on transformations. In some instances this involves regulating word
order, as in the surface order of adjectives before nouns in English
(e.g. 'a charming old white house ...', *'a white old charming house...',
*'a white charming old house ...'; cf. Ross, 1967, pp. 40-41, 61-62),
or it may involve regulating constituent-set membership, as in the case
of Spanish clitic pronouns. The latter case has been discussed in detail
in Perlmutter (1971). In proposing a surface structure constraint for
Spanish clitics, Perlmutter makes the important point that such filters
are positive generalizations about permissible sequences. Although it
is possible to block the ungrammatical sequences by negative constraints,
that is statements about the types of sequences that may *not* occur, in
doing so, it is necessary to use more than one constraint. But in making

a generalization about what does occur, ungrammatical strings are blocked
in a natural way by simple exclusion from the class of permissible
structures. This is exactly the approach that we adopted in formulating
the hierarchical constants of Part I as replacements for negative constraints on transformations.

2.2 'SURFACE STRUCTURE' IN STANDARD THEORY AND MULTIPLE ORDER GRAMMAR

In both ST and MOG we have the following basic components: Categorial Rules, Lexicon, and Transformations (we leave aside semantic interpretation). In addition, the transformational component of ST must
be supplemented by a set of constraints on variables, as discussed in
1.1.; and further, there must be a special set of surface structure constraints that regulate the output of the transformational component by
filtering out certain types of strings which are not well formed with
respect to the order of constituents or constituent-set membership. The
ST model can be characterized by the following chart.

(71)   The Standard Theory Model of Generative Grammar

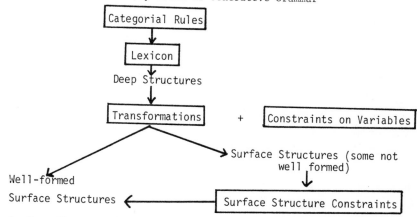

In ST, Surface Structure has always been defined as the point in a derivation where all the transformations have applied, in other words, the
last P-marker of a derivation. With the addition of surface structure
constraints, the picture is less clear. In some languages, certain
classes of surface structures produced by the transformational component

will always be well formed and therefore there are no constraints regulating them. For example, according to Perlmutter (1971, chapter 4) his
constraint on subjects does not apply to Spanish and certain other
languages; but Spanish does have a special constraint on clitic pronouns.
Thus all Spanish sentences without clitics are apparently not subject
to any surface structure constraints and are produced as well-formed
structures directly from the transformational component, but those
with clitics must pass through the clitic filter before they can be
classified as well formed. Conceivably, there are some languages with
no surface structure constraints at all and others where all sentences
must pass through at least one such constraint or another. Thus the
level of surface structure is not well defined. Is it before application of surface structure constraints, after, or both? This arises because the status of these constraints in ST is uncertain. Are they
formal universals in the sense of Categorial Rules, Transformations, etc.,
or are they ad hoc devices tacked on to the theory to accommodate 'leaks'
in the transformational components of specific languages? The latter
description more accurately captures the spirit of their creation.

Let us now turn to MOG. It is clear that in a theory where P-markers
have no single order to their constituents, surface structure cannot be
defined as the stage of a derivation where all transformations have been
applied. There must be some apparatus to assign a specific surface
order to each P-marker issuing from the Transformational Component. We
call such an apparatus a Phrase Structure Ordering Condition (PSOC). PSOC
are formal universals on a par with transformations and the like. (The
form of PSOC will be presented in the following section.) Surface Structure, then, is defined as the stage of a derivation at which all PSOC
have applied. The chart below presents an outline of MOG.

(72)   The Multiple Order Grammar Model of Generative Grammar

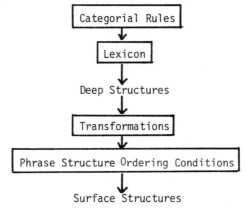

2.3. ASSIGNING SURFACE ORDER IN MULTIPLE ORDER GRAMMAR:

PHRASE STRUCTURE ORDERING FOR ENGLISH

We now take up the formulation of the PSOC mentioned in the previous section. If P-markers are defined as collections of ordered P-markers, then the assignment of surface order to a given P-marker will
necessarily involve a process of selecting one ordered P-marker from
the particular collection that defines that P-marker. This differs both
from ST and from a theory such as that of Sanders (1970, this volume),
which views P-markers as being unordered. In these two theories, surface
order is achieved through the mapping of one P-marker onto another.
For the former it is the mapping of a single ordered P-marker onto a
single ordered P-marker, that is, the final P-marker to issue from the
Transformational Component, while for the latter it is the mapping of
a single unordered P-marker onto a single ordered P-marker. In both cases it is a one-to-one mapping. In MOG, surface order allotment is a
many-one mapping going from many orders to one order, a pairing down and
a discarding of inappropriate orders.

The PSOC which perform this selection function are filters of the
sort suggested by Perlmutter (op. cit.), discussed in Section 2.1.; they
make positive generalizations about permissible surface order. In terms
of the schema for multiple ordering presented in (21b) of 1.3., the

PSOC search through the members ($A_1'...A_{m!}'$, $B_1'...B_{n!}'$, ...) of each
circled node ((A), (B), ...) of the multiordered tree of the final multiordered P-marker of a derivation and they accept one member for each
circled node which meets the conditions of ordering established for that
node. It is assumed that the process moves 'from the bottom up' in the
manner of the cycle, although at this point this is an arbitrary decision.

How many PSOC must there be? Suppose we begin by assuming that there
is one for each nonterminal node of the categorial rules, that is, S,
NP, VP, AP, NOM, Det, and so forth. This would make the set of PSOC
roughly equivalent to a set of context-free categorial rules for surface
structure. For example, the PSOC for S in English would be approximately
the filter shown in (73). (In the interest of economy, we will leave adverbs and particles out of the present discussion; we assume that fronted WH-words are complementizers in Surface Structure.)

(73)   [(C) (V) (NP) (VP)]
        S   S

The sentence types that this enumerates are illustrated below:

(74) a. VP:
          Open the door!
          Who did John say *opened the door?*
      b. NP VP: *John opened the door.*
      c. V NP VP: *Did John open the door?*
      d. C VP: I don't know *how to swim.*
      e. C NP VP: *That John is a fool* is obvious.
      f. C V NP VP: *Who did John see?*

The filter in (73) applies to every $\{S_1'...S_{n!}'\}$ of every S in a multiordered P-marker that has passed through the Transformational Component
and will accept only those $S_1'...S_{n!}'$ whose order and membership meet its
conditions. Thus such orders as *$NP\ V\ VP$, *$VP\ NP$, *$NP\ C\ VP$ will be
rejected.

The PSOC for VP in English is given in (75).

(75) $[\ \overset{\frown}{(C)} \ V \ \overset{\frown}{(AP)} \ \overset{\frown}{(NP_1)} \ \overset{\frown}{(VP)} \ \overset{\frown}{(S)} \ ]$

VP   VP

Some of the surface VP types accepted by (75) are given below:

(76)   a. V: John *left.*

b. V AP: John *is tall.*

c. V NP$_1$: (1) John *saw Bill.*

(2) John *gave money to Bill.*

(3) John gave *Bill money.*

(4) John *talked to Bill about Harry.*

(5) John *talked about Harry to Bill.*

(6) John *mentioned to Bill your going abroad next year.*

(7) John *mentioned your going abroad next year to Bill.*

d. V AP NP: John *is proud of Bill.*

e. V AP S: John *is slow to regognize his faults.*

f. V VP: John *is looking at Helen.*

g. V NP S: John *mentioned to Bill that Helen left.*

h. V S: (1) John *thinks that Helen left.*

(2) John *wants Helen to leave.*

i. C V: *To leave* would be a disaster.

(75) also enumerates certain vacuous combinations such as $*\overset{\frown}{V} \ \overset{\frown}{AP} \ \overset{\frown}{VP}$.

Some of the strings in (76) need further elaboration. Notice that (76c) covers all VPs with one or more NPs, where NP may contain *(D) NOM,* $\overset{\frown}{Prep} \ NP$, or *S*; however, there are certain unacceptable combinations of Direct and Indirect Objects which it does not exclude, e.g. ' *John gave to Bill money*', and '* John *gave money Bill*'. Thus (75) is too general in this respect; in 2.5. we formulate a special PSOC to regulate strings of NPs such as this.

(76f) also deserves some comment. This reflects the analysis of auxiliaries which we have assumed throughout this paper where auxiliaries are main verbs which take obligatory VP complements (cf. 27 of 1.5.).

Note that (75) predicts that if an NP occurs in a VP which dominates an
auxiliary plus a VP complement, the NP will be ordered between the two,
e.g. $V \overset{\frown}{NP} VP$. Through application of the rule known as There-Insertion,
such a surface sentence does come about: 'A man was looking at Helen.' ⇒
There was a man looking at Helen.' The structure for this is given below:

(77)

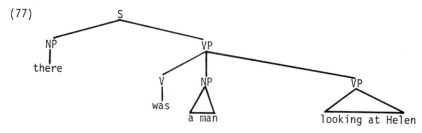

    Finally, (6) and (7) of (76c) show that S dominated by NP (i.e.
Poss-ing nominals) scrambles freely with other NPs in its set, much as
prepositional phrases do, as in (4) and (5) of (76c). S dominated by VP
(i.e. a *That* or *For—To* clause), however, is always positioned as the
rightmost member of its set, as indicated by (76 g,h)). This means that
VPs of the form $V \overset{\frown}{S} \overset{\frown}{NP}$ will be rejected, e.g. ' John *mentioned that
Helen left to Bill'*, ' John *told to leave Bill'*. This is the principal
reason why we maintain the phrase structure distinction between *Poss—ing*
complements on the one hand and *That* and *For—To* complements on the other,
as originally proposed in 1.2.
    Below in (78) is the PSOC for NP:

(78)
$$\underset{NP}{[} \overset{\frown}{} \left\{ \begin{matrix} \text{Prep } \overset{\frown}{NP} \\ \text{(Det)} \overset{\frown}{} \text{NOM} \\ S \end{matrix} \right\} \underset{NP}{]}$$

This represents three basic types of NP: prepositional phrase, NOM preceded by optional Determiner, and S. The PSOC for NOM is shown in (79):

(79)
$$\underset{NOM}{[} \overset{\frown}{} \left\{ \begin{matrix} (AP_1) \overset{\frown}{} \text{NOM} \overset{\frown}{} (S) \\ N \overset{\frown}{} (S) \end{matrix} \right\} \underset{NOM}{]}$$

This details the surface order for the following types of NOM: NOM dominating $\widehat{NOM\,S}$ (relative clause), $\widehat{AP\,NOM}$ (adjective raised from a relative), $\widehat{AP\,NOM\,S}$ (raised adjective plus a relative), $\widehat{N\,S}$ (S with a lexical head noun, e.g. *the fact that S*), and a simple noun.

One might object that the PSOC in (79) is not complete in that it
does not provide for postnominal adjectives as in 'I smell *something
good*'. This would seem to have the structure $\widehat{NOM\,AP}$. However, if we
analyze prenominal adjectives as being derived from relative clauses by
the rules of Relativization, Relative Reduction, and Modifier Shift, the
last of which moves AP out of S and attaches it as a constituent of NOM,
then the sole differences between the derivation of prenominal adjectives
and that of postnominal adjectives is that Modifier Shift applies in the
former but not in the latter. This means that postnominal adjectives will
have the structure of reduced relatives, $\widehat{NOM\,S}$, and will therefore be
properly ordered in a natural way by the PSOC for NOM above. (We reject
Ross' S-pruning convention, which would invalidate this analysis (cf.
Ross, 1967); there are rather strong arguments against this convention,
though we cannot take the time to develop them here.)

In addition to the above categories, there are lower level constituents such as Det and V, which may dominate strings like $\widehat{verb\,af}$,
$\widehat{verb\,af}\,Part$, etc. It is assumed that there are PSOC for these also.

2.4. A GENERAL CONTEXT-FREE PSOC FOR THE MAJOR CATEGORIES OF ENGLISH

If we compare the individual PSOC formulated in the previous
section, certain similarities in the ordering of constituents is immediately apparent. For any constituent set in which any combination of
the constituents S, VP, NP, AP, NOM, N, V, C, Det, Prep occurs, the
following principles of surface order will hold.

(80)   a. C occurs to the left of V (cf. [73] and [75])
       b. V occurs to the left of AP, VP, NP, and S (cf. [73] and
          [75])
       c. AP occurs to the left of NP, NOM, and S (cf. [75] and
          [79])
       d. NP, NOM, or N occurs to the left of S (cf. [74], [78],
          [79])

    e. NP occurs to the left of VP (cf. [73] and [75])

    f. Prep occurs to the left of NP (cf. [78])

    g. Det occurs to the left of NOM (cf. [78])

If general statements of this sort can be made about the surface order
of constituents independently of the nodes that dominate them, then there
is no reason to make a separate PSOC for each constituent type. In fact,
to do so would be to miss important generalizations. For example, by
stating separate PSOC for S and VP, as in (73) and (75), ordering statements like (80a,b) must be made twice. This leads us to propose the
collapsing of all the individual PSOC of the previous section into a
single context-free PSOC.

    Before doing so, let us introduce a notational convention for sur-
face ordering categories. The nodes NP_1, NOM, and N belong to the category 'nominal element', symbolized as $\underline{N}$; the prenominal categories Prep,
Det, AP_1 belong to the group 'descriptor', symbolized as $\underline{D}$. This convention allows us to collapse similar nodes of different hierarchical
levels into a single category; it should not be confused with Chomsky's
$\bar{X}$ convention, which unites different nodes of the same hierarchical level into a single category.

    Armed with the above convention, we give the general CFPSOC for the
major categories of English below:

    (81) General CFPSOC for English

        [(C) (V) ($\underline{D}$) ($\underline{N}$) (VP) (S)]

(81) replaces all the individual PSOC of the preceding section.

    Notice that a theory such as ST can never make a generalization
about surface order such as that in (81) because it scatters the order-
assigning function throughout the categorial and transformational components and thereby provides only an indirect characterization of surface
structure. For example, the fact that V comes before NP and VP in the
constituent-set VP is stated in the PS expansion for VP, while the fact
that V precedes these same two constituents in S is stated separately
by the Subject-Verb Inversion rule. Thus, according to ST, it is mere
coincidence that English orders its verbs to the left in questions and
it is just as likely that it could have ordered them to the right, e.g.

'*John leave did?' ([NP V͡P V͡]).

On the other hand, MOG, with its single, direct, general statement about surface order, suggests that such ordering facts are no accident, but rather they result from a very basic organizational feature of natural language which has been totally missed by ST. We can state it as follows:

(82)   *The Principle of Uniform Ordering*
       A language tends to order its categories the same throughout
       all the constituent-sets of a sentence.

Sanders (this volume) makes a similar statement in his "Invariant Order Constraint", as do Bartsch and Vennemann (1972) in their notion of "Natural Serialization".

In Part 3, certain universals of constituent order which support the above observation will be discussed.

2.5. SPECIAL CONTEXT-FREE PSOC

In Section 2.1., we noted two phenomena for which ST had to create special surface constraints in the form of positive filters: the order of prenominal adjectives according to semantic class and the membership and order of sequences of clitic pronouns in Spanish. In MOG, these same filters are necessary, though they play a supplementary role to that of the general PSOC of (81); that is, they further specify certain members of the general PSOC. For example, the special PSOC for adjectives further specifies members of AP_1 (which belongs to the category $\underline{D}$), filtering out P-markers which contain strings of adjectives that do not adhere to the proper surface order.

Another special PSOC in English is the one which regulates the order of nonprepositional NPs after V. It was noted in 2.3. with reference to (76) that the string V N͡P$_1$ is too general as a description of the surface order of the elements in VP in English, since it will permit such ungrammatical strings as '*John gave to Bill money' and '*John gave money Bill'. This means that NP_1 (written as $\underline{N}$ in (81)), when it is composed of more than one NP, must be further specified by the special PSOC offered below. (We assume that NPs are marked for deep case as in

Matthews, 1967.)

(83)   ...V ([D NOM])   ([D NOM])...
       NP   + PAT NP   NP   NP

This specifies that given a set containing V followed by NP_1, if NP_1
contains any nonprepositional NPs, they must be ordered directly to the
right of V; furthermore, if there are two such NPs, the leftmost must
carry [+Patient] as its deep case. Note that given a direct object and
an indirect object with deleted preposition, there is no way to distinguish the two other than by reference to deep case. (Such use of deep
case is not unknown in other languages; in Tagalog, for example, reduction of identical NPs in coordinate sentences requires identity of deep
case and may operate even when the surface cases are not identical -
cf. Peterson, 1973.)

    Special PSOC capture peculiarities of specific languages. Thus it
is not the case that all languages which have nonprepositional direct
and indirect objects following the verb will order them in a special
way. For example, Moorē, a West African language, may express indirect
objects with a 'serial' verb construction, e.g. '*take* the money *give*
John'. This is roughly equivalent to the prepositional form in English.
Like English, Moorē can reduce the serial form to a verb plus two NPs.
However, in the reduced form, the direct and indirect objects do not have
a special order with respect to each other and therefore two possible
surface sentences come about as a result of the reduction, as illustrated
in (84):

(84)   akulg koo { dawã ligdã.
                   { ligdã dawã. }
       'Kulga gave the man the money.'

So whereas the General PSOC of both English and Moorē order V before NP,
and both languages have reduction rules which apply to indirect object
constructions creating a sequence of two nonprepositional NPs, only English has a PSOC prescribing a special order for those NPs.

2.6. CONTEXT-SENSITIVE PSOC: SUBORDINATE CLAUSE WORD ORDER IN GERMAN

Up to this point, all the PSOC that have been presented have been contextfree; that is, they are applicable to any constituent-set in which the listed elements occur. In some languages, however, a particular order may be restricted to a specific context. Such is the case in German subordinate clauses.

The facts are as follows. In principal clauses, German, like English, orders *tensed* verbs to the right of NP complements and fronts *tensed* verbs in questions, as shown below.

(85)   a.   Hans liest das Buch.
             'Hans is reading the book.'
        b.   Liest Hans das Buch?
             'Is Hans reading the book?'

However, nontensed verbs, that is, participles and infinitives, are always ordered to the right of NP complements, as indicated in (86):

(86)   a.   Hans hat das Buch gelesen.
             'Hans (has) read the book.'
        b.   Hans kann das Buch lesen.
             'Hans is able to read the book.'

In subordinate clauses headed by a complementizer, tensed verbs are ordered to the right of NP complements and to the right of a single auxiliary participle or infinitive.

(87)   a.   Ich weiss,dass Hans das Buch liest.
             'I know that Hans is reading the book.'
        b.   Ich weiss, dass Hans das Buch gelesen hat.
             'I know that Hans (has) read the book.'
        c.   Ich weiss dass Hans das Buch lesen kann.
             'I know that Hans is able to read the book.'

But if there are two or more auxiliary nontensed verbs, a so-called 'double infinitive', then the tensed verb will occur to the right of any NP complements, but to the left of both of the nontensed verbs, as illustrated in (88):

(88)   a. Ich weiss, dass Hans das Buch hat lesen können.

        'I know that Hans was able to read the book.'

      b. *Ich weiss, dass Hans das Buch lesen können hat.

Tensed verbs are never ordered to the right of sentential S-complements:

(89)   a. Ich weiss, dass Elke sagt, dass Hans das Buch liest.

        'I know that Elke says that Hans is reading the book.'

      b. Ich weiss, dass Elke gesagt hat, dass Hans das Buch liest.

        'I know that Elke said that Hans is reading the book.'

      c. *Ich weiss, dass Elke, dass Hans das Buch liest, sagt.

Finally, the position of a tensed verb in a subordinate clause is the same as in a principal clause when the subordinate clause is not headed by a complementizer. Thus when the complementizer *dass* is deleted, (87a) has the surface form shown below:

(90)   a. Ich weiss, Hans liest das Buch.

        'I know Hans is reading the book.'

      b. *Ich weiss, Hans das Buch liest.

These facts are complicated and it is obvious that there can be no single general PSOC which will capture them. In providing a solution, we first posit two T-rules. One provides the proper constituent group-ing for sentences like (88a); it lowers a tensed verb two or more VPs down to a VP which contains a [-Aux] verb, i.e. the principal verb. This rule is presented in (91).

(91)   German Verb Interposition

$$V \quad [\quad\quad V \quad \Rightarrow \quad \emptyset, 2, 1, 3$$

$$\underbrace{+Te}_{1} \quad \underbrace{VP_2}_{2} \quad \underbrace{[-Aux]}_{3}$$

Thus (88a) has the surface structure given below where *hat* has been moved down from the topmost VP.

(92)

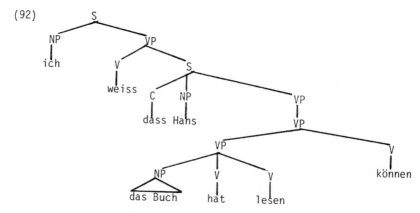

The second rule assures the proper grouping for sentences like (89b) by moving a sentential complement from an embedded VP up to the topmost VP, much like Extraposition in English:

(93)   S-Raising

$$[\quad [\quad [\quad S \Rightarrow 1, 3, 2, \emptyset$$
$$\underbrace{S}_{1} \; \underbrace{VP}_{2} \; \underbrace{VP_1}_{3}$$

This will provide the surface grouping shown below for (89).

(94)

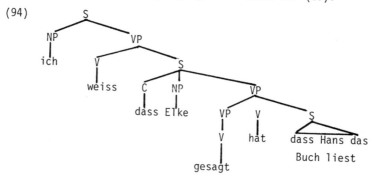

Having provided the above two regrouping rules, we now offer the general PSOC for German given below in (95). (We have omitted the elements co-vered by D.)

(95)   General PSOC for German

$$[\; (C) \quad (\; V \;) \quad (\underline{N}) \; (VP) \quad (V) \; (S) \;]$$
$$+Te$$

Notice that two members, tensed V and the sequence NP VP, are not connected to any other members by the concatenator symbol ⌢. Thus (95) is equivalent to a partially ordered set with two 'floating' members. It makes the following generalizations: (a) S will always occur as the rightmost member of its set; (b) C will always be the leftmost member of its set; (c) nontensed V will always be to the right of tensed C, V, NP, and VP; (d) NP will always occur to the left of VP. It leaves open the ordering of tensed V with respect to (NP) (VP), permitting either V (NP) (VP) or (NP) (VP) V, both of which may occur, but in different contexts.

Next, in order to assure that the alternate orderings mentioned above occur in the proper contexts, we must provide a special context-sensitive PSOC for the constituent-set VP in subordinate clauses which applies after the general PSOC of (95). This is presented below.

(96)   Context-Sensitive PSOC for German:

$$[\qquad [\; C \; [\quad \ldots (\underline{N}) \; (VP) \; V \ldots$$
$$\{VP, \underline{N}, ADV\} \; S \qquad VP_1 \qquad\qquad +Te$$

(96) says: in a VP which is a sister to C in an S dominated by VP, 'nominal element', or ADV (i.e. a subordinate S with a complementizer), select the ordering with tensed verb to the right of $(\underline{N})$ (VP). This condition, then, accounts for the special ordering of the tensed verb in (87a,b,c), (88a), and (89a,b).

Following (96), there must be an 'elsewhere' PSOC which states that in all contexts other that the one stipulated by (96), the 'floating' verb will be ordered to the left of $(\underline{N})$ (VP). This condition appears below.

(97) $$[\ldots \; V (\underline{N}) \quad (VP) \ldots]$$
$$+Te$$

This provides the order of tensed V for sentences like those in (85a,b), (86a,b), and (90a).

2.7. THE ASSIGNMENT OF MULTIPLE SURFACE ORDERS

It is frequently the case in language that when several NPs which are marked for function - say by prepositions or case endings - occur in the same constituent-set, their order with respect to each other may vary quite freely. Two examples of this are given below, one from English, the other from Tagalog. In each case there are twenty-four different variations for each sentence, though we have listed only one for each. This results from the free scrambling of the underlined NPs.

(98) a. The destruction of that village by the Americans with
         napalm in 1969 was a disgrace.

      b. Sumulat ang lalaki ng liham sa babae para kay Juan.
         wrote   the man   a letter to the girl   for John.
         'The man wrote a letter to the girl for John.'

Multiple surface orderings (or 'free word order') such as these cause a problem for systems like ST which posit a single underlying order of constituents in deep structure. First, some order must be selected as basic. Although arguments might be advanced that certain orderings are more convenient than others as the basic order, it is impossible to select in any nonarbitrary fashion one order over all the others. Second, having arrived at a basic order, the other orders must be derived from it by rule.

In order to produce the various possible orders from a single underlying order, ST must add a special type of permutation rule known as a 'scrambling' rule (cf. Ross, 1967: 43). The scrambling rule which provides multiple ordering of prepositional phrases is given below (we assume a node PP here):

(99)   Scrambling of PP: (optional)

$$\underset{1}{X}, \underset{2}{PP}, \underset{3}{PP}, \underset{4}{Y} \qquad 1, 3, 2, \emptyset, 4$$

Scrambling rules have the special properties of being iterative and of applying to their own output. No other permutation rule has both these properties. These special features are what enable scrambling rules to produce multiple surface orders from a single underlying order, as

illustrated in (100), where derivations for the six possible orderings
of a sequence of three prepositional phrases are presented.

(100)   (1) $PP_i\ PP_j\ PP_k$ ⇒ (2) $PP_j\ PP_i\ PP_k$ ⇒ (3) $PP_j\ PP_k\ PP_i$ ⇒

    (4) $PP_k\ PP_j\ PP_i$ ⇒ (5) $PP_k\ PP_i\ PP_j$ ⇒ (6) $PP_i\ PP_k\ PP_j$

Notice that stage (6) need not be derived via stages (2) through (5);
if (99) is applied to the rightmost members of stage (1), stage (6) is
derived directly: $PP_i\ PP_j\ PP_k$ ⇒ $PP_i\ PP_k\ PP_j$. Furthermore, if scrambling
is applied to the rightmost members of stage (6), the original order will
result: $PP_i\ PP_k\ PP_j$ ⇒ $PP_i\ PP_j\ PP_k$. What this means is that so long as
this rule remains unrestricted, any sentence with a sequence of two or
more prepositional phrases has an infinite﹐ number of possible syntactic
derivations. Clearly, we are dealing with no ordinary rule. Just how it
is to be restricted has never been discussed. Some might argue that it
need not be, since there are no ungrammatical sentences produced. We
would respond that if we are attempting to model human linguistic competence at a level of explanatory adequacy, it is absurd to propose that
that competence includes a rule which may apply any number of times to
a finite string with the possibility of no change in the final output
of the string, a result which is at best operationally adequate.

It would seem that the phenomenon of multiple surface ordering also
presents a problem for systems such as Sanders' (this volume) where a
given string has no order at deep and intermediate levels. For in such
a system, the order assigning function must go from no order to many
orders; this is different from going from no order to one or two orders
and might require some special apparatus, as does ST. To our knowledge
this has never been discussed by Sanders.

It is the case, then, that where as in the area of the domain of
operation of transformational rules ST has been found to be too powerful, making it necessary to formulate special constraints to limit its
power, as discussed in Part 1, in the case of multiple surface orders
derived from a single string, ST is too weak, and its power has had to
be increased by the addition of still another ad hoc device, the scrambling

rule. But this rule itself is too powerful and must be limited in some as yet unknown way.

On the other hand, MOG is faced with none of these difficulties because it incorporates multiple order as a general property of P-markers. Optional variations in surface order like those in (98) are captured by subscripted categories such as NP_1 of a PSOC. Since a subscripted category X_1 means any sequence of one or more X, there may be several ordered strings which will meet the conditions of a PSOC containing a subscripted category. Any one of these strings may be selected. If there are further restrictions that apply to the substring covered by the subscripted node, these must be expressed by special PSOC, as discussed in 2.5.

3. UNIVERSAL GRAMMAR

3.1. ON LIMITING THE NUMBER OF POSSIBLE BASES

It has long been a desideratum of linguistic science that a theory of language be narrow enough at the highest level of abstraction to describe a set of structural features which are common to all languages and that such a theory permit no, or at best very little, variation in the representation of these features in the grammars of different languages. In terms of current theory, this has come to be known as the 'universal base hypothesis', which minimally states that the grammars of all languages use the same base, i.e. categorial rules. (We say 'minimally' because others, for example Peters (1970), ascribe to this hypothesis the claim that all languages use the same base component, which includes the lexicon as well as the base rules.) A less ambitious goal is that a linguistic theory should describe a unique set of base rules for each particular language, whether or not it describes the same unique set for all languages.

It is natural that linguists should pursue these ends, for to abandon them would be to relegate linguistic science to a purely descriptive endeavor. In seeking to define a common body of characteristics for all languages, or for any particular language, a linguist attempts to capture, that is to *explain*, the 'unique essence' both of Language in general and of each particular language. He succeeds in this to the degree that he succeeds in constructing ever narrower theories which permit ever lesser

possible variation at the highest levels of abstraction. The question of
alternative bases in Transformational Grammar has been investigated mathematically in work by Peters and Ritchie (1973) in which it is shown that
there are many possible universal bases and consequently many possible
bases for any given language. Although some theoretically possible bases
can be eliminated on empirical grounds, there remains a large number for
which the current theory provides no criteria of selection.

A large part of the indeterminacy of present theory in narrowing the
number of possible bases revolves around the question of linear order. For
example, in McCawley (1970) it is argued that English has a deep structure
order of Verb Subject Object (VSO); the principal argument advanced in
favor of this hypothesis is that it simplifies the writing of certain
transformations. However, Grover Hudson (this volume), using McCawley's
line of argumentation, has demonstrated that a theory which proposes a
deep SOV order for English is exactly equivalent to McCawley's and that
the same is true for a grammar with a deep SVO order. Another example
is the case of German word order mentioned in 2.6. Is main clause or
subordinate clause word order basic? ST provides no clear answer to this
question, since the two alternatives can be shown to be equivalent
(cf. Peters 1970).

The revised theory that we have advanced in these pages eliminates
indeterminacy of the sort described above by eliminating linear order
as a distinctive function at deep and intermediate levels. This puts an
end to the dispute about basic order by declaring it to be empty. Notice
that MOG does not choose between the competing bases of ST; rather,
through the device of multiordering, it declares all of them to be correct.
Thus MOG is, in a sense, an equivalence relation across a class of
grammars with linearly ordered constituents and in this way it embodies
the results of Hudson (op. cit.); a further demonstration of this is
the predictable mirror image statement of every T-rule in MOG, as mentioned in 1.4. Peters (1970) suggests that the solution to the indeterminacy of ST lies in restricting the transformational component. MOG
bears him out, for by redefining the notion P-marker, we also redefine
the operations that T-rules perform. The elimination of distinctive
order brings about the elimination of permutation as a transformational

operation. The power of permutation rules to rearrange any order leads
to the possibility of using many alternative orders in the base.

Beyond settling disputes about deep word order for specific
languages, MOG also clears up the general question of how grammatical
relations are to be represented in deep structure. There are three
logically possible ways to represent grammatical relations in ST:
(a) by configuration, e.g. subject is 'NP of S', object is 'NP of VP'
(cf. Chomsky, 1965); (b) by linear order, e.g. subject is 'the first
NP to the right of V', object is 'the second NP to the right of V'
(this is McCawley's method and also that of modern predicate calculus);
(c) by labeling for deep case, e.g. Agent, Patient, Object, etc.(cf. Fillmore, 1968, and Matthews, 1967). Most linguists have rejected (a) in
favor of either (b) or (c) because it has been found that by generating
the 'subject' as part of the predicate certain basic relations can be
captured which otherwise would be lost. We are left, then, with either
linear order or labeling as a means of marking deep grammatical relations. Current theory provides no clear means of deciding between the
two, leaving it for linguists to disagree over. On accepting MOG, the
option of using linear order is immediately eliminated. Thus the
narrower confines of MOG force a choice between the two alternatives
and in so doing limit the number of possible universal bases.

MOG also cuts down the number of possible bases by forcing a choice
between alternative phrase structure analyses tolerated by ST. In
substituting for constrained variables hierarchical constants which
make precise generalizations about phrase types in terms of hierarchical structure, MOG requires 'distinctiveness' in the phrase structure
delineations of the major phrase types. For example, we noted in 1.2
that there are two analyses for relative clauses in ST, the NP-S analysis
and the Nom-S analysis; given ST, there is no clear way of deciding
between the two. Given MOG, however, we must choose the Nom-S approach
because it *hierarchically* distinguishes relative clauses and nominalizations with lexical head nouns from 'object clauses', while the NP-S
analysis does not. Thus MOG demands that major phrase types such as
relative clause, subject clause, object clause, prenominal possessive,

postnominal possessive, etc. be assigned hierarchical structure which
is distinctive so that T-rules can make proper generalizations about
domains of operation.

3.2. ON SPECIFYING THE NOTION 'POSSIBLE SURFACE ORDER'

If ST is found lacking in its ability to limit the number of
possible bases, the same can be said with respect to specifying the
notion 'possible surface order'. One of the basic criticisms levied by
the transformationalists against structuralism was its preoccupation
with 'surface grammar' and hence with the individual differences between languages, a preoccupation which led to the view, stated in its
extreme by Joos and quoted by Chomsky (1964), that "... languages
could differ from each other without limit and in unpredictable ways".
However, if this conclusion of the structuralists is taken as a view
of surface structure, and this is what generativists claim, then the
ST model of generative grammar in no way disconfirms it. Rather, if
anything, it agrees with structuralism on this point, since, because
of its *indirect* specification of surface structure as the last P-marker
of a derivation, the current generative model tells us nothing about
what sorts of surface structures we might expect to find in natural
language and what sorts not. Given the enormous power of transformations, just about any kind of surface structure imaginable could be
produced by an ST grammar. That there are indeed limits on surface
variation in natural language is indicated by research such as that
of Greenberg (1963) which has uncovered a number of universals and
universal tendencies of surface word order. This is an important feature
of language which generative theory, as it stands, totally fails to
specify.

In contrast to this, the MOG model with its *direct* and general
specification of basic surface order through a single general CFPSOC
makes the claim, stated in 2.4, that "a language tends to order its
categories the same throughout all the constituent-set of a sentence".
Take the ordering of the category S with respect to sister nominal
elements in nominalizations, relative clauses, and object S-complements.

In ST, these constructions are assigned order independently of each
other by individual categorial rules which, in terms of the order-
assigning function, have no necessary theoretical connection. In
effect, this says that it is mere chance that English orders relative
clauses, nominalizations, and object S-complements to the right of
sister nominal elements and that therefore we might expect any of
the other seven combinations to turn up with equal frequency in other
languages: S⌢N, NOM⌢S, NP⌢S; or N⌢S, S⌢Nom, NP⌢S; or N⌢S, S⌢Nom, S⌢NP;
etc. On the other hand, the format of MOG stipulates that we should expect
to find as the normal state of affairs that either one of two ordering
combinations for the three constructions will turn up: N⌢S, Nom⌢S, NP⌢S
or S⌢N, S⌢Nom, S⌢NP and that if a language violates this it will require
a special CSPSOC such as that for tensed verbs in German (cf. 2.6) to
state the deviant orders.

Beyond this, is there more that can be predicted about the occurrence
of the N S versus the S N ordering in the general CFPSOC of languages
or is this merely coincidence? The work of Greenberg cited above sheds
interesting light on this. His researches show that there is a very
strong correlation of invariant Nom⌢S ordering for relatives to a basic
VSO (type I) and SVO (type II) order (in fact, there are no languages
of these types with invariant S⌢Nom ordering in his sample - cf. Greenberg, op. cit., p. 90, Table 10); furthermore, he finds a strong correlation of invariant S⌢Nom ordering to SVO order (type III) (he lists
Hindi and Quechua as exceptions, though in checking Hindi out, we find
that it has S N order for both relatives and nominalisations and therefore it is not an exception - P.J. Mistry, personal communication;
though Quechua has invariant N⌢S ordering for relatives, it is not an
invariant type III language - Marlys McClaran and Irene Dadan, personal
communication). This suggests that the general CFPSOC of an overwhelming majority of the world's languages order the surface categories
S, V, N invariantly as either (a) (S)⌢(N)⌢(V) or (b) (V)⌢(N)⌢(S); let
us call these two basic types L (left) languages and R (right) languages
respectively. This reduces Greenberg's three types to two, types I
and II being subsumed under R languages and type III under L languages.

The fact that throughout his study his types I and II consistently pattern together in opposition to type III is evidence in favor of such a reclassification. Furthermore, as he points out in Universal 6, "All languages with dominant VSO order have SVO as an alternative or as the only alternative basic order", a fact which suggests that the principal difference between these two types is one of optional vs. obligatory subject promotion rather than one of basic word order.

While the general PSOC of L and R languages differ in their ordering of V with respect to N̲ and S, it seems very likely that the ordering of NP and VP is the same in both types, namely NP̂ VP. For the most part, this combination deals with subjects raised from VP to S. We know of no languages which order promoted subjects to the right of VP. Coeur d'Alene, Siuslaw, and Coos, which, according to Greenberg, have a basic Verb-Obj-Subj order (along with Obj-Verb-Subj for the latter two) are possible counter-examples, if it can be shown that their subjects are promoted.

In the case of Complementizers, we can predict with some confidence that L languages order C as the rightmost element while R languages order C as the leftmost element, though Greenberg does not give specific data on this category.

From the observations made above based on the data provided by Greenberg, we can make the following general statement about the grammars of natural languages. The languages of the world can be divided into two major classes according to the form of their general PSOC. With respect to the categories C, V, N̲, S, VP, almost without exception the general PSOC of an L language will have the form [(S) (N̲) (VP) (V) (C)]   and that of an R language will have the form [(C) (V) (N̲) (VP) (S)] . In terms of a schema for universal grammar, we can state this as the general condition in (101) with L and R representing an obligatory choice:

(101)   L   R

[(S) (N) (VP) (V) (C) (V) (N) (VP) (S)]

Besides accounting for the dichotomous ordering facts of relative
and head in the two basic language types and the invariant ordering of
NP and VP across all languages, this formula also explains the following near universal in the ordering of auxiliary verbs in relation to
the main verb: in L languages the auxiliary follows the verb and in
R languages it precedes the verb. Given our formulation of auxiliaries
as verbs with VP complements (cf. 1.5) the general formula above places
V to the right of VP in L languages and to the left of VP in R languages;
VP, of course, represents the main verb. There is only one exception
to this universal in Greenberg's sample, Guarani, an R language (cf. Greenberg, Table 4, p. 84 and note 15). German, also an R language, is a
partial exception (cf. 2.6).

Our general formula for surface ordering does not include the categories Adjective, Adverb, Determiner, or Preposition/Postposition). At
this juncture, we are not prepared to make generalizations about their
positions. (Bartsch and Venneman (1972) have provided a somewhat different
approach to the explanation of universal ordering phenomena by attempting to apply semantic considerations; they have dealt with some of these
categories.)

Although the vast majority of languages conform to the general
formula for surface order, there are exceptions such as Quechua, Guarani,
and German, as mentioned above. Normally, we would expect exceptional
languages to be marked by the presence of special CSPSOC in their grammars.
As in the case of German, this may cause some of the members of the general PSOC to 'float'. Another way that the general formula can be modified is for one of the categories to be split, thereby adding a new member, as in the case of the split of the category V in German.

In sum, we can liken the surface ordering function of generative
theory to a pastry gun the magazine of which is filled with linguistic
structures. Whereas the gun corresponding to the ST model is lacking a
nozzle and squirts out blobs of frosting in any shape or form, that belonging to MOG is fitted with a finely designed nozzle which can be ad-
justed so that it produces patterned squiggles either to the right or
to the left and the squiggle it produces on the one side is near mirror
image of that produced on the other.

MULTIPLE ORDER GRAMMAR
AND THE MOVEMENT OF NP[1]

THOMAS H. PETERSON

0.   INTRODUCTION

Much current work in syntactic theory has been concerned with constraining the power of transformational grammars. While the bulk of these efforts has been directed toward defining the contexts in which movement of NP may occur, that is, the content and form of variables, the present paper is directed toward describing and limiting the types of movement operations performed by NP-movement rules and toward a formal classification of such rules. More specifically, we will be concerned with the direction of movement, the number of movements per rule, and the result of the movement in terms of its effect on grammatical relations. In section 1, we present an outline of NP-movement as described in Standard Theory (hereafter ST), and a sketch of an alternative proposal offered in this paper. The latter involves the application of Multiple Order Grammar (MOG) as described in the preceding article of this volume. In section 2, the basic theoretical assumptions of MOG are reviewed and certain new mechanisms for handling case are presented. Section 3 puts forth the MOG analysis of NP-movement in the form of a block of rules. Section 4 summarizes the view of movement of NP in MOG.

[1] I would like to thank Paul Schachter, Bob Stockwell, Sandy Thompson, Ed Keenan, and Wendy Wilkins for helpful comments on an earlier version of this paper presented at Sandy Thompson's Syntax Seminar at UCLA.

1.   TYPES OF NP-MOVEMENT OPERATIONS

First, we should establish that by "movement" we mean movement
that "chops" in the sense of Ross (1967); thus rules which copy or leave
pronominal traces are excluded from this discussion. The ST rules which
move NP can be divided into two types: (a) rules which effect a change
in grammatical relations, and (b) those which do not. Lists of these
types are shown below.

(1) a. Relation changing rules:

   Passive

   There-insertion

   Subject-promotion (in Case Grammar and McCawley,
      1970)

   Raising ("Pronoun Replacement" in Rosenbaum, 1967)

   Tough movement

 b. Non-relation changing rules (not an exhaustive list):

   WH-question

   Relativization

   Topicalization ("Y-movement")

Looking at ST movement rules from the point of view of the kind of
movement operations they perform, three species can be discerned, as illustrated in (2). (This schema concentrates on the movement and ignores,
for the moment, other operations such as addition or replacement, e.g.
the addition of *there* in There-insertion.)

(2) a. Leftward movement: WH-question

 b. Rightward movement: There-insertion

 c. Criss-cross: Passive

The vast majority of NP-movement rules are of type (2a). There-insertion
is the only relation changing rule of type (2b); Heavy NP shift, if in-

deed this be a rule, is a non-relation changing rule of this type (cf.
Ross, 1967). As for type (2c), criss-cross movement of two NPs, there is
only one rule exhibiting this complex operation which is readily accepted by all camps of ST, the Passive. Lakoff (1970) posits a rule known as
Flip (referred to in Postal (1971) as Psych-movement) which performs
such an operation on *please*-type verbs, e.g. *I please the book   The
book pleases me*. (Also see Subject-object inversion, in Rosenbaum (1967).)
There is some disagreement among theoretical syntacticians as to whether
such a rule as Flip ought to be allowed.

The theory of MOG, outlined in the next section, eliminates linear
(i.e. horizontal) movement as a transformational operation and views movement as being vertical: upward and downward. The system of rules presented in this paper will allow us to make the following general statements
about NP-movement:

    (3) a. All movement of NP is unidirectional: upward.

          b. No rule moves more than one NP (in each cyclic applica-
             tion).

          c. All movement of NP which results in new grammatical re-
             lations is accomplished in two rules: *NP-raising*,
             which raises an NP from a lower S up to the VP of the
             matrix clause, and *Subject-promotion*, which raises
             subject NPs from VP up to S.

Schematically, we can represent the generalizations of (3a, b) as
follows: All movement of NP in MOG is of the sort shown in (4), where x
stands for a sequence of one or more upward brackets (or "hierarchical
constants").

    (4) x NP

This means that the three types of movement in ST, outlined in (2) will
be reduced to one, a considerable limitation on the power of transformations. That the non-relation changing rules of (1b) agree with this generalization is obvious and requires no argument. It is rules such as Passive and There-insertion which contain "downward" (i.e. rightward) movement and, in the case of the Passive, criss-cross movement. Therefore the
bulk of our discussion will concern rules of type (1a). (Non-relation

changing rules have been treated in great detail in the paper which precedes this one in this volume.)

   With respect to the statement in (3c), lest it appear more grandiose
than it really is, we hasten to add that the description to be presented
here does not reduce all the rules in (1a) to two rules, a marvelous
feat, if it were possible; rather our approach is to isolate in two
rules all the movement of NP contained in the rules of (1a). Thus there
will remain a Passive rule, but with the movement removed.

   2.   SOME THEORETICAL ASSUMPTIONS

       As mentioned, the rule format used here is that of Multiple
Order Grammar. Below is an outline of some basic axiomatic elements of
MOG, explicated in detail in the article cited above.

       (5) Axiomatic elements of MOG:

           a. *Non-concatenating categorial rules*
              These are of the type $A \rightarrow \{B,C\}$ and generate "unordered"
              (i.e. non-concatenated) phrase trees.

           b. *P-markers*
              There is a multiple order assigning function which pairs
              each unordered phrase tree having hierarchical relations
              H with the set of all possible ordered phrase trees
              having relations H; the resulting pair is called a
              multi-ordered P-marker; we represent this pair as
              $<u_i, O_i>$ where u_i is some unordered (i.e. non-concat-
              enated) tree and $O_i = \{o_i, o_i', o_i'' \ldots\}$, i.e. the set
              of all ordered trees with the same hierarchical relations
              as u_i; such P-markers have *distinctive* hierarchical (ver-
              tical) relations and *non-distinctive* linear (horizontal)
              relations.

           c. *Transformations*
              A transformation performed on the P-marker $<u_i, O_i>$
              has the following form: the SD is stated in terms of the
              ordered tree $o_i \in O_i$ which most economically mentions
              the essential items of the rule (i.e. all non-essential
              items are ordered out of the path between the essential

items. The SC is a mapping of the unordered tree u_i onto a new unordered tree u_j ($i < j$); thus a transformation T_i is an ordered pair of the form

$$T_i = \langle\langle u_i, o_i \rangle, u_j \rangle;$$ the ordering function of (b) automatically applies to u_j creating a new multi-ordered P-marker.

d. *Phrase Structure Ordering Conditions (PSOC)*

There is a single general context-free PSOC of the form $[\overset{\frown}{A} \overset{\frown}{B} \overset{\frown}{C}]$ where A,B,C are surface ordering categories which correspond to the phrase and category labels generated by the categorial rules; this general condition captures the general facts about ordering for a given language; it selects the appropriate order from the set of all possible orders for each constituent-set of the multi-ordered tree of the final P-marker for a given derivation; it is supplemented by special and context-sensitive PSOC which capture special ordering facts; the PSOC directly define the level of *surface structure*.

The definitions of (5b,c) give the following properties to transformations in MOG: (a) transformational environments are stated in terms of hierarchical structure with ST variables (and the constraints on them) being either eliminated altogether or replaced by positive generalizations in the form of sequences of hierarchical constants; (b) transformations move items up or down in a tree but not to the left or right. Thus all "movement" is performed over some sequence of labelled brackets and transformations no longer *directly* change linear order. For the most part, we will not be concerned in this paper with the PSOC of (5d). Given the above properties of MOG, we designate any theory which posits distinctive linear relations above the surface level as Standard Theory (ST).

Before proceeding with the rules for NP movement, it is necessary to mention some other elements of MOG that will be assumed here without argument.

(6) Other givens of MOG:

a. Constituent Structure Analyses

i. Auxiliaries are main verbs with obligatory VP complements (cf. Peterson, 1974; Emonds, 1970).

ii. NOM-S analysis of NP (cf. Stockwell, Schachter & Partee, 1973).

iii. Prepositional phrases have the structure $\underset{NP}{[}\ P\ \underset{NP}{NP]}$ (cf. Postal, 1971);

all prepositions are generated in deep structure (cf. Stockwell, Schachter & Partee, 1973).

iv. Sentential complements are of two types in deep structure, $\underset{NP}{[}\ \underset{NP}{S\ ]}$ and $\underset{NP}{[}\ It\ \underset{NP}{S\ ]}$. (This will be elaborated below.)

b. Deep grammatical relations are labelled in the manner of a case grammar of the sort in Matthews (1967).

c. The phonological notations of sub- and superscripting for specifying length of sequences, e.g. X_n^m , and of angled brackets, e.g. <> , (cf. Chomsky and Halle, 1968) are extended to syntactic rules.

Finally, we must provide a new mechanism for representing the hierarchy of deep case. In ST case grammars, there is a rule of Subject-promotion which raises the subject NP into subject position, the subject being the highest NP present in the hierarchy of cases. In order for the rule to locate this NP, ST relies on linear order to arrange the NPs after V in the order of the hierarchy. An example of this rule is found in Stockwell, Schachter and Partee (1973), where the highest ranking NP is ordered as the rightmost and the lowest ranking as the leftmost. Subject-promotion promotes to subject position the rightmost NP, whatever rank it may be, i.e. depending on the verb type. The schema in (7) illustrates this (the list of cases is illustrative and not exhaustive):

(7) a. $\underset{VP}{[}V\ +\ Neutral\ +\ Dative\ +\ Instrumental\ +\ \underset{VP}{Agent\ ]}$

b. X AUX $\underset{VP}{[}\ V\ Y\ Prep\ NP\ \underset{VP}{]}\ Z$ $\Rightarrow$ 1, 4, 2, Ø, Ø, 5

---
  1   2   3   4   5

A theory with no distinctive linear relations in deep structure like MOG cannot rely on linear order to locate the subject NP for promotion. Therefore we will use something that is already in the grammar but usually

not assigned until very close to the surface structure, namely surface
case. English has three surface cases: Nominative, Genitive, and Accusative, e.g. *he*, *his*, *him*. These cases are defined by the features
±Genitive and ±Accusative , as shown below:

(8) Nominative = $\begin{bmatrix} \text{-Genitive} \\ \text{-Accusative} \end{bmatrix}$

Genitive   = $\begin{bmatrix} \text{+Genitive} \\ \text{-Accusative} \end{bmatrix}$

Accusative = $\begin{bmatrix} \text{-Genitive} \\ \text{+Accusative} \end{bmatrix}$

(The Genitive, occurring in Poss-ING complements, nominalizations, and
possessives, is the marked form of the Nominative and is derived directly
from the Nominative without regard to deep case; it will not appear further in this discussion.)

Following Matthews (1967) let us assume that every verb has associated with it in its lexical entry a case frame listing the deep cases
with which it may occur; furthermore, we assume that these cases carry
numbers according to their position in the case hierarchy with the highest number going to the highest ranking case and so forth, as shown below.

(9) a. 4 Agent Case   b. Case Frame for the verb *break*
       3 Instrument Case   [(4A) (3I) 1N]
       2 Patient Case
       1 Neutral Case

(In a fuller account, there are more cases and consequently more numbers;
also, these numbers serve to relate surface prepositions to deep case. For
a thorough development, see Peterson (forthcoming).

Immediately it will be asked why it is necessary to have both numbers and
names for cases. As it turns out, there are certain pairs of verbs which
may co-occur with the same deep cases but with a different ranking to the
cases. For example, *die* may occur with an Instrument (of a restricted
class) and a Patient, but the Patient is always promoted over the instrument, e.g. *John died of pneumonia*. *Kill* may also take these two cases,
but the Instrument is always promoted over the Patient, e.g. *pneumonia
killed John*. Thus to *die* we assign the frame [4P (3I)], the Instrument

being optional, and to *kill* we give the frame [(4A∮3I) 2P] , the interlocking parentheses meaning either A or I or both must be present. Note
that ST non-case grammars must have a special syntactic rule such as
Flip (cf. Lakoff, 1970) for verbs such as *die*; similarly, an ST case
grammar would need a special rule to rearrange the linear hierarchy prior
to Subject Promotion.

Given a case frame for each verb, then, the case designations are
transferred in the form of an n-ary feature [nCase] to the NPs that accom-
pany each verb. With regard to surface case, all NPs start out redundantly as Accusative. Thus after transfer of deep case, every NP carries
with it a dual case marking, one for deep case and one for surface case,
as shown in (10).

(10) NP
$$\begin{bmatrix} 4\text{Case} \\ -\text{Genitive} \\ +\text{Accusative} \end{bmatrix}$$

Furthermore, there is a general convention, given in (11), which changes
the surface case of the highest ranking NP in any constituent-set to Nominative:

(11) $\begin{bmatrix} n\text{Case} \end{bmatrix} \rightarrow \begin{bmatrix} -\text{Accusative} \end{bmatrix}$

(n is the highest case number in its set.)

At the level of syntactic deep structure, then, the feature ±Accusative
serves to define the classes "subject" and "non-subject". The numerical
hierarchy and the convention of (11) can be thought of as devices which
translate the semantic relations of deep case, i.e. "Agent", "Neutral",
etc., into the syntactic relations of grammatical case, e.g. "subject",
"object".

We are now in a position to present the rules of MOG which change
grammatical relations.

3. RELATION CHANGING NP-MOVEMENT IN MOG

3.1. MOVEMENT OF NP INTO SUBJECT POSITION

In this section we describe how the relation changing movement

of NP accomplished by the ST rules of Passive, There-insertion, and
Subject-promotion is compressed into a single rule of Subject-promotion
in MOG.

The first MOG rule to be considered is Subject-promotion, shown in
(12).

(12)   Subject-promotion

$$
\begin{array}{cccc}
[& [& ([P) & NP \\
S & VP_1 & NP & -ACC
\end{array}
\quad\Rightarrow\quad 1, 4, 2, \emptyset, \emptyset
$$

$$
\underline{\quad}\ \ \underline{\quad\quad}\ \ \underline{\quad\quad}\ \ \underline{\quad\quad}
$$

$$
1 \quad\ 2 \quad\ 3 \quad\ 4
$$

This rule is an instruction to move any -Accusative NP upward over one
or more intervening VP brackets to the constituent set S and to delete a
sister preposition if one is present. Note that in spite of the fact that
we have used traditional ST notation, this rule does not move NP to the
left; the mirror image of (12) is an exactly equivalent statement. By convention, such rules are written with left brackets. On comparing (12) with
the ST counterpart in (7b), we see that the variables X, Y and Z plus the
extraneous elements AUX and V are not present, having been ordered out of
the SD by selection of the appropriate ordered tree. As an aid to visual-
izing how transformations in MOG operate an ordered tree which meets the
conditions of (12) is presented below.

(13)

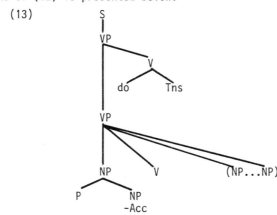

Subject-promotion is a key rule which is fed by a number of other rules.

The first of these rules to be considered is Passive-case change, a rule which involves a change in case, but no movement. It is assumed that a rule optionally deleting the preposition of a Patient phrase occurs before Passive-case change, as in ST, making reduced Patients eligible for passivization. Furthermore, we will suppose that the passive auxiliary be...EN is generated in deep structure and acts as the trigger for the rule, as in Burt (1971).

(14) Passive-case-change

$$\text{be EN} \begin{bmatrix} & \text{NP} & \text{NP} \\ \text{VP} & \begin{bmatrix} +\text{Acc} \\ -\text{Prep} \end{bmatrix} & \begin{bmatrix} -\text{Acc} \end{bmatrix} \end{bmatrix} \Rightarrow \begin{array}{ccc} 1, & 2, & 3 \\ & -\text{Acc} & +\text{Acc} \end{array}$$

$$\underline{\qquad\qquad} \ \ \underline{\qquad} \ \ \underline{\qquad}$$
$$\ \ \ 1 \qquad\quad 2 \qquad 3$$

This rule simply exchanges surface case between the deep subject, which is marked -Acc by (11), and any sister non-prepositional NP.[2] Since (14) feeds Subject-promotion, it is now the case that one rule places the subjects of both active and passive sentences.

It should be noted that (14) is too general for some speakers in that it permits passivization of objects with reduced Indirect Objects, e.g. *This book was given me by my students.* For speakers who reject such sentences, Passive-case change must be made less general and therefore necessarily more complicated. This is easily accomplished by adding certain elements to the environment of the rule. We will not take space to develop this here.

Beyond vastly simplifying the English Passive by eliminating the elaborate criss-crossing of NPs, this analysis also allows for a unified

---

[2] It is left as an open question whether or not ±Prep is actually a feature or merely an abbreviatory notation for a configurational distinction; for in our system −Prep can always be represented as [D NOM] and +Prep as [P NP]. In general, this is true of all such NP   NP "phrase features" in MOG; thus they do not add additional power to the grammar, since their range is always confined to the set of possible grammatical configurations generated by the base rules.

account of passive rules in general. For if we wish to characterize such rules across languages, the identical feature is case change and not necessarily movement. In languages where both the subject NP and the object NPs are ordered on the same side of the verb and are overtly marked for surface case, and where there is so-called "scrambling" of NPs, the surface position (but not the surface case) of the logical subject and object in passive constructions may be the same as in the corresponding active sentences. In Japanese, for example, while the preferred surface order is subject first, sentences with object first are also fully grammatical (cf. Kuno, 1973). (See footnote 3 for discussion of preferred order in MOG.) This is exemplified in the active sentences of (15) and the passive sentences of (16):

(15) $\left\{\begin{array}{l} \text{Mary-ga John-o} \\ \text{John-o Mary-ga} \end{array}\right\}$ korosita

'Mary killed John.'

(16) $\left\{\begin{array}{l} \text{John-ga Mary-ni (yotte)} \\ \text{Mary-ni (yotte) John-ga} \end{array}\right\}$ koros-(t)are-ta

'John was killed by Mary.'

Since whatever basic order we posit in such languages, and whatever corresponding movement we posit in the Passive, the outcome can always be "undone" by scrambling, it is difficult to determine in a non-arbitrary fashion just what the underlying order must be and, consequently, what sort of movement, if any, the Passive brings about. A most interesting critique of theories which define grammatical relations through the device of distinctive word order appears in Hudson (this volume). Arguing against McCawley's proposal that English has a VSO order (McCawley, 1970), Hudson shows that given the power of permutation transformations to rearrange the order of constituents, exactly equivalent grammars can be written for deep SOV, VSO, and SVO orders. Given the power of ST scrambling rules, the same can be done for deep SOV and OSV orders in Japanese. Furthermore, even if we do decide on a particular deep order and then we also decide to introduce movement into the passive rule, it would not be criss-cross

movement of two NPs as in English, but rather simple leftward or rightward movement of the object or subject NP, as the case may be.

The theory of MOG, which posits no single distinctive underlying order and has eliminated permutation rules,faces none of these difficulties
and presents the following picture. The Passive rules of English and
Japanese are virtually identical, the only significant difference being
the lack of the designation -Prep on the [+Acc] NP in the Japanese
rule. (Of course, the phonological shape of the passive auxiliary is also
different.) The apparent obligatory movement of the subject to the front
of the sentence in English is the result of obligatory Subject- promotion.[3]

Now let us turn to the phenomenon known in ST as There-insertion,
which produces sentences such as those in (17) from sentences containing
be and an indefinite subject, e.g. (17a) is derived from *A man was in the
room.*

---

[3] The general PSOC (cf. (5d)) for English orders NP to the left of a
sister VP and to the right of a sister V, i.e. the statement
$[\widehat{(C)}\widehat{(V)}\widehat{(NP_1)}\widehat{(VP)}\widehat{(S)}]$ holds for all constituent-sets of English
(NP_1 = one or more NPs); thus promotion of the subject NP to S automat-
ically results in an SVO order in English. The general PSOC for Japanese, on the other hand, orders NP to the left of both VP and V, i.e.
$[\widehat{(S)}\widehat{(NP_1)}\widehat{(VP)}\widehat{(V)}\widehat{(C)}]$. Therefore promotion of the subject to S
would not necessarily result in a different word order:

However, it would have the effect of not permitting the promoted NP to
scramble with other NPs. Since only thematic *wa* phrases have this property, we assume that promotion in Japanese is restricted to sentences
with thematic *wa*, i.e. they have the structure of (ii).
As for the *preferred* order of S IO DO among non-promoted NPs, this is
accomplished by a special optional PSOC which applies to the sequence
NP_1 of the general PSOC:
(iii)   [NP- ga]   [NP- ni]   [NP- O] . . .
      NP   NP NP   NP NP   NP
Thus in MOG, scrambling is a general property of P-markers and is restricted (at one level) by the application of a general PSOC and (in some
languages) at a lower level by special PSOC such as that in (iii),
which in Japanese is optional.

(17) a. There was a man in the room.

    b. There are some men standing in the door.

    c. There is someone being examined by the doctor.

This rule moves the indefinite subject to the right of a following *be* (the first if there are more than one, e.g. (17c)), and inserts *there* in subject position, thereby creating a new subject.

MOG presents the following account. We assume that a non-anaphoric *there* may be generated in deep structure as a complement of *be* (either main verb *be* or auxiliary *be*).[4] For example, (18) is the structure underlying (17b). (The linear order of constituents in (18) is not significant; such standard ordered trees are to be interpreted as abbreviations for multi-ordered P-markers except when representing surface structures which have passed through the PSOC or when specifically designated as meeting a particular SD, as in (13).)

(18)

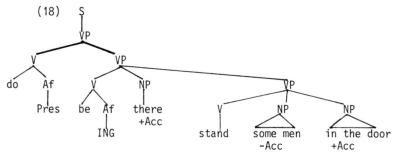

The MOG counterpart to ST There-insertion, like the Passive counterpart, is essentially a case changing rule; it is presented below:

(19)   There-case-change (precedes Subject-promotion)

$$
\begin{array}{ccccccc}
\text{NP} & & & & & & \\
\textit{there} & \left(\begin{bmatrix} \\ \text{VP}_1 \end{bmatrix}\right) & \text{NP} & & 1, & 3, & 2,\ \emptyset \\
+\text{Acc} & & -\text{Acc} & \Rightarrow & -\text{Acc} & +\text{Acc} & \\
 & & +\text{Indef} & & & & \\
 & & \text{sg} & & & & \\
\hline
1 & 2 & 3 & & & &
\end{array}
$$

[4] Since *there* is a contentless non-anaphoric proform, it does not meet the conditions for case transfer and therefore it has no deep case; however, like all NPs, it is redundantly marked [+Accusative].

This is an instruction to transfer the case and number of an indefinite
subject to *there* and to make the indefinite subject [+Acc] ; if *there* is
in a higher VP than the subject, e.g. as in (17b), the rule moves the
indefinite NP into that VP.[5] In the case of copula *be*, e.g. (17a), *there*
and the subject NP are in the same VP and item 2 of the SD of (19) would
be null. Notice that the principle of disjunctive ordering as applied to
subscripted and parenthesized items assures that when there is more than
one auxiliary *be*, as in (17c), the indefinite NP will be moved into the
highest VP. The number of the [-Acc] indefinite NP is transferred to the
NP containing *there* because the verb agrees in number with the deep subject, as in (17b). Finally, in the event that *there* is generated in an S
with no indefinite subject, and therefore (19) cannot apply, then it is
deleted by a rule of There-deletion similar to, or possibly incorporated
in, the rule of It-deletion. Since (19) precedes Subject-promotion,
[-Acc] *there* will automatically be promoted to subject position. Thus the
single rule of Subject-promotion now accomplishes the placement of subject in active, passive, and *there* constructions.

3.2. RELATION-CHANGING MOVEMENT OF NP FROM A LOWER TO A HIGHER S

Relation-changing movement from a subordinate S to a higher S
includes the ST rules of Raising (called Pronoun replacement in Rosenbaum (1967))and Tough-movement. The system proposed here will combine

---

[5] This is a possible caveat to the generalization in (3c) that all movement which results in new grammatical relations is accomplished in *two*
rules, NP-raising and Subject-promotion. For if we consider the indefinite NP which follows auxiliary *be* in sentences like (17b) to be the
surface object, so to speak, of *be*, then (3c) would have to be amended.
The surface structure of (17b) is the following:

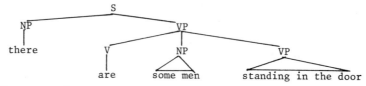

A similar type of movement from a lower to a higher VP within a chain of
VPs occurs in the derivation of at least one sense of sentences of the
sort *I had the work finished* from *I had finished the work* where the deep
object of *finish* becomes the surface object of *have*.

these two rules in a general rule of NP-raising. However, we will begin
by formulating separate rules of Raising and Tough-movement, as in ST.
     Raising involves two types of subject raising, subject to object
position, as in (20a), and subject to subject position, as in (20b):

(20) a. John believes it [she is a liar]   ⇒
                        S   S

        John believes her [∅ to be a liar]
                        S   S

     b. It seems [John is happy]   ⇒
                S   S

        John seems [∅ to be happy]
                 S   S

Hereafter, we will refer to these two types of raising as Subject-raising.
     Recall that in section 3 (6iv), we assigned the following structures
to sentential complements in deep structure.

(21) a.   NP
          |
          S

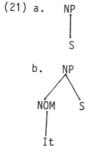

     b.   NP
         ╱╲
      NOM   S
       |
       It

The following discussion is concerned only with type (b), since it is the
type which undergoes raising. This structure was originally proposed in
Rosenbaum (1967). Our analysis of relation-changing NP movement from a
lower S will incorporate features of Rosenbaum's approach and of the
McCawley-Postal treatment (McCawley 1970, Postal 1974). (For the most
part, It-S complements have *for-to* or *that* complementizers and S complements take Poss-ing.)

     An important prerequisite to the system of NP-movement rules pre-
sented in this paper is that the proform *It* be separated from S so that
it may function independently. To accomplish this, we posit an early
obligatory rule of S-detachment which applies to structures of type (21b)

and moves the S out of NP into VP creating the structure in (22).

(22)

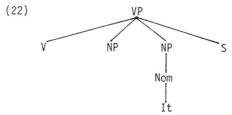

Of course it would be preferable if (22) could be generated directly. However, since deep case is a relation which is applicable only to NP and since we wish to characterize S-complements as having a deep relation to the verb, we must grant them the status of NP at the level of deep structure.

For all verbs and adjectives discussed here, It-S complements are assigned the Neutral case. Verbs of the *seem* class (and adjectives of the *tough* class) have the case frame [4N(2P)] . Therefore their It-S complements are designated [-Acc] by the surface case assigning function in (11). After S-detachment, [It] carries the designation [-Acc] and will
                                        NP   NP
be raised to subject position by Subject-promotion producing sentences like *It seems (to me) that John is happy, It is easy (for me) to like John*. On the other hand, verbs of the *believe* class have the frame [2P 1N] and therefore their It-S complements remain [+Acc]. Thus after S-detachment [It] remains [+Acc] and is not promoted to subject position.   NP   NP

With (22) as the input to Subject-raising, the MOG statement of this rule is formulated below. It utilizes Rosenbaum's features for complementizers: $\lceil+D\rceil$ = *Poss-ing* for *For-to*; $\lceil-D\rceil$ = *that*. This rule is ordered *before* Subject-promotion.

(23) Subject-raising (obligatory)

$$
\begin{array}{ccc}
\text{It} & [\ \lceil+D\rceil \ \ \text{NP} \ \Rightarrow & 3, \ \emptyset, \ 2, \ \emptyset \\
\alpha \ \text{Acc} & \text{S} & \alpha \ \text{Acc}
\end{array}
$$

$$
\underline{\quad\quad 1 \quad\quad} \quad \underline{\quad 2 \quad} \quad \underline{\ 3\ }
$$

(23) is an instruction to raise the subject NP of an S which is sister to

[It] and which has a $\lceil$+D$\rceil$ complementizer and to replace *It* with the
NP   NP
raised NP while transferring the surface case of *It* to the replacing
NP. When *It* is $\lceil$-Acc$\rceil$, as is the case for *seem* verbs, then the raised
NP takes that case (or rather it already carries that case) and is promoted to matrix subject position by Subject-promotion; otherwise the
raised NP is changed to $\lceil$+Acc $\rceil$, i.e. when the matrix verb is a *believe*
type, and can be promoted to matrix subject position only if its case
has been changed by Passive-case change (e.g. see (29b) below).[6]

Next let us consider Tough-movement, exemplified in the sentence
below:

> (24)   It's hard   [to find that house] $\Rightarrow$
>   S   S
>
>   That house is hard   [to find $\emptyset$]
>   S   S

This rule differs from Subject-raising in two ways. First, it moves objects instead of subjects; hereafter we will refer to Tough-movement as
Object-raising. Second, it may operate over unbounded distances, as shown
in (25a); (25b) illustrates that Subject-raising does not have this property.

> (25) a. It's hard to conceive of anyone wanting to try to read
>   this book in one night.
>   This book is hard to conceive of anyone wanting to try
>   to read $\emptyset$ in one night.
>   b. I believe John wants Mary to leave.
>   *I believe Mary John wants $\emptyset$ to leave.

The similarities between the two rules are greater than the differences. They share the following features: (a) both raise an NP from a
predicate sentential complement; (b) the complementizer of the complement
S must be $\lceil$+D$\rceil$; (c) the raised NP assumes a new grammatical relation in
the principal clause; (d) the raised NP replaces the proform *It*. Given

---

[6] At this stage, the rule is too general in that it does not exclude
predicates which trigger Object-raising, e.g. *tough* type adjectives.
This will be remedied when we combine Subject-raising with Object-
raising below.

this considerable list of identical characteristics, it would seem that
these two processes ought to be united in a single general statement of
NP-raising. However, ST has always described Subject-raising and Object-
raising as two separate, unrelated rules. (For an interesting recent attempt to combine the two, see Wilkins, 1976.) Below we will show how MOG
uses standard abbrevatory conventions to present a general account.

In formulating a description of Object-raising, we must first indicate how MOG represents unbounded contexts for movement. Whereas ST requires variables plus certain constraints (cf. Ross 1967, for example),
in MOG variables and their constraints are replaced by hierarchical constants, as mentioned in section 2. In adopting the constituent structure
analyses of (6a), MOG is able to express unbounded movement contexts positively in terms of a recursive sequence of the following finite chain of
brackets: $[_{NP}$ $[_S$ $[_{VP_1}$

or $[_{VP_1}$ $[_{NP}$ $[_S$

depending on what node dominates the sequence. This chain is designated
by the symbol h. By using the phonological convention of sub- and superscripting (cf. Chomsky and Halle, 1968), we can represent sequences of
hierarchical constants such as $[_{VP}$ or h; subscript 1 with no superscript
means a sequence of one or more. (For a complete discussion, see the preceding article in this volume.)

Next we must find a feature which distinguishes matrix predicates
that trigger Subject-raising from those that trigger Object-raising, for
they are mutually exclusive classes. First, the class which triggers
Object-raising is made up exclusively of adjectives, while the class which
triggers Subject-raising contains both adjectives and verbs; secondly,
Object-raising adjectives all have the case frame [4N(2P)] while no Subject-raising adjectives have this case frame.[7] Thus the difference be-

---

[7] This assumes the analysis of Object-raising adjectives where the matrix
predicate contains a Patient phrase which, in most cases, is identical to
the subject of the constituent S and brings about Equi-NP deletion of
the constituent subject (see Chomsky, 1973). When there is no such

tween the two senses of *nice* in (26) are registered in the case frame.

(26) a. It is nice for John [to do that]   ⇒
                                    S   S
        That is nice for John to do.

     b. It is nice [of John to do that]   ⇒
                            S   S
        John is nice to do that.

The Object-raising sense in (26a) carries the frame [4N(2P)], while the
Subject-raising sense in (26b) has the frame [1N]. (It is assumed that *of*
is generated with *nice* and replaces *for* as the constituent complementizer. Note that no Equi is posited in (26b) because it is never possible
for two NPs to appear, as in the case of Object-raising adjectives (cf.
footnote 7).)

     With these facts in mind we posit a rule of Object-raising below.

     (27) Object-raising

$$
\underbrace{\begin{array}{c}\text{+ADJ}\\ \text{[4N(2P)] -Acc}\end{array}}_{1} \quad \underbrace{\text{It}}_{2} \quad \underbrace{\underset{S}{[}[\overset{+D}{]}[\underset{VP_1}{(h_1)} \text{ NP}}_{3} \Rightarrow \underbrace{1,}_{4} \begin{array}{c}4, \emptyset, 3, \emptyset\\ \text{-Acc}\end{array}
$$

This rule gives the following instruction. Given an S which is sister to
an adjective with the case frame [4N (2P)] and sister to a ⌈-Acc⌉ *It*, raise
up to the matrix VP the object NP of that S or the object of an S which
is in a chain of object clauses embedded in that S, transfer the case of
It to the raised NP and delete *It*.

     A comparison of (27) with Subject-raising in (23) shows that the two
rules have many identical features in terms of the operations performed
and the environments. This identity of items enables us to use the convention of angled brackets to collapse the two rules into a general rule
of NP-raising as shown in (28).

     (28) NP-raising

$$
\underbrace{\left\langle \begin{array}{c}\text{+ADJ}\\ \text{[4N (2P)]}\end{array}\right\rangle \alpha \text{Acc}}_{1} \quad \underbrace{\text{It}}_{2} \quad \underbrace{\underset{S}{[}\ [\overset{+D}{]}\langle \underset{VP_1}{[\ (h_1)}\rangle \text{ NP}}_{3} \Rightarrow \underbrace{1,}_{4} \begin{array}{c}4, \emptyset. 3, \emptyset\\ \alpha \text{Acc}\end{array}
$$

identity we get sentences like *It is easy for the rich for the poor*⟩*to
do the work*.

This one rule, then accomplishes all raising of NP from a lower S which brings about new grammatical relations; ST has never been able to present a unified account of this type of movement.[8]

Before closing this section, we must provide for sentences with sentential subjects derived from It S complements. Thus the sentences in (29) have the corresponding variations of (30):

(29) a. It has been suggested by many people that John is a liar.

     b. It was believed by everyone that John had drowned.

     c. It is obvious that John is a fool.

(30) a. That John is a liar has been suggested by many people.

     b. That John had drowned was believed by everyone.

     c. That John is a fool is obvious.

We propose that the sentences of (30) are derived from those in (29) by the rule of S-promotion, given below. This rule follows Subject-promotion.

     (31)   S-promotion

$$[\text{It} \quad] \quad [\underset{\text{NP} \ \text{VP}_1}{\underline{\text{S}}} \quad\quad\quad 3, \emptyset, 2, \emptyset$$

$$\underline{} \quad \underline{}$$
$$1 \quad\quad 2 \quad 3$$

(31) simply replaces *It* of an NP in subject position with an S dominated

---

[8] It should be noted that NP-raising as formulated in (28) is not quite restricted enough. With regard to Object-raising, it must be prohibited from operating when the subject of the constituent S has not been deleted. For example, we get *It is easy for the rich for the poor to do the work* (cf. footnote 7), but not **The work is easy for the rich for the poor to do.* This restriction can easily be included in (28) by a slight amendment to the SD.

A further restriction for some speakers is that when NP-raising extends to a depth greater than one S, i.e. over h, every S in the chain along which the NP is moved must have a +D complementizer. Thus (iv) is acceptable while (v), which has an intervening *that* clause, is not.

(iv) That book is hard [to imagine John [trying [to read $\emptyset$.
                    S   S   S

 (v) *That book is hard [to believe [(that) John tried [to read $\emptyset$.
                  S   S   S

This type of restriction on unbounded movement is handled by "bonding" of the h constant. For a thorough discussion of bonding in Object-raising, see the preceding article in this volume.

by VP.[9] This is the reverse of Rosenbaum's Extraposition (cf. Rosenbaum, 1967; for a treatment similar to ours, see Emonds, 1970).

In the event that +Acc *It* is not deleted by NP-raising, there is a rule of It-deletion which, like Rosenbaum's, is optional for some verbs and obligatory for others. (This varies considerably according to dialect.)

(32) It-deletion

$$[\text{It}]_{\text{NP}} \quad S \Rightarrow \emptyset, 2$$

$$\underline{\phantom{[\text{It}]}} \quad \underline{}$$
$$1 \qquad 2$$

Finally, we present a summary list of the rules presented in this paper and their extrinsic order:

$$\left\{ \begin{array}{l} \left(\begin{array}{l} \text{S-detachment (22)} \\ \text{NP-raising (28)} \end{array} \right. \\ \left(\begin{array}{l} \text{Passive-case-change (14)} \\ \text{There-case-change (19)} \end{array} \right. \\ \left(\begin{array}{l} \text{Subject-promotion (12)} \\ \text{S-promotion (31)} \end{array} \right. \\ \left\{ \begin{array}{l} \text{It-deletion (32)} \\ \text{There-deletion} \end{array} \right. \end{array} \right.$$

4.   CONCLUSION

The generalizations in (3) of section 1 have now been achieved: (a) all movement of NP is unidirectional (upward), (b) no rule moves more than one NP per application, and (c) all relation changing movement of NP is accomplished in two rules (though see footnote 5 for some possible additions to the list). Furthermore, in section 3.1., it was shown that the view of NP movement presented by MOG allows for a unified description of the passive across languages; it was argued that the essential feature of

---

[9] Of course a special condition is needed saying that S is not sister to a verb with the case frame [4N(2P)], i.e. *seem* verbs, since verbs of this class do not take sentential subjects, e.g. *That John is happy seems (to me)*. The corresponding condition in Rosenbaum's treatment is that Extraposition is obligatory for these verbs.

this rule in all languages is surface case change and not movement.

Beyond the above generalizations about NP movement, the theory of MOG suggests a formal distinction between relation changing and non-relation changing rules. The former type raises NP and attaches it under S, as in Subject-promotion, or under VP,   as in NP-raising. The latter type raises an NP and then "re-labels" it as some minor category, as in WH-question and Relativization where a +WH NP is raised and attached under C.[10] (This follows Bresnan 1970; for the MOG version of these rules, see the preceding article in this volume.) The two kinds of NP movement rules are illustrated below.

(33) a. Relation changing rules:

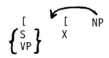

$$\begin{Bmatrix} S \\ VP \end{Bmatrix} \quad \begin{matrix} [\\ X \end{matrix} \quad NP$$

b. Re-labeling rules:

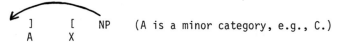

$$\begin{matrix}] \\ A \end{matrix} \quad \begin{matrix} [\\ X \end{matrix} \quad NP \qquad \text{(A is a minor category, e.g., C.)}$$

In sum, on comparing the description of NP movement in ST and in MOG, it can be seen that whereas the former employs a number of different varieties of movement operations in terms of direction, the latter reduces all movement of NP to one basic type. This reduction permits a general formulation for passive rules across languages, something that ST has not hitherto achieved. Finally, MOG provides a formal distinction between relation changing and non-relation changing ("relabeling") rules. Since it presents a more narrowly defined and constrained description of NP movement, MOG, then, is the more restricted and less powerful of the two theories.

---

[10]Since we wish to consider Y-movement to be a relabeling rule, we assume that an NP fronted by this rule is attached under the node C. Another relabeling rule is Possessive-NP movement, which raises NP within NP and relabels it as Det, e.g. *the friend of John's* ⇒ *John's friend.*

IF LINEAR ORDER ISN'T IN THE BASE,
THEN WHERE IS IT?[1]
THE ROLE OF FOCUS IN WORD-ORDER

PAUL WERTH

1. INTRODUCTION

The question of surface word-order has received very wide discussion in the debate on linguistic universals and language typology, but that of serial order in the base has generally been taken for granted, and discussed only perfunctorily (e.g. Chomsky 1965: 124 sqq.) or not at all (there are, of course, exceptions, e.g. Staal (1967)). However, the last few years have seen a growth of interest in the topic, with discussion shifting from papers presupposing ordering and concerned with establishing one order or another (e.g. McCawley 1970) to work questioning or defending the principle of base linearity itself (e.g. Boas 1975, Bach 1975). I shall draw heavily upon the last two works cited in surveying

---

[1] A version of this paper was read to the 1977 Autumn Meeting of the Linguistics Association of Great Britain. I have discussed various aspects of the subject at various times with Nigel Vincent, Rosie Brener, Steve Harlow and Connie Cullen, all of whom I thank. Any faults that remain in this presentation, I bitterly resent and will make every effort to blame on whoever may be at hand at the time. The title of the paper is deliberately ambivalent, or pragmatically ambiguous: as a rhetorical question, it suggests that linearity is certainly in the base, since there could be no other conceivable place for it; as a genuine question, it presupposes that linearity is not in the base, and poses the question: 'Where does linearization begin?'. My attitude in this paper will be somewhat agnostic on the question of linear order, though leaning towards the second interpretation.

arguments both against and for (respectively) an ordered base.

As is well-known, linguistic argument may be assessed at three levels, which, informally stated, are:

> (i) it must correctly predict the observable facts; or, rather
> more rigorously, it must exactly specify surface structures;
> (ii) it must conform to certain general requirements on formal
> systems, including economy, viability and explicitness;
> (iii) it should be compatible with the known (and, indeed, the
> unknown) facts about the human organism, and especially, per-
> haps, psychological and sociological systems.

Levels (i) and (iii) are external to the grammar, dealing with the
empirical data of language itself, the human organism and human social
grouping. Level (ii), though, is clearly grammar-internal, and as such,
is an artificial requirement in the sense that it is highly dependent
upon the assumptions of the particular model being tested, which may to
a greater or lesser extent be arbitrary.

2.   ARGUMENTS FOR AND AGAINST BASE-ORDER

One would imagine that the question of base-ordering would be
an empirical question. It is somewhat disturbing, therefore, to find
that almost all the argument surrounding the question of base-order,
both for and against, is couched in terms of level (ii). Bach's (1975)
discussion is largely a defence of the ordered base using an approach by
way of formal systems theory to claim that the unordered type of base
would impose restrictions upon linguistic data which are not in fact
present. While this method of argument is clearly not completely unem-
pirical, its empirical content rests on the negative assertion that no
evidence exists for an unordered base of any type. Section 3 then exam-
ines arguments that have been, or might be, put forward in support of
an unordered base. For the empirical arguments examined (he rightly dismisses *a priori* arguments), Bach's findings display a mixture of level
(ii) stipulations and some very vague postulates which are level (ii)
insofar as they might be taken as formal conditions on rules of grammar,
and level (iii) if we think of them as restrictions upon the human or-

ganism. Examples of this type of postulate are (i) that children gener-
alize in the direction of fixed word-order, (ii) that, given syntactic
variants, one is always basic, and (iii) the principle that "underlying
structures are just like surface structures unless we can show a reason
why they should not be" (1975: 326; cf. Chomsky 1976a: 8 etc. on the
"logic of markedness"). Bach does not accept this last hypothesis
(which points in the direction of *unordered* bases for free word-order
languages), but points out that a stronger principle, namely the Universal Base Hypothesis, is incompatible with free word-order, given that
certain rules depend upon word-order: thus one would have to assume ordering rules preceding them and disordering rules following them - an
example of the unloved Duke-of-York gambit (Pullum 1976). Bach dismisses
the empirical arguments in this section with some peculiar forms of reasoning, which in one case (329 sq.) indicates that an order-free base
cannot capture some generalizations - which Bach admits however cannot
be captured in the ordered bases with which he is familiar, either; and
in the second case (330 sq.) provides a standard sort of solution to an
ordering problem in Amharic, which he then mentions is perfectly susceptible of an unordered analysis too.

In the fourth and final section, Bach considers arguments against
the unordered base. Again, none of them is overwhelming: several merely
indicate that order is required at *some* stage before surface structure
in order to accommodate certain rules. From these facts, only the weak
argument referred to above is possible: given the necessity for order at
some derivational stage, some kind of simplicity argument suggests that
order must be there all along. Other proponents of basic order include
language typologists (though, as Pullum 1977 shows, the stipulation of
word-order language-types, following Greenberg's pioneering work (e.g.
1963), is not inconsistent with an unordered base hypothesis, in Pullum's
case that of Relational Grammar). However, for those who regard SVO,
VSO etc. as *basic* orders, and therefore capable of differing from language to language, the claims being made for constraining grammatical
theory are at least, rather weak (cf. Bach 1975: 321).

How, then, do the proponents of the unordered base fare? Boas (1975,

ch. 3) sets out to counter Chomsky's (1965: *ibid.*) arguments against the
unordered base (specifically one using a set-system) firstly, by demonstrating that free word-order languages do indeed exist (German, Sanskrit
and Latin are the examples investigated), and secondly, by attempting to
cast doubt on work claiming to show empirically underlying order: in German (Bierwisch 1963, Bach 1962); and in distinguishing between SVO and
SOV languages (Ross's argument from Gapping (1970), and Maling's revision
of it (1972)). However, in connection with Boas's arguments against these
positions, several points may be noted. Against Bierwisch, Boas marshals
counterexamples which, as he says (p. 53), "have a slightly archaic
tinge ... [or are] ... colloquial or dialectical [*sic*] versions of main
clauses". This prompts one to ask: if the counterevidence is always marked as non-normal doesn't this perhaps indicate that it departs (presumably in a rule-governed way) from the basic order for Standard German, i.e.
that it is marked for emphasis or the like? On the demonstration of free
word-order languages, few, I think, would deny that heavily morphologi-
cally-marked languages allow free word-orders as surface possibilities
(although the distinction, if real, between stylistically-preferred and
grammatically stipulated order is not clearcut, particularly in historical perspective). But this alone is not sufficient (or even necessary)
to prove that the underlying serial relationship is equally free, (as
Bach 1975 points out). On Bach's (1962) proposal for German, Boas correctly notes that the stipulation of both linear order and a type of
deep-case context-sensitivity marking leads to redundancy (and in connection with this, we may note that the only type of unordered base proposal with which Bach has any sympathy, or regards as in any way substantial (1975: 328), is one in which grammatical relations or cases or
the like are primitive terms of the base). Avoidance of redundancy is a
powerful, though still level (ii), argument, although Boas chooses to
see this in terms of abstractness and simplicity (p. 57). Simplicity is
a level (ii) criterion which is double-edged, as has often been pointed
out, since it cannot be used as an evaluation measure except in comparing two complete (or at least substantial) grammars: what is simple in
terms of a fragment of description may lead to complication elsewhere.

Abstractness, as Bach is at pains to point out (1975: 324), is not an evaluatory property, and more or less of it, *per se*, is irrelevant in adjudicating between grammars or models of grammar.

Ross's well-known paper (1970) on Gapping as a diagnostic of underlying order, states these conditions:

(1) (A) Gapping deletes all but the first ("forward Gapping") or last ("backward Gapping") of a series of identical verbs in a series of conjoined sentences. "The order in which Gapping operated depends on the order of elements at the time that the rule applies; if the identical elements are on left branches, Gapping operates forward: if they are on right branches, it operates backward". (251)

(B) Gapping is an anywhere rule. Specifically, it can operate both before and after Scrambling (which freely permutes word-order in so-called "free word-order languages").

Ross then uses these principles to adjudicate on the question of Russian and German word-order. They predict that for SVO/SOV languages, the following types of Gapping are possible:

(C) A. SVO + SO ...
     B. SOV + SO ...   Forward Gapping

     C. SO ... + SOV, but not:
     D. *SO ... + SVO   Backward Gapping

Boas expands the German data to allow for OSV and OVS surface-orders (although he does not comment on their status; I shall return presently to the question of emphasis and the so-called Scrambling rule). He points out that Ross's proposal, though it works for many of the sentences adduced, does so by a counter-intuitive route, involving *ad hoc* restraints on Scrambling. Boas's solution to this is to drop the requirement for an ordered base, and to allow Gapping to apply on "a possible surface order of German" (63). But if Gapping operates on surface structure, then the linearity of the base is irrelevant: in other words, even if Boas's solution for German is correct, this tells us nothing about the base. The

input to the rule consists of just those possible surface-structures
which have been derived by whatever means of derivation can be justified
in the usual way. The generalization which seems to come out of Boas's
examples, and which he notes (p. 64) is that Backward-Gapping requires
V-final order. This predicts that even in SVO languages (such as English), surface structures in which the V has ended up in final position
ought to Gap (and given that there are apparently no restrictions on
Forward Gapping for English, they ought to Gap both ways). Boas finds
this confirmed by sentences (2 a-d):

    (2) (a) John came and Bill (SV + SØ)

         (b) John and Bill came (SØ + SV)

         (c) Who fell down and what? (SV + SØ)

         (d) Who and what fell down? (SØ + SV)

But, except with heavily-marked emphasis, (a) and (c) are surely not acceptable[2]; while the clearly acceptable (b) and (d) are (at best - for
Boas's argument) the result not of Gapping but of VP-deletion (cf. *John
and Bill kissed Mary*), or at worst, not from deletion at all, but NP-
conjunction (for the convincing semantic arguments for this latter position, cf. Dik 1968). Furthermore, other V-final surface constructions
don't appear to Gap either way (assuming them not to be spoken with
marked juncture, cf. fn. 3):

        (e) *Who did John see and who did Mary? (OSV + OSØ)

        (f) ?*Who did John and who did Mary see? (OSØ + OSV)[3]

---

[2] They appear to be more acceptable given an adjuct in addition, e.g.
    (i) Yesterday John came, and today Mary.
    (ii) John feebly protested, and Mary vehemently. (Kuno 1973: 11)
But notice that in both cases the adjunct has been shifted forwards,
exposing the verb's rear. It could therefore be argued that Gapping
occurred from a SVA structure (A=adjunct), with the adjunct being
subsequently moved by Adverb-preposing.

[3] The fact that (2f, h, 1) are less unacceptable than the rest seems to
me to show that what we have here is not Gapping, but parenthesis:
    (i) It was Dickens that I was reading and it was Trollope that Mary
       was reading.
    (ii) It was Dickens that I and it was Trollope that Mary Ø was
       reading.
   (iii) It was Dickens that I and Ø Trollope that Mary Ø was reading.

    (g) *It was Dickens that I was reading, and Trollope that
        Mary.   (OSV + OSØ)

    (h) ?*It was Dickens that I, and Trollope that Mary was
        reading.   (OSØ + OSV)

    (i) *Coffee, I like and tea, Mary.   (OSV + OSØ)

    (j) *Coffee, I and tea, Mary likes.   (OSØ + OSV)

    (k) *The man that I spoke to and the woman that Mary are
        teachers.   (OSV + OSØ)

    (l) ?*The man that I, and the woman that Mary spoke to
        are teachers.   (OSØ + OSV)

Furthermore, the existence of acceptable Gappings in English *wh*-ques-
tions like (3), compared with unacceptable ones like (2e):

    (3)   (a) Who did John see and who (*did) Mary?

          (b) Which bill did the Government support and which (*did)
            the Opposition?

          (c) How much does a doctor earn and how much (*does) a
            miner?

demonstrates that Gapping cannot be a surface-structure rule, since it
must precede at least Subject-auxiliary inversion and Do-support (or DO-
drop in the alternative formulation).

    But in any case, Rosenbaum (1977) casts doubt on the universality
of Ross's restrictions on Gapping by broadening his data base to include
Zapotec and many Mayan languages of Central and South America. In these
languages, Backward Gapping from Verb-final position is possible, though
the Verb-final order is not basic but results from Focus-movement. In
fact, Zapotec is a VSO language, so in order to get SOV, two applica-

---

with the second conjunct being (i) truncated, at either end, and (ii)
shifted to the right of its structural parallel. However, apart from
the intonational and junctural evidence, which appears to indicate
the bracketing of (iii) rather than (iv) or (v):

    (iv) *It was Dickens that I Ø (and) Ø Trollope that Mary was
        reading.

     (v) *It was Ø Dickens that I Ø (and) Trollope that Mary was
        reading.

I can furnish no proof for this intuition.

tions of Focus-movement are necessary. The only impossible (or at least
unattested) pattern for Backward Gapping that remains, therefore, is
*SO ... + VSO (and no doubt it won't be very long before that possibil-
ity turns up as well).

I now want to consider briefly the rule of Scrambling, a rule in-
vented by Ross (1967: 41 sqq.) to account for the apparently free word-
order of Latin, (and also in principle, of other languages exhibiting
the phenomenon). Subject to a clause-mate condition, the major categories may optionally be permuted around each other *ad libitum*. Now, native speakers of Latin being rather scarce on the ground, it's a little
difficult to gather native intuitions about the language, but it seems
not unreasonable (and it is the received wisdom) to postulate that the
variant orders which the rule is meant to capture would have been in
fact stylistically distinct, i.e. different sequences of the same morphemes would have born different balances of emphasis. This is stated in
most Latin grammars, for example Kinchin-Smith (1948): "The order of
words in a Latin sentence is usually different from English. The first
word is emphatic, and is usually the subject of the verb, e.g. ...
"*Brutus Luciam amat*". "*Luciam Brutus amat*" would mean "it is Lucia that
Brutus loves". (p. 23). "... unusual word-order in verse is usually justified by something besides the requirements of metre ... In the lines:

> *Nondum praecipites cingebant oppida fossae;*
>
> *non galeae, non ensis erant; sine militis usu*
>
> *mollia securae peragebant otia gentes* ,

fossae is the subject of *cingebant*, *gentes* the subject of *peragebant*;
both subjects gain emphasis by their position at the end of the line."
(p. 157 sq.).(Cf. also Marouzeau 1948).

In poetry, of course, one would expect these emphases also to form
part of the metrical and rhythmical dynamic of the poem, but in both
poetry and prose, (including speech), one would expect Scrambling to be
part of the contextual deixis of the discourse (i.e. in Prague terms,
the Functional Sentence Perspective - although it is an impoverishment
to regard it as a function of the sentence). In other words, a rule such
as Scrambling might fit the bare facts (providing observational adequa-

cy), but is too strong (as Ross himself admits, p. 43) because it is optional, i.e. unconstrained. A contextually-motivated rule is more constrained, linguistically more interesting, and may provide not merely observation, but also explanation ("context" in the case of Latin, as in English, would include semantic and formal textual requirements - cf. the remarks of Kinchin-Smith (1948) quoted above - and in the case of poetry would in addition include metrical and rhythmical determinants).

Let us postulate then that unmotivated free word-order does not exist, i.e. that variations in so-called free word-order languages actually represent discourse-sensitive ordering. For German, Boas provides some indication that this may be the case (though this is not his intended point): to show the falseness of Chomsky's claim that the unmarked word-order of German is SVO (since the morphologically ambiguous sentence (i) *Die Mutter sieht die Tochter* will allegedly always be taken as Subject-first, given normal stress), Boas embeds the sentence in different contexts (p. 42):

> (4)   (a) Die Tochter stand am Fenster und blickte gespannt auf das Tor hinab, das sich öffnete. Die Mutter sah die Tochter.
>
>   (b) Eine Frau stand am Fenster und blickte gespannt auf das Tor hinab, das sich öffnete. Die Mutter sah die Tochter.

According to Boas, the sentence (i) in (4a) will be interpreted as OVS, and in (4b) as SVO. Note that in (4a), *die Tochter* in sentence (i) is repeated, hence it must be *ceteris paribus* the topic, whereas *die Mutter* is focussed as the new comment, but in (4b), *die Mutter* is repeated (though semantically, not formally), and *die Tochter* is the new comment. Since in (4b) *die Tochter* has not been shifted for emphasis, we would expect it to bear extra prominent stress.

Dyirbal (Dixon 1972) is supposedly a language with extraordinarily free word-order (pp. 76, 107-8, 148, 291). Despite this, Dixon suggests (p. 149): "it is likely that considerations of discourse structuring ('given' and 'new', or 'focus', or 'theme' or whatever ...) play some part in determining the actual order of words in a discourse." He goes on

to suggest that a "discourse-generating component" acts on the output of
the syntactic and phonological components (i.e. directly on the phonetic
representation, presumably), "forming a specific discourse appropriate to
some PARTICULAR extra-linguistic situation" (*ibid.* - emphasis Dixon's).
We may suppose that Dixon suggests this arrangement in the belief that
matters of discourse are necessarily matters of performance (a belief
actively encouraged by the MIT school), and that performance should somehow be accounted for only after competence has been taken care of. This
would be perfectly acceptable were there not considerable evidence that
discourse-considerations permeate the construction of all but the simplest and most wooden of sentences, and that furthermore they often provide
explanations for processes that in sentence terms are inexplicable mys-
teries. However, for our present purposes, we merely need to note that
the "extraordinarily" free word-order of Dyirbal is at least restricted
by discourse-considerations.

For Sanskrit, Macdonnel (1927: 178 sq.) says: "The usual arrangement of words in a Sanskrit sentence is: - first, the subject with its
attributes ..., second, the object with its adjuncts (which precede it);
and lastly the verb."

"Adverbs or extensions of the predicate are commonly placed near the
beginning, and unemphatic connective particles e.g. *but* follow the
first word."

"...Instead of the subject any other word requiring emphasis may be
placed at the head of the sentence. ... The subject, if a personal pronoun, is not expressed unless emphatic."

Staal (1967: 63 sq.) is somewhat dismissive of such observations:
"...it may not be difficult to find examples of two Sanskrit sentences
which only differ in the arrangement of the words but where a difference
in meaning is nevertheless felt. It may also be felt that two such sentences would not fit into larger contexts equally well ... While such
differences may well be explicable within the context of a theory of performance, it must be noted that they could not be explained by any theory
of competence which utilizes transformations to effectuate re-ordering,
but adheres to the principle that transformations do not affect meaning.

For according to such a theory different arguments are generated by applying transformational rules, and these result in expressions synonymous with the underlying sentences. (Sometimes different orders may, of course, have to be derived from different deep structures)."

Things have changed somewhat since 1967, of course, but most mainstream linguists, then and now, would surely feel obliged to account for differences in meaning somehow within a grammar of competence. The more difficult problem is concerned with questions of emphasis, focus, contextual function ("functional sentence perspective") and the like, where the vagueness of the term "performance" has become a crucial issue. It is possible - indeed essential in a sentence-grammar - to regard two sequences x and x^1 as synonymous but not contextually-equivalent and to consider the synonymy to be handled by having a single deep-structure x, and the contextual difference to be a matter of performance. However, just as in a sentence-grammar, it is permissible (and necessary) to refer to sentential context, e.g. in the specification of complementation, so in a text-grammar it must be permissible to refer to textual context. The difference between FOR-TO and POSS-ING complements is not semantic, but contextual, relying on the presence of a particular item or arrangement. Similarly the difference between *John saw Mary*, John *saw* Mary, *Mary*, *John saw* etc. relies on the contextual deployment of *John*, *Mary* and other items in the same set. Since both types of regularity are accessible to statement by rule, and are perfectly general in English (and indeed other languages), not being tied to any particular occasion but comprising some of the ordinary constitutive processes of the language, it seems perverse to treat the former in terms of competence, and the latter in terms of performance. (In connection with this, we may note that sentential processes are conventionally regarded in terms of structural description rather than speaker choice, while discourse processes are conventionally regarded in terms of speaker choice rather than structural description. This allows confirmed sentence-grammarians to retain their prejudices, but does nothing to further the study of language). I shall therefore assume that varying surface-orders in "free" word-order languages reflect contextual requirements of emphasis operating on a single linear order specified at some point to the surface.

Similar remarks appear to apply to other languages[4] which have been claimed to be free in word-order, and it is also the case that if we only consider surface word-order, and fail to take contextual determinations into account, even a fixed-order language like English can (cheating a little) show considerable variation (cf. Jespersen 1909-49, vol. VII: ch. 2):

   (5) (a) John has a wife.
            S   V   0
       (b) A wife, John has.
            0   S   V
       (c) A wife, has John.
            0   V   S
       (d) Has John a wife?
            V   S   0
       (e) John a wife has.
            S   0   V
       (f) *Has a wife (,) John.

This only works, of course, if we ignore the difference between statements and questions, neutral and emphatic, and normal and poetic, and furthermore select one of the few main verbs that do not require DO-support. (Though is one were forced to deal with post-surface structure circumstances - as suggested by Boas - there would in addition be all sorts of awkward elisions to account for as well).

Surface-variability, then, does not necessarily tell us anything about base order. Arguments for one or another position have either been couched in terms of vague postulates, amounting to no more than sugges-

---

[4] Cf. Byarushengo and Tenenbaum 1976 who note the effects of emphasis-placement etc. on "free" word-order in Haya, a Lake Bantu language, and Green 1976, who discusses the superficial freedom of Spanish word-order in similar terms. Horvath (1976) notes that focussed elements in Hungarian are shifted to the immediately pre-head position (i.e. N in NP, V in VP, A in AP). Focussed heads, on the other hand, may occur in any post-subject position (though one wonders whether there are, in fact, separate constraints on the non-focal adjunct.

tion and wishful thinking (e.g. that surface-order, *ceteris paribus*, reflects base-order; if this is so, of course, given that surface-orders
vary, no universal statements are possible), or else employ non-empirical (or not *very* empirical) assumptions of the form, 'Given a model of
grammar M, it is easier to state rules a, b and c if we assume x' (where
x is, in this case, either the ordered or the unordered base), (McCawley
1970 is a typical example of this). These facts lead one, inevitably it
seems to me, to the following melancholy conclusion:

> (6) OLD McTAVISH'S DREADFUL WARNING:
>
>> The only evidence which exists in conventional grammars
>> concerning the ordered or unordered nature of the base
>> is evidence against *both* positions.

(Actually, this is merely a special case of Finagle's Law of Universal
Fuzziness (FLUF): 'You can't be sure of anything'.)[5]

3. LINEAR ORDER IN THE TRANSFORMATIONAL COMPONENT

If we can agree, then, that the question of base order is not
directly accessible to empirical argument, a weaker question follows: what
is the earliest point at which serial ordering is demonstrably necessary?
Bach (1975: 331 sqq.) attempts something rather similar, and gets as far
as Extraposition (cf. Anderson 1976: 20 for some comments on this). If,
of course, it could be shown that transformational rules, by their formal nature, required ordered SD's, then on formal grounds (i.e. level
(ii)) there could be no argument. If the first transformation was necessarily ordered, then the terminal output of the base would have to be
ordered. Clearly, however, there are no such formal limitations on transformations: conventionally, transformations operate on trees, which in
the Standard Theory are hierarchically and serially ordered. The hierarchical (dominance) ordering captures constituency-specification, which
is certainly necessary in the statement of SD's, and it is not easy to

---

[5] I am indebted to Geoff Pullum for kindly pointing out to me that FLUF
also applies to itself. I stand by that - maybe there are some things
you *can* be sure of ... if you could be sure what they were, of
course.

think of any convenient and simple alternative (a level (ii) consideration); furthermore, given that the notion of related structures is feasible and real, there is plenty of evidence that they actually operate
using constituent-structures and not, for example, lexical items (giving
levels (i) and (iii) indications of the correctness of the approach).
Using hierarchical information, it is also possible to characterize grammatical relations (or at least subject-of, predicate-of, object-of, cf.
Chomsky (1965: 71); the more oblique relations are more difficult). Serial information, on the other hand, appears to have no such justification in the base, and its conventional inclusion there seems to have resulted more from our linear perceptual processes and the pre-eminence in
the linguistic world of the fixed-order languages than from any strict
constituent-structure requirement. How essential, though, is serial order in the statement of transformations? Conventionally, of course, SD's
are expressed as linear statements (bracketed for hierarchical information): again, is this merely by default, or are there reasons, empirical
or formal, for this linearity? Chomsky (*op. cit.*) regards the question as
"entirely empirical", although his first argument (p. 125) seems to be
formal, (at least negatively so), since he points out that nobody has
ever proposed any non-linear transformations (This omission was swiftly
repaired by Staal 1967, echoed by Boas 1975, to which proposals I shall
presently return).[6] The empirical evidence (which is "overwhelmingly in
favor of concatenation systems over set-systems") is (or is represented
by) the statement that given a set of syntactically related structures,
"there are strong reasons to assign an internal organization and an inherent order of derivation among the items constituting such a set". That
there are such things as basic, neutral, unmarked constructions certainly seems to be true. How strong this is as evidence is, to me at any rate,
not so obvious; (it certainly does not appear to be "overwhelming").
Chomsky, anyway, supports the contention that transformational SD's must
be linearly ordered, though his evidence is not very clear.

    In answer to Chomsky, Staal (1967: 14 sq.) suggests that it is

---

[6] See also Peterson 1977.

"counter-intuitive to assume that rules of concord must be formulated in
terms of strings, though concord itself has nothing to do with order".
He also claims that non-linear rules might be more universal than linear
ones, but again, we have to note that the empirical evidence is weak or
non-existent. In answer to Chomsky's challenge on the form of non-linear
transformational rules, Staal proposes "company-sensitive" (as opposed to
"context-sensitive") rules, which are defined over hierarchically-struc-
tured sets, rather than sequences. These can, according to Staal (p. 77),
be converted with ease into transformational rules bearing structural
indexes, whose output can remain as unordered sets or be regrouped into
concatenations.

Among the elementary transformations, Staal claims (p. 75), additions and deletions are statable without recourse to order, while he suggests that permutations ought to be regarded not as: $x\ y \Rightarrow y\ x$, but as:

$\left\{x,\ y\right\} \mapsto \left\{ \begin{matrix} x\ y \\ y\ x \end{matrix} \right\}$, (where the small braces enclose an unordered set, while

the large braces retain their conventional sense of choice between alternatives).[7] Thus he suggests that Subject-auxiliary inversion (Q-forma-
tion) should not be seen as forming, by a movement rule, a 'secondary'
structure (the interrogative), but that both should be regarded as representing or realizing some more abstract common relationship. I have some

---

[7] Cf. Sanders 1970, 1972, for more extended discussion of permutation
transformations. Peterson 1977 shows that "unordered" is, formally
equivalent to "having all possible orders", (i.e. an 'M-system' in
Bach's 1975 terminology), and his use of such a multiordered base
leads him to assume (pp. 88, 122) that permutation transformations
should be eliminated. However, his chief argument for this seems to be
that "the power of permutation rules to rearrange any order leads to
the possibility of using many orders in the base" (p. 122): a strange
reason for one who, earlier in the same paragraph, has declared:
"R(evised) T(heory) does not choose between the competing bases of
S(tandard) T(heory); rather, through the device of multiordering,
it declares all of them to be correct" ! Paradoxically, too, transformations in his theory have ordered inputs and outputs: "a transformation searches through the multiordered tree until it finds an ordered tree which meets the conditions of its SD" (p. 88). Nevertheless,
there are many valuable insights about constituent sets and surface-
structure constituency in this interesting paper.

sympathy for this viewpoint, particularly since it is harder to claim
primacy or neutrality or unmarkedness among sentence-types (such as
statement, question, command etc.) than it is among 'stylistic' variants
(e.g. *John is easy to please, it is easy to please John, pleasing
John is easy* etc., cf. Chomsky, *op.cit.*)

However, while Staal's suggestions may seem to have some substance
for question-formation, in fact they are unneccessary even within the
Aspects model since the distinction which he complains of is handled
not by transformation, but in the base, whereby a declarative would
be represented as $_s$[Nucleus] , while a question would be $_s$[Q-Nucleus].
His objection could therefore be handled very easily, simply by
marking declaratives with the element 'D' (for example), and allowing
it as a free alternative with Q, Imp etc. (I am, of course, ignoring
the semantic problems at this stage, for instance the mixed types
'whimperative', 'queclarative' etc., see Sadock 1970, 1971).

Furthermore, as soon as one looks at all carefully into movement rules, Staal's suggestion makes no sense. What, for example,
would the more abstract underlying form of non-Dative-movement and
Dative-movement, of non-Subject-raising and Subject-raising, of
non-Extraposition and Extraposition, of non-Topicalization and Topicalization, represent empirically? Staal's suggestion begins to
take on the air of a desperate measure, (although he is still supported by Boas (175 sq.) in this). The other possibility, mentioned
by both Staal and Boas, is the language-specific linearization rule
(though the term itself is not used by Staal), by which order may
be stated on the output of a rule as early in the derivation as a
given language requires it, (which according to Staal would be fairly
early for English, and not at all - or very late - for Sanskrit,
apparently). Of course, if linearization should be required from
the first transformation (as I've already noted), then the distinction between a linear and a non-linear base is vacuous. However, it seems that a distinction might be possible between rules
with an ordered input and those with an ordered output (from an

unordered input); Boas (p. 179 sq.) suggests that only 'stylistic'
rules (in the sense of Chomsky 1965:127) follow the onset of linearization, i.e. all rules with unordered outputs are grammatical
rules. This might (for English) help to characterize such rules
as Dative Movement, Topicalization, Adverb Preposing and Particle
Movement (although I believe - and will elaborate this presently -
it does not help to *explain* them), but it certainly does not
correctly categorize as stylistic such major rules as Wh-fronting,
Passive, Raising and There-insertion, all of which require
linear outputs (and some linear inputs also). Thus, both Wh-Q-
movement and Relative-movement require the wh-marked item to
occupy a specific leftward position (in the highest S and imme-
diately-dominating S, respectively). Passive is rather more
complex in that it requires either linear order (the standard
SD, cf. Huddleston 1976:191, Akmajian and Heny 1976:153, is
'NP-Aux-V-NP', in which the NPs are crucially ordered with respect to each other and to V), or else some way of indicating
grammatical relations (either by direct indication, as in Case
Grammar or Relational Grammar, or by rules of inference from
dominance relationships, as in *Aspects*). Thus a non-linear
model such as Staal advocates must have an input like:

$$(7) \quad (a) \quad _S \left\{ NP, \ _{vp} \left\{ V, \ NP \right\} _{vp} \right\} _S,$$

which is equivalent to:

$$(b) \quad _S \left\{ _{vp} \left\{ V, \ NP \right\} _{vp} \ NP \right\}$$

$$(c) \quad _S \left\{ _{vp} \left\{ NP, \ V \right\} _{vp} \ NP \right\} _S$$

$$\text{and} \quad (d) \quad _S \left\{ NP, \ _{vp} \left\{ NP, \ V \right\} _{vp} \right\} _S$$

Staal claims that for Sanskrit, the correct passivilazation rule
must be unordered, since there are six possible corresponding to
six possible actives, viz:

(8)   *active*   *passive*   *derived structure*

    (a)   SVO   ⇒   OVS   =   S'VX

    (b)   SOV   ⇒   OSV   =   S'XV

    (c)   VSO   ⇒   VOS   =   VS'X

    (d)   VOS   ⇒   VSO   =   VXS'

    (e)   OSV   ⇒   SOV   =   XS'V

    (f)   OVS   ⇒   SVO   =   XVS'

(ignoring verb-morphology; agent-chomage = X). Putting aside for
the moment our doubts about interchangeability of these variants, and our puzzlement about the claim that each active
corresponds to a passive (since the only possible evidence for
this would presumably show simultaneously that the variants were
not in fact interchangeable), we note that stipulating constituent
structure (and specifically a VP constituent) actually precludes
two of the possible orders (namely, VSO or VS'X, and OSV or
XS'V) from appearing either in the input or the output of
the rule. This effectively excludes (8b-c) as possible passives
in Sanskrit, (or indeed any other language, since Staal's
intentions were universalist). This means that the only possible
unordered alternative to the standard ordered SD for passive
(accounting for the variations with subsequent rules, e.g.
Scrambling, or the more restrictive rules based on Focus which
I shall be proposing, and which will be needed in any grammar,
given that these variations are not in fact mutually equivalent)
is one in which grammatical relations are explicitly specified.

    Unlike Passive, Raising seems to require an SD containing
some hierarchical stipulation: at least as much as (Huddleston
1976:112):

(9)   X - $_{NP}$ [*it*] $_{NP}$ - (VGp) - $_S$ [NP - Y] $_S$ - Z

('VGp' must in addition be specified as a raising trigger). But within this structure, and specifically within the embedded S, the NP has to be specified as leftmost in its S, or subject of its S - and in this, it *is* similar to the Passive rule.

There are at least two rules, then, which require their inputs to be stated either in terms of left-right order, or in terms of grammatical relations. Adjudicating between these two alternatives is by no means a simple matter, but some weak evidence for the latter seems to be provided form rules reordering the subordinate clause. Such rules do not in general appear to be possible, and what limited varieties there are do not seem to be acceptable to all speakers. The first point to clear up is that 'leftmost in its S' must mean 'leftmost NP', since other elements (notable adverbials) can precede the shiftable NP with impunity:

(10)   (a) Picasso believes that $_S$[$\left\{ \begin{array}{l} \text{probably} \\ \text{without doubt} \end{array} \right\}$

Rubinstein is a genius].

(b) Picasso believes Rubinstein $\left\{ \begin{array}{l} \text{probably} \\ \text{without doubt} \end{array} \right\}$

to be a genius.

(c) It seems that $_S$[scarcely were the words out of his mouth when the fuzz arrived]$_S$.

(d) The words seem scarcely to have been out of his mouth when the fuzz arrived.

Rules reordering the major constituents of subordinate clauses are, as I have already mentioned, difficult to attest, but 11a, b seem acceptable, whereas their raised equivalents (11c, d) seem quite bad:

(11)   (a) Picasso believes that a genius Rubinstein certainly is.

    (b) Picasso believes that a genius is what
        Rubinstein is.

    (c) * Picasso believes a genius Rubinstein
        certainly to be.

    (d) ?* Picasso believes a genius to be what
        Rubinstein is.

((11d), of course, is good with another sense, in which a third
person, referred to as *a genius*, is believed by Picasso to share
some attribute or function with Rubinstein). (11) seems to suggest
that "leftmost NP in the subordinate clause" is not enough to characterize the NP which undergoes Raising, and that the rule requires the stipulation of grammatical relationship (cf. Postal
1974:286 sqq., and *passim* for further arguments to this conclusion).

    Tough-movement,[8] on the other hand, seems to provide arguments
for reference to left-right positions rather than grammatical
relations:

      (12)   (a) It is difficult (for Richard) to give
             presents to Priscilla.

           (b) Priscilla is difficult (for Richard) to
             give presents to.

           (c) *Priscilla is difficult (for Richard) to
             give presents.

           (d) Presents are difficult (for Richard) to
             give Priscilla.

---

[8] According to Ross 1967, and Lasnik and Fiengo 1974, this is
a deletion rather than a movement rule. Postal and Ross 1971,
Postal 1972, and Berman 1973 argue that it is a movement rule,
while Jackendoff 1975 shows that Lasnik and Fiengo's evidence
in facts fails to adjudicate between the two analyses. I shall
assume that it is a movement rule.

    (e) ?? Presents are difficult (for Richard)
        to give to Priscilla.

    (f) Presents are difficult (for Richard) to
        give.

If these grammaticality judgments are correct (particularly (d) and
(e), which, anyway, do seem to rank in the order given: (d) (just
about) acceptable, (e) (verging on) unacceptable),[9] then what is
indicated is that Tough-movement applies to the final NP of the
constituent concerned (whether it is S, as in Postal 1971:27,
or VP, as in Bresnan 1971:264 sqq. and Brame 1976: 73 sqq.).Thus,
(c) shows that the Dative-moved indirect object will not Tough-
move, while (d), (if acceptable), shows that the direct object,
made final in its constituent by Dative-movement, will Tough-move.
(e), on the other hand, shows that the direct object does not
easily move (if at all) from its pre-Dative-movement nonfinal
position, though, as (f) shows, there is no problem for the direct
object if no indirect object is present in final position.

[9]
Interestingly, Berman's (1973:37 sq.) judgments are the reverse. She marks the following sentences:
    (i) Presents are impossible to buy for John.
    (ii) *Presents are impossible to buy John.
    (iii) *John is unpleasant to be kicked by.
For me, (ii) and (iii) are perhaps slightly dubious (though
(iii) is fine with the *get* passive), but (i) is considerably
more doubtful for me. I find (i) salvageable where *for John*
= 'on John's behalf' or 'as far as John is concerned' (i.e.
a preposition-phrase), rather than 'with John as recipient'
(i.e. indirect object). Berman points out the possibility of
dialect-variation on precisely these sentences, but remarks
that insofar as her judgments represent a real dialect, her
conclusions are valid for that dialect at least. What they are
not, of course, is universal. In the case of the present paper,
on the other hand, it is not my intention to propose any uni-
constraints, but simply to point out that there are some cyclic
transformations that require a linearly-specified input (however language- or dialect-specific they may otherwise be).

The apparent clarity of this restriction, however, is marred firstly by the difficulty of arriving at acceptability judgments in some cases, and secondly by the fact that prepositional objects do not behave with such co-operative submissiveness, and neither do Datives under verbs which do not allow Dative-movement:

(13) (a) Sonatas are difficult fo play on this violin.

(b) Daffodils are awkward to plant under this bush.

(c) This conclusion was impossible to prove to Sid.

These exceptions (indicating the squishiness of the rule), may be mitigated, if not explained, by reference to the NP Accessibility Hierarchy proposed by Keenan and Comrie (1972) and identical to the Grammatical Relation Hierarchy of Relational Grammar (cf. Pullum 1977:271):

(14)   Subject > Direct Object > Indirect
       Object > Prepositional Object > POSS-NP
       > Obj.-Comp-Particle

Some people (e.g. Johnson 1977:153, Woodbury 1977:308) now make a subdivision within this hierarchy around the Indirect Object; thus Subject, Direct Object, and less clearly,[10] Indirect Object are 'pure' relations, while the rest (sometimes including Indirect Object) are 'impure', which in this case apparently means 'less syntacitically specified' or 'more semantic' (cf. Vincent, forthcoming). It will be seen that our dubious cases fall into the 'impure' set; (Subject, of course, does not enter into Tough-Movement). This observation does no more, of course, than in-

---

[10] Woodbury (*op. cit.*) actually expresses it thus:

$$
\begin{array}{l}
\text{primaries} \left\{ \begin{array}{l} \text{subject} \\ \text{object} \end{array} \right\} \\
\text{non-primaries} \left\{ \begin{array}{l} \text{indirect object} \\ \text{other} \end{array} \right.
\end{array}
\left. \begin{array}{c} \\ \\ \\ \end{array} \right\} \text{terms}
\quad \text{non-terms}
$$

It will be seen that, although Indirect Object is a "term", it is not a "primary". The latter term is not defined (moreover, in in the same volume, Lawler 1977:224 has Subject and Direct Object as primaries, and Direct Object (again) and Indirect Object as "secondaries").

dicate where the rule tails off.

Wh-exclamation-movement provides another example (a slightly stronger one) of a rule which evidently requires linearity rather than grammatical relations in its statement. Like Tough-movement, Wh-exlamation movement fronts a rightward element in either a simple or complex clause:

(15)   (a) I am wh-such an idiot[11] ⇒ What an idiot I am__!

[11]The evidence for this derivation of wh-exclamations is both synchronic and diachronic. First, note that the *such* and *so* forms do not occur in exclamations with *wh* forms:
(i) *What such an idiot I am__!
(ii) *How so beautiful a rose is__!
Secondly, there is a class of very similar rhetorical questions (often bearing exclamatory force) which uses degree terms semantically related to *such* and *so*:
(iii) *What kind of* fool do you take me for__?
(For a possible response, cf. the old-fashioned: *Such a one as this*)
(iv) *Just how* beautiful can a rose be__?
(cf. *Just so beautiful, and no more.*)
Thirdly, *such*, like wh-exclamations (see below), patterns exclusively with true indefinites which are singular and countable:
(v) *John married such the beautiful woman.
(vi) ?*The cat is such a domestic quadruped.
(vii) *John drank such (some) wine!
Fourthly, the forms *such* and *so*, apart from being morphologically related (pOE*swalic, 'so-like' OE *swilc* and *swa*) are also connected, via *which* (pOE*hwalic, 'what-like') to the interrogative etc. *wh*-forms *who* (hwa), *what* (the neuter of *who*), *how* (the instrumental of *who*, but perhaps alternatively a suffixed form, cf. Gothic *hwaiwa*, IE*kwoivos, 'what like'. Could this suffix be *swa*?). Cf. also Latin *talis, qualis*. Moreover, the earliest exlamations of this type, (based on nominals), have *which* rather than *what*: *Which a great thing is affeccioun!* Chaucer *Miller's Tale* (A 3611). Fifthly, both *such/so* and wh-exclamations can only be attached to an item which semantically is evaluative, e.g. qualitative adjective phrases and nouns denoting qualities:
(viii) *This is such a machine-gun.
(ix) *What a machine-gun this is!
(x) *Molepipe kicked such a third policeman.
(xi) *What a third policeman Molepipe kicked!
(xii) *The editor's decision is so final.
(xiii) *How final the editor's decision is!
Sixthly, *such* and *so* function in parallel to *what* and *how*, with regard to their position in an adjective phrase:
(xiv) He was *such a funny* man ≡ *What a funny* man he was!
(xv) He was so funny a man ≡ How funny a man he was!

    (b) A rose is wh-so beautiful ⇒ How beautiful a rose
                                            is__!

    (c) John believes that I am ⇒ What an idiot John be-
        wh-such an idiot   believes I am__!

There are various restrictions on this movement, e.g. that it can only
apply to indefinites (genuine ones, i.e. excluding generics):

    (16)   (a) *What the beautiful woman John married!

           (b) ?*What a domestic quadruped the cat is!

((16b) is probably O.K. as a joke, but seems to lack a *raison d'être*).
More relevantly for our present purposes, the rule tends to select (though
again not exclusively) the rightmost of a series of NPs:

    (17)   (a) What a big man Rocky hit__!

           (b) ?*What a big man hit Rocky![12]

           (c) What a big man Rocky was hit by__!

           (d) *What a big man was hit by Rocky!

---

[12]Quirk and Greenbaum (1973: 203) accept wh-exclamation movement from
Subject position:
        (i) What an enormous crowd came!
I find these just acceptable with intransitives, but increasingly unacceptable with transitive, ditransitive and subordinating constructions:
        (ii) ?What a skilled player kicked the final goal!
        (iii) ?What an officious warden gave a parking ticket to John!
        (iv) ??What a strange analyst expected me to reveal all my
             innermost thoughts to him!
These are all "savable" by first shifting the Subject rightwards, e.g.
by clefting (thus providing a new Subject):
        (v) What a skilled player it was __ that kicked the final
            goal !
        (vi) What a strange analyst it was __ that expected me...
It is perhaps significant that in a whole page of examples of wh-exclamations, Jespersen (1909-49, vol. V: 499 sq.) notes only one made on
the Subject, taken from *The Tempest* (i.e. dating from 1616) and originally punctuated with a question-mark (though most modern editions have
substituted an exclamation-mark): *What a strange drowsiness possesses
them*? (He suggests, incidentally, (498), that these constructions may
have developed from indirect questions). It might be that exclamations
on the Subject are merely excessively rare, rather than actually ungrammatical, but this fact, taken with the clear preference for a separate Subject (even a dummy one; cf. (v, vi) above, and also with
There-insertion: *What an enormous crowd there was*!) suggests to me
that a wh-exclamatory Subject is generally avoided, and is perhaps on
the way to becoming ungrammatical.

(e) What a nice present John gave __ (?to) Mary!

(f) What a beautiful girl John gave that present $\begin{smallmatrix} to \\ *\emptyset \end{smallmatrix}$ __ !

(g) What a beautiful screen Carruthers produced a large
    bottle from under an old table behind__!

(h) *What an old table Carruthers produced a large bottle
    from under __ behind a beautiful screen!

However, (17i) shows that the 'pure' grammatical relation Direct Object
can be shifted even when followed by several 'impure' prepositional objects:

(i) What a large bottle Carruthers produced __ from un-
    der an old table behind a beautiful screen!

Similarly, as (17c) shows, the non-Dative-moved Indirect Object (i.e.
with *to*) is not entirely unacceptable with the Direct Object wh-moved
away.

Turning from English to other languages, we note that Japanese, according to Kuno (1973: 330 etc.) has a rule of Indirect Object Marking
which attaches the postposition *ni* to the second of three unmarked NP's,
and a rule of Object Marking which attaches *o* to the first nonsubject
unmarked NP to the left of the main verb if it is [-stative], and *ga* if
it is [+stative]. The Subject, on the other hand, is evidently given in
some way, since the rule of Subject Marking simply states, "Attach *ga*
to the subject NP". (Kuno provides no PS rules, indeed no formalization
of any kind. We must assume that NP's may be generated in strings of up
to at least three). A simple sentence therefore receives the following
marking (p. 330):

(18) (a) (i) DS: [John]$_{NP}$ [Mary]$_{NP}$ [okane]$_{NP}$ [yatta]$_V$
                                            [-stative]

     (ii) IO Marking: [John]$_{NP}$ [Mary]$_{NP}$ *ni* [okane]$_{NP}$
          [yatta]$_V$

     (iii) Subj. Marking: [John]$_{NP}$ *ga* [Mary]$_{NP}$ ni
           [okane]$_{NP}$ [yatta]$_V$

     (iv) Obj. Marking: [John]$_{NP}$ ga [Mary]$_{NP}$ ni
          [okane]$_{NP}$ *o* [yatta]$_V$

(b) John ga Mary ni okane o yatta
'John gave Mary money'.

A complex sentence, though, which according to Kuno also undergoes Equi
and other deletion rules, shows that case marking applies cyclically,
and furthermore that it cannot be stated in terms of the grammatical relations which obtain at the end of each cycle. If we compare intransitive and transitive causative constructions, we can see the rules operating in terms of left-rightness rather than grammatical relations:

(19) (a) John ga Mary *o* ik-sase-ru

go-cause

'John makes Mary go'.

(b) John ga Mary *ni* hon *o* yom-sase-ru

books read-cause

'John makes Mary read books' (cf. Kuno, pp. 341 sqq.)

Notice that in each case *Mary* bears the same relationship both to *John*
and the verb (given that Japanese is not an ergative language), but that
the nearest NP to the verb is marked *o*, while the second nearest (not
being the Subject) is marked *ni*, so that *Mary* is marked differently in
the two instances. (In both cases according to Kuno, *Mary* starts out as
the Object (presumably) of the upper S, and the subject of the lower S,
the latter subsequently undergoing Equi-NP-Deletion[13]).

   It is, of course, quite clear that all rules *can* be stated in a serial order - they generally have been, in conventional TG. But the only
times they absolutely must be so stated (assuming there were no other
means) are when the SD must contain two or more instances of the same
category (e.g. NP, PP) within the same constituent. But, of course, as
we have seen, there are other means for pinpointing some particular element: bracketing, indexing, or marking grammatical relations (GRs), to
name the most obvious. Of these, bracketing and marking GRs appear to be
in most cases equivalent, and the former is traditionally used in most
SDs (GRs in this tradition - Chomsky 1965 - being derivable from brack-

---

[13]Whether or not this analysis is correct, it is irrelevant to the
  placement of the postpositions in question.

eting). What I am here calling indexing - the explicit marking of certain elements for later treatment[14] - is also widely employed in certain traditional rule-statements. Many of the conventional rules, though, may be stated with equal felicity using these alternative means:

(20)	INDEXING	BRACKETING	GRs	SERIAL ORDER
Raising	-	+	+	+[15]
Passive	?[16]	+	+	+
Equi	17	+	+	+[18]
Tough[19]	-	?	?	?
Dative	+[20]	+[21]	+[22]	+[23]

[14]Cf. Postal's (1972: 214 sqq.) warnings on the use of *arbitrary* indexing features. I exclude triggering elements which are already present (and which figure in Raising, Equi, Tough and Dative, at least).

[15]e.g. "First NP in embedded S (assuming R-trigger in higher S)".

[16]As in Chomsky 1965.

[17]In this case, by identity-indexing.

[18]e.g. "First NP in embedded S (assuming identity-indexing with NP in higher S)".

[19]My preceding remarks appear to show the inadequacy of each of these conventions taken separately (though perhaps serial order is the least unsatisfactory).

[20]Indexed in the sense that [+Dat], or its equivalent, is necessary in most statements of the rule to exhaustively specify the moved element.

[21]Assuming that [Indirect-Object-of] can be specified hierarchically.

[22]Indirect Object is a primitive term (a 3) in Relational Grammar.

[23]e.g. "Third NP in S, following class p of prepositions (containing at least *to*, *for*)". There are obvious drawbacks to this formulation, not least that not all PPs introduced by *to* or *for* are actually Indirect Objects:

*John bought a car for $\frac{1000}{his\ own\ use}$ ≠ *John bought $\frac{1000}{his\ own\ use}$ a car;*
*Che showed the way to freedom ≠ *Che showed freedom the way.* Even restricting the NP in question to animates does not fully overcome the problem: *Clyde bought the painting for Melvyn. ≠ ?Clyde bought Melvyn*

	INDEXING	BRACKETING	GRs	SERIAL ORDER
wh-rel.	+[24]	-	-	-
Extraposition	-[25]	+	+	?
wh-Q	+	-	-	-
wh-exlam	+[26]	?	?	+
Reflexive[27]	+	+	-	+
There	-	+	+	+
Question[28]	+	?	?	?

Most of these rules are generally accepted as being crucially in the cycle (as opposed to being merely consistent with it: e.g. Affix

the painting. (in the 'on behalf of' sense).

[24] An essentially-indexed rule, to which bracketing is irrelevant (since it is unbounded), in which grammatical relations do not appear to figure (since although the *wh*-word may be regarded as a derived subject, the subject in the structure preceding the application of the rule is not demoted or chômeurized), and in which serial order is not apparently important (since - restrictions such as the Complex NP Constraint aside - NPs from any position may undergo the rule, although there are language-specific differences: see Keenan and Comrie (1972)).

[25] See Bach 1975 for indirect arguments to show that Extraposition must be linearly stated. In Relational Grammar, the phenomenon is apparently handled by inserting a dummy 1 (Subject- viz. *it*), demoting the S 1 to 1 (chomeur) and linearizing it rightwards later.

[26] Indexed (with *wh*-), but perhaps not as crucially as *Wh*-Rel and *Wh*-Q. The rule seems broadly speaking to require serial order, in that there is a strong tendency to shift the *final* NP, (see the preceding discussion).

[27] Identity-indexed; bracketed in the sense that it is restricted to NPs within a single S (the clause-mate condition), but not restricted in terms of GRs. However, serial in the limited sense that reflexivization generally operates forwards on the nearest identity-indexed NP.

[28] Indexed by the presence of Q (though this element is present right from the base). Partial bracketing or GR analyses seem possible (in that both may stipulate the subject, around which certain verbal elements are inverted by the rule. Serial order is possible, provided that the first NP has resulted only from cyclic reordering, or is the 'deep' first NP.

Hopping[29] and DO-Support in Akmajian and Heny 1976). There is, however,
a great deal of vagueness about the precise formulation of the rules,
but one property which apparently does keep them conceptually together
is that in a certain sense, which I shall define, they are practically
all 'discourse-conditioned'.

4.   DISCOURSE-CONDITIONING

The notion of 'discourse-conditioning', as far as I can tell,
is due to Jorge Hankamer (especially 1974), and is also mentioned in
Pullum (1977: 266) and Williams (1977: 102). Hankamer's characterization
is as follows:

> I use the term 'discourse-conditioned' to mean that the rule
> is unable to apply except under specific discourse conditions
> (these 'discourse conditions' may include extralinguistic con-
> text). The test of a rule's being discourse-conditioned in this
> sense is its inability to apply in a sentence which initiates
> a discourse, does not resume a previously-initiated discourse,
> and where there is no relevant extralinguistic context." (p. 221)

By this test, the "out-of-the-blue" test, such rules as Topicalization,
Left Dislocation, inversions and emphatic fronting are categorized as
discourse-conditioned, whereas Passive and *There*, for example, are not
(in these examples, '#' means "can not be uttered out of the blue"):

(21)   (a) # My basement, army ants have invaded.

(b) # My basement, army ants have invaded it.

(c) # Army ants, they've invaded my basement.

(d)   My basement has been invaded by army ants.

[29]Affix-Hopping is a clear case of a rule requiring both a serial input
and a serial output, (though this is denied by Boas 1975: 31 sqq.).
However, although it may be characterized as operating cyclically, it
is not crucially ordered to precede any cyclic rule, nor do there
seem to be any rules in which it could mistakenly operate over S bound-
aries (e.g. a rule such as Raising to Subject which could be taken to
bring the triggering verb (e.g. *seem*) into sequence with the subordinate verb, thus allowing Affix-Hopping to operate across the S boundary - but given the presence of the usual *for-to* complementizer or
some sort of boundary-symbol, Affix-Hopping would in fact be blocked).
There is therefore no reason to suppose that this rule, like other
"housekeeping" rules of a morphological nature, is necessary cyclic.

(e)   There are army ants in my basement.
(Hankamer's examples and judgments). The trouble with this is that the
notion of discourse-conditioning - which is, I think, potentially a useful one - remains vague in Hankamer's presentation, and the diagnostic
test, as he himself admits (p. 231) is by no means straightforward in
application or interpretation. For example, the Passive (22a) clearly
cannot be discourse-initial (for quite separate reasons):

      (22)   (a) The man has been detained by Lanarkshire police.
and yet other reasons rule out (22b) as discourse-initial:

      (b) His basement has been invaded by army ants.
In fact, I would argue that Passives clearly *are* discourse-conditioned,
and that the reason why (21d) can apparently be discourse-initial is
that the Ego and its belongings (and the Addressee and its belongings)
are *automatically* in the Universe of Discourse. The initial element in
(21d) refers to a presumed participant in the discourse; no such presumption without previous explicit information is possible for (22a, b).
All three are nevertheless equally discourse-conditioned. Furthermore, I
can quite easily imagine (21a) as initiating an out-of-the-blue list of
misfortunes:

      (23)   What a day![30] My basement, army ants have invaded. My
              mother, she got mugged. My car, the police towed away...
And, of course, topicalized, preposed and inverted sequences are very
common as elegant openings in written English with no particular impact
of deviance or deliberate defiance of expectation:

      (24)   (a) In a small valley near Leamington Spa stood an an-
              cient public convenience.
           (b) Difficult though it is to elicit, Attribute Pre-
              posing is common in all styles of speech.
((b) is Hankamer's example, judged by him to be non-discourse-initial).
Hankamer's thesis in his paper is:

      (25)   *All discourse-conditioned rules are noncyclic.*

---

[30]Hankamer allows "a certain amount of ritual preamble"; discourse-
initial thus means "initial in the informative portion of the discourse" (p. 231) (whatever *that* means!).

(By the latter term he means not crucially ordered before any cyclic
rules.) I have already shown, I believe, that Passive is in fact a discourse-conditioned rule, even in Hankamer's terms, so that no more is in
fact required to disprove (25) - nobody would deny that Passives are cyclic. I shall be making the claim that all movement rules[31] in fact are
discourse-conditioned (in a rather more defined sense than Hankamer's),
and that since most of them are clearly in the cycle, they also discon-
firm (25). Hankamer's main aim, however, is to show that Pseudo-clefting
(which he calls WH clefting) is noncyclic, but even in this he is, I
think, more or less incorrect. There appears to be sufficient variation
in the acceptability of some of the sentences involved to cast doubt on
the iron-cladness of Hankamer's assertion. Some of his starred sentences
appear reasonably acceptable to me:

> (26)   (a) What he was doing turned out to be washing himself.
>
> (b) What they're doing appears to be amusing each other.
>
> (c) What I want him to write on the board is how Clefts
> work.
>
> (d) What there was in the closet turned out to be a
> roach.

(a) shows interaction between Pseudo-clefting and Raising to Subject
(from: *It turned out that what he was doing was washing himself*); (b)
likewise, though (b) is ambiguous (*contra* Hankamer) between a Pseudo-
cleft and a Headless Relative interpretation (both from: *It appears that
[what they're doing is amusing each other]*$_s$, with the embedded S itself
ambiguous between: PC: *They're AMUSING each other*. (*What are they doing?
What they're doing is AMUSING each other*), and HR: *Whatever it is they're
each doing is amusing the other*: though this latter sense is more com-
fortable without the reciprocal); (c) according to Hankamer (pp. 227 sq.)
could neither be clefted nor a headless relative. He bases the former
claim on his conclusion that these Pseudo-clefts cannot be cyclic (though
as far as I can see no cyclic rule crucially intervenes here); (d) shows

---

[31]Strictly, 'all movement rules shifting an element to the leftmost position in its own S , or the highest non-performative S' . This excludes
Raising to Object, for example (see subsequent discussion).

interaction with *There* preceding, and Raising to Subject following (a fairly classic "sandwich" argument for the cyclicity of Pseudo-cleft! But see Higgins (1976) for an interpretative account). In general *all* the *wh*-rules (with the partial exception perhaps of *wh*-Rel. movement) are said to be unbounded and last cyclic or post-cyclic (if there is a distinction). Pseudo-cleft, at least, appears to cast doubt on this supposition. Moreover, there is another rule which is clearly discourse-conditioned and pragmatically almost identical to Pseudo-clefting, but which appears to be cyclic, and that is Clefting, as the following examples show.

(27)   (a) Rowena likes massage.

(b) It's massage that Rowena likes.

(c) Piers believes it to be massage that Rowena likes.

(d) It is believed by Piers to be massage that Rowena likes.

(27a) represents the base structure from which the focussed element *massage* is clefted, to give (b). (27c) and (d) show that clefting must take place on the S_1 cycle before Raising and Passive can operate on the S_0 cycle to lift the expletive *it* and invert it to top-subject position. [32]

---

[32] Hankamer claims (p. 232) that clefting is a rule which embeds the clause to be clefted in a superstructure, so that it applies one cycle up (like Raising or Tough, for example). This does not appear quite appropriate, though, since both kinds of cleft (along with a related rule I have called "pseudo-relative" - see Werth 1976, 1977, forthcoming) in fact create their own superstructure in that they form a new predicator:

(i)   Jack likes Glenmorangie.

(ii) It is Glenmorangie that Jack likes.

(iii) What Jack likes is Glenmorangie.

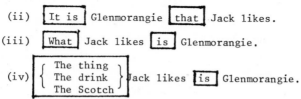

(iv) { The thing / The drink / The Scotch } Jack likes is Glenmorangie.

Since this requires a new sort of machinery in the cycle (although one formally related to and perhaps identical with Chomsky-adjunction, as I argue in the references cited), it might provide a disincentive to claiming that such rules are cyclic. However, it seems to me that the **data** are reasonably clear in indicating the cyclicity of these rules.

Furthermore, there may be morphological evidence to show that, in Relational Grammar terms, Clefting is a relation-changing rule (of a slightly different kind), since clefted subjects take on object morphology: *It's* ME *that likes Glenmorangie*.

It seems, then, that there is ample evidence to cast doubt on both sides of Hankamer's proposed constraint (25). There exist clearly cyclic rules which are nevertheless discourse-conditioned, as well as clearly discourse-conditioned rules which are nevertheless cyclic. It is obvious therefore that we cannot take the property of discourse-conditioning (or perhaps 'discourse-sensitivity' would be more accurate) as diagnostic or indicative of post-cyclic rules of grammar, for example (as Pullum (*op. cit.*) hopes).

5.   EMPHASIS-PLACEMENT FROM DISCOURSE

Rather, I would argue that the role of discourse in syntax is much more intimate than Hankamer's approach suggests. As I have argued elsewhere (Werth 1976, 1977, forthcoming), discourse-function *motivates* and *relates* many rules which in a sentence-grammar insensitive to discourse have to be regarded as separate and ad hoc. The machinery which I have proposed to carry out this function allocates FOCUS, CONTRAST and REDUCTION (collectively, EMPHASIS) in response to the cumulative exigencies of the discourse. By this means, the progression of information and repetition is able to be presented to (cf. Hetzron 1975) and decoded by the listener in a comprehensible form. *Focus* (F) marks new or revived information as prominent; *contrast* (C) on an item implicitly makes it deny some other item (which must be semantically linked or syntactically parallel with it); while *reduction* (R) occurs in repeated semantic material subsequently referred to.

Informally stated, the rules for emphasis-placement are:

(28) (a) (i) Mark each major lexical item F, (cf. the Choms-

A separate point is that the *it* of (27d) might be taken as a sort of portmanteau-realization (cf. Matthews 1972: 65) combining the base-generated *it*-complement of *believe* with the transformationally derived empty *it* of the Cleft.

ky/Halle rule assigning 1's to items in lexical
categories);

(ii) If an item or its (partial) synonym is mentioned or implied previously in the same text,

$$F \rightarrow R$$

(unless it initiates a new sub-text)

(iii) Under the semantic condition for contrast
(roughly, if an item is preceded by its negative, or an alternative in the same semantic
set),

$$\left\{ \begin{matrix} R \\ -F \end{matrix} \right\} \rightarrow C$$

(Notice that since an item marked C is necessarily preceded by some previous imputation of itself, even though a negative one, it cannot be
founded on focus).

There are, therefore, four categories of emphasis: F, -F, R, C. (To these, we shall later
add a fifth).

A brief example of these will suffice:

(28) (b) A: This whole *topic* of a *day* in the *country*, or
LIFE in the [country] I should say, is perhaps
a very ENGLISH thing to *talk* about because we
are *such* an *urban community* that we *think* of
it as *important* and an *event* when we *go* to the
[country]. This might *not* be so in AUSTRALIA,
for example?

B: *No*, I think WE *tend* to [go to the country] just
to [go] SOMEWHERE. We don't [go] *out* just to
look at the *birds* or anything like *this*, unless
it's in a NATIONAL PARK *district*.

A: You *pass* THROUGH the [country].

B: *Yes*, and we have a *place* to *go* and we don't
sort of STOP, 'cos *all* the *trees* are the *same*.

(cf. Dickinson and Mackin (1969: 90)).

KEY: *italics*   = Focus
     CAPITALS = Contrast
     [ ]   = Reduction

(I have omitted hesitations, etc., and the
Emphasis-marking is my own.)

The constituent sentences of (28) tend to be rather simple in construction, and have by and large undergone few of the cyclic movement transformations in which we are primarily interested. They therefore illustrate what I claim is precyclic (actually prelexical) emphasis-marking,
which without those movement transformations is realized as stress-as-
signment of one form or another, but which in other circumstances could
act to motivate one or another of the movement rules (as I have shown in
the papers cited). Focus (italics) normally marks new material (*topic,
day, country* in the first sentence) or old material reintroduced (*go* in
the last sentence). Contrast (capitals) marks the denial of another item
in the Universe of Discourse (i.e. either in the linguistic context:
LIFE (~ *day*), STOP (~ *go*); or else in the extralinguistic context: ENG-
LISH (~ 'Australian', ~ 'American', ~ 'Norwegian', the nationalities of
the other speakers)). Reduction (square brackets) marks material repeated to keep it unambiguous in the discourse, but destressed to prevent it
from assuming the prominence of new information (e.g. [country] and [go]).
Two caveats are necessary here: first, it should be noted that contrast
and reduction are actually more closely connected with each other semantically, than either is with focus, since both are fundamentally *phoric*
(referring as they must to some previously mentioned element or some
element present in the situation: reduction positively, contrast negatively). Secondly, weak stress or "absence" of stress cannot be absolutely equated with reduction, since there are weakly-stressed major
lexical items which are not reduced, because they are not repeated. I
am referring, of course, to the so-called weak impersonals *someone, one,
you, people* etc., which are typically weakly-stressed, though they may
be freshly-mentioned. We may regard them as a special sub-set of $F_r(WF)$.

The foregoing constitutes a hypothesis about the nature of discourse-conditioning, which is seen as a process of checks and balances
in the presentation of information for communicative purposes. In order

to understand the operation of this process however, it is necessary to recognize also the existence of two things: (i) unmarked nuclear stress, and (ii) so-called 'Topic-Comment Articulation'. Unmarked nuclear stress is normally a pitch-turn or prominence on the final lexical item in an S^{33}. It carries no particular impact of contrast or expressiveness. If there is a sequence of focusses in an S, the nucleus will be the last, since this will coincide with the final lexical item (assuming that the rule F → R does not apply to it).

The dynamics of discourse-conditioning derive, I postulate, from the interaction between the process of emphasis-placement from the discourse, and the process of nuclear-stress placement in the sentence. It may happen, for example, that the final lexical item is in fact repeated, and therefore reduced, distorting the unmarked pattern of nucleus last. One way of restoring the equilibrium is to move the reduced element leftwards (by Topicalization). Or, it may be the case that the final lexical

---

[33]Schmerling 1976 points out a large number of "normally-stressed" examples with the nucleus on a non-final item, e.g.
    (i) By the way, Jóhn diêd (where ´ = primary, ^ = secondary, and
                                     = tertiary stress, as is usual)
In (i), John's death is unexpected; we should therefore expect the lexical item *died* to impart new information and therefore be focussed. Contrast this with:
    (ii) After a series of operations, Jôhn díed,
where the death is expected: yet *died* is stressed. We may presumably regard the latter case as contrastive, where *died* represents a member of a set of conditions suffered by John. (i), on the other hand, seems to me to be equivalent in expressiveness to:
    (iii) You know Jóhn? He díed.
In such a case, it may be argued that *John* is contrastive, along the lines of 'one member of the set of our mutual acquaintances'. (iii) then analyses emphatically as *You know John? He died*; suggesting that
                                            C   R   F
(i) is, similarly, *John died* (whereas (ii) is *John died*), i.e. in (i),
                                 C F   R   C
the secondary-stress is actually a primary phonetically lowered to make the adjacent contrast more salient. Similar well-known examples actually have a reduced element to the right (usually reduced semantically), e.g.
    (iv) The kettle's boiling.
         F/C   R
since in such cases, the predicate is highly redundant semantically.

item is contrastive, and therefore emphatic. But since the final lexical item is nuclear, and therefore stressed anyway, the contrast may not be distinctive enough. One way of restoring the contrastiveness is to move the emphatic element leftwards (by Y-movement).

Topic-comment articulation is a concomitant feature of the unmarked nuclear stress sentence, with a relatively heavily-stressed right end corresponding to the comment. It ensures that there is a relatively lightly-stressed left end, corresponding to the topic. This reflects the fact, of course, that repeated information is, *ceteris paribus*, marshalled first, while new information is reserved for the final impact of the sentence. The rules of Topicalization and Y-movement which I have mentioned, constitute a kind of push-effect (to borrow a term from historical linguistics). There is a corresponding drag-effect when the leftmost position is particularly lightweight, e.g. when it contains one of the weak impersonal forms already mentioned.

6.   EMPHASIS AND MOVEMENT-RULES

The combination of these factors can result in the various movement rules of grammar. In order to illustrate this, however, it would obviously be insufficient merely to present isolated sentences displaying Raising, Tough, Passive, etc. Instead, they must be shown embedded in the context which gives them their form. Examples therefore follow in this format (mostly from Levine 1971):

(29)   *Raising to Subject*

(a) Sir,

In this week's issue of the *Observer*, John Crosby refers to England as an island.

...England is *not* an island. She is only threefifths of an island ...

John Crosby writes: *This gentleman seems to think an island must be surrounded by water* ...

(The Observer)

(b) ... something to put in your mouth which is supposed to slim you without any need for you to control your

eating ...   ... *it is likely to be thyroid hormone*
(John Yudkin)

(c) How do you know that red is red? *The colour may appear to be blue to everyone else's eyes.*
(Magnus Pyke)

(30) *Non-raising to Subject*

(a) The English consider themselves sportsmanlike, reserved, tradition-loving, conventional and intelligent; astonishingly enough, Americans agree ...
The close agreement found in English and American groups is probably due to the fact that these stereotypes derive from books, films and other cultural media shared by both groups. (i) *It is unlikely that a comparison between stereotypes held by Spaniards, Turks or Russians would show much agreement* ... (NOT: *Stereotypes held by Spaniards, Turks or Russians are unlikely to* ...)
To judge by German writings, (ii) *it appears that, to the Germans, the average Englishman is 'a clever and unscrupulous hypocrite'* ... (NOT: *the average Englishman appears, to the Germans, to be* ...)
(H. J. Eysenck)

(b) MISS LESTOR: Would my Right Honourable Friend not agree that the agitation and the racialist statements which have been made by [Mr. Sandys] and [Sir C. Osborne] over the last few years have produced what they wanted - the acceleration of immigrants from Kenya and other parts of the world which has forced us into a position that is abhorrent to many of us on this side of the House?
MR. CALLAGHAN: This is asking me for an opinion. If I am asked for it, I will give it. *It seems to me that three factors have contributed to the situation over the last few months* ...

(NOT: *Three factors seem to me to have contributed ...*)

(Hansard)

(31) *Raising to Object*

(a) There are experimental ways of investigating stereotypes ... There is even agreement between different
nations; for instance, the Americans and English a-
gree with respect to other groups, and even, though
less markedly, themselves. The Germans, for instance,
are regarded as scientifically minded and industrious by English and Americans alike ... Italians ...
Negroes ... The Irish ... Jews ... The Chinese ...
(i) *The English consider themselves sportsmanlike,
reserved, tradition-loving, conventional and intelligent ...* (ii) *The Americans consider themselves
industrious, intelligent, materialistic, ambitious
...* (iii) *The English agree that Americans are materialistic and pleasure-loving, but also consider
them generous, talkative and ... boastful.*

(H. J. Eysenck)

(32) *Non-raising to Object*

(a) I don't know how much truth there is in the things
Mr. Bunetta and Mr. Bonaro and the others have said.
I don't doubt them, understand. (i) *I believe that
they spoke up in good conscience and good faith.*
(ii) *And I believe that Mr. Douglas defended his
choice in good conscience and good faith.* (NOT: *I
believe them to have spoken up ... I believe Mr.
Douglas to have defended ...*)

(David Karp)

(b) As soon as the engine starts, release the starter
switch and warm up the engine at a fairly fast i-
dling speed ... *Research has proved that the practice of warming up an engine by allowing it to idle
slowly is harmful.* (B.M.C: Morris 1100 *Handbook*)

(NOT: *Research has proved the practice of warming up an engine ... to be harmful*).

(c) Like ministers in the parliamentary debates on immigration, [Patrick Gordon Walker] deliberately met the prejudices of the ignorant with a statement calculated to exacerbate them. Of course, one should be careful about *believing that Mr. Gordon Walker says anything deliberately or with calculation.*
(NOT: *believing Mr. G. W. to say anything ...*)

(Economist)

(d) # *I believe that every parent in the country who understands the problem of teachers' salaries is on our side in the campaign for high pay.*

(N.U.T. pamphlet)

(NOT: *?I believe every parent who ... to be on our side ...*)

(33) *Passive*

(a) ... But success has brought its share of worry for Mr. and Mrs. Harrison.
Since their mammoth win *they have been plagued by an endless succession of callers and spongers.*

(The People)

(b) Positioning the lips is a problem that recurrently challenges the ingenuity of the embalmer ... the lips tend to drift apart. (i) *Lip drift can sometimes be remedied* by pushing one or two straight pins through ... the lower lips and then ... between the two front upper teeth. If Mr. Jones happens to have no teeth, (ii) *the pins can just as easily be anchored in his Armstrong Face Former and Denture Replacer.*

(Jessica Mitford)

(c) Both councils have been complaining about the clearance of leaves and dirt from roads and pavements

within their area. A month ago Clr. Ashton said that
in some cases pavements were inches deep in leaves
from last autumn ... *Clr. Ashton said that even now
a brush had still not been put to work on the pavements.*

(Huddersfield Weekly Examiner)

(34) *Non-passive*

(a) ... It was my first experience of doctors who handle
you without speaking to you or, in a human sense,
taking any notice of you ...
There was another treatment coming, the mustard poultice ... *Two slatternly nurses had already got the
poultice ready ...*

(George Orwell)

(NOT: *The poultice/It had already been got ready by
two slatternly nurses ...*)

(b) 'Fancy living? You can keep your champagne and your
posh hotels. I'm just a plain, simple man ...'
It will take a lot to change this ruddy-faced York-
shire lad. *Certainly the rich life won't do it.*
(NOT: *Certainly it won't be done by the rich life.*)

(c) Mr. Allison isn't a newcomer to the poetry trade.
While still at Oxford he ran an outfit called Har-
lequin Poets and was 'staggered by its success'. He
believes (i) *people should read poetry ...* (ii) *just
as they read novels ...*

(Observer)

(NOT: *... poetry should be read (by people) ... just
as novels are read (by them)*).

(35) *Tough*

(a) ... But he hasn't used British Ceramic Tiles because
of their looks alone. Ceramic tiles are stain-proof,
steam-proof, *they are extremely easy to clean and
extremely difficult to damage.*[34]

(Advert)

(b) ... Although veal escalopes are much used because
veal is a meat that goes well with the flavour of
wine or cream sauces, you will find that pork does,
too. Pork fillet, *which is easy to find in most su-
permarkets these days,* can be trimmed of all excess
fat ...

(Katie Stewart, *The Times* 5/10/77)

(c) '... We must persuade the Europeans that the doctor
holds disloyal, anti-British opinions ... let them
suspect his loyalty even for a moment, and he is
ruined.'

'It would be a hard thing to prove', objected Ba Sein.

(George Orwell, *Burmese Days*)

(36) *Non-tough*

(a) ... Turkish baths, or some similar and probably more
costly way of sweating hard ... You learn in school
that a pint of water weighs a point and a quarter,
and (i) *it is quite easy to lose a pint by sweating.*
And (ii) *it is just as easy to put this pint back
into your dehydrated tissues* as soon as you begin to
drink again.

(John Yudkin)

(NOT: *a pint is quite easy to lose by sweating; this
pint is just as easy to put back ...*)

(b) Never overtake unless you *know* that you can do so
without danger to yourself or others. Be specially
careful at dusk and in fog or mist, when *it is more
difficult to judge speed and distance.*

(Highway Code)

[34]This happens to be the only example of a *Tough*-moved structure in the
whole of Levine 1971, a book of some 133 pages of mixed-variety texts.
This may be, of course, an extremely significant indication of the
relative infrequency of the construction in English. Equally, it could
be a very boring coincidence. (35b, c) are taken from other sources, in
order to give more than a single example of the construction.

(NOT: *when speed and distance are more difficult to judge.*)

(c) ... His face was now an old man's ... He smiled without sadness and with an extraordinary detachment. 'It makes me wonder how they are grouping themselves about the coming vacancy' ... '*It is surprisingly easy to face that kind of fact*'.

(C. P. Snow)

(NOT: '*That kind of fact is surprisingly easy to face*')

(37) *Cleft and pseudo-cleft*

(a) At five in the morning the nurses came round, woke the patients and took their temperatures, but did not wash them. If you were well enough you washed yourself, otherwise you depended on the kindness of some walking patient. *It was generally patients, too, who carried the bedbottles and the grim bedpan, nicknamed la casserole.*

(George Orwell)

(b) It is interesting to examine Pop Culture to see what it borrows and what it invents. The involvement of 'high culture' with Pop in the postwar era is a thing which has been much discussed. *What has been less thoroughly examined is the tendency of Pop to take what it needed from the avant-garde.*

(*The Times*)

(c) ... Mr. Healey's visit might well have passed off with nothing worse than some ill-tempered, ill-mannered shouting. *It was Mr. Patrick Gordon Walker, Secretary for Education and Science, who transformed the Cambridge incident into something of real political significance.*

(*Economist*)

(d) ... the natives of this country ... like to employ
their own breed in preference to coloured aliens ...
Why assume that this rejection is prejudice against
them? ... The coloured invasion threatens our whole
security. The alien has his foot in our door ... *It
is not the colour of their faces, but their numbers
which we dislike.*

(Daily Telegraph)

(e) ... I think you ought to know what I think of your
thanks - and most of you ... I will pass over the
insult you have given to Mr. Isler. I don't think he
will be much disturbed by it ... *But what sickens
and disgusts me is that I have shown the abysmal
lack of good taste and good judgment to become associated with you.*

(David Karp)

(38) *Non-cleft and non-pseudo-cleft*

(a) ... there has been nothing to equal the 338, 356
Percy collected last September ...
'Fancy living? *You can keep your champagne and your
posh hotels ...*'

(The People)

(NOT: **It's your champagne and your posh hotels you
can keep* / **What you can keep is your champagne and
posh hotels.*)

(b) ... There was another treatment coming, the mustard
poultice, seemingly a matter of routine, like the hot
bath. *Two slatternly nurses had already got the poultice ready ...*

(George Orwell)

(NOT: **It was two slatternly nurses who had already
got the poultice ready* / **The ones who had already
got the poultice ready were two slatternly nurses.*)
(NOR: **It was the poultice that two slatternly nurses*

*had already got ready / *What two slatternly nurses
had already got ready was the poultice.*)

(c) The Eagle Tower is the finest of all the towers, and
is part of the work of 1285-94 ... It is first called
the Eagle Tower in 1316 ...

The origin of the name of the tower is not certain.

(Guide to Caernarvon Castle)

(NOT: ?**It is the origin of the name of the tower
that is not certain.*

?**What is not certain is the origin of the name of
the tower.*)

(39) *Combined Raising and Passive*

(a) ... the ad-men have been hotting up social classes
quite a profitable bit.

We are now all classified as either A, B, C_1, C_2, D
or E ...

(i) *D people are contemptuously thought likely to
buy a souvenir in Blackpool and cook steak in
casseroles on Sunday ...*

(ii) *C_2 people are reckoned to buy cheap 'knowledge'
books on their doorsteps ...*

(iii) *... A people, who are reckoned by ad-men to be
A 1 people...*

(*Morning Star*)

(b) ... there is considerable agreement between different people in any one nation regarding the most
characteristic traits of other nations ... The Americans and English agree with respect to other
groups ...

(i) *Negroes ... are considered to be supersti-
tious, lazy, happy-go-lucky ... by both Americans and English.*

(ii) *Jews are believed to be shrewd, mercenary, industrious, intelligent ...*

(H. J. Eysenck)

In examples (29) - (38), I have taken the unusual step of examining not only certain movement rules in context, but also of looking at instances where the rule could by all accounts have applied, but did not. This allows us to see not only the pattern of emphasis which accompanies (to use a neutral term) a particular movement rule, but also the pattern which seems to go along with the non-application of that rule. Preliminary findings indicate clear distinctions between these phenomena, although there is obviously much room for further and more extensive research.

The examples in (29) show that the raised items (respectively: *this gentleman, it, the colour*) are all reduced (R): *this gentleman* is given in the situation, as an alternative way of referring to the signatory of the letter, i.e. it is a "semantic repetition", *it*, which is here pronominal rather than expletive, is therefore a previously-mentioned item (= *something to put in your mouth* ...); and *the colour* is given semantically, since it is superordinate to the previously-mentioned *red*, and constitutes an alternative reference.

The converse examples in (30) show that the non-raised items tend to be contrastive. Thus, in (30ai), though *stereotypes* is repeated, it forms part of a Complex NP containing contrastive material (*Spaniards, Turks or Russians ~ English and Americans*). The embedded predicate *would show much agreement*, however, is clearly repeated material, and therefore reduced. In (30aii), *the average Englishman* is contrastive since, although the concept has appeared before, it is in a different role: here, the Englishman is under discussion himself, where previously he has been the discussant. We might call this "reversed contrast" - it also occurs in sentences of the '*then* SHE *insulted* HIM' type. In this case, though, the embedded predicate contains focussed material. In (30b), although *factors* may in some sense be regarded as repeated (from '*x* produces *y*' or the like), *three* is contrastive in that the previous speaker suggests only *one* factor. The predicate of the embedded S, on the other hand, seems to repeat some of its preceding context in that it summarizes.

The other type of Subject Raising (Postal's B-raising) is exempli-

fied in (31). (31ai) has a raised item which may be contrastive or reduced: it may contrast with the other objects of English consideration
(*Germans, Italians* etc.) or it may be reduced in that it is a reflexive
pronoun and therefore repeated. We may note however that the complement
of the deleted *to be* contains material which is certainly focussed, and
may be contrastive (with the attributes of other nations mentioned before). (31aii) is, on the face of it, structurally identical with (31ai);
however, it is not contextually identical, precisely because its structure is a repetition. For this reason, it is more likely that the contrastive element in (31aii) is not *themselves*, but *Americans* (contrastive stress on *themselves* seems quite unnatural to me). *Themselves* is
presumably, then, reduced, as is *them* in (31aiii) which cannot be contrastive. The strings of adjectives are again certainly focussed and
possibly contrastive.

In (32ai), the unmoved subject *they* may be reduced, or with some
probability, contrastive (with *Mr. Douglas* in the following S). *Mr.Doug-
las* in (32aii) is certainly contrastive, however. *Good conscience and
good faith* in (32ai) is certainly focussed and possibly contrastive
(with *doubt/don't know how much truth*, by implication), whereas in (32a
ii) the same phrase is likely to be reduced. In (32b), the item *research*
is F or perhaps WF, while *proved* is F here; *the practice of warming up
an engine by allowing it to idle* is substantially a direct repetition,
and thus reduced; while *slowly* contrasts with *fairly fast*. *Harmful* is,
of course, focussed. In (32c), however, *Mr. Gordon Walker* is repeated
and reduced as is most of its predicate, except for the word *anything*
which is contrastive with the 'something said' implicit in *statement*.

The passive examples (33) all have reduced subjects (i.e. ex-ob-
jects) and focussed or contrastive predicates. In (33a), *they* is repeated and reduced, whereas *plagued with an endless succession of callers
and spongers* is new, focussed material. In (33bi), *lip drift* is repeated
(... *lips* ... *drift apart*), whereas most of the material from *remedied*
on is focussed. In (33bii), *pins* is repeated, and in this case the predicate verb *anchored* is too, in that it semantically shares structure
with 'push *x* through *y*' (presumably). However, the rest of this predi-

cate is contrastive with *teeth*. In (33c), *brush ... put to work* is semantically repeated (implied by *clearance ... presumably*), *pavements* is actually repeated, while *even now ... still* is contrastive (with *a month
ago*).

The examples (34), where the passive option has not been chosen, are
not in total accord. (34a) has a subject which is perhaps reduced (implied by the situation) and possibly contrastive (with *doctors*, perhaps);
the poultice, though, is repeated and reduced. (34b) has *the rich life*,
which sums up, and therefore semantically repeats, *champagne and ... posh
hotels*, but on the other hand contrasts with *a lot*, since it implies 'not
enough' in this context (though precisely *how* it does is difficult to
formulate). The final *it*, of course, being pronominal, is reduced here.
(34c), however, has the apparently weak topic subject *people*, normally
regarded as a prime conditioner of passivization since it normally appears to exert a drag-effect on its object NP, which in this case is repeated, but could be contrastive, since it occurs in a parallel structure. However, in truth, there seem to be two perfectly acceptable alternative readings for the sentence in question:

> (34) (c') ... people should *read poetry* ... just as they
>   read NOVELS ...
>   (c'') ... people should *read* POETRY ... just as they
>   read NOVELS ...

In both readings, *novels* is contrastive, but in (34c') *poetry* is focussed
(though in fact, in this context, reduced), whereas in (34''), it is contrastive. It will be noted, however, that *read* is focussed in both first
conjuncts, and then reduced, because repeated, in the second conjuncts.
I think it is possible to show that passivization (like the other movement rules we are examining) is very considerably conditioned by patterns of emphasis of the type I have described. This is not the occasion
to go into full details of this claim, but briefly, given a structure of
the form $S-V-O_1-(O_2)$, i.e. transitive or ditransitive, and all possible
permutations of R, F (including WF), and C, certain tentative generalizations about passivization may be formulated. Remember that the unmarked emphatic structure of a sentence is:

(40) (a) *Topic*   *Comment*

R.....................F

(b) *John* and *Bill came* to *see* me *yesterday.*

[They've] just *acquired* a *new car.*

R   F   F   F

However, as we've seen, the important thing about topics is not that
they display reduced stress, but that they are phoric, i.e. they repeat
or refer back to some element in the situational or verbal context. This
property is shared by R and C, but not by F and WF:

(c) *John* and *Bill came* to *see* me *yesterday.*

JOHN'S just *acquired* a *new car.*

C   F   F   F

(d) *John* and *Bill came* to *see* me *yesterday.*

Fred's just *acquired* a *new car.*

F   F   F   F

Notice that there is nothing actually unacceptable[35] about the discourse
(d), but that in order to be understood as a discourse, it must incorporate a deletion in the second sentence of the form *They said that...,*
which begins, note well, with a R.

If we look now at the emphatic status in passives of the shifted
object (direct or indirect) certain generalizations appear to be possible. An object element marked R or C is much more shiftable in general
than one marked F; this tendency is considerably enhanced when the subject is WF. In such cases, it seems clear a phoric element (R or C)
moves in order to restore the unmarked topic-comment structure of (40).
I referred to this earlier as a drag-effect. With C, moreover, I believe
we must also recognize a push-effect: a contrastive stress at the end
of a sentence may be insufficiently distinct from the ordinary (focussed)
nuclear stress normally occurring there. In order to make the contrast

[35]In fact, we are often talking about fairly subtle degrees of acceptability or probability in many of these cases, rather than anything
that could be represented as downright ungrammatical (though for some
discussion of the meaning of this term in relation to the contextu-
alization of sentences, see Werth 1976: 29 sqq.).

more distinctive, therefore, it may be shifted away from the final position.

These remarks imply the following predicitions:

(41)   (a) The most unstable active sentences, i.e. those most
           conducive to passivization will have the emphatic
           structure

$$\left\{ \begin{array}{c} WF \\ F \end{array} \right\} \cdots\cdots\cdots \left\{ \begin{array}{c} R \\ C \end{array} \right\}$$

       (b) The most stable active sentences, i.e. those least
           conducive to passivization, have the emphatic struc-
           ture

$$\left\{ \begin{array}{c} R \\ C \end{array} \right\} \cdots\cdots\cdots\cdots F$$

If we now return to the examples of (33) and (34), we may note that
these predictions are by and large supported. The emphatic structure of
the active sentences we may assume to underlie the passives of (33) all
bear out the predictions of (41a):

(33a)   An *endless succession* of *callers* and *spongers* has
              F   F   F   F
           plagued [them]
              F   R

(33bi)   One can *sometimes remedy* [lip drift] ...
           WF   F   F   R

(33bii)   One can *just* as *easily* [anchor] [the pins] in his
           WF   F   F   R   R
           A.F.F.D.R.
                C

(33c)   Somebody had STILL not [put a brush to work] on
           WF   C   R
           [the pavements] even NOW
                 R   C

Conversely, the emphatic structures of the active sentences indicated
in (34) tend to bear out the prediction of (41b):

(34a)   [Two slatternly nurses][36] had already *got* the
                   R   F

           [poultice] *ready*
                R   F

(34b)   The RICH LIFE *won't do* [it]
                   C   F   F   R

(34ci)   People should *read poetry* ...
           WF   F   F

(34cii)   ... just as [they] [read] NOVELS
                          R   R   C

Here, (34a) bears out (41b) exactly; the others are less precise (having either the predicted initial or final emphatic structure, but not both). In such cases, we may suppose, the passive is not particularly encouraged, though it *may* take place. This in turn suggests that perhaps passivization does not occur *unless* the conditions of (41a) are present. However, this is probably an overambitious claim. At any rate, to the predictions of (41a, b), we may add (c):

> (41)   (c) Intermediate types will be more or less conducive
>   to passivization:
>   more: WF ... F; less: $\left\{ {R \atop C} \right\}$ ... C, or F ... F

The *tough*-moved examples of (35) tend to agree in their emphatic structure. In every case, the shifted element is reduced (so that it restores the topic - otherwise realized by *it*, a non-phoric expletive

---

[36] It will have been noted that the whole NP has been marked as reduced here, even though it is only *nurses* that is implied by the situation, while *two* and *slatternly* cannot be. There seem to me to be two good reasons for this. Firstly, the rule of passivization is sensitive (in the way described above) to the emphatic status of the *subject*, and not of merely leftward elements; secondly, most adjectives in English are non-restrictive, i.e. they provide further information about their head of a non-crucial kind: they are usually therefore not strongly marked in stress. Restrictive adjectives (i.e. 'two nurses from the slatternly group, as opposed to the fastidious group') are usually contrastive. Even so, they are subordinate to the emphatic marking of the head, and what *this* suggests is, that emphasis-placement and passivization are ordered before relativization, whiz-deletion and adjective inversion.

form), and then pronominalized. Thus, in (35a), *they* is repeated and reduced, and pronominalized (and then deleted in the second conjunct),
while *easy* and *clean* contrast with *difficult* and *damage* respectively.
In (35b), *pork fillet* is repeated, reduced and pronominalized as *which*,
while the whole predicate *easy ... days* is focussed. In (35c), *that the
doctor holds disloyal, anti-British opinions* is repeated and pronominalized to *it, hard* is focussed, (though *thing* is presumably a WF, while
prove contrasts with *suspect* and *persuade*.

The unmoved examples of (36) on the other hand, though all arguably
repeated and reduced, are not however pronominalized. I can't see why
this fact should be significant, unless pronominalization represents a
further and distinct stage of reduction. Thus in (36ai) *quite easy* is
focussed, *lose* is focussed, but *pint* and *sweating* are both repeated and
reduced. In (36aii), *just* is probably contrastive, easy is reduced, and
pint is reduced, but *put ... back* is contrastive (with *lose*). In (36b),
it might be argued that all the lexical items are new and similarly
speed and distance might be said to be implied in some way by *overtake*.
(36c) is also rather hard to characterize:[37] *easy* might well be contrastive here (since *difficult* is evidently expected), *face* is focussed,
but that kind of fact is presumably semantically repeated here (since it
refers to *the coming vacancy*, shortly to be created by the Master's own
impending death).

The examples of cleft and pseudo-cleft in (37) show clearly that
clefts require the shifted element to be contrastive, while for pseudo-
clefts, it may be either focussed or contrastive. Thus, in (37a) *patients,*
despite several repetitions, is contrastive with *nurses*: the implication
is that it is contrary to expectation. The whole predicate is new information and consequently focussed. (37b), a pseudo-cleft, contrasts *less*
(*thoroughly examined*) with *much* (*discussed*). Focussed items are *tendency*
and *avant-garde*, while *Pop* is reduced (straight repetition), as is *take
what it needed* (semantic repetition of *what it borrows*). In (37c), the

---

[37]Notice that this example of Tough-movement, in my own text, has the
shifted element contrastive, as is thè word *also*. *Hard* though is reduced, as is *characterize*.

shifted item is *Mr. Patrick Gordon Walker* ..., which contrasts with *Mr. Healey*, while the predicate of the sentence focusses *transformed* and *real political significance* (though the latter could well be contrastive with *passed off with nothing worse*), while *the Cambridge incident* is reduced, and *something* is a WF. (37d) incorporates a complex contrast in the shifted element:

C   R   C

not the [colour of their faces], but their numbers.

Dislike semantically repeats parts of *rejection* and *prejudice*. (37e), another pseudo-cleft, shifts the conjoined predicates *sickens and disgusts me* which are certainly focussed, and in addition *me* is probably contrastive (with ... *he (will be much disturbed...)*). The predicative *that S* (originally the subject) is mostly focussed.

Examples where cleft or pseudo-cleft could have taken place, but did not, as in (38), show that if an element is reduced, either by repetition or implication, it cannot be clefted or pseudo-clefted. In these cases, those transformations would result in actually ungrammatical sequences (or as near as discourse-grammar gets to ungrammatical - "uncontextualizable" is more accurate, if less euphonious). So, in (38a), *champagne and posh hotels* is reduced by implication from *fancy living*. The only likely contrastive element is *keep* (by some sort of implied denial of *give*, in "the champagne etc. you're trying to give me"), and this is not available for clefting and can only be pseudo-clefted with accompanying pro-forms: *What you can do with your champagne and posh hotels is keep them*, (though ... *shove them up your arse* is perhaps more natural). In (38b), as we've already seen in (34a), *two slatternly nurses* is reduced by implication, and *poultice* is reduced by repetition. Neither is therefore available for clefting or pseudo-clefting in this context. In (38a), the situation is not so absolute, since *origin* could be contrastive (with the implied 'FACT *of the name of the tower*'). Otherwise, though *name of the tower* is repeated, *origin* will be focussed. In this case, it will not be available for clefting, but will be for pseudo-clefting.

Before proceeding on to the combined shifts, let us summarize the conclusion reached so far, with regard to the relationship between move-

ment rules and emphasis. The relevant emphatic structure for each rule
and "non-rule" is schematized below:

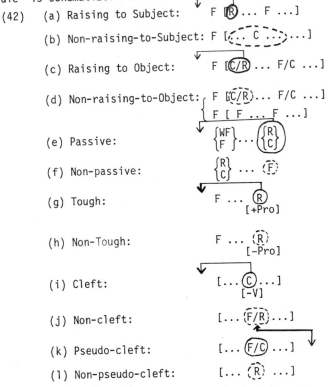

 (42) (a) Raising to Subject: F [R ... F ...]

    (b) Non-raising-to-Subject: F [... C ...) ...]

    (c) Raising to Object: F [C/R ... F/C ...]

    (d) Non-raising-to-Object: F [C/R)... F/C ...]
              F [F ... F ...]

    (e) Passive: {WF / F} ... {R / C}

    (f) Non-passive: {R / C} ... (F)

    (g) Tough: F ... R [+Pro]

    (h) Non-Tough: F ... (R) [-Pro]

    (i) Cleft: [... C ...] [-V]

    (j) Non-cleft: [... (F/R) ...]

    (k) Pseudo-cleft: [... (F/C ...]

    (l) Non-pseudo-cleft: [... (R) ...]

Scrutiny of the majority of these items enables us to advance the
following hypothesis:

 (43) *Word-ordering hypothesis*

    Elements undergo movement in order to restore the
    emphatic structure of topic-comment, i.e. {R / C} ... F.

(43) then applies to (42a), (42e), (42g) and (42i), since in each of
these cases an element marked R or C is moved leftwards of an element
marked F or WF. (42k) partly follows the same principle in that it ends
up with a stressed (F or C) item to the right, apparently. However, as
I have shown in Werth (forthcoming), there are good reasons for regard-

ing Pseudo-Cleft as a left-moving rule (moving the rest of the original
structure - necessarily R - to the left, leaving the F or C element be-
hind at the right-hand end, isolated and delayed for extra emphasis). By
this description, pseudo-cleft also fits in with hypothesis (43). This
only leaves (42c) outside God's ordinance, and in particular, as the
astute reader will have already noted, there is a non-raised emphatic
structure identical to the raised one. There are, I think, several reasons for this. Firstly, insofar as the topic-comment deployment is only
weakly requisite, violations of it are only weakly dubious. Secondly,
Raising to Object is more a tree-reorganization rule than a movement
rule. Perceptually, that is to say, the non-finitization of the subordinate predicate is probably more prominent than the movement of the
subject around the complementizer *that*, which is necessarily deleted
here, and often deleted in any case. Thirdly, of course, this rule does
not move into *leftmost* position, so that in fact topic-comment structure remains unaffected by it. For these reasons, therefore, it is difficult to argue that Raising to Object is a discourse-conditioned rule
at all. The remainder, however, appear to be governed - at least weakly - by hypothesis (43).

7.   THE POSITION OF EMPHASIS-PLACEMENT

Where does all this lead our earlier discussion on the place
of linearity in a grammar? If we can in fact argue that those movement
rules which move an element to the leftmost position in the sentence
are governed by the emphatic structure of the underlying tree, which is
in turn dictated by the arrangements of the discourse, then it ought to
be the case that the placement of emphasis could shed some light on the
question of linearity.

Prima facie, it appears that emphasis-placement must precede the
movement-rules specified, since otherwise it cannot act to motivate
them. It might still be argued, of course, that although emphasis-*placement* precedes these rules, the actual movement *transformations* (whose
very application necessarily presupposes ordering) may occur later (taking as a model for this sort of arrangement, the treatment of Q, Imp,

etc. in the *Aspects* grammar). This will not do, of course, because most
of the rules in question (and perhaps all) are *cyclic*, and any movement
which takes place at all must take place in the cycle.[38] If such movement is indeed affected (not to say effected) by emphatic structure,
then emphasis-placement from discourse is at least cyclic, and probably
*pre*cyclic. There is actually independent evidence for this latter position, from so-called anaphoric islands. It was noticed by Postal (1969)
that despite a great deal of evidence for prelexical transformations,
lexical items on the whole blocked the anaphoric processes from applying to their internal structure once lexicalization had occurred. Thus,
although the "non-lexicalized" (44a) is good, the lexicalized (44b) is
not:

> (44) (a) The girl with blond hair$_i$ caught it$_i$ in the fan.
>
>   (b) *The blonde$_i$ caught it$_i$ in the fan.[39]

[38] This does not actually appear to be necessarily true in Relational
Grammar, since the equivalent rules in the cycle will by and large
simply change grammatical relations in the appropriate way, with
the actual *movement* (or its equivalent) being handled by later
linearization rules. This could not work, of course, with those
movement rules which are not relation-changing rules, e.g. WH-movement.

[39] Any obscene meaning ascribable to (44b), however, might be taken as
counterevidence to the anaphoric island proposal, since coreference
would presumably occur with a subtree of the prelexical structure
of *girl*. Obscene meanings often seem to operate outside the rules,
however (cf. Tic Douleureux 1971).
The transformationalist rule for Pronominalization is of the form:

$$\text{SD: } X - NP_i - Y - NP_i - Z, \text{ where Y includes } S_n^1 \text{ (i.e. at least}$$
$$\phantom{\text{SD: }} 1 \quad 2 \quad 3 \quad 4 \quad 5 \qquad\qquad\qquad\qquad \text{one S - 'a mi-}$$
$$ \text{nimally complex}$$
$$\text{SC: } 12345 \qquad 1234+ \text{ [+PRO]}5 \qquad\qquad\qquad S')$$

The lower bound of the SD is a minimally-complex S; the upper bound
is infinite, though like relative-clause embedding, subject to
performance restrictions. The SC may furthermore be conditioned by the
precede-and-command constraint (restraining backwards pronominalization), unless Hankamer's unpublished suggestion (quoted by Higgins
1976: 219) that backwards pronominalization is discourse-conditioned
(cf. section 4 above) is correct.

Pronominalization is only one manifestation of anaphora, and a complex type at that. Underlying the process of pronominalization is the process of reduction; since they are normally phoric, pronouns may also be contrastive (by a separate process), but never focussed. The further semantic operations which actually bring about the process of pronominalization, however, have never, to my knowledge, adequately been catalogued. (I am referring to the processes of progressive semantic deletion). But evidence for anaphoric island status based exclusively on pronominal coreference is bound to be incomplete. If we extend the evidence to *contrastive* elements, we can see that it is in fact possible to build bridges between anaphoric islands:

(45) (a) *John married* a *blonde*. MY [wife] has DARK [hair].

*MY *wife* has *dark hair*.

(b) *John's* an **organist* . MY [parents] are still ALIVE.
           orphan

(c) *Melvyn's* an old **bugger*   *I* went to ETON.
               Harrovian · It was ETON *I* went
                                          to.

(d) *Elspeth* is a *Mancunian*. However, she was brought UP
    in GLASGOW./ It was GLASGOW she was brought UP in.

(e) *Elspeth* is a *lesbian*. *However, she was brought UP
    in GLASGOW./ *It was GLASGOW she was brought UP in.

(f) *Rodney strangled* his *guard*. I subsequently
    [killed] MINE with a KNIFE.
    KNIFED MINE.

(g) *Rodney kissed* his *guard*. I subsequently
    *[killed] MINE with a KNIFE.
    KNIFED MINE.

(h) *Jethro* ISN'T a *malingerer*. He really IS [ill]
                                                 *[tall].

These examples provide evidence for lexical decomposition (a) because the pattern of reduction and contrast with lexicalized structures is identical with the pattern for non-lexicalized structures, and can only be described explicitly by reference to them; and (b) because otherwise no explanation could be found for the ungrammaticality of the starred

parts of (45b), (c), (e) and (h). Furthermore, and relevant to our present purpose, (45) shows that R, F and C must be allocated from discourse
prelexically,[40] since the stress-pattern on subsequent sentences in the
discourse is identical with that which would follow the unlexicalized (or
"less lexicalized") equivalents:

(45) (a') *John* <*took* as *wife*> a <[girl] with *blond hair*>
            MY [wife] has DARK [hair].

      (b') *John* is <one such that his *parents* are   *dead.*

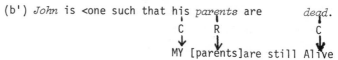

            MY [parents]are still ALIVE

Note that only the lexically decomposed versions offer the correct emphatic environments for subsequent discourse.

8.   IMPLICATIONS FOR CURRENT MODELS OF GRAMMAR

        The status of lexical items, and the point or points at which
lexicalization takes place, have, of course, been hotly-debated issues
in recent linguistics. In ST, and as far as I can tell, EST, proof that
any process is prelexical is equivalent to proving that it takes place
in the base. In a fairly recent paper, Chomsky (1976b: 336) provided the
following schematic representation of his EST model:

(46)
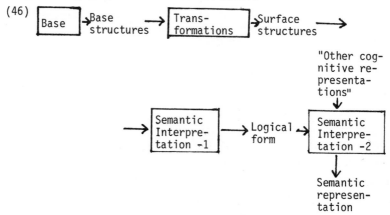

Of particular interest to the present paper is the content of SI -2,

[40]This means, of course, that the informal rules for emphasis-placement, given
above as (28), are incorrect, since they mark lexical items. A more accurate,
and in fact mor interestingly constrained and predictive, set of rules will
mark emphasis on *predicates* in underlying semantic subtrees. See Werth (forthcoming) for more detailed discussion.

which Chomsky describes as rules associating the logical form (LF) along
with "other cognitive representations" with "fuller representations of
meaning". The rules of SI -2 are in general not rules of sentence-grammar, Chomsky states, and they include rules of anaphora (p. 324), including the rule interpreting *the others* in such sentences as:

   (47)   (a) Each of the men likes the others.
          (b) Each of the men wants John to like the others.
          (c) Each of the men seems to John to like the others.
          (d) Each of the women likes some of the books;
              each of the men likes the others.   (pp. 322 sqq.)

Chomsky takes (47d) as demonstrating the discourse nature of the *others*
rule, since he claims that *others* here must refer to *books*. This is
clearly one - and probably the commonest - interpretation; but the sequence may also be understood as comparing what the two gender groups
like: the women, some of the books, and the men, each other. In this latter interpretation, as my gapped representation shows, the reciprocal
rule may apply without changing meaning. And, as (47e, f) show, even the
apparent interpretation bias of (47d) may be neutralized, or reversed to
embrace only the reciprocal sense:

   (47)   (e) Each of the women likes some of the men;
              each of the men likes the others.
          (f) Each of the women likes all of the men;
              each of the men likes the others.

Others requires some preceding reference to a proper subset X' of some
contextually-defined set X; *others* then refers to that proper subset
which is the complementary of X', call it ~X', so that X' + ~X' = X. In
(47e), X' could be either *some of the men* or each of the men; the reference of *others* is therefore ambiguous (as it is in (47d): the preference
for *some of the books* is purely a matter of pragmatics). In (47f), X'
could only be *each of the men*, since *all of the men* cannot be a proper
subset of the *men*. (*Some* simply denotes a proper subset, while *each* denotes all possible proper subsets of just one member (where X $\geq$ 2),
selected distributively across the set). *Others* is clearly anaphoric,
then, and like all anaphors may be intra- or extrasentential. The ques-

tion remains, though, is Chomsky correct in placing such rules in SI -2 simply because their domain may be extrasentential? The model (46) which Chomsky is aiming for is a surface-structure interpretation model exclusively (unlike earlier versions of EST). In this model, pronouns and other anaphors are generated *in situ* and then interpreted by rules of construal, regulated by various filters. In most cases, it seems quite clear that these are simply mirror-images of generative semantic mapping rules regulated by global constraints. Chomsky's SI -2 is then equivalent to Lakoff's transderivational constraints. Would it be *lèse majesté* to suggest that this version of EST is a mere notational variant of GS? In fact, the suggestion is probably inaccurate, since the questions of lexical insertion and use of "trace" still remain, (though the latter has been specially concocted to solve problems which arise solely from the form of the EST model, and which in GS (or in ST, for that matter) are not problematic at all).

Both SI -2 and transderivational constraints, I would argue, are piecemeal attempts to incorporate some discourse-processes into sentence-grammar. By placing SI -2 where he does, Chomsky is claiming that such processes affect the final semantic representation, but not the logical form or syntactic structure. I have given grounds for believing that the processes of emphasis placement which are motivated by anaphora and related conditions actually underlie and are influential upon some of the rules of the syntactic cycle, and also must precede at least some lexical insertion. If this is the case, then the rules for pronoun and *others* interpretation in the Chomsky model have three distinct stages:

 (i) pronoun and *others* generation   (Base)

 (ii) emphasis-placement   (Base or pre-cycle)[41]

[41] Chomsky (1976b: 344) has a rule of FOCUS in SI -1 (i.e. contributing to the logical form of the derived interpretation). It is a construal rule whose function is to extract that x which is under discussion, e.g. assigning to

 (i) Bill likes JOHN
 (ii) BILL likes John

the logical forms:

 (i') the x such that Bill likes x - is John;
 (ii') the x such that x likes John - is Bill.

(iii) surface-structure interpretation   (Surface-structure,
post-SI -1)

(ii), of course, does not form part of the Chomsky canon, but as I have
shown, its existence and effect have to be accounted for in any model.

If I have succeeded in my aim of tying emphasis-placement in with
the syntactic rules of the cycle, and given that it is dependent upon
anaphora, then rules of anaphoric interpretation clearly cannot follow
even shallow structure, let alone surface structure or logical form (in
EST). Since certain transformational rules are dependent upon R, F or C,
and underlying R, F and C is anaphora (or its absence), then the representation of anaphora must be deeper than the representation of those
rules. In the paper referred to, Chomsky does not dwell upon the content
of SI -2, except to imply strongly (pp. 323, 336) that it includes dis-
course-related rules, but not the rules of sentence-grammar. He therefore
apparently distinguishes, for instance, between two quite distinct sets
of rules for interpreting anaphora - within sentences (SI -1), and between sentences (SI -2). This is clearly a consequence of the artificial
restriction of the domain of grammar to the sentence. Chomsky's model
cannot handle the interaction between emphasis and either movement-rules
or lexicalization. Furthermore, it must regard emphasis as an unpredictable and adventitious phenomenon, occurring randomly somehow to trigger
off such SI -1 rules as FOCUS, but otherwise assigned by the phonological
component automatically.

The Generative Semantic model, as it has been extensively specified
in the work of J. D. McCawley, G. Lakoff, P. A- M. Seuren etc., is normally, like EST, a sentence-grammar, although it may easily be adapted
for the domain of discourse (cf. Van Dijk 1972, 1977). The evidence for
emphasis-placement which has been presented in the foregoing allows us to
place the rule in the cycle, at least, but since lexicalization in the
GS model is said to take place at various points among the transformations, we can produce no clear knock-down argument for emphasis-placement being prelexical.

However, if Newmeyer 1976[41] is correct, the rule of Predicate-

---

[41] Newmeyer's argument is an interesting and ingenious one, depending in

Raising (upon which lexicalization is founded in GS) is precyclic. This, if true, would be a bitter blow indeed to the Generative Semanticists, though Newmeyer argues that it merely allows a rapprochement between the transformationalist and lexicalist camps. From our point of view, however, it would locate lexicalization (and hence emphasis-placement)

part on the non-existence of lexical items "containing" applications of such cyclic rules as *There*-insertion, *Tough* and Passive. If Predicate-raising were cyclic, his argument goes, then the apparent lack of interaction between it and these rules would have to be explained by separate and *ad hoc* conditions. But if Predicate-raising were *precyclic*, its application would destroy the environment for the other rules, thereby blocking them naturally. However, the processes of lexicalization are in general so poorly understood that the non-appearance of a lexical item cannot be taken as hard-and-fast evidence for any supposition. Furthermore, it seems to me that such lexical items are for the most part in principle quite possible, and some may even exist, e.g.:

(a) (i) PASSIVE + $\begin{smallmatrix}\text{RAISING TO}\\\text{OBJECT}\end{smallmatrix}$ [[CAUSE] [BE MADE]] $\overset{\text{PR}}{\Rightarrow}$ *to commission*
                                                              (a painting etc.)

(ii)   [[CAUSE] [BE SEEN]] ⇒ *to reveal*
                        (cf.[[CAUSE] [SEE]]   ⇒ *to show*)

Newmeyer's examples with *Tough* seem to me to be not quite so clearly impossible as he claims, since they seem to have some sort of relationship with Nominalized predicates (e.g. *facilitate delivery/discussion/admission* etc., where *facilitate* = [[CAUSE] [(MORE) EASY]]). I suspect that there is an action predicate in there as well, viz. [DO], and the removal of this from *deliver*, *discuss* etc. triggers off Nominalization. Evidence for this is provided by the non-existence of non-nominalized action predicates after *Tough*, Raising to Object and PR, and perhaps more significantly, the complete disappearance of *do* itself:

(b) (i) S_0[The instructions caused that S_1[it be (more) easy for me S_2[I do the assignment]]] ⇒ TOUGH,
                                                          RAISING TO OBJECT
     (ii) The instructions caused the assignment to be more easy for me to do.
     (iii) [[CAUSE] [(MORE) EASY [DO]]] ⇒ *facilitate*
     (iv) The instructions facilitated the assignment for me (*to do).

Furthermore, DeRijk (1974) shows that PR must follow Raising to Object (though assuming that the raised predicate must be initial in its S_1 an assumption also made by McCawley, though solved by stipulating a general predicate-first order). Finally, lexical items such as *suicide*, *self-service*, *autobiography* and perhaps *masturbate* would seem to require the prior application of the Reflexivization rule.

firmly among the precyclic rules in GS.

If this is the case, then it is difficult to see how the recent EST model advocated by Chomsky ((46) above) could possibly handle facts of emphasis-placement and its effects. (46) caters for discourse-information insofar as SI -2 contains (at least programmatically) such data. However, if the data from focus, contrast and reduction do turn out to be intimately tied up with the functioning of cyclic rules then textuality is not a peripheral aspect of sociolinguistic performance, but a central aspect of linguistic competence.

This is not the occasion to argue in detail for one text model rather than another, but in general terms, the sort of model suggested by the foregoing facts is one in which the constituent propositions (Ps) in a text are generated in series:

(48)   Text
       component $\rightarrow P_1$ & P_2 & ... & P_n

The connective '&' is rewritten into one of the logical or pragmatic connectives Λ, V, $\supset$, $\equiv$, $\rightarrow$, etc., and there is a condition on the sequence of P's thus connected that their elements (i.e. Predicates and Arguments: the semantic structure of each P) be emphatically structured under the conditions of (28a) (i), (ii) and (iii), i.e. by reference to the semantic structure of the preceding P's in the text.[43] This condition bears affinities with, and indeed is essentially a descendant of Van Dijk's (1972) global coherence constraint. I have tried to show, however, that the effects of coherence are farther-reaching than a mere condition of textuality. Further questions do, of course, arise: assuming that each P in (48) is expanded by PS-type rules or dependency-rules etc., and then transformations, derivational constraints, relation-changing rules or the like, is each P taken to the surface or to some intermediate point before

---

[43]The essential nature of a text, therefore, — as here presented — is a Markov series (cf. Brainerd 1976). Discontinuous texts, however, are perfectly possible, particularly in conversational discourse. Moreover, further structuring of texts, between the level of the initial state and that of P is often postulated, particularly in narrative and other literary forms (cf. Reid et al. (1968), for example). It might be, though, that in spontaneous discourse, any further structuring is determined by the subject-matter.

the ensuing P is dealt with, or are they somehow expanded simultaneously? In other words, is there any evidence that the coherency-relation-
ship between Ps is necessarily at the level of phonetic realization,
surface, shallow, deep or semantic structure? Are there different levels
of coherence?[44] These are substantive and empirical questions which I
leave for later research.

9.   CONCLUSION: IMPLICATIONS FOR LINEAR ORDER

For each sentence in a discourse, therefore, the final word-
order depends on the nature of the text in which it is embedded, and
specifically, upon the deployment of emphasis (focus, reduction and contrast) in the preceding text. Conversely, different word-orders representing the same propositional content are seen as occurring within different texts, displaying different emphatic structure. This predicts that
in so-called "free-word-order" languages, such as Sanskrit, the different-
ly-ordered renderings of the same propositional content will be associated with different texts.[45] In more "fixed" word-order languages (i.e.
those in which grammatical relations are not signalled by inflection),
we would expect these differences to become "grammaticalized" into established constructions (Cleft, Passive etc.).

To sum up, then, given the Topic-Comment Articulation, (for English,
but there also seems to be ample evidence for this as a linguistic universal, cf. the papers in Li (1976)), emphatic structure is linearized
to conform with it. Serial order is established at a very early stage in
the transformational component (by the arguments adduced for the placement of emphasis from the discourse). Since the grammar must deal with

[44]For instance, it may be that certain stylistic devices affecting word-
   order (such as parallelism, chiasmus etc.) may be 'low-level' reordering rules, not affecting the cycle at all, and not, note well, conditioned by emphatic structure (though they might carry emphatic effect).

[45]N. C. Collinge assures me that this is indeed the case in Sanskrit.
   The remarks made about Latin and German in section 2 would seem to
   bear this out too.

ordered trees from such an early point, there is presumably no particular advantage in assuming that the rules of the base should be unordered, with a very early transformational rule ordering trees. Furthermore, there appear to be no early transformational rules absolutely *requiring* un-ordered trees. I conclude, then, that the slight (and arguable) loss of economy engendered by stipulating order in the base is more than balanced by the advantage of dealing with the same kind of tree throughout.

ACCOUNTING FOR YIDDISH WORD ORDER
OR
WHAT'S A NICE NP LIKE YOU
DOING IN A PLACE LIKE THIS?

BEATRICE L. HALL

1. INTRODUCTION

Yiddish[1] is a continental West Germanic language which shares a common origin with Modern Standard German and to some degree is mutually intelligible with it. Yiddish is, however, clearly a separate language from German on both social and historical grounds and on purely grammatical ones: it has its own grammatical norms and its own supra-dialectal standard.

---

[1] The variety of Yiddish reported on here is, essentially, that of my own Yiddish speech as influenced by Literary Yiddish -- the classic Yiddish authors of the late 19th and early 20th Centuries, and the contemporary Yiddish daily press. I am myself a Yiddish-English bilingual. I was born and raised in the New York area, but my Yiddish speech reflects the dialect of my parents, both of whom came from White Russia. The orthographic representation which I have used is systematic phonetic -- in essence a transliteration of Literary Yiddish orthography representing no surface sandhi phenomena and ignoring silent aleph. Hebrew words have been treated as if written in Yiddish and hence completely spelled out. The symbols I have chosen throughout have their IPA values, except that all vowels are lower and laxer than their cardinal equivalents.
I am grateful to Martin Pam for suggesting the subtitle for this paper and for many hours of discussion of the problems involved in comparative and theoretical word order studies.

I have chosen to explore the facts of Yiddish word order in depth
here both because they are inherently interesting and have received very
little attention from modern grammarians and because of the light which
data from Yiddish may cast on the history of the syntactic development
of the other West Germanic languages.

Yiddish sentences in their surface structure show a somewhat greater freedom of the order of constituents than is found in Standard German. Someone approaching Yiddish without a realization of what its
total word order pattern is might be led to conclude that word order
in Yiddish is almost as free as that found in Latin, Greek, or Biblical Hebrew and that almost any constituent may occur almost anywhere
at the whim of the speaker.

As a matter of fact, any given Yiddish surface word order is the
result of a complex series of rule interactions and rule options, exercised or not. If at any point the wrong series of rule options in constituent movement and in stress and intonation contour assignment is
chosen, then the result will be either an ungrammatical sentence or an
infelicitous one. I have undertaken this study of the system of interaction of the syntactic options of Yiddish in the belief that an examination of the constraints on constituent movement in one apparently free
word order language for which informed native speaker intuitions are
available may be useful in helping linguists understand the general
nature of other languages which, like Yiddish, exhibit several possible
linear orderings of sentence constituents.

2.   THE SIMPLE SENTENCE AND THE EXTRAPOSITION OF NP'S TO THE RIGHT

The basic facts of Yiddish syntax are much the same as the
corresponding facts of other West Germanic languages. In simple, present tense S's, the surface word order is SVO:

1.   Avrom zet Soren.[2]   Abraham sees Sarah.
2.   Sore zet Avromen.   Sarah sees Abraham.
3.   Avrom git Soren a matone yedn šabes.
      Abraham gives Sarah a present every Saturday.

---

[2] Personal names and some relationship terms are marked by the oblique
case marker -n.

Unlike the other West Germanic languages, Yiddish has lost the simple past tense of all verbs, even *zayn* 'to be' and *hobn* 'to have'. The periphrastic past tense is constructed identically with that of German, *hobn* being used as the Aux with transitive verbs and *zayn* with strong intransitives.

4.   Avrom hot Soren a matone nextn gegebn.
      Abraham gave Sarah a present yesterday.

5.   Avrom iz in Kasrilovke geven.
      Abraham was in Kasrilovke.

However, we can already see here a significant difference between Yiddish and German in that Sentences (4) and (5) can also be:

4a)   Avrom hot Soren nextn gegebn a matone.

  b)   Avrom hot a matone nextn gegebn Soren.

  c)   Avrom hot Soren a matone gegebn nextn.

  d)   Avrom hot gegebn Soren a matone nextn.

5a)   Avrom iz geven in Kasrilovke.

If the objects are pronominalized, they must occur to the left of the main verb:

6a)   Avrom hot es ir dan gegebn. Abraham gave it to her then.

  b)   *Avrom hot Soren dan gegebn es.

  c)   *Avrom hot a matone dan gegebn ir.

  d)   *Avrom hot gegebn es ir dan.

  e)   *Avrom hot gegebn ir es dan.

  f)   * Avrom hot es ir gegebn dan.

  g)   ?Avrom iz geven dortn.

There are several points which are worth noting about these structures. The first, a minor one, is that here Yiddish shares with German the obligatory switch of order as between pronominalized and non-pronominalized direct and indirect object NP's. One might say that the order indirect object - direct object which is found when both objects are full NP's is the underlying one and that the act of pronominalization interchanges the order. One might also say that the true underlying order is that found when both objects are pronouns and that Yiddish has a rule similar to the rule of Indirect Object Movement of English

which is blocked if the NP's are pronouns and if the indirect object
receives contrastive stress. That is, one can say:

7.   Ix hob dos bux *Avromen* gegebn.   I gave Abraham the book.
if *Avrom* receives contrastive stress. In this case *Avrom* is in some
sense highlighted and the implication is that the NP is being compared
or contrasted with another.

While either of these underlying orders is possible, there do not
seem to me to be any compelling reasons for selecting one in preference
to the other. Whichever order is selected as underlying, the selection
is arbitrary and one has to postulate an ad-hoc rule nowhere else needed
in the grammar to account for the other order.

The major point to be noted about sentences (4) through (7) is that
the unmarked word order is

8.   Subject-Aux-IO-DO-Adverbial-Verb.

All other word orders are to some extent marked. What I mean by 'marked'
in this context is simply that certain variants of word order can only
felicitously be followed by some conjuncts and not others. Thus:

9.   Avrom hot Soren nextn gegebn a bux ...
      Abraham gave Sarah a book yesterday ...

can be followed by

10a) ... un haynt a kuš   ... and today a kiss,

but not by

10b) (!)... ober leyenen, hot er es aleyn geleyent.
     ... but as for reading, he read it himself.

(Note: The symbol (!) indicates a well-formed structure which is used
infelicitously in a given context.)

So too, each of the other variants in (4) through (7) has a possible
felicitous context which has called forth the transformation which put
the given NP in a highlighted or marked position. The only really
neutral, unmarked order is that in (8). The variant orders are all
achieved by extraposition. One major way, then, in which the grammar
of Yiddish differs from that of German is that Yiddish, but not Modern

Standard German, freely permits full NP's and adverbials to be extraposed to the right of a verb in final position. Any other analysis seems
to me to be untenable; to argue that the NP's are generated after the
V and moved leftward would be to ignore the unmarked nature of preverbal position, and the marked nature of postverbal position.

Aside from the internal switch in order of the direct and indirect
objects with pronominalization, we have here the significant fact that
the unmarked order for full NP's is also the only possible order for
pronouns.

In the sentences above I have shown extraposition to the right with
simple NP's. In these cases, as I have stated, the application of the
rule is completely optional on the sentence level; rightward extraposition is an option which can be exercised to bind a sentence more
closely rhetorically to the one which is going to follow it. Moreover,
if the option to extrapose is not exercised, an infelicitous sentence
never results. There is, however, one case where the rule of rightward
extraposition becomes variably obligatory -- this is in the case of
so-called 'heavy' NP's, that is, expanded NP's which have either one
or more adjectives or relative clauses associated with them. The exact
nature of this condition is hard to state since it varies from speaker
to speaker. One variable is the amount of exposure of a given speaker
to German, his degree of 'dayčmeriškayt'; the greater this is, the
heavier the non-extraposed NP he will tolerate. For my own taste and
stylistic feeling

11.   Ix hob dem alten man gezen.
      I saw the old man.

is quite within the realm of acceptability;

12.   Ix hob dem alten man mit dem bord gezen.
      I saw the old man with the beard.

is still fine unextraposed, although extraposition without contrastive stress is also a viable syntactic option.[3]

Since the condition on Heavy NP Extraposition is a stylistic
variable it is difficult to find unequivocal cases where extraposition
must occur. Nontheless, I believe that most speakers would find a sentence such as

13.   ??   *Ix hob dem alten man mit dem langen bord vos hot

                 mit mayn korev Berelen gearbet gezen.
                 I saw the old man with the long beard who worked
                 with my relative Berele.

unacceptable if not extraposed. One factor, certainly, is not merely
length: in Sentence (13) what makes extraposition virtually mandatory
is the fact that the NP ends in a verb. Thus

13a.   Ix hob dem alten man mit dem langen bord vos arbet mit

           mayn korev Berelen gezen

is much more acceptable unextraposed.

3.   EMBEDDED SENTENCES AND THE COMPLEMENTATION CYCLE

       The form of Yiddish sentences with the auxiliary verbs *hobn*
'have' and *zayn* 'be' is essentially like that of the corresponding German sentences. The unmarked order is:

14.   Subject - Aux - (NP) - (NP) - (Adv) - Verb$_{\text{past participle}}$

This order is also found when the Aux is a modal verb such as *veln*[4]

---

[3] It should be noted that in my own idiolect
                 Ix hob gezen Avromen.   I saw Abraham
sound odd without contrastive stress on *Avrom*. The rule, which may
just be my personal one, seems to be that, with a 'light' NP, extraposition is possible only if some other element occurs between the
Aux and the verb, e.g.
                 Ix hob nextn gezen Avromen.   I saw Abraham yesterday
is perfectly acceptable, although *Avrom* does not receive contrastive
stress.

[4] *Veln*, which is historically a conflation of *viln* 'to want' and *vern*
'to become', is today a defective verb which has no function other
than to mark the future. The rules in Yiddish for when the future
must obligatorily be marked are complex and beyond the scope of this
study. Suffice it to say that in Yiddish the future is more often
morphologically marked than in German.

'future auxiliary', *viln* 'to want', *muzn* 'must', *kenen* 'can', *darfn* 'have to', *megn* 'may', *toren* 'to dare', *zoln* 'shall', *flegn* 'used to'; or an aspectual verb such as *onfangn* 'to begin', *oyfhern* 'to stop', *haltn in* 'to continue'. What modals and aspectuals share in common is that the verb which they command is always an infinitive; NP objects can be extraposed over the infinitive in the same way as I outlined above for past participles. Thus we may have

15a. Ix vil dem altn man zen.

b.   Ix vil zen dem altn man.

I want to see the old man.

16a. Der beker fangt on di šabesdike xales donerštik opbakn.

b.   Der beker fangt on donerštik opbakn di šabesdike xales.

The baker begins to bake the Sabbath bread on Thursday.

Yiddish, like German, but unlike English, does not allow the infinitive in a complement sentence except when there is Equi-NP Deletion:

17. Ix vil geyn.   I want to go.

18. Er vil az ix zol geyn.

He wants me to go. (Lit.: He wants that I should go.[5])

19. Er hot faynt rusiš študiren.

He dislikes studying Russian.

20. Er hot faynt az ix študir rusiš.

He dislikes my studying Russian.

21. Er hot faynt vos ix študir rusiš.

He dislikes the fact that I study Russian.

22. Ix veys az er iz ⎰gegangn kayn Xelm ⎱
                       ⎱kayn Xelm gegangn.⎰

I know that he went to Chelm.

As sentences (18), (20), and (21) show, a major difference between Yiddish and German is that in Yiddish tensed verbs in embedded clauses do not move to clause-final position. Such movement would result in ungrammatical sentences:

---

[5] Yiddish, having lost all trace of the subjunctive, requires *zoln* to indicate the modality implicit here. Compare the Modern English equivalence of

I insisted that he go.

and

I insisted that he should go.

18a.   * Ix vil az er geyn zol.

20a.   * Er hot faynt az ix rusiš študir.

21a.   * Er hot faynt vos ix rusiš študir.

22a.   * Ix veys az er kayn Xelm gegangn iz.

These then, in their barest outlines, are the facts of complementation in Yiddish. The question now is, the nature of the rules which most
economically and naturally account for these structures. Specifically,
what underlying word order and what transformations should be postulated for Yiddish.

What is immediately obvious is that the device of using an SOV
underlying word order which has been proposed many times for German is
completely unjustified for Yiddish. In Yiddish there are *no* sentences
in which the word order is S O V$_{[+ tensed]}$, either as a main clause or an
embedded one.[6] It might be argued that nevertheless Yiddish is under-
lyingly SOV, but has lost the surface possibility of exhibiting SOV word
order with finite verbs; this would be, for example, Ross's argument
based on his Penthouse Principle (Ross, 1973). I have argued elsewhere
(Hall and Hall, 1978) that the consequences which Ross has claimed
follow from the Penthouse Principle are invalid on both logical and empirical grounds. Suffice it to say here that an SOV underlying order
would require in Yiddish the formulation of a rule such as Verb Fronting:

23.   NP   NP   V   oblig
       1   2   3   =====>
       1   3   2   Ø

[6] It is worth noting that the mutual intelligibility between Yiddish
and German absolutely breaks down for the Yiddish speaker if a tensed
verb in an embedded S is moved to final position. Such sentences as
those in (18a) – (22a), even though there is complete lexical identity
and even when pronounced with Yiddish surface phonetics, seem to the
average Yiddish speaker to be not simply deviant but incomprehen-
sible.

This rule seems to be motivated solely by the fact that Yiddish word order happens not to be SOV. It fails to explain *why* the verb moves and, as such, is only an ad-hoc device to bring the surface which the rules produce as a result of one's theoretical preconceptions into line with the facts of the language. In fact, it is almost impossible to account in any simple way for the set of verbs to which such a rule would apply in Yiddish, since the set includes both all finite verbs, whether auxiliary or main verbs, and all modals, both finite and non-finite. That is, Yiddish modal sentences can be:

24a.   Ix muz dem man zen.
       I must see the man.

  b.   Ix hob gemuzt dem man zen.
       I had to see the man.

  c.   *Ix hob dem man zen gemuzt.

If, however, one starts with another underlying word order, either SVO or VSO, then the rule itself can be as simply formulated and its condition can be stated more naturally. I shall argue in Section 6 below that, in fact, Yiddish is best analyzed as being loosely verb-initial, and that verb initial is the optimum starting point in that it requires fewer transformational passes on a large class of sentences. For the arguments which follow here, let us assume verb initial. Whether verb initial or verb second is chosen, the course of these arguments is in no way changed. The reformulated rule of Verb-to-the-End would be:

25.   V   NP   NP   X
      1   2   3   4   ======>

      Ø   2   3   4   1

       Condition: 1 = non-finite.

This rule, too, poses a problem. Specifically, it does not apply to the non-finite forms of modals and aspectuals: exactly the same set of verbs which require the next lower verb[7] to be an infinitive, and which

----

[7] Here, of course, I am following Ross (1969) in treating the tense auxiliaries, modals, and aspectuals as main verbs.

therefore can be said on independent grounds to form a natural class.

To visualize this blockage of the rule in (25), let us first look at its non-blocked application in a sentence such as

26.   Ix hob Dovidn gezen.
       I saw David.

27.

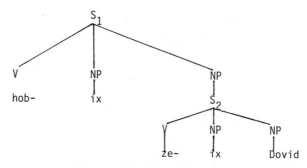

Equi-NP Deletion, case marking and non-finite Verb-to-the-End will operate on S_2, yielding

28a.

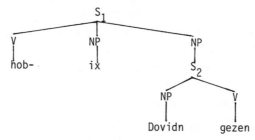

Agreement and Subject Fronting will apply to S_1 yielding

28b.

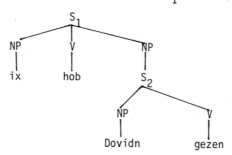

In the case of sentences which contain modal or aspectual verbs, this rule of Non-Finite Verb-to-the-End is blocked, as can be seen in a sentence like

29.   Er hot gezolt kenen Dovidn a matone gebn.
      He should have been able to give David a gift.

the underlying representation of which is:

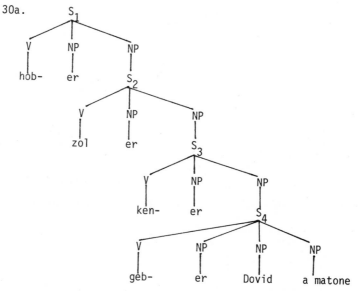

30a.

On S₄ Equi-NP Deletion and Non-Finite Verb-to-the-End will operate, yielding

30b.

On S_3 Equi-NP Deletion will operate, but NOT Non-Finite Verb-to-the-End, yielding

30c.

Similarly on S_2 Equi-NP Deletion but not Non-Finite Verb-to-the-End apply:

30d.

Finally, on S_1 Agreement and Subject Fronting apply:

30e.

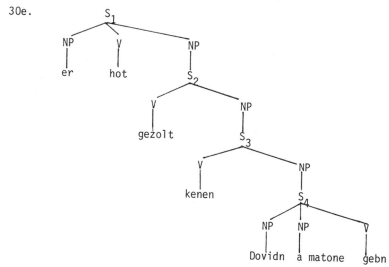

    If we look at the two cases where Non-Finite Verb-to-the-End has failed to apply, that is, S_2 and S_3, we find that in both cases such movement would require that the verb pass over a verb the subject of which had been deleted by Equi-NP Deletion. I shall term this condition on the rule Pass-Over Blocking. I have no ready explanation for why this blockage occurs. As can be seen from sentences like:

31.   Der onhoyb fun di harhandlungen iz frier geplant geven oyf
       montik. *Forward,* 17 January 1978 (p.1, col. 1)
       'The beginning of the negotiations was earlier planned for
       Monday.'

the blockage would seem to require not only Equi-NP Deletion of the subject but also that the lower verb be an infinitive. While, as I have said, I cannot motivate the Pass-Over Blocking, exactly the same blocking condition also seems to operate in Dutch; furthermore a similar rule condition is also found in such diverse languages as Kurdish, an Iranian language, and Soso, a Mande language spoken in Guinea and Sierra Leone.

In the above derivations I have assumed not only that all auxiliaries are main verbs (following Ross, 1969) but also that they are transitive verbs. In the case of the tense auxiliaries *hobn, zayn, veln,* this
assumption makes the process of derivation somewhat more straightforward,
but it is not crucial for this argument. The same result could be
achieved by Subject Raising. However, in the case of the modals it is
crucial. If the failure of *kenen* in Sentence (29) to pass over *gebn* is
due to Equi-NP Deletion, then equally the failure of *gezolt* to pass
over *kenen* must be due to Equi-NP Deletion. If *kenen* is thus shown to
be transitive, *zoln* must also be transitive since both are modals. If the
blocking condition is indeed Equi, but the modals are seen as intransitive, one should then get:

32.   * Er hot kenen gezolt Dovidn a matone gebn.

where *gezolt* has passed over *kenen* but been blocked, as *kenen* was, by
the Equi-NP Deletion in the lowest sentence. However, (32) is ungrammatical.

To conclude, I have tried to show that there exists a unitary explanation for the complementation structures of Yiddish if one assumes that
the linear order of the constituents in the underlying representation is
VSO or SVO. To assume an SOV order would, I believe, make such an account
at least much more complex. If one postulated that the starting point for
the derivation were SOV in a sentence such as (29) above, *Er hot gezolt
kenen Dovidn a matone gebn,* then stating the conditions on verb fronting, which would involve the inverse of Pass-Over Blocking, would require that the rule read that it apply to all finite verbs and also to
nonfinite modals and aspectuals. These do not form a natural class.

4.   NP CLIMBING

Yiddish shares with German the ability to move any constituent,
whether NP or Adverbial, from the predicate into sentence-initial position for purposes of focus or emphasis. As in German, a constituent which
is so fronted need not be a member of the highest clause, just so long
as the process of complementation is one in which the lower clauses
have lost their subjects through Equi-NP Deletion. This results in sentences such as

33.   Arabiš hob ix šoyn a lange vayle gemeynt onfangen študiren.
       I have long meant to begin to study Arabic.

Here one can see that, in Yiddish as in German, fronting any constituent before the verb results in the order X-Verb-Subject, the implications of which I shall discuss in detail in Section 6 below.

     In addition to this kind of leftward movement of constituents into
initial, focused position, there also exists in Yiddish yet another type
of leftward movement, which can be seen in a sentence such as

34.   Er hot zayn toxter a kleydl gevolt koyfn.
       He wanted to buy his daughter a dress.

No matter what theory of word order one starts from, *zayn toxter* and
a kleydl can only be seen as the indirect and direct objects of *koyfn*;
that is, schematically the underlying representation must be

35.

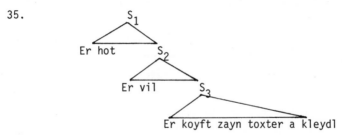

paralleling

36.   Di mame vil az der tate zol zeyer toxter a kleydl koyfn.
       The mother wants the father to buy their daughter a dress.

What has occurred, then, is that the noun phrases *zayn toxter* and
a kleydl have been dislocated leftwards by some grammatical process.
This process cannot be Raising since the NP's which have been moved do
not become grammatically a part of the higher clause, which is the ulti-
mate effect of Raising. What has occurred can also not be Leftward Extraposition for focus for a number of reasons:

     (a)   The focused positions of Yiddish are either sentence initial
or sentence final. Constituents which are moved to either of these positions stand in some sort of semantic contrast to the preceding or
following sentences. Such focused NP's are always at least minimally

stressed and potentially can be set off by comma intonation from the
rest of the sentence. None of these facts are true of NP's such as
zayn toxter and *a kleydl* in Sentence (34).

(b)   The effect of this particular leftward dislocation is precisely the opposite of focus: NP's which have undergone this movement
are semantically least-marked.

(c)   In a given Yiddish sentence, while two or more constituents
may be extraposed to the right, only one constituent may ever be focused
leftward to sentence initial position. It is always ungrammatical for
two or more elements to precede the finite verb.[8] However, in Sentence
(34) we have seen that both objects of *koyfn* have been dislocated leftwards.

Since this leftward dislocation of NP's to a position following the
finite verb is not Raising and is not Focus Extraposition, then what is
it? I would suggest that what we are dealing with here is the manifestation
of a widespread de-focusing device which is found in many, but by no
means all Indo-European languages.[9] I have termed this transformation
NP Climbing since its effect is to cause object NP's of the lowest verb
to "climb" into what would be object position of the topmost verb in the
tree. As the name Climbing suggests, it seems to me that, unlike Raising,
which is in some sense performed on the lower NP by the higher S, this
transformation is a spontaneous movement by the lower NP into the highest
possible non-marked object position, regardless of the nature of the
higher S's. That Raising is an action performed *by* a higher S on an NP
is shown by the change of grammatical status of the raised NP; on the

---

[8] There are two classes of exceptions to this statement: (1) the conjunctions *un* 'and', *ober* 'but', *oder* 'or', *oyb* 'if, whether', *ven* 'when,
if', *az* 'that', etc. and (2) the relative/interrogative/indefinite pronouns when embedded, e.g.
        Ix veys vemen er hot gezen.   I know whom he saw.
I shall return to this topic in Section 6 below.

[9] The fact of pronoun climbing was seen by Jakob Wackernagel (1891) and
is, in essence, the phenomenon described by the law which bears his
name. However, Wackernagel failed to see that full NP's, as well as
pronouns, are affected by Climbing -- a fact which invalidates his argument that pronouns climb because they are by nature clitic. I discussed this in detail in Hall, Hall and Sheerin (1973).

other hand, the spontaneous upward movement of Climbing is shown by
the fact of the grammatical non-participation of the climbed NP's in
the syntax of the surface S where they occur.

The Climbing Transformation could be formally stated as a rule
something like[10]

37. $\begin{bmatrix} V & NP & \begin{bmatrix} V & [NP & (NP) & V] \\ & & S & & & S \end{bmatrix}_S \end{bmatrix}_S$

SD: 1   2   3   4   5   6   =======>

SC: 1   2   4 $\left\{ \begin{matrix} \emptyset \\ 5 \end{matrix} \right\}$ 3 $\left\{ \begin{matrix} 5 \\ \emptyset \end{matrix} \right\}$

Conditions: (a)   6 must be non-finite
             (b)   If 5 is climbed, 4 must be.

The parentheses around the third NP and the curly braces in the structural change have been used so that the movement of the objects of both
simple transitive verbs and of ditransitives can be accounted for within
one rule. Condition (b) provides that the second object (whether direct
or indirect) may only climb if the first object has. These conditions can
be visualized more easily with examples:

---

[10] Although I have stated the transformation in this rule, I am less than
happy with its formulation. My major objection is a fundamental one:
of necessity, this kind of rule writing does not have any way to indicate that while the word order has changed, the grammatical relationships have not. It seems to me that it is a major failure of our science
that our rules are incapable of distinguishing grammatically significant changes from simple permutations with no grammatical consequences.
    If, instead of proceding to formulate an explicit rule, as I have
done, one were to follow the common contemporary practice of indicating the transformation by means of one tree becoming another, derived,
tree, the result would have been even more misleading in that the
climbed NP (or NP's) would be shown as immediately dominated by the
topmost S. This tree would cause one to believe that a grammatical
change had happened – something which has in fact *not* occurred.

38.   Movement of the Object of a Simple Transitive Verb

    a.   Ix hob gevolt Avromen zen.

    b.   Ix hob Avromen gevolt zen.
       I wanted to see Abraham.

    c.   Ix hob gevolt im zen.

    d.   Ix hob im gevolt zen.
       I wanted to see him.

39.   Movement of the Objects of a Ditransitive Verb

    a.   Er hot gevolt Rivken dos seyder hayom tsaygn.

    b.   Er hot Rivken gevolt dos seyder hayom tsaygn.

    c.   Er hot Rivken dos seyder hayom gevolt tsaygn.

    d.   *Er hot dos seyder hayom gevolt Rivken tsaygn.
       He wanted to show Rebecca the agenda.

    e.   Er hot gevolt es ir tsaygn.

    f.   Er hot es gevolt ir tsaygn.

    g.   Er hot es ir gevolt tsaygn.

    h.   *Er hot ir gevolt es tsaygn.
       He wanted to show it to her.

Thus we can see that the rule is not sensitive to whether the NP's which will climb are full NP's or pronouns, but rather simply to their sequential order; if one is to see the difference in order which exists between direct and indirect objects when they are pronouns and when they are full NP's as having been arrived at via a transformation, then, obviously, this transformation must precede Climbing.

As can be seen from the following sentences, the focus of one NP to sentence-initial position[11] neither blocks nor necessitates climbing.

40a.   Yisroyl hot gevolt Feygln a mayse dertseyln.
       Israel wanted to tell Feygl a story.

    b.   Feygln hot Yisroyl gevolt a mayse dertseyln.

    c.   Feygln hot Yisroyl a mayse gevolt dertseyln.

    d.   A mayse hot Yisroyl gevolt Feygln dertseyln.

---

[11] Let me note in passing that the focus of one NP to sentence initial position does not preclude the focus of some other NP to sentence final position, e.g.
    Der bobn hot dos yingl gemaxt a matone.
    The boy made his grandmother a present.

e. A mayse hot Yisroyl Feygln gevolt dertseyln.
f. Yisroyl hot a mayse gevolt dertseyln Feygln.
g. Yisroyl hot gevolt a mayse dertseyln Feygln.
h. Yisroyl hot Feygln gevolt dertseyln a mayse.
i. Yisroyl hot gevolt Feygln dertseyln a mayse.   etc.

These sentences suggest that Focus must precede Climbing. The transformation as formulated in the rule given in (37) states that the second of two NP's, whether nouns or pronouns, may only climb if the first has. However, in a sentence such as (40c) above, we find that a full-NP direct object has climbed, although the indirect object has not climbed, but rather been focused -- that is, the second NP of the string has climbed but not the first. If one were to order Climbing before Focus then one would have to say that Climbing is obligatory, since otherwise one could not produce 40c. Thus one would be led to the logical contradiction that an optional rule becomes obligatory if and only if one plans to later apply a second optional rule. On the other hand, if Focus applies first to the indirect object, then the direct object in a sentence such as (40b) meets the structural description of the rule in (37) and the rule of Climbing is free to apply, thus yielding (40c).

These, then, are the syntactic facts concerning Climbing. The question now remains, what is its semantic/rhetorical function. The answer is, I believe, that in the broadest terms, Climbing is a de-focusing or de-emphasizing transformation. It is impossible to utter a sentence such as

41a. Ix hob gevolt dos bux leyenen.
      I wanted to read the book.

felicitously unless the object NP *dos bux* receives at least some degree of sentence stress; the article *dos* can never reduce to [d$^{\theta}$s]. However, if the object NP climbs, then, while a degree of stress is still possible, the most normal rendition of the sentence is unstressed and, in allegro speech, *dos* will reduce to [d$^{\theta}$s]:

41b. Ix hob dos bux gevolt leyenen.

      [xɔd$^{\theta}$s bʉx gvolt leyɛnɛn]

There are in a Yiddish sentence which contains a transitive verb
used with the past tense of a modal or aspectual four possible positions
for a definite object: (1) the position immediately before the transitive verb; (2) the position immediately before the modal or aspectual
verb; (3) sentence initial position; (4) sentence final position. These
four possible positions for NP's interact in complex and, to me as a
native speaker, still largely mysterious ways with the systems[12] of sentence stress and intonation to provide the network of semanto-rhetorical
linkings of the language. A complete theory of discourse as applied to

[12] In Yiddish there are three major systems of sentence stress and intonation: (a) conversational, which is the least marked; (b) narrative,
which is marked by a musical intonation pattern called 'nigen' in
Yiddish (from the Hebrew word for melody), and which is quite distinctive; (c) logical argumentation, which one may term 'pilpul' intonation -- this is the intonation pattern used in Jewish schools for
legal and religious argumentation and carried over into secular life
for any purpose which requires argumentation and the statement of a
line of reasoning. There is a certain quasi-chanted effect about pilpul intonation, but it is much less melodic than the narrative nigen.
These three intonation types are so absolutely distinctive that every
speaker of Yiddish is aware of them and of their stylistic import.
While each has its own proper realm, they are frequently mixed in the
course of a single discourse. A major discourse unit frequently will
begin with the unmarked, conversational intonation style, and then
shift to either the narrative style or to the argumentative style, or
both, depending on the semantic content. Olsvanger (1947:viii f.)
discusses the melody of Yiddish narrative briefly and impressionistically. He does not differentiate, as I have attempted to do, between
the melody of sequential narration and the melody of logical argumentation. The example which he gives in musical notation (p. ix) is
actually logical argumentation, although this is not clear from his
discussion.
    The significant thing about Yiddish narrative intonation and
about the intonation of Yiddish logical argumentation is that they
both represent marked departures from the rhythm and melody of every-
day-speech. The melody of Yiddish narration is undoubtedly derived
from the traditional chant used to read the Bible aloud. However,
the narrative 'nigen' is by no means a simple reproduction of the
Biblical chant.

Yiddish would be able to account for both the specific surface positions of NP's within any given sentence and the stress and intonation pattern which they would receive in terms of the sentence's position in its discourse unit -- whether the given NP was being asserted or presupposed, whether it gave new information or merely recapitulated old information, whether it was being highlighted or contrasted, on the one hand, or deemphasized, on the other. Although I, as a native speaker, can react with approval or disapproval to a given sentence configuration in terms of other preceding or following sentences, I am as yet unable to propose rules which will account formally for my intuitions.

5.   VERB-SUBJECT STRUCTURES IN YIDDISH[13]

There is, however, one word order in Yiddish which is discourse

[13] Maurer (1924 and 1926) has investigated the question of verb initial sentences in German in some detail. It is difficult to evaluate his conclusions for two reasons:
1) Since Maurer does not have a theory of verb position as a discourse-governed phenomenon, he frequently does not give enough context for the reader to decide what is going on.
2) Maurer seems to have started his investigation with the thesis that all verb initial, non-question structures are in some way aberrant and as a result his work gives the impression throughout that what he is trying to do is not explain the structures which he does find but rather explain them away (e.g. his treatment of the sentence "Hat mich der Teufel eingesperrt." 1926:200).

As a plus for Maurer it should be noted that he carefully discriminates the type of verb-initial, quasi-existential introductory sentence found in folk song imitations ("Sass ein Eichhorn/auf dem Heckendorn ...", "Sah ein Knab' ein Röslein steh'n ...") and subject-verb inversion in the protasis of conditions without *wenn* (though he does misanalyze these latter egregiously (1924:144)) from other types of verb-initial structures.

The question whether the Narrative Sequential verb-initial structures of Yiddish are a Yiddish innovation or whether they are a continuation of an older Germanic and Indo-European rhetorical device is an important one. It is my strong belief that a careful reexamination of the evidence will show that such sequences do exist in the literary monuments of many if not all of the older Western Indo-European languages and that here we are dealing with an Indo-European survival rather than a new structure which has arisen spontaneously within Yiddish or one which has somehow come into being through Hebrew-Aramaic or Slavic influence.

specified, but under such explicit conditions that it can be discussed, even in terms of what little is known about discourse. Consider the following text[14]:

42.   A yid iz amol gekumen bazuxn zaynr a xavr in Pariz. *Hot* der fraynt getraxt vu im tsu nemen, az es zol farinteresirn a yidn. *Hot* er im genumen in Yidišn beys-oylem tsu tsaygn im Roytšildz keyvr. *Kukt* der yid un kukt un dreyt zix arum tsum xavr un zogt, "Zest, Yankl, dos heyst gelebt!"

> Once a Jew came to visit a friend in Paris. His friend thought about where to take him so that it would be inter- esting to a Jew. So he took him to the Jewish cemetery to show him Rothschild's grave. The Jew looked and looked and turned around to his friend and said, "See, Jake, that's what you call living!"

The first thing to be noted about this paragraph is that every sentence which is not paragraph initial is verb initial. The condition here is that in a continuous narrative, sentences which maintain the same topic and which do not contain a leftward focused element must be verb initial. If this condition is violated the result is gross in- felicity, if not outright discourse ungrammaticality. For example, in the specimen text, if the second sentence were to read

43.   (!) Der fraynt hot getraxt ...

---

[14] Throughout this section I have drawn my examples from the genre of the traditional East European Jewish humorous folktale, the *vits*. An ex- cellent collection of such tales is to be found in Immanuel Olsvan- ger's *Röyte Pomerantsen* (1947) and the reader who wishes to find additional examples of the structures which I discuss here is re- ferred to it. (For the non-Yiddishist Olsvanger's work has the double advantage of being in Roman alphabet and being provided with notes and a glossary). Although I have checked my intuitions and the analysis I have based on them rather extensively against the language reported in Olsvanger's tales, for reasons of economy I have chosen to rely on my own Sprachgefühl and retell parts of the traditional stories in such a way that they would illustrate precisely those grammatical points which I wished to exemplify.

While I have chosen to show narrative sequencing solely in humorous folktales, the grammatical structure is by no means con- fined to this literary genre – indeed, it is a part of both everyday speech and of conscious literary narrative. Like any other rule of grammar, when the conditions for its use arise, it is applied.

then the reader's reaction would be the kind of double-take one does when the rules of pronominalization are misapplied.[15] The synonym *der fraynt* seems no longer to be coreferential with *xavr* - suddenly a third character would appear to have been introduced into the story. So too if the third sentence were to read

44. (!) Er hot im genumen in Yidišn beys-oylem ...

the flow of the narrative would be broken.

The claim which I am making here is that just as the speaker of Yiddish can distinguish between the sentences and the non-sentences of his language, and can further distinguish between 'major' sentences, completely understandable in themselves, and 'minor' sentences, understandable only within some context, so too he can distinguish, intuitively, between sequences of sentences which hang together and form a discourse unit, what I shall here term a *Narrative Sequence*, and those which do not.

---

[15] It has long been recognized that there are rules of pronominalization (or of pronoun interpretation, if one wishes to view the matter thus) which unite the parts of complex sentences and sentences which are serially ordered as part of a unified paragraph. Many of these rules are so self-evident that they have been simply taken for granted. Thus, in a sentence such as

i. He came into the room and John took off his hat.

in English and, I suspect, in most if not all other languages, *he* and *John* cannot be interpreted as being coreferential. In addition to such obvious rules prohibiting pronominalization there are, as well, rules which require it. For example,

ii. John came to New York in 1972. (!) In New York John found work as a subway guard.

Although the second sentence of this sequence is perfectly grammarical, it is not a possible sentence in its position in this sequence of sentences. The failure of pronominalization breaks the flow for the reader because this is just as much a violation of the grammatical rules of English as any sentence-level failure to apply an obligatory rule is a grammatical error.

In the construction of a Narrative Sequence there are a number of rules which interact. Each of the rules in itself is fairly simple, but the pattern of their interaction is complex. Just as there is a necessary sequential relationship between pronouns and the nouns to which they refer, so also there is a sequential relationship between the position of the grammatical subjects within the sentences of a Narrative Sequence. Specifically,

(i) The subject may not be sentence initial in the second or following sentences, as has already been shown.

(ii) If S_2 has the same subject as S_1, then it must be pronominalized; no epithet or synonym may be used:

45. Moyše Kopoyer hot zix gedarft onton.

      Hot er zix ongeton di šix af di hent ...

  (!) Hot Moyše zix ongeton ...

  (!) Hot der nar zix ongeton ...

      Moyše Kopoyer (a famous folk fool) had to get dressed.
      He put his shoes on his hands ...
      (!) Moyše put on ...
      (!) The fool put on ...

(iii) A synonym is permissible if the subject of S_2 is an object in S_1, e.g. in (42) S_1 *xavr*, S_2 *fraynt*.

(iv) Without breaking the Narrative Sequence, certain objects and adverbials can be preposed. Although the conditions on precisely what can be preposed are complex and, to me, still unclear, as a general rule the items which can be preposed most frequently tend to be personal or adverbial pronouns, but not epithets.

46. Letstn yor bin ix geforn kayn Varše. Dortn hob ix zix azoy farblonjet ...

      Last year I went to Warsaw. There I lost my way so badly ...

However, if an epithet is used for *Warsaw*, e.g. *di Poylise hoyptstot* 'the capital of Poland', then, this Narrative Sequence is infelicitous:

47. Letstn Yor bin ix geforn kayn Varše. (!) In der Poyliše hoyptstot hob ix zix ...

However, epithets such as 'di Poylişe hoytştot' can be used quite freely in Yiddish; impressionistically, it would seem much more frequently than in English:

48.   Ven er iz geven a yungerman hot mayn feter gevoynt in Varşe.
      Dos kulturele lebn in der Poylişe hoyptştot iz geven zeyer a
      rayxer ...
         When he was a young man my uncle lived in Warsaw. The
         cultural life of the Polish capital was very rich ...

Here the second sentence is part of a thought paragraph with the first and is, according to Yiddish style ideals, completely felicitous, but it clearly does not form part of a Narrative Sequence.

(v)   When S_2 is in Narrative Sequence with S_1 the intonation
      pattern which it exhibits is different from the intonation
      pattern which is found on a sentence which, while logically
      following from S_1, is not in Narrative Sequence with it. For
      example, the following texts both show possible ways in which
      a Yiddish joke could begin. In the first specimen, (49), the
      narrative sequencing begins with S_2 and S_1 is simply an ex-
      pository introduction. In the second specimen, (50), the
      narrative theme begun in S_1 is continued in S_2 which is in
      Narrative Sequence with it. In both instances I have marked
      an intonation curve directly beneath S_2. It will be seen
      that in (49) the first words of S_2 are pronounced on an even
      high tone, while in (50) the initial tone contour is high
      with a protracted melodic glissando to a low tone.

49.   Eyner a yid iz geforn kayn Pariz bazuxn zayner a xavr.
      Der fraynt hot im şoyn lang nit gezen ...

         A man went to Paris to visit his friend. His friend had
         not seen him for a long time ...

50.   Eyner a yid iz geforn kayn Pariz bazuxn zayner a xavr.

Dem fraynt hot er šoyn lang nit gezen ...

      A man went to Paris to visit his friend. He hadn't seen
      his friend for a long time ...

Lest it be thought that the difference in intonational contour is
due to object preposing in S_2 of (50), contrast this with the normal conversational contour of the same sentence in a non-narrative context:

51.   Dem fraynt hot er šoyn lang nit gezen.

To complete the picture of Narrative Sequence intonation contours,
note the contour on S_2 of (42):

52.   Hot der fraynt getraxt vu im tsu nemen ...

      hot dr fraynt getraaxt vu: im tsu nemn

[―――――――――ᴧᴧ――――――――――]

(vi)   For emphasis within a Narrative Sequence, a non-pronominal
       subject in S_2 or following may be 'floated', i.e. postposed
       to non-second position. Although subject postposing in
       Yiddish normally requires the insertion of the dummy subject
       es, this is not the case in Narrative Sequences:

53.   Eyner a yid iz geforn kayn Pariz tsum erštn mol.

      Hot im bagegnt in stantsie zayn fraynt ...
      A man came to Paris for the first time.
      His friend met him at the station ...

Here the subject of S_2, zayn fraynt, has been extraposed rightward past
the past participle and the adverbial for purposes of emphasis and shift
of rhetorical focus within the narrative sequence. It is a rhetorical
strategy to permit additional information to be given without inter-
rupting the flow of the narrative, e.g. S_2 could continue:

54.   ... vos hot in Pariz šoyn lang gevoynt.
      ...who had lived in Paris for a long time.

Contrast this with the same focusing in a non-narrative context:

55.   Es hot im bagegnt in stantsie zayn fraynt ...

Sentence (55) could be a sentence from a letter or other report of
a series of events. Narrative Sequencing seems to be triggered by the
rhetorical need to build up to a denouement, a 'punchline'.

If the subject is to be extraposed rightwards, then there are two
possible positions which it may occupy:

(a)   If the sentence contains a reflexive, the subject may simply
      be extraposed immediately to the right of its own reflexive.
      There are other verb-subject structures, specifically yes/no
      questions and declarative sentences with focused constituents,
      which also permit this movement:

56a. Hot dos kind zix ongeton?
   b. Hot zix dos kind ongeton?
       Has the child dressed himself?
   c. Di hoyzn hot Berele zix ongeton.
   d. Di hoyzn hot zix Berele ongeton.
       Berele put on his pants.

While the sentential meaning within each of these two utterance
pairs is identical, the rhetorical force is quite different; (56a) is
simply a question; (56b) expresses astonishment, or impatience - implicit in the question is the kind of rhetorical-semantic focusing often
associated with English contrastive stress. So too in (56c) the object
di hoyzn has been maximally focused and the subject *Berele* has been
left unmarked, while in (56d) the subject too, has been focused, although
weakly so.

(b)   In Narrative Sequences the subject may also be extraposed to
      absolute clause-final position, e.g.

57.   Hot zix di grine hoyzn ongeton Berele.
      Berele put on the green pants.

Here the rhetorical effect is a 'rabbit-out-of-the-hat' one -- the act
of delaying the subject until the last possible moment has the effect
of surprise and maximal emphasis. This kind of unmarked subject extraposition is a property of Narrative Sequencing and of focused statements;
it is not shared by questions. Thus,

58.   *Hot zix di grine hoyzn ongeton Berele?
is impossible as a question, although questions are par excellence the
other verb-initial structure of Yiddish.

In a non-narrative embedded sentence, if the object (but not an adverbial) is focused to clause-initial position, then the subject may be
floated to clause-final position, e.g.

59.   Ix veys az di grine hoyzn hot zix ongeton Berele.
      I know that *Berele* put on the green pants.
Otherwise the dummy subject *es* must be inserted.

In addition to the Narrative Sequence, Yiddish also has those verb-
subject structures which one would expect from a normal West Germanic
language such as German and Dutch or Older English: Yes/no questions,
wh-questions, focused object and adverbial statements, focused adjectives.
Examples of these are as follows:

60.   Iz er gekumen kayn Pariz?   Did he come to Paris?

61.   Ven iz er gekumen kayn Pariz? When did he come to Paris?

62.   Letstn vox iz er gekumen kayn Pariz.
      He came to Paris last week.

63.   Zayn xavr hot er gezen in Pariz.
      He saw his friend in Paris.

64.   Kleyn iz er, obert xots dem, štark.
      He's small, but nevertheless strong.

65.   A kleyninker iz dos eyfele, un a ziser.
      The baby is small and sweet.

6.   THE POSITION OF THE SUBJECT IN THE UNDERLYING WORD ORDER
      OF YIDDISH

The question which remains is how to account for the verb-subject
structures of Yiddish in terms of the phrase structure rules and transformations of a generative grammar. It would be quite possible to write
a 'subject-verb inversion rule' such as the following (assuming verb-
second underlying order):

66.
$$\begin{Bmatrix} Q \\ \text{Nar. Seq.} \\ NP_{obj} \\ Adv \\ Adj \end{Bmatrix} \quad NP_{subj} \quad V \quad X$$

1	2	3	4	=======>
1	$\emptyset$	3	2	4

However, this rule is less than adequate, even though it is mechanically
sufficient, primarily because the structures in Position 1, which trigger
the transformation, do not form in any sense a natural class. One might
argue that NP_{obj}., Adv. and Adj. share in common the fact that they are
focused non-subject constituents. However, the Narrative Sequential sentence is, rhetorically, a non-focused sentence; again, although it is
conventional to treat Q as a constituent, the status of this symbol,
which has been introduced for notational convenience, is certainly
different from that of NP, Adv, or Adj, which have real segmental phonological correlates.[16]

The argument that languages such as German and Yiddish have a condition which requires that the verb be the second constituent in a declarative sentence is, I believe, a case of misreading the symptom as the
cause: it is, of course, the case that in the vast majority of sentences, the verb is the second constituent. However, the question is whether
this is the result of a condition on the verb or a condition on the
possible positions of NP's.

----

[16] It is worth noting in passing that when Q does have a phonological
correlate, Yiddish *oyb*, German *ob*, English *whether*, it does not trigger
'subject-verb inversion' but rather one finds in German normal subordinate clause word order, and in Yiddish and English normal subject-
verb-object order, although the rule in (66) would predict 'inversion'.
I shall return to this point below.

There are three possible word orders which one might set up for
Yiddish: SOV, SVO, or VSO. Given the power of transformational rules,
it is certainly mechanically possible to derive the occurring sentences
of Yiddish from any of these orders. Of these, SOV is, as I have shown
above, the least attractive because it is the farthest from any occurring
surface structure. Furthermore, if one starts from SOV, then one would
have to say that Yiddish (and presumably German too) has an arbitrary
condition on the verb that it be the second element in a sentence. For
Yiddish, this word order also poses the further problem that in the most
rhetorically unmarked sentence, the Narrative Sequential one, this structure must be derived by a highly marked rule moving the verb to initial
position.

   If one starts from an SVO underlying order, then, still, one has
to maintain that, in addition to conditions on NP positions, there is a
condition on the verb that it be the second element, which is the only
motivation for the rule of 'subject-verb inversion' postulated in (66)
above, since its only function is to ensure that only one constituent
may precede the verb. As a matter of fact, it is not an absolutely general condition in Yiddish that only one constituent may precede the
verb. Not only may coordinating conjunctions -- *un* 'and', *oder* 'or',
ober 'but' -- precede the verb without inversion, so too inversion is
not caused by the complementizer *az* 'that', the indirect question marker
oyb 'if, whether', and the relative/interrogative/indefinite pronouns
vemen 'whom', *vos* 'what' or 'who', *velxer* 'which', etc. when they are
embedded. One might argue that the coordinating conjunctions and *az*
are not constituents of the sentences which follow them; however, this
argument cannot be raised for the relative/interrogative/indefinite
pronouns.[17] Under an SVO underlying word order hypothesis the Narrative
Sequential verb-initial sentence type still poses a problem because, in
order to arrive at a rhetorically unmarked sentence, one is forced to

---

[17] The fact that the relative pronoun does not block subject fronting
is a problem no matter what theory of Yiddish word order one starts
from since no theory allows for the verb to be in third position.

apply a marked transformation. In the case of the adverb and object preposing transformations, SVO underlying word order is the least satis-
factory because it requires two separate transformations -- one to prepose the focused element, a second to postpose the subject after the
verb.[18]

If one starts with VSO word order as underlying, then there are, I
believe, a number of advantages of economy, of naturalness, and of greater explanatory power. In the first place, verb second surface position
need no longer be seen as a condition on the verb. Rather, the simple
act of focusing any sentential constituent results in the verb ending
up in second position; if what is focused is an object or an adverbial,
then only that constituent which is focused need be moved. Since the
subject follows the verb in the underlying structure, there is no need
to move it. In the case of both yes/no questions and the Narrative Sequential, the underlying word order is the surface word order. There are,
I believe, natural reasons for this. In the case of Narrative Sequential
verb-initial sentences, what ties an S_2 to its preceding S_1 is the action
of the verb. It is therefore rhetorically natural that the linking element between sentences be the first word of the second sentence. In
yes/no question, what is being questioned is the entire sentence, so
that no one element in it can be elevated to greater prominence by being further focused. For example, in a question such as

67.   Iz Xayim do gekumen nextn?
       Did Chaim come here yesterday?

an affirmative answer requires that *Chaim, come, here,* and *yesterday* be
equally true. A negative answer can negate any one of the four elements
equally -- no, it wasn't Chaim; no, it wasn't here; no, he didn't come;
no, it wasn't yesterday. By this analysis, sentences in a Narrative Sequence and yes/no questions are the least marked sentence types of the
language and thus allow the least amount of transformational manipulation.

---

[18] The mechanical possibility of subsuming both of these movements into
one rule should in no way disguise the fact that there are two separate transformational processes involved.

In the case of simple declarative sentences which contain no focused adverbial or object, then a transformation is required to move the
subject into initial position. This transformation is, I believe, well
motivated on a number of grounds, both semantic-rhetorical and phonological.

A sentence with subject-initial, whatever else its function may be,
is making an assertion about the subject which is, to this extent, at
least weakly focused. This is clearly evident in the case of third person pronouns.[19] In the sentence

68.   Er iz gekumen.
       He came.

er must be uttered with at least some degree of stress, while *iz* can reduce to just [+]. However, in a Narrative Sequence such as

69.   Iz er gekumen.
       He came.

er is normally unstressed and clitic to the preceding verb, which itself
can never reduce.

Furthermore, in a sentence which is subject initial, if the subject
is a full NP (i.e., not a third person pronoun), there always exists a
disjuncture after the subject. In allegro speech this disjuncture is
realized as a slight intonation fall on the subject NP; in more deliberate speech styles there is a perceptible comma intonation after the
subject.[20] However, in the case of verb-subject structures, whether in
Narrative Sequences or questions or the result of preposed focused constituents, such a disjuncture is never possible. Whatever the speed of
speech, the verb and its subject are one breath-and-intonation unit. There
is no possibility of a comma intonation before the subject.

---

[19] I am excluding from consideration here the first and second person
'pronouns' since there exist no nouns to which they refer. By their
very nature, third person pronouns are merely referents, the least
marked occurrence of the nouns to which they refer.

[20] In cases where the subject is followed by forms of *zayn* and *hobn*
which have become enclitic to it, by an adjustment rule the disjuncture is moved after the auxiliary.

A further fact which has a bearing here is the possible position into which sentential adverbials may be inserted. In Yiddish, as in English, sentential adverbials may always be inserted between a subject and a following verb, e.g.

70.   Miriam, xotš dem, hot es nit gevolt ton.
      Miriam, nevertheless, didn't want to do it.

However, a sentential adverbial inserted between a verb and a following subject is bizarrely ungrammatical[21]:

71.   *Hot xotš dem Miriam es nit gevolt ton.

It is fairly widespread in the world's languages that comma intonation is a concomitant of the dislocation of a constituent.[22] Since initial subjects can be separated from the verbs which follow them by a comma intonation, and since clearly the comma intonation is not a phonological property of the subject itself, or of initial sentence position, then this would seem a fairly strong argument that the underlying word order of Yiddish is VSO.

---

[21] Compare the equivalent English structure:
      *Had {nevertheless / however} Mary known it, she wouldn't have done it.

[22] Not surprisingly, the facts of Yiddish here closely match those of English. Compare:
      i.   Yoysef volt gegangn ven er volt gehat gelt.
      ia.   Joseph would have gone if he had money.
      ii.   Ven er volt gehat gelt, volt Yoysef gegangn.
      iia. If he had money, Joseph would go.
where the facts of command show that (i) and (ia) are the basic sentences; these sentences, in both languages, are deviant if a comma intonation is introduced after the first clause in (i) and (ia), or omitted after the first clause in (ii) and (iia). So too, in both languages, a preposed adverbial - clearly a constituent which has been moved -- may always be followed by a comma intonation.

7.   CONCLUSION

In this paper I have tried to discuss the major facts of the complete word order system of Yiddish. I believe that it is important to try
to see the word order system of a language *as a whole* with the various
rules interacting and each having its own semantic role, rather than con-
centrating simply on the rules of one of the subsystems: verb movement,
NP extraposition or whatever.

If one were to look at the surface facts of Yiddish word order, without regard to the rules which underlie it, one would see seeming chaos:
SVO, OVS, VSO, S Aux OVX, S Aux VOX, S Aux VXO, S Aux V_1OXV_2, S Aux O
V_1OV_2 and so forth and so forth, through all of the transformational
possibilities that I discussed above. What I have tried to show here is
that although all of these word order variations exist, *the word order
of Yiddish is anything but free*. Rather, there are as many or more non-
occurring orders of the mathematically possible ones, as there are orders which yield grammatically well-formed sentences. Furthermore, I
have tried to show that every complex word order -- for example O Aux
SOV_1V_2Adv -- can only be seen as having arisen as the result of the application of a series of simple well-motivated transformations, each of which
is, in itself, highly restricted, both in scope of application and seman-
tic/rhetorical effect. I have dealt less fully with the semantic implications of Yiddish word order variation than I would have liked, both
because the scope and focus of this paper were restricted and because,
although much important work has been done during the last ten years on
such areas as conversational postulates, and the illocutionary force of
utterances, there still exists no way of really stating, even anecdotally,
the relationship of a sentence in a discourse to the preceding and
following sentences. As a native speaker I have the strong feeling that

72.   Leyen hob ix gevolt a bux gebn.
      I wanted to give Leah a book.

is slightly different in its emphasis from

73.   Ix hob gevolt a bux gebn Leyen.

and that both of these sentences maintain a slight difference from

74.   Ix hob gevolt a bux Leyen gebn.

as well as from all of the other possible permutations. The establishment of a way to talk meaningfully about such variations is one of the major tasks which is yet before us as a science.

Nonetheless, I am certain that such rules exist and that their discovery and formulation is, so to speak, just over the horizon. I further believe that once such rules have been worked out for a modern language, such as Yiddish, in which there is relatively free word order which can be analyzed with the help of native speaker input, then the seemingly capricious variations which one finds in the order of constituents in ancient languages such as Latin, Greek, and Biblical Hebrew will yield themselves to a surer analysis than any as yet proposed. This is not to say, of course, that the rules of Yiddish word order and the rules of Latin word order are the same; in many cases clearly they are not. Nonetheless, I do believe that an overall framework which can explain how the pieces of a Yiddish joke hold together will also be able to say much about the structure of a letter of Cicero's.

All of the above is to say that I believe that all sentence-level free options become either obligatory or conditioned on the discourse level.

PROBLEMS IN THE DESCRIPTION
OF GERMAN WORD ORDER

MARTIN D. PAM

1. THEORETICAL BACKGROUND

Since the development of transformational grammar, syntactic
study has shown an ever-increasing concern for problems of word order.
Indeed, the number of books and articles which have appeared on word order have established this area of syntax as an independent sub-division
of syntax worthy of investigation in its own right. This is not to say
that word order is neglected in the traditional grammars. These, however,
have tended to concentrate on the use of inflectional forms - that is,
noun declensions and verb conjugations - to express basic relations like
subject of, object of, and predicate. In other words, such grammars
approach syntax from the point of view of cataloguing the formal elements
which may serve in the basic functional roles available in sentences. The
arrangement of words into linear order plays a separate, often peripheral, role in the syntactic description and is frequently limited to a

* This is a revised, and somewhat expanded, version of a paper read at
  the University of Hull on March 3, 1978. I would like to thank those
  who attended the lecture for their helpful comments, particularly Eric
  Fudge for getting me to reconsider my definition of embedded sentence.
  My thanks also to Günther Deimer for his helpful contribution to my
  thinking in this area, to Jürgen Meisel for sharing with me the insights of his working group on second language acquisition, and to
  Dieter Kastovsky for his careful reading of the original paper and the
  many suggestions he made for its improvement. But most of all, I would
  like to thank R.M.R. and Beatrice L. Hall for their comments on the
  original paper, and for encouraging me to examine some of their in-
  sightful hypotheses concerning Germanic word order.

listing of basic sentence types and correlating them with functions like
statement, question, and command, or with the distribution of old and
new information and emphasis in sentences.

The emergence of word order as a fascinating arena where opposing
theories of grammar could contend for superiority was greatly facilitated by the shift away from morphologically-oriented descriptions to a
basic model type where the central preoccupation is that of discovering
and explaining the (assumed) relationship among sentences having the
same meaning but exhibiting a different order and/or different types of
constituents.

Look, for example, at the sentences in number (1):

(1) a. I am *easy* to please.   cf.   I am *eager* to please.

   b. It is *easy* to please me. cf. (*)It is *eager* to please
      me.[1]

   c. To please me is *easy*.   cf. * To please me is *eager*

   d. Pleasing me is *easy*.   cf. * Pleasing me is *eager*

   e. It is *easy*, pleasing me. cf. * It is *eager*, pleasing
      me

In (1a), the sentences with *eager* and *easy* have the same structure:
Pronoun, Be+Adjective, To-Infinitive. But whereas the sentence with
easy can be paraphrased by (1b-e), the sentence with *eager* cannot. Paraphrase means that *in some sense*, all of the sentences with *easy* are
equivalent. That is, despite the formal differences among the five sentences - including the linear arrangements of words - we understand in
every case that the First Person Singular is the Recipient of pleasure
rather than the Provider of pleasure, and that the adjective *easy* refers
to the effortlessness with which some unspecified agent can provide this
pleasure.

Traditional grammar makes a useful distinction here between grammatical relations and logical relations. In sentence (1a), for example,
the pronoun *I* is the grammatical subject of the predicate *be easy* but
the logical object of the verb *please*; whereas in (1b), the pronoun *it*

---

[1] The asterisk is in parentheses here because of the grammatical reading
which is possible if *it* actually has a referent.

is the grammatical subject of the predicate *be easy* and the pronoun *me* is the grammatical, as well as logical, object of the verb *please*. In these examples, the grammatical relations are nicely indicated by the morphology, the grammatical subject occurring in the nominative case, *I*, and the grammatical object occurring in the oblique case, *me*. It is one of the crucial functions of transformational grammar to give a formal description of these relations - a description which would explain the relationships among the sentences of (1).

This is done by assigning to each sentence two types of analytical representations - a surface structure, in which grammatical relations are expressed either by the linear sequence of words alone, by inflectional endings, or by both; and second, a deep structure, in which the logical relations which underlie the linear sequence are expressed. The deep structure is the output of the categorial, or base, component, which defines the possible logical relations that can be expressed, while the surface structure is the output of the rules of the transformational component, which may insert grammatical markers, or delete and reorder elements, thereby accounting for such phenomena as ambiguity and paraphrase. It follows, then, that if the sentences in (1) all share the same logical relations, they must be assigned the same deep structure; and that the differences in linear sequence, and so on, are the result of the application of different transformations to the common deep structure from which they are derived. This relationship is represented in number (2):

(2)   Deep Structure

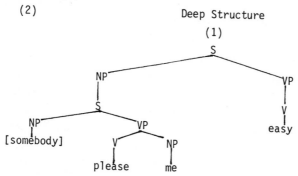

⟹ Surface Structure (1a), (1b), (1c), (1d), (1e).

Here we come to the crux of the problem of word order within transformational grammar. The following excerpt from Chomsky's *Aspects of the
Theory of Syntax* (1965) has been taken by many linguists as a basic
tenet of transformational grammar:

> The rules of the categorial component carry out two quite
> separate functions: they define the system of grammatical
> relations, and they determine the ordering of elements in
> deep structures... The transformational rules map deep
> structures into surface structures, perhaps reordering
> elements in various ways in the course of the operation
> (pp. 123-4).

(Notice that in Chomsky's terminology, 'grammatical relations' corresponds to what we have called 'logical relations'.) Chomsky goes on to
reject attempts by other linguists to limit the role of the categorial
component to defining these relations. The result is that many linguists
(e. g., Bach 1975) have devoted a great deal of effort to trying to find
rational criteria which would automatically select a particular linear
order for a deep structure which underlies a number of surface structures
with a variety of surface word orders (see section 3). The basic difficulty, of course, is that deep structures are not available for direct
observation - just as there is no sentence (1), only (1a), (1b), (1c),
(1d), and (1e).

Those linguists, however, who subscribe to the basic goals of transformational grammar but reject Chomsky's view of the dual function of the
categorial component have sought to invalidate Chomsky's position in one
of two ways: Some have tried to show that all transformational rules operate solely with grammatical categories and therefore need not specify
linear order. For example, referring to the deep structure in number (2),
the fact that the rule of Raising, which is required in the derivation of
surface structure (1a) from deep structure (1), can be stated purely in
terms of attaching the object of *please* directly to the NP which is the
subject of the main clause, without any reference to its linear position
in the sentence, would be one such argument against Chomsky's position
being necessarily valid. Other linguists have tried to show that there are
general principles which determine all the possible linear sequences of
words in surface structures, so that all so-called sentence types, for

example, would be contextually determined. All these linguists would claim that there is no basic underlying word order from which surface structures may or may not vary - or they would at least have very strong reservations about this.

2.   AN OVERVIEW OF GERMAN WORD ORDER

Four major factors are involved in determining German word order. Two of these are demonstrated by the sentences in number (3):

(3) a. Hans *wohnt* in der Stadt.   John lives in the city.

b. *Wohnt* Hans in der Stadt?   Does John live in the city?

c. Ich weiß, daß Hans in   I know that John lives in
der Stadt *wohnt*.   the city.

d. Ich weiß, Hans *wohnt*   I know John lives in the city.
in der Stadt.

By comparing (3a) with (3b), we see that the function of a sentence is one relevant factor in determining word order type: A contextually-neutral declarative sentence with a simple verb has the subject in initial position and the verb in second position, with all verb complements following the verb. This is the case in (3a). In a question, however, we find the verb in initial position, with the subject immediately following it.[2] This is the case in (3b). Sentences (3c) and (3d) show a completely different kind of constraint on German word order; namely, in a subordinate clause introduced by a subordinating conjunction, the verb occurs in clause-final position.[3] Thus, in (3d), where the subordinating conjunction *daß* - 'that' - does not appear, the verb occurs in second position, just as it would in a main declarative clause like (3a).[4]

[2] I.e. in syntactically marked yes-no questions. As in English, there are also intonationally marked yes-no questions, with SVO word order.

[3] This includes relative clauses as well as complement clauses and subordinate clause types.

[4] Actually, although on intuitive grounds (3d) is perceived by speakers of German as a single sentence, it clearly has been derived by a different transformational process than was involved in the derivation of (3c). Not only is the speaker surer of the truth value expressed by the subordinate predicate in (3c), but, unlike structures of the type

But notice that the verb in a subordinate clause cannot occur in clause-initial position. The ungrammaticality of number (4) shows this:

(4) *Ich weiß, *wohnt* Hans in der Stadt

The reason number (4) is ungrammatical is simply that a clause-initial verb signals a question, as in sentence (3b); and only *main* clauses can mark a sentence as a statement or a question.

The other two factors affecting German word order are quite different from the two we have just looked at. First of all, whereas the difference between a statement and a question, or between a main clause and a subordinate clause, essentially involves the position of the verb, the phenomena which we will look at now involve noun phrases and other complements as well as verbs. Second, these phenomena are directly related to the discourse situation. Look first at the sentences in number (5):

(5) a. Ich *sehe* ihn oft in der Stadt.   I often see him in
    b. Oft *sehe* ich ihn in der Stadt.   the city.
    c. Ihn *sehe* ich oft in der Stadt.
    d. In der Stadt *sehe* ich ihn oft,

In every case the verb is the second constituent of the sentence, as we would expect in a declarative main clause. But as (5b-d) show, any complement may occur in initial position, if it is to be emphasized or if it is to be topicalized. Sentences (6a) and (6b) illustrate an emphasized verb and a topicalized verb respectively:

(6) a. *Arbeiten* tue ich gern,   It is *work* I do gladly and
       und nicht *faulenzen*,   not *loafing*.
    b. Arbeiten tue ich *gern*,   Work I do *gladly* and not
       und nicht *ungern*,   *ungladly*.

In (6a), the verb *arbeiten* is emphasized, because it is being contrasted with its opposite, *faulenzen*. In (6b), the verb *arbeiten* is merely topicalized; it is the adverb *gern* which is emphasized with *its* opposite, *ungern*. A number of points emerge from these examples: First, as to the *position* of *arbeiten* - as we saw before, a finite verb in initial posi-

---

(3c), the truth values of the two predicates in (3d) do not necessarily have to be the same, This difference is, in fact, marked by the different intonational contours of the two types.

tion signals a question; so a verb cannot be emphasized or topicalized simply by placing it in initial position. It must occur in the infinitive form, followed, in second position, by a conjugated form of the verb *tun - to do*. A second observation we should make concerns the role of stress in these sentences. Stress and word order are interdependent linked variables; if I skimp on the role of prosodic features in general, it is because I feel that most of what is relevant in German word order can be said without reference to them. And finally, the emphasis on the adverb *gern* in (6b) suggests that sentence-*final* position can also be used as a position for emphasized elements. The interaction between sentence-initial position and sentence-final position as positions of emphasis and topicalization can be seen in the short discourse in number (7) - a discourse which is very common in radio broadcasts:

> (7) Sie hörten die 9. Symphonie   You have heard the 9th
> von Ludwig van Beethoven. Es   Symphony by Ludwig van Beet-
> spielten die Berliner Phil-   hoven. The Berlin Philhar-
> harmoniker. Die Leitung hat-   monic played. The conductor
> te Herbert von Karajan.   was Herbert von Karajan.

The first sentence is a normal subject-verb-object sentence opening the discourse. The second sentence is an example of emphasis by word order in which the subject occurs in final position. Obviously, the logical (or deep structure) subject of this sentence is the phrase *die Berliner Philharmoniker*. It occurs here in final position because the subject is *not* normally emphatic in initial position. The pronoun *es - it -* is introduced into initial position in order to preserve the principle that the verb occurs in second position in declarative main clauses. The third sentence is an example of topicalization by word order in which the object occurs in initial position.[5] Thus, the principles of emphasis and topicalization with regard to word order involve having a given

---

[5] This sentence is actually ambiguous in that the differential selection of stress and intonation contour can topicalize the object or emphasize the subject. In the latter case, this sentence would be parallel to the second with the difference that since there is a noun phrase which can occur in initial position, the insertion of the pronoun *es* is not necessary.

constituent occur in a position where it would not occur in a contextually-neutral sentence. Since the subject and verb complements occur on
opposite sides of the verb, both in contextually-neutral sentences and
in discourse-conditioned sentences, it is difficult to see how the rules
of German word order can be formulated without reference to some basic
order. And those constraints on the position of the verb which have
nothing to do with discourse conditions - like the main clause/subordi-
nate clause dichotomy - they, too, would be difficult to formulate without reference to some basic order. The so-called "basic order" which I
keep referring to need not necessarily be in the deep structure. But if
it is not in the deep structure, what sort of arbitrary transformational
rules do we have to postulate in order to establish such a basic order?[6]

3.   UNDERLYING WORD ORDER

If we wish to give a Chomskian description of the German sentences we have seen so far, we have to choose one particular linear order
to uniformly represent the deep structures of all clauses. We have seen
that the verb can occur in initial position in German surface structures,
as well as in second position and final position. We have also seen that
any constituent of the sentence may precede or follow the verb. The theoretically possible choices, therefore, are those in number (8), where
Object is to be understood as referring to *any* verb complement:

(8) Verb-Subject-Object	see (3b)	
Subject-Verb-Object	see (3b), (3d), (5a)	
Subject-Object-Verb	see (3c): subordinate clause	
Verb-Object-Subject		
Object-Verb-Subject	see (5b-d)	
Object-Subject-Verb		

As an initial procedure, let us take the first three orders in number (8)

---

[6] Note that the sort of linearization rules proposed by Boas (1975) imply
that word order is arbitrary and unimportant. Such rules also make it
difficult to capture the notion of marked and unmarked word orders, a
notion which is in fact quite useful, especially in its historical implications.

as possible candidates for the linear order of German deep structures, noting that whichever order is chosen, certain movement rules will have to be postulated to derive the other occurring surface orders. The consequences of choosing one of these three orders are displayed in number (9). The trees here deviate from Chomsky's model in that his Verb Phrase label is not used. This is because the label VP requires that the verb and its object be contiguous, which is clearly impossible in verb-subject-object order, where the subject intervenes between the verb and its object. Therefore, the subject will be defined as the first NP on the left in deep structure, and the object or complement as any other NP:

(9) a. Underlying VSO:

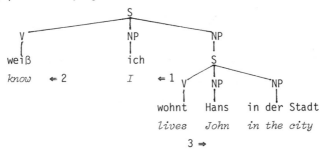

1. Object-Fronting / emphasized or topicalized statement
   (Daß Hans in der Stadt wohnt, weiß ich.)
2. Subject-Fronting / context-neutral statement
   (Ich weiß, ...)
3. Verb-to-the-End / daß _____
   (Ich weiß, daß Hans in der Stadt wohnt.)

b. Underlying SVO:

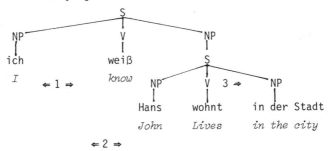

1. Subject-Verb Inversion / question
   (Weiß ich, ...)
2. Subject-Object Inversion / emphasized or topicalized
                                    statement
3. Verb-to-the-End / daß _____

c. Underlying SOV:

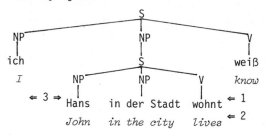

1. Verb-to-Initial-Position / question
2. Verb-to-Second-Position / statement
3. Subject-Object Inversion / emphasized or topicalized
                                    statement

With underlying VSO word order as in (9a), two movement rules have
to be postulated for the main clause - first, a fronting rule which
places the object or *any other* complement, for that matter, in initial
position if it is to be emphasized or topicalized in the resulting statement; and second, another fronting rule, which places the subject in initial position if the resulting sentence is to be a context-neutral statement. These rules do not apply if the sentence is to be a question, since
the deep structure already *is* that of a question. Finally, we need a
rule - let us call it Verb-to-the-End - which moves the verb of the subordinate clause to the end of that clause if a subordinating conjunction
is present. If there is no subordinating conjunction, then the rule of
Subject-Fronting applies, just as in a main clause. It is interesting to
note that the subordinating conjunction *must* be present if the subordinate clause begins the sentence - as a result of Object-Fronting - or if
the sentence is a question. This is shown in number (10):

(10) a. Ich weiß, *daß* Hans in der Stadt wohnt.

     b. Ich weiß, Ø Hans wohnt in der Stadt.

     c. Weiß ich, *daß* Hans in der Stadt wohnt?

     d.*Weiß ich, Ø Hans wohnt in der Stadt

     e. *Daß* Hans in der Stadt wohnt, weiß ich.

     f.* Ø Hans wohnt in der Stadt, weiß ich

Underlying SVO word order is illustrated in (9b). This is the surface order of main clause context-neutral statements. So this time, it is question word order which has to be derived. It is actually rather arbitrary
to specify the rule needed to place the verb in initial position as an
inversion rule; it could just as easily be called a Verb-Fronting rule.
The emphatic or topicalized object-verb-subject order *must*, however, be
formulated as an inversion rule, or we would either get an ungrammatical
object-subject-verb sequence, or we would have to add another rule to
change this to the required object-verb-subject sequence. The subordinate
clause requires the same Verb-to-the-End rule as in (9a).

    Coming finally to (9c), we find that the underlying order here is
that of a subordinate clause which is marked as such by a subordinating
conjunction. If no such conjunction is actually present, then the verb
will have to be moved to second position, as will be the case in the main
clause. Question order will be derived by moving the main verb into initial position, and an emphasized or topicalized object will have to change
position with the subject as in (9b).

    Notice that we could have chosen for our deep structures one of the
other alternatives listed in number (8) - that is, VOS order, OVS order,
or OSV order. But this would only have led to more complicated descriptions. In (9a), for example, we would have needed an additional rule of
Subject-Object Inversion for questions, since number (11) is ungrammatical:

    (11) *Weiß, daß Hans in der Stadt wohnt, ich

And this brings us to the actual point of the exercise illustrated
by numbers (8-11): Which of the six theoretically *possible* word orders
are we to choose as *basic* for a description of German word order?

Linguists generally like to think that the answer to such questions is purely empirical - that is, given enough time, energy, wisdom, and insight one will inevitably come up with a *correct* solution which will exclude all others because it will reflect how language *really works*. The problem, however, is that the description of linearity cannot be dealt with empirically in transformational grammar. As I pointed out above, deep structures are not directly observable. The concept of Deep Structure is a *theoretical construct* which represents certain systematic relations within language; and although transformations often give the impression of describing processes which are a part of the speaker's linguistic competence, the fact is that transformations are also just descriptive devices of a particular grammatical model.[7] Psycholinguistic research has convincingly demonstrated that actual linguistic performance works along lines that are only very roughly analogous to transformational rules.[8]

If this is indeed the case, then the question of underlying word order has to be seen as a strictly model-internal problem. In such a situation, one might be tempted to reduce this problem to one of personal aesthetics - for example, the notion of symmetry has frequently played such a role in the development of many structural models of description; and within transformational grammar, the notion of "possible rule" frequently gets defined in terms of personal taste, as in the choice between an inversion rule and a simple movement rule in (9b). For those linguists, however, who insist that Linguistics is a science rather than an art, there must be certain criteria which determine an objective choice from among competing hypotheses such as those in (9). The most fundamental criterion, of course, for any hypothesis is that it accurately describes the relationship among the elements occurring in the

[7] Even those who claim a certain psychological reality for the transformational model are usually careful to point out that transformational derivations do not necessarily represent a one-to-one correspondence with the actual processing of sentences.

[8] What little we know about the processing of linguistic data shows that it is, if anything, more complex. For a convenient summary of work on this area see Presch (1977).

data. But beyond this the criteria generally chosen are not always well defined or easy to apply. Chief among these criteria are *naturalness* and *simplicity*.

Two arguments of the naturalness type have been developed by R.M.R. and Beatrice L. Hall. The first involves their claim that German has underlying VSO word order. It is based on the fact that when a subject pronoun follows the verb, this pronoun tends to coalesce with the verb. This does not happen when the pronoun precedes the verb:

(12) a. Kennste ihn?   Do you know him?
     b. Du kennst ihn. You know him.

In (12a), the voiced *d* of the pronoun has been assimilated to the voiceless *t* of the verb and the vowel of the pronoun has been reduced.[9] In an analogous way, the Halls point out that while there is a potential pause between a subject and verb in a subject-verb statement, there is no such pause possible in a verb-subject question. The examples they use are given in number (13):[10]

(13) a. Sah Hans Maria?   Did John see Mary?
     b. Hans (#) sah Maria. John saw Mary.

The Halls would attribute the non-reduction of the initial subject pronoun in (12b) and the potential pause between the subject and a following verb in (12b) and (13b) as evidence for the movement of the subject out of its basic position after the verb.

Another argument of this type developed by the Halls is that the surface position of pronouns may be a more reliable guide to the underlying position of noun phrases than full nouns, not to mention longer phrases. A simple example from English may be seen in number (14):

(14) a. *I find *that you have done your work already* good
     b. I find *it* good *that you have done your work already*.

What we have here is a case where the object of the verb *find* is so long that it presents a potential perceptual problem for the hearer if it occurs between the predicative phrase *find ... good*. Therefore, this ob-

---

[9] Compare also Swabian [kɛnš(ə)n] and Yiddish [kɛnstm̩].

[10] Analogous arguments are presented for Yiddish by Beatrice L. Hall (in this volume).

ject is moved to the right, so that *find* and *good* can occur closer together. But the original position of the object is marked by the pronoun
it, which preserves the original structure of the sentence, but is short
enough not to be a problem perceptually. We will soon see similar cases
of this in German, when we come to analyze such predicative phrases.

Similar types of naturalness criteria would include the constraint
that deep structures should differ as little as possible from surface
structures and that therefore no underlying order should be postulated
unless it actually occurs in the language. One might also argue that
only so-called "unmarked orders" - that is, contextually-neutral orders
should be chosen. This has led to the controversy over Joseph Greenberg's
work. Greenberg noted that certain types of linguistic features tend to
go together. For example, if a language has as its normal surface word
order SOV, it is likely to express case relationships by means of postpositions instead of prepositions and modifiers are apt to precede the
words they modify. In VSO languages, the situation is exactly the opposite: case relationships are expressed by means of prepositions, and
modifiers follow the words they modify. SVO languages, while showing the
characteristics of both of these groups tend to be more like VSO languages than like SOV languages. In those cases where the language being
investigated shows a discrepancy with Greenberg's correlations, many
linguists have concluded that the language in question must have the underlying order of verbs and noun phrases which one would expect on the
basis of whether the language has prepositions or postpositions, or
whether the modifiers precede or follow the words which are being modified.

All of the arguments or criteria I have mentioned so far are in
some rather vague sense natural. They all try to approach something like
an empirical basis for determining how to deal with the problem of underlying word order. As such, they are far more interesting than arguments based on the more mechanistic criterion of simplicity; for simplicity is an axiom of scientific methodology and as such it is operationally sound. But it cannot be taken for an a priori characteristic of
human language. It is especially interesting to look for cases where the

criterion of naturalness and that of simplicity lead to contradictory results. For example, one corollary of simplicity is that the best description - note, *best*, not necessarily *correct* - is the one that requires the fewest and simplest rules in order to derive surface structures from deep structures. This means that it could happen that we would, for some language, have to choose as an underlying word order an order which never actually occurs in the language.[11]

This, then, is the veritable jungle of word order studies. I will devote the rest of this paper to a suggestion by the Halls that by postulating underlying VSO order for German and extending the range of opportunities for the application of the rule of Verb-to-the-End, we can describe both naturally and simply a vast and very characteristic part of German grammar. We will also look at some of the problems raised by their analysis.

4.   VERB COMPLEXES

In German, there are three constructions where the behavior of the verb forms is similar to the behavior of verbs in sentence (3c), which is here repeated as (15a):

(15) a. verb + verb

Ich *weiß*, daß Hans in der Stadt *wohnt*.	I know that John lives in the city.

b. verb + infinitive

Ich *sehe* Hans in der Straße *laufen*.	I see John running in the street.

c. modal + infinitive

Ich *will* Hans in der Stadt *besuchen*.	I want to visit John in the city.

d. auxiliary + past participle

Ich *habe* Hans in der Stadt *besucht*.	I (have) visited John in the city.

[11]For many languages this would be a direct consequence of the Universal Base hypothesis in many of its forms. In this regard, it would be interesting to contrast the SOV analysis which would be imposed upon English by Ross's Penthouse Principle with McCawley's VSO analysis.

In each case, the first verb form in the sentence is a finite verb - 1st
person singular present tense. This finite verb occurs in second position
in the sentence. The second verb form may also be a finite verb, as in
(15a), or a non-finite verb - an infinitive, as in (15b) and (15c), or
past participle, as in (15d). The non-finite verb forms in (15b-d) occur
in sentence final position just as the finite verb form in (15a) does.
The description of German word order would obviously be simplified by
deriving all of these sentences from the same kinds of deep structures,
as in number (16):

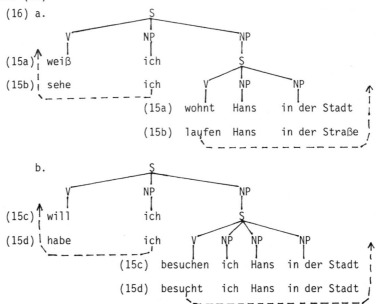

As the tree diagrams show, the positions of the verb forms in all four
sentences of (15) can be described by the rule of Subject-Fronting applying in the main clause and the rule of Verb-to-the-End applying in
the embedded clause. What distinguishes (15b-d) from (15a) is that they
require the application of further rules while (15a) does not. For example, (15c) and (15d) require the rule of Equi-Noun Phrase Deletion;
for although the first person *ich* is the subject of the verb *besuchen*,
just as it is the subject of the main clause verb, the repetition of an

identical subject in a subordinate clause is not allowed here. The deletion of the subject in the subordinate clause has two consequences:
first, it marks the subordinate clause as such, because main clauses retain their subjects; second, without an explicit subject, the verb has
no noun phrase with which to agree and must therefore appear in a non-
finite form.

However, this poses the problem of why in the subordinate clause
in (15b) the verb is in the infinitive form since its subject, *Hans*, has
not been deleted. Again, the solution is that (15b) has undergone another, but analogous, rule which removes the subject from the embedded
clause: the rule of Raising, which we mentioned earlier. This becomes
obvious if we change the name *Hans* to the corresponding personal pronoun, which is *er* in the nominative, *ihn* in the accusative. We then get
the sentence in (17):

(17) Ich sehe *ihn* in der Straße laufen.

The occurrence of the accusative *ihn* shows clearly that the subject of
the lower sentence has been raised to the position of object in the main
clause.

So despite the fact that we have four different types of constructions here, we can explain one aspect of their behavior which they have
in common - namely, the position of the verb forms. We have done this by
extending the definition of an embedded sentence to include strings containing non-finite verb forms. These non-finite verb forms trigger the
rule of Verb-to-the-End, just because they mark a subordinate clause. We
thus have the situation which is summarized in number (18):

(18) Subordinate Clause Marker	Type of Verb Form	Position of Verb Form
Ø	finite	second
daß	finite	final
infinitive	non-finite	final
participle	non-finite	final

The subordinate clause may either remain intact, in which case it will
contain a finite verb, or it may lose its subject through Equi-Noun
Phrase Deletion or Raising, in which case it will contain a non-finite

verb. In the first case, the subordinate clause may not be signalled by
any overt marker, in which case the verb appears in second position; in
all other cases, the subordinate clause *is* marked overtly, and the verb
must appear in final position. This can be seen again in the triplet
given in number (19):

(19) a. Wir meinen, Ø wir *haben*   We believe we are right.
        recht.

     b. Wir meinen, daß wir recht   We believe that we are
        haben.   right.

     c. Wir meinen, recht zu haben.   We believe (ourselves) to
                                       be right.

The real fun begins as soon as we start to increase the number of
embeddings. Note, for example, the sentences in number (20), which have
the constructions Modal + Infinitive and Auxiliary + Past Participle:

(20) a. Er weiß, daß ich sie   He knows that I will speak
        morgen sprechen werde.   to her tomorrow.

     b. Er behauptet, daß ich   He claims that I saw him
        ihn gestern gesehen habe.   yesterday.

Both sentences have the deep structure configuration of (21):

(21)

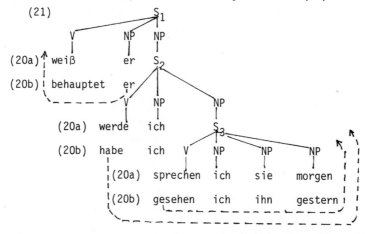

The broken arrows in the tree diagram show that if Verb-to-the-End is
applied to each of the embedded sentences, the correct order of verb

forms will result. And, as we have seen before, the absence of the subordinating conjunction *daß* in S_2 will prevent Verb-to-the-End from applying to S_2, yielding the sentences in (22):

(22) a. Er weiß, ich werde sie morgen sprechen.

     b. Er behauptet, ich habe ihn gestern gesehen.

When we increase the complexity of sentences in which the Verb +
Infinitive construction occurs, we find that an additional movement rule
may optionally apply. Such a case is found in number (23), where both
the *a* sentence and the *b* sentence are fully acceptable:[12]

(23) a. Ich höre, daß er zu
      kommen beabsichtigt.   I hear that he intends

     b. Ich höre, daß er be-   to come.
      absichtigt zu kommen.

These variants are derived from the structure in (24), the *b* sentence
undergoing the additional rule of Extraposition:

(24)

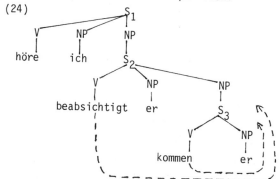

The extraposition of S_3 seems, however, to be obligatory if we have the
Verb + Verb construction, as the ungrammaticality of (25a) shows, in
contrast to the fully grammatical (25b):

(25) a. *Ich weiß, daß er, daß ich
      morgen komme, behauptet.   I know that he claims

     b. Ich weiß, daß er behauptet,   that I am coming to-
      daß ich morgen komme.   morrow.

[12] Note that if the verb *kommen* has complements associated with it, the *b*
sentence is preferred. This is due to the problem of Heavy NPs; see below.

Formally stated, Heavy NP Extraposition is obligatory if the subordinate clause is introduced by *daß*.[13] The deep structure of this sentence has the same configuration as in (24). Notice that it is always the lowest embedded sentence that is extraposed. This can be seen in sentence (26) and its representation in number (27):

> (26) Ich weiß, daß er versucht hat,   I know that he (has)
>   es zu machen.   tried to do it.

(27)

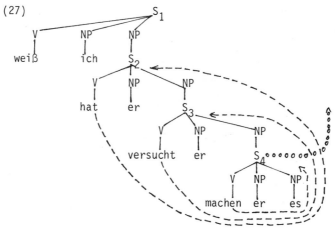

Modern Standard German has a very interesting little peculiarity which rather upsets this nice orderly mechanism which we have so carefully built up. There is a small class of verbs, consisting mainly of the modals, which appear in the infinitive instead of the past participle if they are governed by an auxiliary verb and if they in turn govern another verb. This can. be seen by contrasting the sentence (28a) with (28b):

> (28) a. Ich habe es nicht *gekonnt*.   I haven't been able
>   (to do) it.
>   b. Ich habe es nicht machen   I haven't been able to
>   *können*.   do it.

In (28a), the verb *können*, English *can*, is part of an Auxiliary + Past Participle construction. Adding the verb *machen*, English *do*, as a further

[13]It is possible in German, unlike English, to formally define one class of Heavy NP as consisting of any non-reduced subordinate clause.

embedding should not alter the form of *können*, but it does. Let us now suppose that (28b) is itself embedded. This would give us a tree like (29) (omitting the negative *nicht*):

(29)

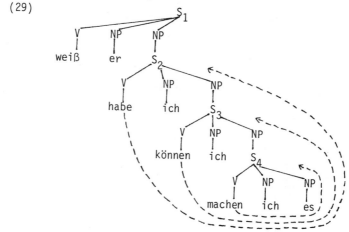

If we simply apply Verb-to-the-End to each of the embedded sentences we will get the ungrammatical (30):

(30) *Er weiß, daß ich es nicht machen können habe

Even with Extraposition applied either to the lowest embedded sentence or to S_3 is the sequence unacceptable, as (31) and (32) show:

(31) *Er weiß, daß ich können habe, es nicht machen

(32) *Er weiß, daß ich habe es nicht machen können

Note that the ungrammatical (32) is also what we would get if we somehow blocked the application of Verb-to-the-End in S_2. This sentence, whose correct form is given in (33),

(33) Er weiß, daß ich es nicht habe machen können.

He knows that I was unable to do it.

poses a problem for any theory of German word order.[14] The only thing that seems certain is that the construction in question has to be described in terms of the so-called "double infinitive", in (33) the

[14]R.M.R. Hall and B.L. Hall (personal communication) suggest that it may be an instance of obligatory NP Climbing. See B.L. Hall (this volume).

machen können.

5.   COMPLEX VERBS

    Complex verbs in German seem to behave exactly like the verb
complexes which we have just been looking at. This can be seen in the
sentences in (34):

>   (34) a. verb + separable prefix
>
>   Das Auto *fuhr* den Mann *um*.   The car ran the man down.
>   b. verb + adjective
>
>   Ich *machte* es ihm *klar*.   I made it clear to him.

In both of these sentences we have a finite verb form in second position,
followed by a predicate-completing morpheme in sentence-final position.
And when these sentences are embedded, we get the same sentence-final
reversal of predicative elements we saw before. This is shown in (35):

>   (35) a. Ich weiß, daß das Auto den   I know that the car ran the
>   Mann *umfuhr*.   man down.
>   b. Ich weiß, daß ich es ihm   I know that I made it clear
>   *klar machte*.   to him.

The tree diagram in (36) shows the intended derivation of these sentences:

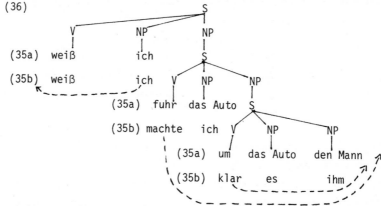

In this way, the analysis by the Halls brings together a wide variety of
seemingly disparate phenomena into one homogeneous operational mechanism.

6.   CONCLUSION

The Halls' analysis requires two pieces of formal apparatus: First, it is necessary that every verb form - whether finite or non-finite - have its own sentence in deep structure. Second, the rule of Verb-to-the-End has to apply in every clause marked as subordinate, although subsequent extraposition may disguise the fact that such a rule has applied.[15]

Let us call the first piece of apparatus the "constituency problem". The *problem* here is that there are a number of facts which make it difficult to operate within a system where all verb forms have equal status in deep structures. One such fact is that two verb forms may function together as a single constituent. We saw earlier that a finite verb occurs in second position in a declarative main clause, and that any *single* constituent may occur in initial position. So, whereas (37a) is a perfectly good German sentence, (37b) is not:

(37) a. Oft sehe ich ihn in der Stadt.   I often see him in the city.

    b. *Oft in der Stadt sehe ich ihn

What we mean by single constituent may include any level of structure representable in a tree diagram. So let us look at sentence (38) and its representation in (39):

(38) Man muß dich nur erreichen können.   One just has to be able to reach you.

(39)

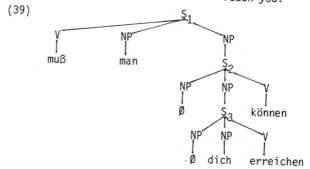

Except under the limitations of Pass-Over Blocking; see B.L. Hall (this volume).

The tree in (39) represents an intermediate stage in the derivation where
Verb-to-the-End has applied in the embedded sentences, and where Equi-
Noun Phrase Deletion has deleted repetitions of the impersonal pronoun
man. Assuming that Subject-Fronting does not take place to yield sentence
(38), the question is what elements may be preposed for purposes of emphasis or topicalization. The answer appears in number (40):

      (40) a. Nur *erreichen* muß man dich können.

          b. Nur *dich* muß man erreichen können.

          c. ?Nur *dich erreichen* muß man können

          d. *Nur *können* muß man dich erreichen

          e. Nur dich erreichen *können* muß man.

(40a) and (40b) are not problematic. In each case, a single constituent
in the lowest sentence has been preposed. (40c), in which the whole of
S_3 has been preposed is odd, not for grammatical reasons, but for purely
pragmatic ones: by preposing two lexically independent constituents, one
is in fact emphasizing both, implying that there must be a double contrast somewhere in the discourse. This problem does not arise in structurally similar sentences where the object of the lowest verb is a reflexive pronoun, as in (41):

      (41) Nur *sich entscheiden* muß   One just has to be able to

          man können.   make up one's mind.

This sentence is completely equivalent to the slightly preferred (41a):

      (41) a. Nur *entscheiden* muß man sich können.

The crucial examples here are (40d) and (40e), where one wants to emphasize the verb *können* in the context of a sentence like "One just has
to be able to reach you, one doesn't necessarily have *to want* to". Sentence (40d) is not just odd; it is completely ungrammatical, although it
fulfills the requirement of being a single constituent. The only explanation that seems plausible to me is that one cannot prepose a higher
constituent without carrying along everything which that constituent
dominates.

    The problem which now faces us is the behavior of the embedded verb
forms in sentence (42):

(42) Es ist <u>in Zürich</u> <u>kurz nach 1300</u> <u>geschrieben worden</u>.

It was written in Zurich shortly after 1300.

Each of the three underlined portions of this sentence represents a pre-posable unit. In the deep structure of this sentence, the past partici-ple *geschrieben* is certainly dominated by the passive auxiliary *worden*. But while there is no difficulty about preposing the complex *geschrieben worden*, it is impossible to prepose *geschrieben* by itself.

This suggests that auxiliaries have a much more intimate relation-ship with the verbs they govern; it is not just a matter of simple dom-inance. The problematic nature of auxiliaries is frequently seen in col-loquial German, where the past participle sometimes occurs as the lone representative of the past tense, without the usual auxiliary. This can be seen in the subordinate clause in number (43), where the omitted aux-iliary is placed in parentheses in the position in which it would normal-ly occur:

(43) Er hat es gemacht, weil sein   He did it because his
     Vater Klavier *gespielt* (hat).   father played the piano.

This phenomenon also occurs in poetry, as in the following lines from the poem "Eingang" by Clemens Brentano:

(44) Die Armut durch die Stoppeln geht,

   Sucht Ähren, die *geblieben*;

   Sucht Lieb, die für sie untergeht,

   Sucht Lieb, die mit ihr aufersteht,

   Sucht Lieb, *die sie kann lieben*.

   Poverty goes through the stubble,

   Looking for ears which are left,

   Looking for love which will perish for it,

   Looking for love which will rise with it,

   Looking for love which can love it.

The phrase in the second line - *die geblieben* - is a relative clause, marked with the relative pronoun *die*, referring to *Ähren*. In its full form, the phrase would be *Ähren, die geblieben sind*.

We will return to this poem in a minute, for its interesting last line. I just want to point out that while the auxiliary may be deleted

in the expression of past time, there is an increasingly frequent expression of past *perfect* time by means of a *double* auxiliary, as in sentence (45b) as opposed to more standard (45a):

    (45) a. Ich *hatte* das gemacht.   I had done that.

        b. Ich *habe* das gemacht *gehabt*.

Just as in (42), preposing here works as though the embedded auxiliary
and the past participle are a single unit:

    (46) a. Gemacht *hatte* ich das, als ...

        b. Gemacht gehabt *habe* ich das, als ...

All of these little facts make it seem a bit suspect to represent auxiliaries as though they had the same status as normal lexical verbs.

    Turning now finally to the rule of Verb-to-the-End, two sorts of
comments seem in order. First of all, I gave the impression earlier that
the only place where Verb-to-the-End fails us is where we have a double
infinitive. Only in Literary German does this appear to be strictly so -
Literary here in the sense of a prescriptive grammar. The last line of
the poem in number (44) is a good example of the freedom *not* to apply
Verb-to-the-End in that genre. Again we have a relative clause, here mod-
ifying the word *Lieb*. We would normally expect Verb-to-the-End to apply
to the modal *kann* as well as to the main verb *lieben*, giving *Lieb, die
sie lieben kann*. But for reasons of rhyme and rhythm, the rule is *not*
applied. Of course, poetry is notorious as an art form in which the rules
of normal language use can be stretched and even broken, as is further
illustrated by the fact that in the first line of the poem, the verb *geht*
appears in third position, although this is a main clause. But like the
case of the deleted auxiliary, the non-application of Verb-to-the-End is
also found in colloquial German, as in sentence (47):

    (47) Da waren schon welche,   At that time there were already

        die haben gesegelt.   some (people) who were sailing.

So despite what I said earlier about the double infinitive, the problem
of the position of embedded auxiliaries is really quite general - and,
for an operational description of German word order, quite serious.[16]

---

[16]Recent studies of the production strategies employed by foreign workers

There seems to exist in colloquial German a type of sentence nowhere accountable for in modern theory. Specifically, these are sentences which seem to consist of two sentences where the second is subordinate but not marked as such so that both sentences permit main clause transformations, for example:

(48) Dies sind Probleme, die kann man lösen.

in which the intonation contours and the stress patterns clearly show that what would normally be interpreted as a relative pronoun is interpreted as a demonstrative pronoun.

The structures which I have pointed out as constituting a problem for the Halls' VSO theory for German pose exactly the same problem for Ross's SOV theory or the Standard SVO theory. This is a large problem which merits further investigation.

learning German in an unguided language acquisition situation suggest that there may be two separate rules involved in the positioning of predicative forms. The research group headed by my colleague Jürgen Meisel in Wuppertal would represent a sentence like *Er sagte mir, daß er nach Hause gegangen ist* (He told me that he went home) with the tree

Following the *Aspects* model, the group believes that both verb forms – the auxiliary *ist* and the past participle *gegangen* - are dominated by the same S node. The rule which moves the past participle into final position may be called Particle Movement, since the group treats all non-tensed verb forms in the same manner as they treat verbs with prefixes, like the example in (34) and (35). Unlike the Halls, the group considers sentence (34a) a simplex, with no embedding. The rule which moves the auxiliary to the end of a subordinate clause is the same Verb-to-the-End rule postulated by the Halls. The reason for separating the two cases is that some of their test subjects systematically apply the rule of Particle Movement while never applying Verb-to-the-End in the more restricted sense. As more detailed results of the group's work become available, it should be possible to ascertain more precisely the psychological processes involved.

DEUTSCHE WORTSTELLUNG
UND
MONTAGUE GRAMMATIK

ARNIM VON STECHOW

ENGLISH SUMMARY

There is a lot of descriptive literature on German word order but there are only a few attempts to treat this subject within the framework of a formal grammar. This article concentrates on declarative sentences and tries to capture some important features of their order by means of a Montague-Grammar.

Declaratives exhibit two basic types of word order: *second position* and *final position* of the finite verb.

(1) (Second position) Kasper *schenkt* seiner Freundin einen Rettich.
     (Kasper gives a radish to his girl friend.)

(2) (Final position) (daß) Kasper seiner Freundin einen Rettich *schenkt*.
     ((that) Kasper gives a radish to his girl friend.)

There is a further pecularity in German. Any 'constituent of the main verb' (Satzglied) can occupy the 'front position'. Thus, (3) and (4) are equally possible instead of (2):

(3) Seiner Freundin *schenkt* Kasper einen Rettich.
(4) Einen Rettich *schenkt* Kasper seiner Freundin.

The same holds for adverbs, prepositional phrases and other constructions. So, all of the following sentences are grammatical:

(5) Max *rennt* immer schnell zum Bahnhof.
     (Max always runs quickly to the station.)

(6) Immer *rennt* Max schnell zum Bahnhof.
(7) Schnell *rennt* Max immer zum Bahnhof.
(8) Zum Bahnhof *rennt* Max immer schnell.

There are certainly pragmatic principles governing the choice of one word order rather than another . But this aspect is completely neglected in this article.

As in English, there are discontinuous constituents in German; but
in German, this phenomenon is much more widespread.

(9) Kasper *ruft* seine Freundin *an*.

    (Kasper *calls* his girl friend *up*.)

Besides   discontinuous verbs the compound verb forms typically exhibit
a discontinuous structure.

(10) Kasper *hat* seine Freundin *angerufen*.

    (Kasper has called up his girl friend.)

The words in italics in (9) and (10) are what is called in German grammar
"Satzklammer" ("sentence bracketing"). The first word of the "Satzklammer"
is the finite verb, whereas the last word is an 'affix-part' of it.
The affix-part has a stable position but the finite part changes its place
according to the sentence type as in (11) and (12):

(11) (Final position)

    (daß) Kasper seiner Freundin *angerufen hat*.

(12) (Initial position)

    Hat Kasper seiner Freundin *angerufen?*

The phenomena exposed so far seem to call for a description within
a transformational approach. This has been tried by Bach, Bierwisch and
others. In paragraph 2 of this article a typical drawback of a "classical"
transformational solution is shown. Bierwisch generates a sentence like
(3) from (2) as its "source". (2) roughly has the following "underlying
structure". (For more details, see page 336.)

(2a)

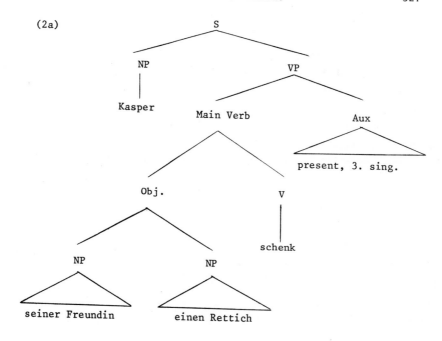

Then, by a series of movement transformations (2a) is transformed into

(3a)

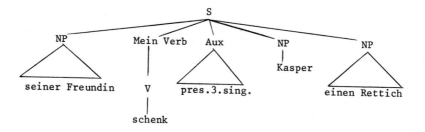

(2a) is the underlying structure of (2). Yet, whereas the tree (2a) is
well-structured, the tree (3a) is 'flat'. It has lost its depth because
the movement transformations destroyed the original structure.
To my mind, this indicates that a classical transformational approach does
not provide for a natural way of reconstructing the syntactic structures
of (2) and (3). The actual nature of these structures might be doubtful,
but whatever the structures of these sentences are, they should be the same
with the only exception that the finite verb occupies a different position.

There is another approach to natural language which apparently gets
along very well with the problem of word order: It is Cresswell's method
of shallow structures. Cresswell's idea is roughly as follows:
He uses a λ-categorial language for the semantic representation of the
sentences of the natural language. By means of "λ-abstraction" any order
of the "non-logical" words of the language can be accounted for.
For instance, sentence (3) can be represented in the following way.

(3b) $((\lambda, v_{NP}, (v_{NP}, (\lambda, z_N, ((\lambda, u_{NP}, (u_{NP}, (\lambda, y, (\textit{Kasper}, (\lambda, x_N, (\textit{schenkt},$
$x_N, y_N, z_N)))))), (\textit{seine}, \textit{Freundin}))))), (\textit{ein}, \textit{Rettich}))$

When we delete the "logical" symbols in (3b) that is, the parentheses,
the variables and the lambdas, then we get the string (3c) which is almost
identical with sentence (3).

(3c) *Kasper schenkt seine Freundin ein Rettich*

Unfortunately, this method does too much. It can be shown that it yields
a common reading for the following two sentences:

(12) Kasper kommt und Hotzenplotz geht.

(Kasper comes and Hotzenplotz goes.)

(13) Kasper geht und Hotzenplotz kommt.

(Kasper goes and Hotzenplotz comes.)

Yet, (12) and (13) certainly have no reading in common. This criticism,
which is due to John Ruttenberg, is exposed in detail in paragraph 3.

In the sections (4) to (15) a fragment of German is described within the framework of a Montague Grammar. As the article's title indicates, particular attention is paid to problems of word order.

Calling the syntactic and semantic method adopted here "Montague-Grammar" is perhaps somewhat misleading. Certain features which are dear to the orthodox Montaguean are lacking completely. For instance, the semantics of the language are not given by means of a translation into the language of intensional logic. The German words are interpreted directly instead and to each syntactic rule a semantic operation is associated which tells how the meanings of the "input constructions" of the rule combine into the meaning of the output construction of the rule. The spirit of this procedure is very close to that of Montague's article "English as a formal language".

The syntactic rules developed in this fragment are determined very strictly by a principle which Barbara Partee calls the "well-formedness constraint" (cf. (47)). This principle roughly says that the construction of a sentence should, at each step, proceed from well-formed parts to a well-formed part of the sentence. In particular, this principle has the consequence that no artificial symbols (dummies, stars, indexed pronouns and so on) are allowed in the derivation of a sentence. I have tried to apply this principle as rigidly as possible. The results are quite promising. The only thing which is still lacking is a well-developed theory of anaphora. Such a theory will be necessary in order to treat the full range of phenomena which Montague accounted for in his article "The proper treatment of quantification in ordinary English". Montague's approach itself does not conform to the well-formedness constraint and therefore it cannot be adopted to German (or English) without modifications.

The reason why I call my grammar a Montague-Grammar is this:
Montague had the (very old) idea that syntax is a recursive procedure
for determining the syntactic categories of a language. You assign the
words of a language to certain syntactic categories. Then you have syntactic
rules which tell you how to combine constructions of certain categories into
a new construction of a particular new category. Furthermore, each syntactic
rule has its semantic interpretation. It was Montague who successfully put
forward this simple and obvious idea. And my fragment is developed exactly
along these lines.

I shall now give a rough idea how the different word order of sentence
(2) and (3) are accounted for in my fragment. The derivation of (2) can be
sketched by the following tree:

(14) Derivation of (2)

1. *schenkt,* VP (*nom,dat,akk*) end
      2. *einen Rettich,* NP akk
3. *einen Rettich schenkt,* VP (*nom,dat*) end, (V1)
      4. *seiner Freundin,* NP dat
5. *seiner Freundin einen Rettich schenkt,* VP (*nom*) end, (V1)
      6. *Kasper,* NP nom
7. *Kasper seiner Freundin einen Rettich schenkt,* S_{end}, (S1)

The syntactic categories are actually much more complicated than in
(14). But the basic idea of the construction should be clear. We start
with the finite verb *schenkt* which needs an accusative, a dative and a
nominative complement in order to yield a sentence. Furthermore, the verb
is in final position. All this is codified in the syntactic "subcategories"
"(*nom,dat,akk*)end". The rest is done by the syntactic rule (V1) and (S1).
The details will be explained later.

The derivation of (3) initially proceeds exactly as the derivation of (2). Yet, at a certain point, a different rule is applied:

(15) Derivation of (3)

1. *seiner Freundin einen Rettich schenkt,* VP (*nom*) end, (cf. 14.5)
2. *schenkt seiner Freundin einen Rettich,* VP (*nom*) zweit, (V4)
   3. *Kasper,* NP *nom*
4. *Kasper schenkt seiner Freundin einen Rettich,* S_{zweit}, $(S5_o)$

The difference in word order which obtains between (14.7) and (15.4) comes in at step 2 of derivation (15). By application of rule (V4), the finite verb *schenkt* moves to the front of the intransitive verbphrase (15.1) in order to yield the intransitive verbphrase (15.2). Thus, (V4) is a sort of movement transformation. Yet, it is not a transformation in the usual sense, mapping trees into trees. It is rather a syntactic operation which puts the verbphrase in the order which is needed if we want to get a nonsubordinate declarative sentence. The syntactic structure of (15.4) and (14.7) are the whole trees (15) and (14) respectively. If we compare the two structures, we see that they are identical up to the generation of the verbphrase (14.5) (=15.1). Afterwards different rules apply. (15) is slightly more complicated than (14). This is a result of the fact that the final position of the verb is the "unmarked" one in this approach. This assumption is commonly made, but it might be wrong, of course.

A rule like (V4) is not formulated as easily as the picture (15) suggests. The technical details are tricky and sometimes tedious. Furthermore, much more complicated constructions than those presented in this summary are treated in the article. For instance passive sentences, relative clauses, modal verbs, infinitive complements and so on.

The semantics of the fragment is given very informally in a Cresswell style. The semantic parts are mostly short, but there is one exception: I have written a rather longish paragraph about "Kasper seeks a unicorn" and "The mayor allowably presides necessarily".

The last section contains a brief discussion of alternative ways of formulating the syntactic rules in a Montague framework. Furthermore, I will say something about proposals by Bach, Partee and Thomason.

0. EINLEITUNG

Von der rechten Art, Syntax zu betreiben

Daß Richard Montagues Leistungen auf dem Gebiet der Semantik natürlicher Sprachen bahnbrechend sind, wird unter Linguisten heutzutage mehr und mehr anerkannt. Weniger allgemein dürfte dagegen die Überzeugung sein, daß auch seine Leistungen zur Syntaxtheorie wegweisend sind. Dies spiegelt sich in zahlreichen Arbeiten des letzten Jahrzehntes wider: man läßt das Prestige des von Chomsky begründeten transformationalistischen Ansatzes für das Gebiet der Syntax unberührt und versucht, Montagues semantische Theorie damit zu vermitteln. Derartige Arbeiten sind zuweilen ein wenig apologetisch. Ich verweise dazu auf den Artikel etwa von D. Lewis (72), B. Partee (77), E. Bach (76), U. Egli (74) oder R. Cooper & T. Parsons (76). Solche Versuche sind verdienstvoll, weil sie zeigen, daß man ein und dieselbe Sache - die Sprache - aus verschiedener Sicht betrachten kann. Die Divergenzen liegen dann oft nur in der Sprache, nicht in der Sache. Dennoch ist es nicht ganz so. Allen transformationalistischen Ansätzen ist es nämlich gemeinsam, daß man irgendwo noch unterscheidet zwischen 'Oberflächen-' und 'Tiefenstruktur' von Sätzen. Das mag für einige Randfälle ein nützliches Begriffspaar sein. Wird diese Unterscheidung aber strapaziert, so schafft sie nach meiner Meinung mehr Probleme, als sie zu lösen gestattet. Diese Ansicht verlangt natürlich eine Begründung, nachdem Chomsky die Notwendigkeit der Unterscheidung von Oberflächen- und Tiefenstruktur mit "überwältigender Evidenz" bewiesen hat. Die Begründung versuche ich in Abschnitt 2 zu geben, wo ich mich mit Bierwischs *Grammatik des deutschen Verbs* auseinandersetze. Meine Gegenposition dazu lautet: "Nimm die syntaktische Form der Ausdrücke einer Sprache ernst bis in jedes Detail, wenn du eine tragfähige Gesamtbeschreibung einer Sprache fertigbringen willst!" Ich glaube, das ist eine Position, die ganz im Geiste Montagues ist. Denn anders als Chomsky hat Montague genau dies getan.

Die Arbeit, die am konsequentesten in diese Richtung gegangen ist, ist "English as a formal Language". Hier werden die Sätze des Englischen mehr oder weniger direkt gedeutet. Gemessen an dem damaligen Stand der

Grammatiktheorie ist dies ein entscheidender Fortschritt, der Montague nur
möglich war, weil er eine sehr reiche semantische Theorie benutzte. (Den
sogenannten "generativen Semantikern" war zu dieser Zeit ein derartiges
Vorgehen vermutlich deshalb verwehrt, weil sie nicht über die dazu nötigen
logischen Methoden verfügten, die dafür Montague mit Meisterschaft be-
herrschte.)[1]

Während - wie gesagt - betreffs Montagues Leistungen zur Semantik
unter all denjenigen, die sich intensiv damit beschäftigt haben, kein Zweifel besteht, ist die Beurteilung seiner syntaktischen Theorie sicher nicht
so einhellig positiv. Ich bin nun der Meinung, daß gerade in dem syntaktischen Apparat, den Montague entwickelt hat, Möglichkeiten stecken, deren
Tragweite bisher noch nicht in das allgemeine Bewußtsein der Gemeinschaft
der Sprachwissenschaftler gedrungen ist. Ich habe wiederholt größere Frag-
mente des Deutschen syntaktisch beschrieben oder an solchen Beschreibungen
mitgewirkt, stets in generativ orientierten Ansätzen.[2] Ferner habe ich natürlich die Literatur nach Maßgabe meiner Kräfte verfolgt. Ich habe dabei
immer gefunden, daß keiner der generativen bzw. transformationellen Ansätze mit der deutschen Wortstellung in einleuchtender Weise fertig wird.
Der vorliegende Aufsatz ist nur ein Versuch, die Montaguesche Syntaxtheorie auf diesen Gegenstandsbereich anzuwenden. Mich selbst befriedigen die
Perspektiven, die dieser Versuch eröffnet hat, weit mehr als die meiner
früheren Bemühungen und mehr als die mir bekannte theoretische Literatur
zur deutschen Wortstellung. Wie bei jeder systematischen Syntax, so fehlt
es natürlich auch hier noch an allen Ecken und Enden. Ich habe aber das
Gefühl, daß der eingeschlagene Weg vielversprechend ist. Dies sage ich
nicht, um das Fragment zu rühmen, das ich später vorlege, sondern um meine
Überzeugung auszudrücken, daß Montagues Art und Weise, Syntax zu treiben,
vielleicht nicht die beste aller möglichen ist, aber doch die beste der
mir bekannten.

[1] Vgl. etwa G. Lakoff (1972)

[2] Vgl. Brockhaus and v. Stechow (1971), Kratzer, Pause, v. Stechow (1974),
v.Stechow (1975)

Wenn ich sage, daß ich eine Montague-Grammatik entwickle, dann ist das nicht so zu verstehen, daß ich die Regeln des Meisters nehme, sie mehr oder weniger direkt ins Deutsche übertrage und um einige Zusätze vermehre (sogenannte "Extensions of PTQ"). Ich habe vielmehr den ganzen Formalismus ungeniert den Erfordernissen der deutschen Syntax angepaßt. Was herausgekommen ist, ist stellenweise sehr verwandt mit dem, was man in traditionellen deutschen Syntaxen liest.[3] Und das ist gut so. Ich halte es für einen der ganz großen Vorzüge des von Montague bereitgestellten Formalismus, daß man die Ergebnisse traditioneller Forschung mehr oder weniger direkt in ihn übertragen kann. Allgemein kann man sagen, daß ich den in Montagues Syntaxen noch vorhandenen Restlogizismus restlos beseitigt habe. Unter anderem gibt es bei mir keinerlei sogenannte indizierte Pronomina wie er_1, er_2, ... usw. mehr, die für die Montaguesche Behandlung der Quantifizierung zentral sind. Meine Syntax ist radikal oberflächenorientiert. Ich werde in Abschnitt 5 noch näher erklären, wie das zu verstehen ist. Ich habe übrigens, als diese Arbeit schon weitgehend fertiggestellt war, einen Aufsatz von B. Partee zu Gesicht bekommen, in dem für ein ganz ähnliches Vorgehen plädiert wird, das ich hier praktiziert habe.[4]

Auch mein Vorgehen als Semantiker orientiert sich nicht sklavisch an Montague. Insbesondere benutze ich nicht die Sprache der intensionalen Logik, die meines Erachtens in erster Linie zum Zwecke der Fregeexegese geschaffen wurde, und die nur dem Eingeweihten verständlich ist. Ich stehe vielmehr in der Tradition von David Lewis' "General Semantics" und besonders von Max Cresswells *Logics and Languages*. Meine skrupellos inhaltlichen Redeweisen werden jeden orthodoxen Montagueaner schockieren, müßten aber einem an der Sprache Interessierten eigentlich gefallen. Im übrigen ist das zentrale Anliegen dieses Ansatzes kein semantisches, sondern ein syntaktisches. Es ist aber nun einmal so, daß ein Montaguegrammatiker keine Syntaxregel schreibt, ohne auch über die inhaltliche Seite nachzudenken. Ich habe das stets getan, wollte dabei aber jeden unnötigen technischen Aufwand vermeiden.

[3] Vgl. etwa Blatz (1895) oder Jørgensen (1976).
[4] Vgl. Partee (1977).

So viel ich Max Cresswell auf dem Gebiet der Semantik verdanke, so
hart gehe ich übrigens mit seiner Auffassung von Syntax ins Gericht. Sein
Buch scheint mir ein Paradebeispiel dafür zu sein, in welche Schwierigkeiten sich der Sprachtheoretiker manövriert, wenn er die Syntax nicht ernst
genug nimmt. Dies zu zeigen ist das Ziel von Abschnitt 3. Ursprünglich war
meine Haltung zu diesem Punkt übrigens nicht so dezidiert. Diese Arbeit
geht auf einen Aufsatz aus dem Jahre 1976 zurück, in dem ich die deutsche Wortstellung im Rahmen der Cresswellschen Theorie zu behandeln versucht habe. Ein Briefwechsel mit Manfred Bierwisch und besonders die Arbeit
von J. Ruttenberg (1976)   haben mich eines Besseren belehrt. Abschnitt
3 kann von allen, die an mehr theoretisch orientierten Fragen nicht so
interessiert sind, überschlagen werden.

Zum Schluß möchte ich noch Inge Tedjajuwana für ihre Unterstützung
bei der Ausarbeitung der Syntaxregeln danken. Für kritische Bemerkungen
danke ich meinen Kollegen im Sonderforschungsbereich 99 "Linguistik". Ganz
besonders wertvoll waren mir Hinweise von I. Heim und W. Sternefeld.

1.   EINIGE TATSACHEN ÜBER DAS DEUTSCHE VERB

Ich möchte hier einige Fakten über das deutsche Verb ins Ge-
dächtnis rufen. Dies geschieht mit dem Ziel, die Merkmale zu erarbeiten,
nach denen die Verben auf jeden Fall unterklassifiziert werden müssen,
will man ihrem syntaktischen Verhalten einigermaßen gerecht werden.

Bekanntlich gibt es im Deutschen drei Grundstellungen des finiten
Verbs: Anfangs-, Zweit- und Endstellung.[5]

Resümieren wir zunächst einige wichtige Eigenheiten der Zweitstellung. Erich Drach hat meines Wissens als erster mit Nachdruck darauf hingewiesen, daß das Deutsche keineswegs eine Subjekt-Verb-Objekt-Sprache ist,
sondern daß ein beliebiges "Satzglied" vor dem Finitum stehen kann.[6]

---

[5] Für eine derartige neutrale Charakterisierung im Gegensatz zu "Frage-,
Haupt- und Nebensatzstellung" spricht sich mit guten Gründen Glinz aus.
(1970,   S. 71 f.). Z.B. hat in dem Satz "Er sagt, er müsse sich be-
trinken" das finite Verb des Nebensatzes Zweitstellung.

[6] Vgl. Drach (1940)

(1) a. Max rennt immer schnell zum Bahnhof.

    b. Immer rennt Max schnell zum Bahnhof.

    c. Schnell rennt Max immer zum Bahnhof.

    d. Zum Bahnhof rennt Max immer schnell.

Ich will dabei voraussetzen, daß wir wissen, was ein Satzglied ist, hier das Nominal *Max* sowie die Adverbialien *schnell, immer* und *zum Bahnhof*.[7] Falls alle die genannten Satzglieder hinter dem Verb stehen, muß ein suppletives *es* an den Anfang.

    e. Es rennt Max immer schnell zum Bahnhof.

Nehmen wir einmal an, e. spiegele die normale Reihenfolge der hier vertretenen Satzglieder wider. Dann sieht es so aus, als dürfe man im Deutschen jedes Satzglied an die Stelle des *es* setzen, wobei die übrigen Glieder ihre Abfolge beibehalten.[8] Diese Gesetzmäßigkeit wollen wir die *Drachsche Regel* nennen.

Etwas komplizierter gestalten sich die Verhältnisse bei Verben mit obligatorisch abtrennbarem Affix, wie etwa *abholen* ("trennbare Verben").

    (2) a. Max holt Richard Burtons Frau vom Bahnhof ab.

       b. Richard Burtons Frau holt Max vom Bahnhof ab.

       c. Vom Bahnhof holt Richard Burtons Frau Max ab.

       d. Es holt Max Richard Burtons Frau vom Bahnhof ab.

holt und *ab* bilden die sogenannte "Satzklammer". Die Drachsche Regel gilt auch hier, wobei *ab* allerdings nicht als Satzglied gerechnet wird.

---

[7] Ich möchte keineswegs suggerieren, daß die genaue Festlegung von Satzgliedern im einzelnen unproblematisch ist. Zum Beispiel sind u.U. Adverbiale und Nominalphrasen Satzglieder, Artikel dagegen nicht. Kriterien für die syntaktische Bestimmung von Satzgliedern werden beispielsweise in Engelen angegeben. Vgl. Engelen (1973).

[8] Wolf Thümmel hat mich darauf aufmerksam gemacht, daß die gängige deutsche syntaktische Terminologie teilweise der Sexualsphäre entstammt: "Satzglied, Kopula, Spannsatz, Anfangs-, Zweit- und Endstellung". Das ist für mich noch kein Grund, diese Terminologie aufzugeben, etwa zugunsten von MS_6, SitP, Σ_3 oder KopKj., einer Nomenklatur, die von Clément & Thümmel propagiert wird.

        e. Abholt Max Richard Burtons Frau vom Bahnhof.

e. versteht man zwar, aber wir wollen diesen Satz nicht als wohlgebildet ansehen.[9]

Für eine Syntax des deutschen Verbs gilt, daß man den abtrennbaren Teil eines Verbs auf jeden Fall kennzeichnen muß. Was seine Herkunft betrifft, so kann er bekanntlich sehr verschiedenen Wortarten angehören; man denke etwa an: rad+fahren, schwer+fallen, durch+sägen. Die Unterkategorie "abtrennbarer Teil" wird übrigens bei der syntaktischen Beschreibung eine noch weit wesentlichere Funktion erhalten, als man das auf Anhieb denken sollte.

Noch eine letzte Bemerkung zur Satzklammer: Satzglieder mit besonderem Eigengewicht (etwa ab 25 Kilopond) werden manchmal aus der Satzklammer an das Ende ausgeklammert.

        f. Max holt Richard Burtons Frau ab vom Bahnhof
          in Wellington.

Diese Möglichkeit werde ich im folgenden aber nicht berücksichtigen. Als ungrammatisch werde ich dagegen

        g. Max abholt Richard Burtons Frau vom Bahnhof.

klassifizieren.

Nun möchte ich etwas zur sogenannten Valenzproblematik sagen. Ein Verb wie *schenken* verlangt drei nominale Ergänzungen im Nominativ, Dativ und Akkusativ, und zwar in der genannten Reihenfolge. Daß diese Glieder erfordert werden, sieht man an der Unvollständigkeit der folgenden Sätze:

    (3) a. + Ihm schenkt das Buch

        b. ? Er schenkt ihm.

        c. ? Er schenkt das Buch.

---

[9] Besonders im poetischen Gebrauch kommen Sätze dieser Art natürlich vor: "Eintritt Franz Mohr". Bei besonderer Betonung sagt man auch ohne weiteres "An kam er nie". Bezeichnenderweise trennt man hier aber Affix vom finiten Teil in der Schrift. Wenn man e. übrigens zulassen will, werden die Syntaxregeln einfach noch einfacher.

In (3) a. ist die Nominativergänzung fortgelassen. Das führt zu einem ganz unverständlichen Satz. Bei einer Äußerung von b. müßten wir wohl fragen *Was?* und bei einer von c. *Wem?*.

Daß die Reihenfolge Nominativ-Dativ-Akkusativ die normale ist, sieht man daran, daß die folgenden a.-Konstruktionen jeweils besser als die b.-Konstruktionen sind:

(4) a.   Peter schenkt seinem Bruder ein Buch.

    b. ? Peter schenkt ein Buch seinem Bruder.

(5) a.   Schenkt Peter seinem Bruder ein Buch?

    b. ? Schenkt Peter ein Buch seinem Bruder?

(6) a.   Weil Peter seinem Bruder ein Buch schenkt

    b. ? Weil seinem Bruder Peter ein Buch schenkt

In allgemeinen erhalten wir stets einen guten Satz, wenn wir bei dem Verb *schenkt* der Drachschen Regel die Reihenfolge Nominativ-Dativ-Akkusativ zugrundelegen, während dies nicht gewährleistet ist, wenn wir eine andere Kasusabfolge ansetzen.

Dies zeigen die Siebenersätze im Gegensatz zu den Achterbeispielen, wo einmal die Normalreihenfolge Pate steht und das andere Mal die parasitäre Abfolge Nominativ-Akkusativ-Dativ. (Man hätte natürlich etwa auch Akkusativ-Nominativ-Dativ nehmen können.)

(7) a.   Es schenkt Peter seinem Bruder ein Buch.

    b.   Peter schenkt seinem Bruder ein Buch.

    c.   Seinem Bruder schenkt Peter ein Buch.

    d.   Ein Buch schenkt Peter seinem Bruder.

(8) a. ? Es schenkt Peter ein Buch seinem Bruder.

    b. ? Peter schenkt ein Buch seinem Bruder.

    c.   Ein Buch schenkt Peter seinem Bruder.

    d.   Seinem Bruder schenkt Peter ein Buch.

Die Sätze (8) c. und (8) d. sind in Ordnung, weil sie auch durch Anwendung der Drachschen Regel auf (7) a. erhalten werden können, und (7) a. ein wohlgeformter Ausdruck ist.

Die Drachsche Regel ist aber nicht ganz ohne Ausnahmen. Zum Beispiel
kann man sagen

(9) a.   Wir schenkten es seinem Bruder.

Aber nicht

b. + Wir schenkten seinem Bruder es.

Dies ist so, obwohl der Konstruktion (9) b. die "normale" Kasusabfolge zu-
grundeliegt. Ebenfalls geht nicht:

c. + Es schenkten wir seinem Bruder.

Ich will hier nicht über die Gründe für die Mißbildungen (9) b. und
(9) c. spekulieren. Man kann versuchen, die Ursachen für derartige Ein-
schränkungen zu ergründen, um sie dann in Regeln zu fassen. Aber schon
Bierwisch bezweifelt, daß es sinnvoll ist, eine Syntax bis in alle diese
Einzelheiten vorwärtszutreiben. Er meint, man müsse zwischen wichtigen und
marginalen Erscheinungen unterscheiden.[10] Damit kann ich mich einverstanden
erklären, jedenfalls für die Zwecke dieses Aufsatzes.[11]

Ich möchte also festhalten, daß die für ein Verb typischen Ergänzungen und ihre Reihenfolge auf jeden Fall bei der syntaktischen Klassifikation berücksichtigt werden müssen. Ich will mich dabei in keiner Weise
auf das heikle Thema einlassen, wie man die Ergänzungen im einzelnen rechtfertigt. Es gibt dazu eine umfangreiche Literatur, die ich nicht einmal
annähernd überschaue.[12]

(Ich bin übrigens nicht sicher, ob man die jeweilige Valenzfestlegung
durch grundsätzliche Überlegungen unabhängig von bestimmten Beschreibungs-
zwecken begründen kann.) Um Mißverständnisse zu vermeiden: Verben verlangen
nicht nur Kasusgruppen im engeren Sinne als Ergänzungen, sondern etwa auch

[10] Vgl. Drach (1940:14).

[11] Bach hält nicht viel von einer solchen Haltung. Er meint, je mehr Details man berücksichtigt, desto näher käme man der eigentlichen Struktur
einer Sprache. Siehe Brockhaus and v. Stechow (1971:15).
Zweifellos ist auch diese Ansicht richtig.

[12] Vgl. etwa Engelen (1973), Flämig (1960), Helbig and Schenkel (1969).

Adverbiale oder Infinitivkonstruktionen. Z.B. verlangt *wohnen* eine Nominativergänzung plus ein lokales Adverbial. Man kann nicht sagen

(10) a. + Er wohnt.

wohl aber

                    b.   Er wohnt dort.

Sätze wie

                    c.   Er wohnt preisgünstig.

könnte man vielleicht als elliptisch ansehen, als zurückgehend auf

                    d.   Er wohnt in einer Wohnung, die preisgünstig ist.

oder dergleichen mehr. (Was weggelassen ist, muß wohl der Kontext klarmachen.) Ich werde zu Konstruktionen dieser Art übrigens nichts sagen, sondern verweise etwa auf R. Steinitz.[13] Das mag genug (wenn natürlich auch viel zu wenig) zur Valenzproblematik sein.

Es bleibt mir nun noch zu bemerken, daß sich im Deutschen das finite Verb in Person und Numerus nach dem Subjekt richtet.[14] Deswegen müssen Numerus und Person bei der syntaktischen Klassifizierung berücksichtigt werden. Schließlich benötigt man noch stets eine Angabe, ob ein Verb mit *sein* oder *haben* konjugiert wird.

Zusammenfassend läßt sich also sagen, daß zumindest mit den folgenden syntaktischen Merkmalen für das Verb zu rechnen ist.

    1) Stellungstyp: Anfangs-, Zweit- und Endstellung

    2) Typische Ergänzung (Valenz)

    3) Kennzeichnung des Affixteils

    4) Person und Numerus

    5) Konjugation mit sein und haben.

Diese Merkmale geben aber nur erste Anhaltspunkte. Wie wir später sehen werden, erfordern die tatsächlichen Verhältnisse ein weit detaillierteres Begriffsinventar.

---

[13] Vgl. Thomason (1976).

[14] Das gilt nicht für Kopulasätze: "Dies sind zwei Kälber".

2. DIE DEUTSCHE WORTSTELLUNG BEI BIERWISCH

Immer noch die ausführlichste generativ orientierte Arbeit zur deutschen Wortstellung ist nach meiner Kenntnis Manfred Bierwischs *Grammatik des deutschen Verbs*. Ich möchte diese Schrift hier benutzen, um eine unschöne Konsequenz aufzuzeigen, die ein klassisch transformationalistisches Vorgehen meines Erachtens unweigerlich nach sich zieht, und zwar im Zusammenhang mit den sogenannten Umstellungsregeln.[15] Bei der Beschreibung der deutschen Wortstellung spielen derartige Regeln dann eine Rolle, wenn es darum geht, die verschiedenen Stellungen des finiten Verbs zu beschreiben. Bierwischs Vorgehen ist hier typisch transformationalistisch. Er zeichnet die Endstellung des Verbs aus und leitet die übrigen Stellungen daraus ab. So liegt etwa dem Satz (1) b. der Satz (1) a. zugrunde.

(1) a. (daß) Kasper seiner Freundin einen Rettich schenkt

b. Kasper schenkt seiner Freundin einen Rettich.

Man sollte denken, daß die syntaktische Struktur von b. derjenigen von a. sehr ähnlich ist. Wir haben ein finites Verb mit drei nominalen Ergänzungen in fester Reihenfolge, nur steht das Verb in b. nach der ersten nominalen Ergänzung, in a. dagegen nach der dritten. Ich würde mir nun für a. und b. "Oberflächenstrukturen" wünschen, die bis auf den genannten Unterschied völlig gleich aussehen. Das aber ist in einer Syntax der chomskyschen Art nicht ohne weiteres möglich. Schauen wir einmal, weshalb. Bierwisch weist dem Satz (1) a. etwa die folgende Tiefenstruktur zu:

---

[15] Bei den Amerikanern: "movement rules".

(2) a.

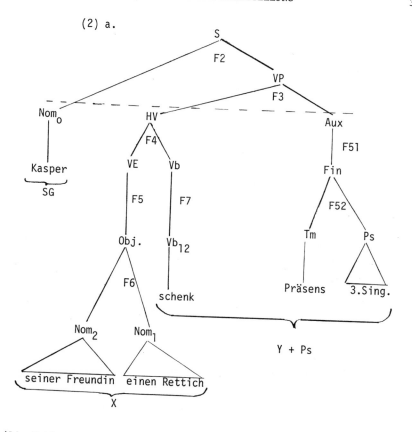

(Die Zahlen an den Verzweigungen geben die Nummern der Bierwischschen For-
mationsregeln an. Die gestrichelten Linien sowie die Zeichen SG, X, Y und
PS beziehen sich auf die Regel, die gleich diskutiert werden wird.) Es
ist klar, daß dieser Baum ein vernünftiger Kandidat für die Oberflächenstruktur von (1) a. ist.

Es gibt nun eine Umstellungsregel, welche aus (2) a. die zu (2) b. gehörige Oberflächenstruktur herleitet, und zwar die folgende (vgl. Bierwisch
(1973:111).

(T16) "Verb-Umstellung-Hauptsatz"

$$SB: \quad (\left\{ \begin{array}{c} (SG)(W) \\ \\ Imp \end{array} \right\} \quad , X, /Y + Ps)$$

SV: $\quad X_1 X_2 X_3 \rightarrow X_1 X_3 X_2$

wobei: $X \neq I + Z \quad Y \neq L / U$

$X_1 \neq$ leere Kette, wenn $X_2 = H_1 + PP(P1)K_0 + H_2$

Bedingung: obligatorisch L, U, H_1, H_2 beliebige Ketten.

Ich habe diese Regel hier aufgeschrieben, um ein Gefühl für die Verständnisschwierigkeiten zu vermitteln, die man bei der Lektüre von transformationellen Arbeiten stets zu bewältigen hat. Wie in 99 % der generativen Grammatiken ist nämlich auch hier nicht detailliert erklärt, wie der benutzte Formalismus genau funktioniert. Beispielsweise würde ich aufgrund der Strukturbeschreibung (SB) von T16 den Schnitt so durch den Baum legen, wie das die gestrichelte Linie in (2) a. zeigt. (SG steht bei Bierwisch für "Satzglied". Darunter fallen unter anderem auch die Nom_0, d.h. nominativische Nominalkomplexe.) Das hätte aber zur Folge, daß nur der Aux-Komplex an die zweite Stelle rückt, was Bierwisch aber nicht intendiert. Der Schnitt muß also irgendwie so gelegt werden, daß er den mit SG, X und Y+Ps indizierten Klammern entspricht.[16] Wenn wir von dieser Interpretation von T 16 ausgehen, dann führt eine Anwendung dieser Regel auf (2) a. zu der folgenden Struktur:

---

[16] Transformationsregeln wirklich sauber zu formulieren, scheint eine Wissenschaft für methodenbewußte Pedanten zu sein. Ich möchte deshalb betonen, daß mich Fehler nicht interessieren, wenn offensichtlich das Richtige gemeint ist. Da es mir in diesem Aufsatz aber unter anderem auch um Methoden der syntaktischen Beschreibung geht, erlaube ich mir derartige Hinweise auf Schwierigkeiten. Sorgfältig eingeführte Formalismen für Transformationsregeln findet man bei ihrem Erfinder, Chomsky, übrigens nie. Vgl. dazu etwa Ginsburg and Partee (1969), Peters and Ritchie (1973) oder Pause (1976).

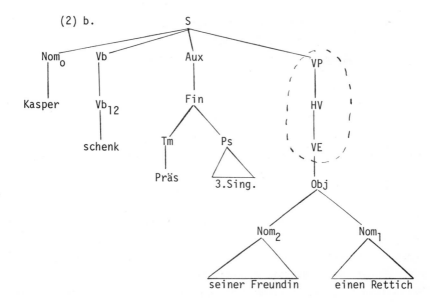

(2) b.

Weil die Objektgruppe "seiner Freundin einen Rettich" für sich alleine
sicher nicht als eine Verbgruppe (VP) interpretiert werden kann, gibt es
bei Bierwisch eine Konvention zur Knotenreduktion, aufgrund derer die mit
der gestrichelten Linie eingekreisten Knoten VP, HV und VE fortfallen.[17]
Diese müssen wir uns also aus der Zeichnung (2) b. wegdenken. Damit erhalten wir durch die Transformation T16 ein wesentlich "flacheres" Gebilde
als die Ausgangsstruktur (2) a. Und noch mehr reduziert sich die Struktur,
wenn wir die Oberflächenstruktur für den Satz (2) c. herleiten wollen:

(2) c. Seiner Freundin schenkt Kasper einen Rettich.

Die Tiefenstruktur dafür ist wieder (2) a. Allerdings muß man, bevor man
T16 anwenden kann, zunächst das Dativobjekt an den Anfang des Satzes bringen. Das leistet die Regel "Satzglied-Umstellung".

---

[17] Die Konvention besagt, daß "für jeden Ast, der bei der Permutation 'ge-
schnitten' wird, der Knoten, von dem er ausgeht, eliminiert wird und
alle Äste beim nächsthöheren Knoten neu angefügt werden." (Bierwisch
(1973)).

Ich will diese hier nicht bringen, sondern mich mit dem Hinweis begnügen, daß die oberflächennahe Struktur von (1) c. dann im Endeffekt so aussieht:

(3) c.

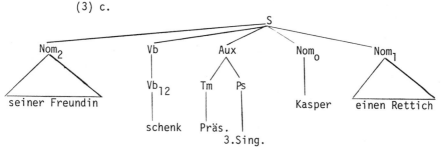

Hier ist das Werk der Zerstörung – wenn man von der Struktur (2) a. ausgeht – weit fortgeschritten. Und das liegt nicht etwa an den speziellen Regeln von Bierwisch. Jeder, der einmal intensiv mit Umstellungsregeln gearbeitet hat, weiß, daß sie reiche Strukturen wie (2) a. zerstören müssen. "Konstituenten", die an einem einzigen Knoten hängen, kann man dagegen beliebig und ohne nachteilige Folgen für die Struktur vertauschen. Warum wählt man dann nicht als Tiefenstruktur für (1) a. ein ärmeres, permutationsfreundlicheres Gebilde, also etwas Ähnliches wie (3) c.? Nun, die Antwort ist meines Erachtens die, daß eine Struktur wie (2) a. letztlich semantisch motiviert ist. (3) c. dürfte nicht besonders geeignet dafür sein, wenn es darum geht, die Bedeutung von (1) c. zu bestimmen. Da greift man auf (2) a. zurück.

Wir halten das Ergebnis dieses Paragraphen fest, daß ein klassisch transformationeller Ansatz dem Satz (1) a. auf der einen und den Sätzen (1) b. und (1) c. auf der anderen Seite völlig verschiedene Oberflächenstrukturen zuweist, obwohl diese Sätze praktisch gleich gebaut sind und sich nur durch die Stellung bestimmter Glieder unterscheiden.
Man kann eine syntaktische Theorie, die Derartiges zur notwendigen Folge hat, zwar nicht als unsinnig abtun. Sicher aber ist es erlaubt zu sagen: so eine Theorie ist sehr häßlich.

3.   KANN MAN SYNTAX WEGERKLÄREN?

Betrachtungen zu einem Versuch von Cresswell

Max Cresswell (1973) schlägt ein Verfahren vor, das scheinbar gut mit Stellungsphänomenen der bisher diskutierten Art fertig wird. Es ist dem Vorgehen der Transformationsgrammatik in mancher Hinsicht extrem entgegengesetzt. Cresswells Grundidee ist es, eine "semantische Sprache" zur Darstellung der Tiefenstrukturen zu benutzen, die keine spezielle Wortstellung auszeichnet. Diese Tiefenstrukturen werden zunächst durch einen simplen Umformungsprozeß auf manchmal recht oberflächennahe "Seichtstrukturen" (shallow structures) abgebildet. Es soll dann eine Art Filter geben, der die in der Sprache nicht realisierten Seichtstrukturen abfängt

Dieser Ansatz führt in große Schwierigkeiten. Das hat meines Erachtens John Ruttenberg völlig überzeugend gezeigt. (1976)   . Ich bin Angelika Kratzer zu Dank dafür verpflichtet, daß sie mich auf Ruttenbergs Kritik aufmerksam gemacht hatte. Sie hat übrigens schon vor dem Bekanntwerden der Ruttenbergschen Arbeit dieselben Einwände geäußert.) Ich will hier nicht sämtliche Argumente Ruttenbergs bringen, sondern nur das Wichtigste.

Ich entwickle in diesem Abschnitt einige technische Begriffe, die für den Hauptteil des Aufsatzes nicht gebraucht werden. Der an Syntaxtheorie nicht interessierte Leser kann deshalb diesen Paragraphen getrost überschlagen.

Die von Cresswell benutzte semantische Sprache ist eine kategoriale Sprache mit Abstraktionssymbol λ. Sie wird λ-kategoriale Sprache genannt. Ihr Bauprinzip ist das einfachste der Welt.[18]

Zunächst gibt es sogenannte syntaktische Typen. Dazu gehören zwei Grundtypen, nämlich der Typ S der Sätze und der Typ N der Namen. Sodann lassen sich nach der folgenden Regel zusammengesetzte Typen bilden:

---

[18] Ich halte mich in der Darstellung mehr an David Lewis' "General Semantics".

Wenn τ, $\sigma_1,..,\sigma_n$ Typen sind, dann ist auch $(\tau/\sigma_1,...,\sigma_n)$ ein Typ.
Eine λ-kategoriale Sprache L^λ wird durch ein Lexikon festgelegt. Das ist
eine Funktion *Kon*, die jedem Typ eine Menge von Symbolen zuordnet. Für die
meisten Typen σ ist Kon_σ die leere Menge. Kon_σ ist die Menge der Konstanten vom Typ σ. Die Vereinigung aller Mengen Kon_σ ist die Menge der Konstanten von L^λ.

Das Lexikon gibt man am besten in Form einer Liste an, deren Einträge jeweils aus einer Konstante plus dem syntaktischen Typ besteht, zu dem diese gehört. Ein Beispiel für ein Lexikon ist das folgende:

3.1 *schimpft*
   lacht $\qquad$ S/N

   schenkt $\qquad$ S/N,N,N

   ein $\qquad$ (S/(S/N))/(S/N)

   Rettich $\qquad$ S/N

   Hotzenplotz
   Kasper $\qquad$ N

   und $\qquad$ S/S,S

Zusätzlich zu den Konstanten gibt es dann noch gewisse logische Symbole,
nämlich das Abstraktionssymbol λ und eine abzählbar unendliche Menge Var_σ
von Variablen für jeden Typ σ. Wir verlangen, daß die Variablenmengen
verschiedener Typen keine gemeinsamen Zeichen erhalten. Ferner darf es
keine Überschneidungen zwischen Variablen und Konstanten geben.
Auf der Grundlage von *Kon*, *Var* und λ können wir induktiv die Ausdrücke
(Terme) *Tm* für jeden Typ σ definieren:

3.2 *Tm* ist diejenige Funktion, deren Argumente die Typen sind und
   deren Werte die kleinsten Mengen sind, die den folgenden Bedingungen genügen. Für beliebige Typen $\sigma,\tau,\sigma_1,...,\sigma_n$ gilt:

a. $Var_\sigma \subseteq Tm_\sigma$;

b. $Kon_\sigma \subseteq Tm_\sigma$;

c. Wenn $\alpha_1, \ldots, \alpha_n$ beziehungsweise zu $Tm_{\sigma_1}, \ldots, Tm_{\sigma_n}$ gehören und δ ein Element von $Tm_{\tau/\sigma_1, \ldots, \sigma_n}$ ist, dann ist

$(\delta, \alpha_1, \ldots, \alpha_n) \in Tm_\tau$.

d. Wenn $x \in Var_\sigma$ und $\alpha \in Tm_\tau$, dann $(\lambda, x, \alpha) \in Tm_{\tau/\sigma}$.

Ein Ausdruck δ vom Typ $\tau/\sigma_1 \ldots \sigma_n$ heißt *Funktor*. δ macht aus Ausdrücken der Typen $\sigma_1, \ldots, \sigma_n$ einen neuen Ausdruck vom Typ τ. Ausdrücke der Form (λ, x, α) heißen *Abstrakte*. Abstrakte sind natürlich ebenfalls Funktoren. Die runden Klammern dienen hier zur Darstellung von Folgen.

Aufgrund dieser Festlegung sind die folgenden Ausdrücke Sätze:

(1) a. (*lacht*, *Kasper*)

    b. (*und*, (*lacht*, *Kasper*), (*schimpft*, *Hotzenplotz*))

    c. ((*ein*, *Rettich*), (λ, x_N, (*schenkt*, *Hotzenplotz*, *Kasper*, x_N)))

Jedem Satz der λ-kategorialen Sprache L^λ entspricht nun eine Seichtstruktur. Diese erhält man aus ihm durch Weglassen der inneren "Klammern" und der logischen Symbole. Die Seichtstrukturen für unsere Sätze sind der Reihe nach

(2) a. (*lacht*, *Kasper*)

    b. (*und*, *lacht*, *Kasper*, *schimpft*, *Hotzenplotz*)

    c. (*ein*, *Rettich*, *schenkt*, *Hotzenplotz*, *Kasper*)

Seichtstrukturen sollen in der Regel schon wie deutsche Sätze aussehen. Wir sehen, daß dies allenfalls für (2) a. der Fall ist, der vielleicht eine Darstellung des Satzes

(3) a. Es lacht Kasper

sein könnte. Cresswells Semantik stellt übrigens sicher, daß (3) a. auch dieselbe Bedeutung wie (2) a. hat. Die Struktur (2) c. ist vielleicht ein Kandidat für die Darstellung des Satzes

(3) c. Einen Rettich schenkt Hotzenplotz Kasper.

Wieder stellt die Semantik sicher, daß (2) c. im Sinne von (3) c. gedeutet wird. Es muß allerdings unbedingt verhindert werden, daß die Seichtstruktur (2) c. in den Oberflächensatz (3) d. überführt wird, denn dieser bedeutet etwas ganz anderes:

     (3) d. Ein Rettich schenkt Hotzenplotz Kasper.

Wie dies verhindert werden soll, ist mir völlig nebulös. Und Schwierigkeiten dieser Art führen meines Erachtens dann schließlich Cresswells Ansatz ad absurdum.

Der Seichtstruktur (2) b. entspricht kein deutscher Satz, obwohl ihre Tiefenstruktur (1) b. im Sinne des Satzes

     (3) b. Kasper lacht und Hotzenplotz schimpft

gedeutet wird. Die Wortfolge von (2) b. ist einfach nicht realisiert im Deutschen. Aus rein syntaktischen Gründen muß (2) b. deswegen weggefiltert werden.

    Wir werden später sehen, daß es in einer λ-kategorialen Sprache einen Ausdruck gibt, der dieselbe Bedeutung wie (1) b. hat und dessen Seichtstruktur ganz ähnlich wie (3) b. aussieht. Das hält Cresswell für einen der großen Vorzüge seines Ansatzes.

Ich komme darauf zurück, möchte aber zuvor etwas mehr dazu sagen, wie man Seichtstrukturen aus λ-kategorialen Ausdrücken gewinnt. Bereits John Ruttenberg (1976) hat bemerkt, daß Cresswells Redeweise vom Wegstreichen der inneren Klammern und der logischen Symbole in keiner Weise präzise ist. Wenn die Ausdrücke (1) a. bis c. Ketten wären, wie man das aus der Linguistik, Logik etc. meist gewohnt ist, dann wüßte man genau, was hier gemeint ist. Sie sind es aber nicht, sondern es handelt sich um Folgen. Cresswell (1973) weist zwar explizit auf diesen Umstand hin, entwickelt aber nie die einschlägige Begrifflichkeit. Das ist ihm von seinen Kritikern oft vorgehalten worden.[19]

Ich will dies hier für ihn nachholen. Die Begriffe sind nicht schwierig und werden später, wie gesagt, sowieso benötigt.

---

[19] Z.B. von Rennie in seiner Kritik an Cresswell.

3.3 DEFINITION. Sei M irgendeine Menge und n = {0,1,...,n-1} die ersten n natürlichen Zahlen. Dann ist jede Funktion s von n in M eine *n-
stellige Folge von Elementen vom M.* Wenn n = 0, d.h. wenn n die leere
Menge ∅ ist, dann ist s die *leere Folge ∅.*

Man kann natürlich auch Folgen von Folgen betrachten, und das geschieht genau bei der Definition der kategorialen Ausdrücke.
Zum Beispiel ist (1) b., also

    (*und*, (*lacht, Kasper*), (*schimpft, Hotzenplotz*))

eine dreistellige Folge, deren zweites Glied die zweistellige Folge

    (*lacht, Kasper*)

ist. Mengentheoretisch wird (1) b. folgendermaßen dargestellt:

    (1) ba. {<0, *und*>,<1,(*lacht, Kasper*)>,<2,(*schimpft,*

            Hotzenplotz)>}

Wenn man bedenkt, daß (*lacht, Kasper*) und (*schimpft, Hotzenplotz*) ihrer-
seits wieder Folgen sind, entpuppt sich (1) ba. als die Menge:

    (1) bb. {<0, *und*>,<1,{ < 0, *lacht*>,<1, *Kasper*>}> ,

            <2,{ < 0, *schimpft*>,<1, *Hotzenplotz*>}>} .

Diese stellt man übersichtlicher als Baum dar:

    (1) bc.

Eine andere, von Montague meistens benutzte Darstellungsweise ist
die folgende:

    (1) b'c.

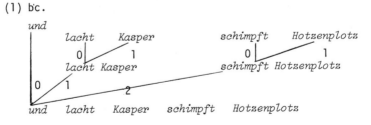

Es sollte klar sein, daß alle diese Notationen genau auf dasselbe
hinauslaufen. Die Moral, die wir daraus ziehen, ist, daß wir es bei einem
λ-kategorialen Ausdruck nicht etwa mit einer Kette von Symbolen zu tun haben, sondern eben mit einem Baum. D.h., der Ausdruck (1) b. ist nicht nur
linear geordnet, sondern auch hierarchisch.[20]
Man kann diese Strukturierung dazu ausnutzen, um einen recht allgemeinen
Begriff des Vorkommens eines Konstituenten innerhalb eines Ausdrucks zu definieren.

Zunächst kann man aus zwei Folgen s und t durch "Hintereinander-
schalten" eine neue Folge st bilden. Falls $s = (s_0,...,s_{n-1})$ und $t = (t_0,
...,t_{m-1})$, dann ist st die n+m-stellige Folge $(s_0,...,s_{n-1},t_0,...,t_{m-1})$.
Die Verknüpfung von s mit der leeren Folge ändert nichts, d.h. wir haben:
$s\emptyset = s = \emptyset s$.[21] Nun legen wir fest:

3.4 DEFINITION. Sei α eine beliebige Folge.

a. α *kommt in* α *an der Stelle* $\emptyset$ *vor.*

b. Wenn β eine Folge der Gestalt $(\beta_1,...,\beta_n)$ ist, die in α an
der Stelle s vorkommt, dann *kommen* β_1 ...,β_n *in* α beziehungsweise *an den Stellen* $s(0)$.,...,$s(n-1)$ *vor.*

(Wenn β an der Stelle n in α vorkommt, nennen wir $<n,\beta>$ auch
ein *Konstituentenvorkommnis* von β in α.)

---

[20] Alles, was Tesnière mit seinem *ordre linéaire* versus *ordre structural*
im Sinne hatte, läßt sich hier leicht rekonstruieren.

[21] Eine Definition der Verknüpfung von Folgen (des Hintereinanderschaltens),
die dies leistet, ist etwa die folgende: Sei s eine n-, t eine m-stelli-
ge Folge. Dann ist st: $= s \cup \{ <p,q> : <p-n,q> \in t\}$.

Nach dieser Definition kommt etwa Hotzenplotz in (1) b. an der Stelle (2,1) vor. Man kann das den Bäumen (1) bc. und (1) bd. direkt ablesen, indem man die Wegnummern sammelt, die von der Wurzel zum Symbol führen. Aufgrund unserer Festlegung gibt es übrigens für (*lacht, Kasper*) ein Konstituentenvorkommnis in (1) b., nicht aber für (*Kasper, schimpft*). Das stimmt völlig mit dem üblichen Sprachgebrauch überein.

Wir sind nun endlich in der Lage, präzise zu sagen, was bei Cresswell mit dem Wegstreichen der inneren Klammern und der logischen Symbole gemeint ist. Dies leistet die Anwendung der folgenden Funktion f auf irgendeinen λ-kategorialen Ausdruck.

3.5 Die *Seichtstruktur* $f(\alpha)$ für den λ-kategorialen Ausdruck α wird folgendermaßen definiert:

a. Wenn α eine Variable ist, dann ist $f(\alpha) = \emptyset$.

b. Wenn α eine Konstante ist, dann ist $f(\alpha) = (\alpha)$.[22]

c. Wenn α die Gestalt $(\delta, \alpha_1, \ldots, \alpha_n)$ hat, dann ist $f(\alpha)$
   $= f(\delta) f(\alpha_1) \ldots f(\alpha_n)$.

c. Wenn α das Abstrakt (λ, x, β) ist, dann ist $f(\alpha) = f(\beta)$.

Nach dieser Definition ist die Seichtstruktur von (1) c. die anfangs genannte Folge (1) c:

(*ein, Rettich, schenkt, Hotzenplotz, Kasper*).[23]

---

[22] D.h. $\{<0, \alpha>\}$.

[23] $f((1)\ c) = f(ein, Rettich)\ f((\lambda, x_N, (schenkt, Hotzenplotz, Kasper, x)))$
         nach 3.5 c.
   $= f(ein)\ f(Rettich)\ f(schenkt, Hotzenplotz, Kasper, x)$
         nach c. und d.
   $= (ein)\ (Rettich)\ f(schenkt)\ f(Hotzenplotz)\ f(Kasper)\ f(x)$
         nach b. und c.
   $= (ein)\ (Rettich)\ (schenkt)\ (Hotzenplotz)\ (Kasper)\ \emptyset$
         nach a. und b.
   $= (ein, Rettich, schenkt, Hotzenplotz, Kasper)$
         nach der Definition der Verknüpfung
         von Folgen.

Cresswells Begriff der Seichtstruktur eines Ausdrucks ist damit also zu-
friedenstellend präzisiert.

Wir wollen als nächstes zeigen, daß in einer Theorie, die eine λ-katego-
riale Sprache mit der Methode der Seichtstrukturen kombiniert, jede Wortstellung gleichberechtigt ist. Was damit genau gemeint ist, beinhaltet
der folgende Satz.

3.6 Satz

Sei α ein beliebiger λ-kategorialer Ausdruck, dessen Seichtstruktur $f(\alpha)$
die Form $(\alpha_1,\ldots,\alpha_n)$ habe. Sei π eine beliebige Permutation von $(1,\ldots,n)$.
Dann gibt es einen λ-kategorialen Ausdruck β mit den folgenden Eigenschaften:

      a. $f(\beta) = (\alpha_{\pi_1},\ldots,\alpha_{\pi_n})$

      b. β ist durch λ-Konversion in α überführbar.

Ich muß hier eine Bemerkung dazu machen, was es heißt, daß ein Ausdruck
in einem anderen durch λ-Konversion überführbar ist. Damit ist eine syntaktische Relation gemeint, deren präzise Formulierung einigen technischen Aufwand mit sich bringen würde. Ich will deshalb nur eine Defini-
tionsskizze geben. Zunächst bezeichnen wir durch $\alpha(\beta/x)$ den Ausdruck, den
man durch simultane Ersetzung der freien Variablen x durch β in α erhält,
unter Wahrung der üblichen Vorsichtsmaßnahmen (d.h. keine Variable, die
frei in β vorkommt, darf in $\alpha(\beta/x)$ plötzlich gebunden vorkommen). Wir
legen dann fest:

3.7 Definition

Sei $\alpha \in Tm_\tau$, $x \in Var_\sigma$ und $\beta \in Tm_\sigma$.
Dann ist der Ausdruck $((\lambda,x,\alpha),\beta)$ in den Ausdruck $\alpha(\beta/x)$ durch λ-Konver-
sion überführbar.[24]

---

[24] Man kann die λ-Konversion allgemeiner definieren. Für meine Zwecke genügt diese Definition aber.

Das Wichtige ist nun, daß in jeder Standardsemantik für L^λ in einander durch Konversion überführbare Ausdrücke dasselbe bedeuten. Damit besagt Satz 3.6, daß es zu jeder Seichtstruktur eine beliebige Permutation gibt, die in einer Lesart dasselbe bedeutet. (Jede Tiefenstruktur einer Seichtstruktur legt eine Lesart derselben fest.) Dies wird verheerende Konsequenzen für Cresswells Ansatz haben. Bevor ich Satz 3.6 begründe, noch ein Beispiel für eine λ-Konversion: (1) d. läßt sich durch λ-Konversion in (1) a. überführen.

> (1) d. $((\lambda, x_{S/N}, (x_{S/N}, \textit{Kasper})), \textit{lacht})$
>   a. (*lacht*, *Kasper*)

f(1) d. ist (2) e., und damit ist (1) d. ein guter Kandidat für die logische Repräsentation des deutschen Satzes (3) f.

> (2) e. (*Kasper*, *lacht*)
> (3) f. Kasper lacht.

Ich gebe nun eine Skizze für den Beweis von 3.6 an.[25] Sei α beliebiger kategorialer Ausdruck, dessen Seichtstruktur f(α) die Form $(\alpha_1, \ldots, \alpha_n)$ habe. Sei π eine beliebige Permutation von $(1, \ldots, n)$. Dann gibt es in α eindeutig bestimmte Konstituentenvorkommnisse $<s_1, \alpha_1>, \ldots, <s_n, \alpha_n>$. Wir ersetzen nun in α diese Vorkommnisse durch $<s_1, x_1>, \ldots, <s_n, x_n>$, wobei $x_1, \ldots, x_n$ "neue" Variablen sind, und zwar vom selben Typ wie $\alpha_1, \ldots, \alpha_n$ beziehungsweise. Den so erhaltenen Ausdruck nennen wir X(α). Man mache sich an Beispielen klar, daß X(α) nur noch aus logischen Symbolen besteht. Wir bilden nun den neuen Ausdruck

$$((\lambda, x_{\pi n}((\ldots((\lambda, x_{\pi 2}, ((\lambda, x_{\pi 1} X(\alpha)), \alpha_{\pi 1})), \alpha_{\pi 2}))\ldots)), \alpha_{\pi n})$$

Dies ist der gesuchte Ausdruck β.

Wir machen uns an einem Beispiel klar, daß diese Konstruktion stimmt. Wir gehen von (1) b., also von

> (*und*, (*lacht*, *Kasper*), (*schimpft*, *Hotzenplotz*))

aus. Die Seichtstruktur von (1) b. ist (2) b.

---

[25] Ein exakter Beweis ist vermutlich langwierig. Wahrscheinlich drückt 3.6 aber einen seit Jahrzehnten bekannten Sachverhalt aus. Die Beweisidee steht bei Ruttenberg (1976:3). Ich selbst habe das Bestehen dieses Sachverhaltes in (1960:36) vorausgesetzt und plausibel gemacht.

(2) b. $(und_1, lacht_2, Kasper_3, schimpft_4, Hotzenplotz_5)$.

Wir betrachten nun die Seichtstruktur

(4) $(Kasper_3, lacht_2, und_1, Hotzenplotz_5, schimpft_4)$.

Wenn man (1) b. als Ausgangspunkt wählt, dann liegt ihr die Permutation

$$\pi = \begin{pmatrix} 1 & 2 & 3 & 4 & 5 \\ 3 & 2 & 1 & 5 & 4 \end{pmatrix}$$

zugrunde, was ich durch die Indizes bereits angedeutet habe. Es gilt nun, einen Ausdruck β zu finden, dessen Seichtstruktur gerade (4) ist und der sich durch λ-Konversion in (1) b. überführen läßt. Nach Konstruktion sieht β folgendermaßen aus:

(5) $((\lambda, z_{S/N}, ((\lambda, z_N, ((\lambda, x_{S/S,S}, ((\lambda, y_{S/N}, ((\lambda, y_N,$

$(x_{S/S,S}, (y_{S/N}, y_N), (z_{S/N}, z_N))),$

$Kasper)), lacht)), und)), Hotzenplotz)), schimpft)$.

Man sieht auf den ersten Blick, daß f(5) = (4) ist. Wenn man ein wenig überlegt, dann sieht man auch bald ein, daß sich (5) in (1) b. durch λ-Konversion überführen läßt.

Die Folgen dieses Ergebnisses für Cresswells Ansatz sind nach meiner Meinung katastrophal. Aus 3.6 ergibt sich nämlich sofort, daß die Seichtstruktur

(6) $(Kasper, schimpft, und, Hotzenplotz, lacht)$

eine gemeinsame Lesart haben muß mit der Seichtstruktur

(4) $(Kasper, lacht, und, Hotzenplotz, schimpft)$,

denn nach 3.6 kann man effektiv einen Ausdruck β finden, dessen Seichtstruktur (6) ist, und der sich durch λ-Konversion in (1) b. überführen läßt.[26] (6) ist aber offensichtlich die Seichtstruktur des Satzes

(3) e. Kasper schimpft und Hotzenplotz lacht.

Und dieser Satz bedeutet unter keinen Umständen dasselbe wie

(3) b. Kasper lacht und Hotzenplotz schimpft.,

dessen Seichtstruktur (4) ist.

---

[26] Diese Kritik überträgt sich voll auf den Ansatz von D. Lewis (1972).

Cresswell ahnt am Ende seines Buches, daß Schwierigkeiten dieser Art auftreten könnten: "Tatsächlich regt sich der Verdacht in mir, daß sie (die Prinzipien der λ-Konversion) am Ende zu viel leisten könnten, daß schließlich jede Wortfolge als Darstellung praktisch jeder Tiefenstruktur angesehen werden könnte. Deshalb brauchen wir Akzeptabilitätsprinzipien". (1973:229). Derartige Akzeptabilitätsprinzipien können nur so aussehen, daß "perverse" Abstrakte wie etwa die in (5) vorkommenden weggefiltert werden. Cresswell benötigt in seinem Buch zur Erzeugung der von ihm gewünschten Wortstellungen aber laufend "perverse" Abstrakte. Ich sehe auf Anhieb keine Möglichkeit, hier zwischen gutartiger und bösartiger Perversion zu unterscheiden. Die λ-Konversion ist das zentrale logische Prinzip der λ-kategorialen Sprachen, an dem sich wohl kaum ungestraft herumbasteln lassen dürfte. Ich habe deshalb keine Ahnung, wie sich die in diesem Abschnitt geschilderte Konsequenz vermeiden läßt, es sei denn, man wirft die Abstraktion über Bord. Aber damit würde dann gerade Cresswells Lieblingswerkzeug versinken, mit dem er die meisten Stellungsphänomene der natürlichen Sprache bearbeiten möchte.

Ich selbst ziehe aus diesen beiden letzten Abschnitten den folgenden Schluß. Cresswell geht von einer semantischen Sprache aus, die viel zu viele Stellungsmöglichkeiten (nämlich alle denkbaren) zuläßt. Für die Syntax einer natürlichen Sprache ist damit nichts gewonnen, denn man muß sagen, was von diesen Möglichkeiten realisiert ist. Der klassische Transformationalist geht dagegen von einer viel zu stellungsarmen semantischen Sprache aus. Er muß deshalb in gewisser Weise einem lahmen Esel das Tanzen beibringen. Ich glaube, das Beste ist ein Mittelweg zwischen diesen beiden Extremen.[27]

[27] "Das Gute", so sagt der Stagirit in der Nikomachischen Ethik, "ist ein Meson zwischen zwei Akra".

4. VORBEMERKUNGEN ZUR SYNTAX EINES FRAGMENTS DES DEUTSCHEN

Ich habe schon in Abschnitt 1 gesagt, daß der wichtigste Unterschied zwischen den von Montague entwickelten Syntaxen und der meinigen ist, daß ich den dort teilweise noch vorhandenen Logizismus vermeide. So benutzt etwa Montague noch indizierte Pronomina he_1, he_2, he_3,..., die in der Syntax des Englischen die gleiche technische Rolle spielen wie die Variablen x_1, x_2, x_3,... in der Prädikatenlogik. Nun gibt es im Englischen und im Deutschen freilich nichts dergleichen, und deswegen gibt es auch in meinem Fragment so etwas nicht. Allerdings sind derartige Variablen ja eingeführt worden, um bestimmte technische Aufgaben zu lösen, z.B. um die sogenannte Quantifikation zu erfassen oder um den deiktischen Gebrauch von Pronomina zu erklären. Letzterer macht keine Schwierigkeiten. (Steinitz (1969). Was die Quantifikation betrifft, so habe ich in meinem Fragment nur einfache Fälle erfassen können. Kompliziertere würde ich nach den Ideen von R. Smaby angehen, vgl. (1975) und (1976). Ich habe keinen Zweifel, daß man ohne indizierte Variablen auskommt, denn das tun wir ja alle Tage.

Das leitende Prinzip, nach dem ich meine Syntaxregeln formuliert habe, ist, daß diese der *Wohlgeformtheitsbedingung* genügen müssen.[28] Dies besagt folgendes: Syntaxregeln fassen wohlgeformte Ausdrücke zu wohlgeformten Ausdrücken zusammen. Bei dem syntaktischen Aufbau eines Ausdrucks dürfen keine technischen Hilfszeichen (z.B. "dummies") benutzt werden, die später wieder verschwinden. Barbara Partee nennt dies Prinzip "well-formedness constraint". (1977).

Ein weiterer Grundsatz (jedes Montague-Grammatikers) ist, daß syntaktische Regeln stets semantisch vernünftig sein müssen. Meistens formuliert man dieses Prinzip ziemlich stark, indem man sagt, daß es für jede Syntaxregel eine "semantische Operation" gibt. Diese legt die Bedeutung

---

[28] Bei B. Partee "well-formedness constraint", siehe Partee (1977).

des mithilfe dieser Regel gebildeten Ausdrucks in Abhängigkeit der Bedeutung der Ausdrücke fest, auf die die Regel angewendet wird. Man nennt dies
das *Fregeprinzip*. Obwohl ich das Prinzip in dieser strengen Form für falsch
halte, werde ich es im folgenden einmal voraussetzen. Da ich hier eine Syntax entwickle, skizziere ich die semantische Seite der Regeln nur jeweils
ganz kurz.

Die Darstellung der folgenden Paragraphen soll im Prinzip so exakt
sein, daß sie strengen Ansprüchen genügt. Sämtliche technischen Begriffe
werden aber immer erst dann eingeführt, wenn man sie braucht. Und zwar
grundsätzlich anhand von Beispielen. Mir soll es recht sein, wenn der Leser
am Ende fragt, wann denn nun endlich die *Theorie* kommt. Er hat sie dann in
Wirklichkeit schon längst gelesen. Möge es ihm ergehen wie jenem Mann in
Rottweil, der gewettet hatte, ein ganzes Schwein zu essen. Nach vielen Vor-
gerichten bat er, ihm nun endlich die Sau zu servieren, sonst wäre er am
Ende noch vorher satt. Er hatte sie selbstverständlich bereits verspeist.

Im Mittelpunkt meines Fragments steht das deutsche Verb mit seinen
verschiedenen Stellungsmöglichkeiten. Nun weiß jeder, daß man nicht über
das Verb reden kann, ohne über vieles andere zu reden ("La langue est un
système où tout se tient ..."). Dies soll die Auswahl der verschiedenen
Phänomene des Deutschen rechtfertigen, die im Inhaltsverzeichnis aufge-
führt sind. Nicht unbedingt gerechtfertigt ist damit allerdings der Titel
des Aufsatzes, der auch "Ein Fragment des Deutschen in einer Montague-
Grammatik" hätte lauten können. Ich komme nun zu den ersten Regeln.

5. SYNTAKTISCHE UND SEMANTISCHE GRUNDBEGRIFFE

Ferner: DIE MORPHOLOGISCHEN REGELN DES FRAGMENTES

Betrachten wir den Satz

(1) Kasper muß den alten Mann verprügelt haben.

Es ist klar, daß die einzelnen Formen sinnvollerweise morphologisch analysiert werden müssen. Das kann etwa folgendermaßen aussehen:

Kasper	ist ein Eigenname im Nominativ Singular Maskulinum
muß	ist ein Modalverb der dritten Person Singular
den	ist ein Determinator im Akkusativ Singular Maskulinum
alten	ist ein schwaches Adjektiv im Akkusativ Singular Maskulinum
Mann	ist ein Nomen im Akkusativ Singular Maskulinum
verprügelt	ist ein Partizip Perfekt Aktiv
haben	ist der Infinitiv eines Hilfsverbs

Beobachtungen wie diese motivieren die folgenden morphologischen Regeln.

(M1) Wenn α ein Nominalstamm ist mit dem inhärenten Geschlecht a, β ein Kasusmorphem und γ ein Numerusmorphem, dann ist $\alpha\beta\gamma$ ein Nomen vom Geschlecht a, im Kasus β und mit dem Numerus γ.

Das Genus-, Kasus- und Numerusmorphem ist natürlich nicht immer "realisiert". Ich stelle sie deswegen hier als *abstrakte* Morpheme dar. Die *Kasusmorpheme* werden dargestellt durch

nom	(das Nominativmorphem)
geni	(das Genitivmorphem)
dat	(das Dativmorphem)
akk	(das Akkusativmorphem)

Die abstrakten Genusmorpheme sind

mas	(das Maskulinummorphem)
fem	(das Femininummorphem)
neut	(das Neutrummorphem)

Die *Personalmorpheme* werden dargestellt durch

   1. pers   (erste Person)

   2. pers   (zweite Person)

   3. pers   (dritte Person)

Die Numerusmorpheme sind *sg* (das Singularmorphem) und *pl* (das Plural-morphem).

Wir legen durch ein Lexikon fest

   Mann   ist ein Nominalstamm im Maskulinum

   Frau   ist ein Nominalstamm im Femininum

   Kind   ist ein Nominalstamm im Neutrum

Die Regel (M1) erlaubt uns dann die folgende Ableitung:

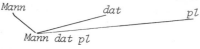

Ich nehme nun an, daß es morphophonetische bzw. morphographemische Regeln gibt, die aus *Mann dat pl Männern* machen. Diese Annahme ist natürlich problematisch. Für eine ernsthafte Morphologie benötigt man wesentlich mehr Merkmale. Zum Beispiel arbeitet Wurzel unter anderem mit den Merkmalen *Pluralumlaut, Nominativerweiterung, r-Stamm, s-Plural, stark.* Die Berücksichtigung solcher Unterscheidungen würde den morphologischen Teil so verkomplizieren, daß er ein Vielfaches des gesamten Aufsatzes ausmachen würde. Es geht mir hier nur darum zu zeigen, an welcher Stelle sich die Morphologie in die Beschreibung eingliedert und wie sie grundsätzlich aussieht.

    Zurück zur Regel (M1). Die Variablen α, β, γ stehen für endliche *Zeichenketten*. Das sind endliche Folgen von Buchstaben.[29] Die Buchstaben sind: $a, b, c, \ldots, z, 0, 1, \ldots, 9, \ldots$ *A* bezeichnet denselben Buchstaben wie

---

[29] Die folgenden Klärungen geschehen im Anschluß an verschiedene Arbeiten von Bennett, (1974).

a, *B* wie *b* und so weiter. Ferner ist das *Leerzeichen* (der Blank) ein Buchstabe. Es wird durch den Zwischenraum bezeichnet. Z.B. ist die Zeichenkette

> *Kasper muß*

die Folge

> $(K, a, s, p, e, r, \ , m, u, ß)$.

Wie man Folgen hintereinanderschaltet (=verkettet), habe ich in Abschnitt 3 erklärt. Dem üblichen Schreibgebrauch folgend, notiere ich Ketten einfach durch Hintereinanderschreiben der Buchstaben. Bestimmte Zeichenketten sind *Ausdrücke (unseres Fragmentes)*. Nämlich solche, die laut Lexikon bestimmte morphologische Eigenschaften haben wie Nominalstamm Maskulinum zu sein etc. und solche, die mithilfe von Syntaxregeln aus anderen Ausdrücken hergeleitet sind. Z.B. ist *Mann dat pl* ein Ausdruck unseres Fragmentes.

Dieses letzte Beispiel zeigt, daß ich eine stillschweigende *Konvention* verwendet habe: Wenn ein Ausdruck unseres Fragmentes mit einem anderen verkettet wird, dann steht stets das Leerzeichen dazwischen. Mit anderen Worten: Wenn α und β Ausdrücke sind, dann bezeichnet αβ die Folge α( )β, d.h. α verkettet mit der Folge, deren einziges Glied das Leerzeichen ist, verkettet mit β.

Ich arbeite im folgenden nicht mit morphologischen (und syntaktischen) Eigenschaften, sondern alleine mit *syntaktischen Kategorien*. Eine syntaktische Kategorie ist eine Menge von Zeichenketten. Die Kategorien werden induktiv definiert, und zwar im Prinzip genau so, wie die λ-kategorialen Terme definiert worden sind (vgl. 3.2).

Ein *Lexikon* gibt zunächst an, zu welchen Kategorien die Wörter und Morpheme unseres Fragmentes gehören. Es gibt dann *Syntaxregeln*, die aus Ausdrücken bestimmter Kategorien einen Ausdruck einer anderen Kategorie machen.

Technisch gesehen ist das Lexikon eine Funktion *Lex*, die Kategoriennamen Mengen von Zeichenketten zuordnet. Als Kategoriennamen benutze ich
komplexe Symbole, und zwar unendlich viele. Für die meisten Kategoriennamen *A* ist *Lex*(*A*) = ∅. Ich gebe diese Symbole hier nicht auf einen Schlag
an, sondern führe sie mit dem Fortschreiten des Gedankenganges ein.

Das Wort *Kasper* wird etwa syntaktisch beschrieben als

>   *Kasper* ∈ *Lex* *(EN nom sg mas)*.

Kasper gehört also zur Menge, die das Lexikon (*Lex*) dem komplexen Symbol
EN *nom sg mas* zuordnet. Diese Notation ist noch zu pedantisch. Ich benutze
deshalb im folgenden einfach die Kurzschreibweise

>   *Kasper* ∈ EN *nom sg mas*.

So etwas nenne ich einen *Lexikoneintrag*. Er ist inhaltlich zu lesen wie anfangs beschrieben.

Was ist das komplexe Symbol EN *nom sg mas* selbst? Man kann es auf
verschiedene Weisen rekonstruieren. Für meine Zwecke genügt es, es als
Folge anzusehen. Es ist die Folge (EN, *nom, sg, mas*), deren erstes Glied
also EN ist, deren zweites Glied das Kasusmorphem *nom* ist usw. Jede Folge
der Form

>   EN kas(a) num(b) gen(c)

ist ein Kategorienname. Dabei bedeutet kas(a), daß an dieser Stelle der
Folge ein Kasusmorphem einzusetzen ist, nom(b), daß das dritte Glied der
Folge ein Numerusmorphem sein muß und gen(c), daß das letzte Glied der
Folge ein Genusmorphem sein muß. Mit anderen Worten:

>   EN *nom sg mas*
>   EN *geni pl neut*
>   EN *dat sg fem* etc.

sind sämtlich Kategoriennamen. Im folgenden werde ich die pedantische
Unterscheidung zwischen Kategoriennamen und Kategorien vernachlässigen
und einfach von der Kategorie EN *nom sg mas* sprechen. Ich nenne EN *Hauptkategorie* und die Teile kas(a), num(b) etc. *Unterkategorien*. Für den

Fall, daß der Teil in Klammern bei einer Unterkategorie (übrigens immer eine Folge) eine Variable ist, sage ich, daß die Unterkategorie *unspezifiziert* ist. Falls dort etwas Geeignetes eingesetzt ist, rede ich von einer *spezifizierten* Unterkategorie. Die Notation kas(*nom*) bedeutet dasselbe wie *nom*. D.h., für den Fall, daß eine Unterkategorie spezifiziert ist, heißt dies, daß an der entsprechenden Stelle das Richtige eingesetzt worden ist. Komplexe Symbole kann man natürlich auch so notieren wie etwa Chomsky in den Aspects. D.h., das bisher diskutierte komplexe Symbol könnte man darstellen als

$$
\begin{array}{c}
\text{EN} \\
| \\
\begin{bmatrix} + \text{ nom} \\ - \text{ pl} \\ + \text{ mas} \end{bmatrix}
\end{array}
$$

oder dergleichen. Wem das vertrauter ist, der kann den Artikel in diesem Sinne umgestalten. Er wird denn zehnmal so lang.

Nach diesen Klärungen können wir die Regel (M1) kürzer formulieren:

$$
\text{(M1a)} \quad
\begin{array}{ll}
\alpha & \in \quad \text{CNST gen(a)} \\
\beta & \in \quad \text{Kas} \\
\gamma & \in \quad \text{Num} \\
\hline
\alpha\beta\gamma & \in \quad \text{CN gen(a) kas(}\beta\text{) num(}\gamma\text{)}
\end{array}
$$

Ich habe hier den "Wenn-Teil" der Regel (M1) vom "dann-Teil" einfach durch einen Strich getrennt und die einzelnen Voraussetzungen untereinander geschrieben.

Um mit dieser Regel arbeiten zu können, benötigen wir die folgenden Lexikoneinträge:

5.1 *nom, geni, dat, akk* ∈ Kas.

Pedantisch formuliert:

Lex(Kas) = {*nom, geni, dat, akk*}

  sg, pl ∈ Num

  {*mas, fem, neut*} = Gen

  $\left.\begin{array}{l} Rettich \\ Mann \end{array}\right\}$ CNST *mas*

  Frau   CNST *fem*

  Kind   CNST *neut*

CN erinnert an "common noun", d.h. in CN sind die Appellative. CNST ist die Kategorie der *Nominalstämme*. Der Rest versteht sich von selbst. Wir können nun die folgende Aussage beweisen:

5.2 *Rettich akk sg* ∈ CN *mas sg akk*

Beweis:

1. *Rettich* ∈ CNST *mas*   (nach 5.1)

2. *akk* ∈ Kas   (nach 5.1)

3. *sg* ∈ Num   (nach 5.1)

4. *Rettich akk sg* ∈ CN *mas sg akk*

   (Anwendung von (M1 *mas*) auf 1, 2 und 3)

Diesen Beweis können wir natürlich auch als Baum beschreiben:

1. *Rettich*, CNST *mas* 2. *akk*, Kas 3. *sg*, Num

    4. *Rettich akk sg*, CN *mas sg akk*, (M1 *mas*)

Man muß sich nur darüber im klaren sein, daß so ein syntaktischer Baum und eine Ableitung in einem formalen System vollständig gleichwertig sind.

Ich möchte nun sagen, wie syntaktische Regeln ganz allgemein aussehen. Sie haben die folgende Form: [29a]

_____

[29a] Zur Darstellung, vgl. die Bemerkung auf S. 366 oben.

5.3 FORM DER SYNTAXREGELN

Jede Syntaxregel r_i hat die folgende Form:

Seien $\alpha_1, \ldots, \alpha_n$ beziehungsweise Ausdrücke in $Kat_{A_1}, \ldots, Kat_{A_n}$,

dann ist $F_{r_i}(<\alpha_1, A_1>, \ldots, <\alpha_n, A_n>) \in Kat_B$.

Hier stehen die Variablen $A_1, \ldots, A_n, B$ für Kategoriennamen, also für komplexe Symbole der besprochenen Art. F_{r_i} ist eine n-stellige syntaktische Operation, die aus Ausdrücken zusammen mit ihrem Kategoriennamen einen neuen Ausdruck macht. Um dieser allgemeinen Form zu genügen, müßte (M1) folgendermaßen formuliert werden:

(M1a) $\alpha \in Kat_{CNST\ gen(a)}$

             $\beta \in Kat_{Kas}$

$$\frac{\gamma \in Kat_{Num}}{F_{(M1a)}(<\alpha, CNST\ gen(a),\ <\beta, Kas>, <\gamma, Num>)}$$

     $\in Kat_{CN\ gen(a)\ kas(\beta)\ num(\gamma)}$

(M1a) ist ein Regelschema, das für drei Regeln steht, je nachdem, ob man für *a mas*, *fem* oder *neut* einsetzt. $F_{(M1a)}$ ist diejenige Funktion, deren Wert für beliebige $<\alpha, CNSTa>$, $<\beta, Kas>$, $<\gamma, Num>$ $\alpha\beta\gamma$ ist, d.h. die Folge $\alpha(\ )\beta(\ )\gamma$. Hier ist die Operation $F_{(M1a)}$ lediglich die Verkettung. Und so wird es meistens sein.

Die Regelschemata, die ich im folgenden angebe, stehen sehr oft für unendlich viele Regeln im Sinne der Theorie. Sie werden meistens nicht exakt indiziert, weil alle Regeln eines Schemas stets denselben "semantischen Effekt" haben, falls dies nicht besonders vermerkt ist.

Es ist übrigens ganz wesentlich, daß die syntaktischen Operationen auch von den Kategoriensymbolen abhängen, denn in diesen merke ich mir entscheidende morphologische und syntaktische Information. Es gibt hier alternative Vorgehensweisen [30], die meines Erachtens auf keinen Fall konzeptuell

---

[30] Cf. Thomason, Partee, Bach, Bennett et al.

einfacher werden als die Meinige. Ich komme im Schlußabschnitt noch darauf
zu sprechen.

Bei der Angabe des Formates der Regeln habe ich die Notationen Kat_{A_1},
Kat_{A_2} ... benutzt. Damit sind natürlich die Kategorie A_1, die Kategorie A_2.
..., gemeint. Die *Kategorien* werden induktiv definiert. Zunächst ist für
jedes Kategoriensymbol A *Lex*$(A) \subseteq Kat_A$. Ferner gehört dann noch zu A, was
durch die Syntaxregeln hineinkommt. Sonst nichts.

Damit ist der syntaktische Formalismus völlig präzisiert. Ich werde
im folgenden die Regeln natürlich nie so pedantisch wie das Schema (M1a)
angeben, weil ich auf Lesbarkeit Wert lege. Es sollte aber klar sein, daß
man die Pedanterie so weit wie Montague treiben kann.

Bevor ich nun endlich wieder zur Sache, nämlich zum Deutschen, komme,
eine Bemerkung zur *Semantik*. Jede Syntaxregel hat eine semantische Seite.
Bei Montague ist das eine semantische Operation. Wenn r_i eine Syntaxregel
der in 5.3 beschriebenen Form ist, und wir voraussetzen, daß die "Eingabe-
Ausdrücke" $\alpha_1, ..., \alpha_n$ der Regel die Bedeutungen $b_1, ..., b_n$ haben, dann ordnet
die zu r_i gehörige semantische Operation $f(r_i)$ $<b_1, A_1>, ..., <b_n, A_n>$ eine
neue Bedeutung zu. Diese ist natürlich die Bedeutung des durch die Syntaxregeln gewonnenen neuen Ausdrucks. Ich werde die semantische Seite der Regel stets nur inhaltich skizzieren, und zwar meistens nur in Fußnoten,
weil dieser Aspekt der Theorie hier aus Platzgründen nicht abgehandelt
werden kann.

Die Bedeutungen der Lexikoneinträge müssen direkt beschrieben werden.
Für unsere bisherigen Beispiele sieht das so aus: Der Nominalstamm *Mann*
bezeichnet die Eigenschaft, Mann zu sein. Eine *n-stellige Eigenschaft* ist
eine (partielle) Funktion von n-stelligen Dingfolgen in Propositionen.
Eine *Proposition* ist etwas, was je nach Umständen wahr oder falsch (oder
sinnlos) ist, d.h. eine partielle Funktion von möglichen Umständen in
Wahrheitswerte. Die Proposition p *ist wahr* in dem Umstand c gdw. $p(c) = 1$;

falsch in c, wenn $p(c) = 0$. Eine n-stellige Eigenschaft ω *trifft zu* auf die Dinge $a_1,\ldots,a_n$ unter den Umständen c gdw. $\omega(a_1,\ldots,a_n)(c) = 1$. Umstände selbst kann man rekonstruieren als Tripel <w,z,o> bestehend aus einer möglichen Welt, einem Zeitintervall z und einem Ort o.[31] Die Eigenschaft, Mann zu sein, ordnet also einem Individuum a die Proposition zu, daß a ein Mann ist. Das ist die Proposition, die unter den Umständen c wahr ist, wenn a ein Mann in c ist. Alternativ gesprochen: Die Eigenschaft, Mann zu sein, trifft auf das Individuum a unter dem Umstand c genau dann zu, wenn a in c ein Mann ist.

(M1) wird so gedeutet: α bezeichne die Eigenschaft ω. Falls $\gamma = sg$, so bezeichnet auch $\alpha\beta\gamma$ ω. Falls dagegen $\gamma = pl$, so bezeichnet $\alpha\beta\gamma$ diejenige Funktion f, so daß für jedes c gilt: $f(c) = \{a : \omega(a)(c) = 1\}$. So etwas wie f heißt *Gattungsbegriff.*

Es folgen nun weitere morphologische Regeln:

(M2)   *Einfache finite Verbformen*[32]

$$\alpha \in \begin{bmatrix} \text{HST typ(a)} \\ \text{MST erg(b)} \\ \text{VST erg}(b_1,\ldots,b_n) \text{ abtr}(\varepsilon) \text{ hiv(a) sgl(c)} \end{bmatrix}$$

$\beta \in$ ET

$\gamma \in$ Pers

$\delta \in$ Num

$$\alpha\beta\gamma\delta \in \begin{bmatrix} \text{HVP pers}(\gamma)\text{num}(\delta)\text{typ(a)} \\ \text{MVP erg(b)num}(\delta)\text{pers}(\gamma) \\ \text{VP pers}(\gamma)\text{num}(\delta)\text{erg}(b_1,\ldots,b_n)\text{stell(end)} \\ \text{sgl(c)abtr}(\varepsilon) \end{bmatrix}$$

---

[31] Vgl. dazu etwa Kratzer (1977) oder Kaplan (1977).

[32] Verbstämme drücken Eigenschaften aus. Semantisch hat diese Regel unter anderem den Effekt, daß diese temporalisiert werden. Ich kann, was hier vorgeht, ohne eine ernsthafte Kontexttheorie aber nicht beschreiben. Vgl. Bäuerle (1977), Kratzer (1977) und Schapk-Dolt (1977). Ich tue im folgenden so, als wäre klar, was temporalisierte Eigenschaften sind. Ich werde also etwa von der Eigenschaft, die Suppe gegessen zu haben, sprechen. Sie wird von Kasper erfüllt, wenn dieser die Suppe gegessen hat.

Die äußeren Klammern bedeuten hier, daß die unterschiedenen Fälle jeweils in eindeutiger Korrespondenz stehen.

5.4 EIN BEISPIEL

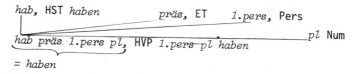

HST steht für "Hilfsverbstamm", ET für "einfaches Tempus". Zur letzt-genannten Kategorie gehört *präs* und *prät*, d.h. das Präsens- und das Prä-teritummorphem. HVP ist die Hilfsverbphrase, d.h. die finite Form des Hilfsverbs. Dem Baum 5.4 sind die vorausgesetzten Lexikoneinträge unmittel-bar anzusehen. Zusätzlich setzen wir an:

5.5 *tu*   HST *tun*

    sei   HST *sein*

    muß   MST erg(0-Inf)

    könn   MST erg(0-Inf)

    hab   MST erg(zu-Inf)[33]

---

[33] Zu den Bedeutungen dieser Stämme. Sie sind sämtlich Funktionen, die aus einer einstelligen Eigenschaft wieder eine machen. Statt "Die Bedeutung des Ausdrucks α der Kategorie A" schreiben wir kürzer "V(α,A)". Die Be-deutung von α hängt dabei meistens nur von der Hauptkategorie ab. Es gilt dann für eine beliebige einstellige Eigenschaft ω, ein beliebiges Individuum a und einen beliebigen Umstand c: V(*tu*,HST)(ω) trifft zu auf a in c gdw. ω in c auf a zutrifft. V(*hab*,HST) = V(*sei*,HST) = V(*tu*,HST).

V(*muss*,MST) macht aus einer n-stelligen Eigenschaft ω_n wieder eine n-stellige Eigenschaft. Es gilt: V(*muss*,MST)(ω_n)(a_1,...,a_n)(c) = 1 $\Longleftrightarrow$ In jedem Umstand c', in dem der Fall ist, was in c sein muß, gilt:

$\omega(a_1,...,a_n)(c') = 1$

V(*hab*,MST zu-Inf) = V(*muss*,MST), allerdings auf deontische Verwendung eingeschränkt. V(*Muss*,CN) ist dagegen die Eigenschaft, Muß zu sein. Es ist übrigens nicht verboten, daß ein Wort α der Kategorie A mehrere Be-deutungen hat. Dann ist V(α,A) eine Menge. V(*könn*,MST) wird analog zu V(*muss*,MST) bestimmt.

Es ist klar, daß MST Modalstamm heißt. Die Merkmale "O-Inf" bzw. "zu-Inf" erinnern daran, daß *müssen* einen Infinitivsatz ohne *zu* als Ergänzung verlangt, *haben* als Modal einen mit *zu*. Vgl.

> (2) Kasper muß einen Rettich haben.
>
> (3) Kasper hat einen Rettich zu haben.

Bei den Unterkategorien der Verbstämme schlägt sich bereits die gesamte syntaktische Komplexität des Verhaltens der Verben nieder. Im Augenblick kann ich die Einträge deshalb noch nicht motivieren. Beispiel:

5.6   1. *anbiet*   VST erg(nom,dat,a) abtr(an) hiv($haben$)sgl(+)

                              a = akk, zu-Inf

    2. *wünsch*   VST erg(nom,dat,daß-S)abtr(-) hiv($haben$)sgl(+)

    4. *schenk*   VST (nom,dat,akk)abtr(-) *haben* sgl(+)

    5. *hab*   VST (nom,akk)abtr(-) *haben* sgl(+)

    6. *verprügel* VST (nom,akk)abtr(-) *haben* sgl(+)

    7. *lach*   VST (nom) abtr(-) *haben* sgl(+) [34]

VST heißt "Verbstamm". Die Unterkategorie erg ("Ergänzungen") gibt die Valenz an. Hier darf eine höchstens dreistellige Folge angesetzt werden, die aus Kasusmorphemen oder zusätzlich dem Morphem *es*; und den Merkmalen "pass", "daß-S", "O-Inf" oder "zu-Inf" besteht.

---

[34] Zur Semantik: Alle VST drücken Eigenschaften aus.

V(*anbiet*,VST(nom,dat,akk)) trifft zu auf (a_1,a_2,a_3) gdw. a_1 bietet a_2 a_3 an. (Den Umstandsparameter lasse ich unter Umständen fort.) V(*anbiet*,VST nom,dat,zu-Inf) ist mehrdeutig. Für beliebige Individuen a_1,a_2 und eine beliebige Eigenschaft ω ist dies nämlich {daß a_1 dem a_2 $\omega(a_1)$ anbietet, daß a_1 dem a_2 $\omega(a_2)$ anbietet}. V(*wünsch*)(a,b,p)(c) = 1 gdw. a wünscht dem b p in c. V(*hab*,VST) trifft zu auf (a_1,a_2) gdw. a_1 a_2 besitzt. Später wird die Semantik komplizierter werden.

Es gibt hier gewisse Beschränkungen, die aus den Lexikoneinträgen ersichtlich werden. Die Unterkategorie "abtr" kodiert den abtrennbaren Teil des Verbs, "hiv" markiert das für zusammengesetzte Verbformen verlangte Hilfsverb. In "sgl" ("Satzglieder") merkt man sich die Satzglieder der Verbgruppe. Meistens sind das mehrere, d.h. an dieser Stelle steht in der Regel eine Folge von Ausdrücken. Satzglieder sind immer auch abtrennbar. Nicht aber ist der abtrennbare Teil des Verbs auch stets ein Satzglied. Beispiel:

5.7 1. *auslach* VST (*nom,akk*)abtr(*aus*) *haben* sgl(+)
 2. *schwerfall* VST (*es,dat*,zu-Inf)*sein* sgl(*schwer*,+)
 abtr(*schwer*)

Falls in einer Unterkategorie der Strich "-" steht, bedeutet dies, daß die leere Folge an dieser Stelle einzusetzen ist. Das Kreuz "+" in der Unterkategorie "sgl" markiert die Position des Hauptverbs relativ zu den Satzgliedern.

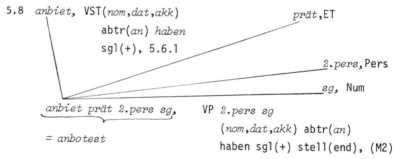

5.8 *anbiet,* VST(*nom,dat,akk*)   *prät*,ET
 abtr(*an*) *haben*
 sgl(+), 5.6.1   2.*pers*,Pers
          sg, Num

anbiet prät 2.pers sg, VP 2.*pers sg*
          (*nom,dat,akk*) abtr(*an*)
= *anbotest*   *haben* sgl(+) stell(end), (M2)

Die Unterkategorie "stell" enthält eine rein syntaktische Information. Für unser Fragment kommen als Spezifikationen

"zweit" für "Zweitstellung des Finitums"
"end" für "Endstellung des Finitums"
"rels" für "Relativsatzstellung"

in Frage. Wie man sieht, zeichne ich bereits im Lexikon die Endstellung des Verbs aus. Das ist nicht nötig, hat sich aber für mein Fragment als praktisch erwiesen. [35]

---

[35] Ebenso wird es bei Bach (1962) und Bierwisch (1973) gemacht.

Eine Bemerkung zur Darstellung. Ich halte mich in der Notation nicht
strikt an die kanonische Folge der Unterkategorien. Das ist deshalb zu-
lässig, weil das Kategoriensymbol aus meiner Schreibweise stets eindeutig
rekonstruierbar ist.

Es könnte übrigens an dieser Stelle so aussehen, als seien die Unterkategorien ad hoc. Sie sind es nicht. Wer die Mühe aufbringt, mein Fragment
im Detail zu studieren, wird hoffentlich zu der Überzeugung kommen, daß die
hier kodierte syntaktische Information unbedingt benötigt wird. Am Anfang
sieht dieses Verfahren noch kompliziert aus. Später sieht man, daß es nicht
unelegant ist.

Ich gebe nun die restlichen morphologischen Regeln an:

(M3)   *Flektierte Adjektive*

$\alpha \in$ ADJST, $\beta \in$ Gen, $\gamma \in$ Kas, $\delta \in$ Num, $\varepsilon \in$ Fle

---

$\alpha\beta\gamma\delta\varepsilon \in$ ADJ $\beta\gamma\delta\varepsilon$

ADJST heißt natürlich "Adjektivstamm".
Fle sind die beiden abstrakten Flektionsmorpheme *strk* ("stark") und *schw*
("schwach"). Beispiel:

5.9 *alt*, ADJST   *mas*, Gen   *nom*, Kas   *sg*, Num   *strk*, Fle

---

alt mas nom sg strk, ADJ *mas nom sg strk*, (M3)

= *alter*

Die Semantik von Adjektiven skizziere ich hier nicht einmal andeu-
tungsweise.[36] Man könnte natürlich auch Eigennamen, Personalpronomina und
Artikel morphologisch analysieren. Es ist vollkommen klar, wie das vor
sich geht. Ich verzichte aber darauf und führe später die flektierten Formen bei Bedarf jeweils direkt ein. Interessant ist lediglich noch die
Morphologie der Infinitive und der Partizipien des Perfekts Aktiv. Sie
wird durch die folgenden Regeln beschrieben:

---

[36] Vgl. dazu etwa Kaiser (1978).

($M4_1$) *Einfache Infinitive* (i = 0,1)[37]

$$\alpha\beta \in \begin{bmatrix} \text{HST typ(a)} \\ \text{MST erg(b)} \\ \text{VST erg}(b_1,\ldots,b_n)\text{abtr}(\alpha)\text{ hiv(a) sgl(c)} \end{bmatrix}$$

$$\alpha\gamma\beta\ inf \in \begin{bmatrix} \text{HINF typ(a) art(d)} \\ \text{MINF erg(b) art(d)} \\ \text{VINF erg}(b_1,\ldots,b_n)\text{ hptv}(\alpha\gamma\beta\ inf)\text{ sgl(c)} \\ \text{art(d) diat(akt)} \end{bmatrix}$$

Dabei ist: γ = $\emptyset$ und d = 0-Inf, falls i = 0,

γ = *zu* und d = zu-Inf, falls i = 1.

α kann natürlich leer sein.

Die Regeln ($M4_0$) dienen der Bildung der 0-Infinitive, die Regeln ($M4_i$) der Erzeugung von zu-Infinitiven. Beispiel:

5.9 *schwerfall,* VST (*es,dat,*zu-Inf) hiv(*sein*) sgl(*schwer*,+)

abtr(*schwer*), 5.7.1

schwer zu fall inf,

= *schwerzufallen,* VINF erg(*es,dat,zu-Inf*) hptv(*schwer zu fall inf*) sgl(*schwer*,+) art(zu-Inf) diat(akt), ($M4_1$)

Die Hauptkategorien verstehen sich von selbst. In der Unterkategorie "art" merkt man sich, ob es sich bei der Infinitivphrase um einen 0-Infinitiv oder einen zu-Infinitiv handelt. In der Unterkategorie "hptv" kodiert man den "Hauptverbkomplex" der Konstruktion. Warum das wichtig ist, das wird später noch klar. Die Unterkategorie "diat" dient der Markierung der Diathese. Einfache Infinitive sind immer im Aktiv. Die einschlägigen Merkmale sind "akt" (Aktiv) und "pass" (Passiv). Die Diathese wird wichtig

---

[37] Semantisch hat diese Regel keinen Effekt. Infinitive drücken Eigenschaften aus.

für Konstruktionen mit *tun*, das stets einen Infinitiv aktiv als Ergänzung verlangt.[38] *inf* ist das Infinitivmorphem, also *en*.

(M5) *Partizip Perfekt Aktiv*

$$\alpha\beta \quad \in \quad \left[\begin{array}{l} \text{HST typ(a)} \\ \text{MST erg(b)} \\ \text{VST erg}(b_1,\ldots,b_n) \text{ abtr}(\alpha) \text{ hiv(a) sgl(c)} \end{array} \right.$$

$$\alpha\text{part}\beta\text{perf} \in \left[\begin{array}{l} \text{HPPf typ(a)} \\ \text{MPPf erg(b)} \\ \text{VPPf erg}(b_1,\ldots,b_n) \text{ hptv}(\alpha \; part \; \beta \; perf) \\ \quad \text{hiv(a) sgl(c) diat(akt)} \end{array} \right.$$

Es ist klar, daß α leer sein kann. Bei regelmäßigen Verben ist *part* durch *ge* realisiert und *perf* durch *t*. Aber das ist natürlich nicht immer so, wie die folgenden Beispiele zeigen:

5.10 *schwerfall*, VST (*es*,*dat*,zu-Inf) *sein*

$\quad$ | $\quad\quad\quad\quad\quad$ sgl(*schwer*,+) abtr(*schwer*), (5.7.1)

$\underbrace{schwer\ part\ fall\ perf}$, VPPf (*es*,*dat*,zu-Inf)

= *schwergefallen* $\quad\quad\quad$ hptv(*schwer part fall perf*)

$\quad\quad\quad\quad\quad\quad\quad\quad\quad$ *sein*(*schwer*,+) akt, (M5)

5.11 *verprügel*, VST (*nom*,*akk*) abtr(-) *haben* sgl(+), (5.6.6)

$\quad$ |

$\underbrace{part\ verprügel\ perf}$, VPPf (*nom*,*akk*) hptv(*part verprügel perf*)

= *verprügelt* $\quad\quad\quad$ *haben* sgl(+) diat(akt), (M5)

Die Morphologie ist etwas unübersichtlich. Dafür gibt es dann bei den eigentlichen Syntaxregeln - von ganz wenigen Ausnahmen abgesehen - keine morphologischen Operationen mehr. Syntax ist mehr oder weniger Kombinatorik von schon Vorhandenem.

---

[38] Die Regel für *tun* wird nicht angegeben. Hausaufgabe für den Leser.

6. NOMINALPHRASEN

Mich interessiert der Aufbau der Nominalphrasen für mein Fragment nur am Rande. Es läßt sich aber einfach nicht vermeiden, wenigstens etwas zu ihrer syntaktischen Struktur zu sagen.

Die wesentliche Idee, die ich hier vertrete, ist, zwischen den definiten auf der einen und den übrigen Termen auf der anderen Seite schon syntaktisch zu unterscheiden. Viele meinen, es sei ein Fortschritt von Montagues Theorie, daß man diese Unterscheidung gerade nicht braucht.[39] Ich bin hier also anderer Meinung. Man wird bei der Behandlung der Relativsätze sehen, warum. Allerdings werden auch bei mir alle Terme zu einer Oberkategorie, der Kategorie der Nominalphrase (NP), zusammengefaßt. Das geschieht durch die folgenden *Anhebungsregeln*.

$$(No) \qquad \frac{\alpha \in EN \; num(a) \; kas(b) \; gen(c)}{\alpha \in NP \; \textit{3.pers} \; num(a) \; typ(b)}$$

Ein Beispiel:

6.1   *Kasper,* EN *sg nom mas*
$\quad\quad$|
$\quad\,$ *Kasper,* NP *3.pers sg nom,* (N$_0$)

6.2   *Hotzenplotz,* EN *sg akk mas*
$\quad\quad$|
$\quad\,$ *Hotzenplotz,* NP *3.pers sg mas,* (N$_0$)

Die Unterkategorie "typ" bei der Nominalphrase wird in aller Regel durch ein Kasusmorphem spezifiziert. Lediglich bei sogenannten Präpositionalobjekten (im Unterschied zu Präpositionalphrasen) kann hier eine Präposition stehen (vgl. die Regel (N5)).

Die Bedeutung einer Nominalphrase ist stets ein *Charakter*.[40] Das ist eine Funktion von möglichen Umständen in Mengen von Eigenschaften. Die Bedeutung von *Kasper* als EN ist das Individuum Kasper. Die Bedeutung des NP *Kasper* ist dagegen die Funktion, die jedem Umstand die Menge der

---

[39] Z.B. Cresswell, Partee oder Thomason.

[40] Vgl. dazu Lewis (1972).

Eigenschaften zuordnet, die Kasper in ihm hat. Der semantische Effekt der Regel (N1) kann also etwa so beschrieben werden: Wenn das EN α das Individuum a bezeichnet, dann bezeichnet das NP α diejenige Funktion f, so daß für ein beliebiges c f(c) = die Menge der Eigenschaften, die in c auf a zutreffen.

Personalpronomen werden ganz anders behandelt. Ich verzichte aber auf Regeln, weil ich hier keine Pronominalsemantik leisten kann. Sie würde zu vielen Änderungen Anlaß geben. Ich kenne bisher nur einen Autor, dessen Pronominalsemantik mir tendenziell richtig zu sein scheint, nämlich R. Smaby.[41] Für die Zwecke dieses Fragmentes kann man sich Personalpronomina als NPs vorstellen.

Appellative haben in der Sprache eine Doppelrolle. Sie können als Prädikat oder als Gattungsnamen auftreten. Ich berücksichtige dies bereits in der Syntax. Ein Satz wie

(1) Kasper haut Klaubrüder, die böse sind

hat zwei Lesarten, eine restriktive und eine explikative. Diese lassen sich etwa so umschreiben

(2) Kasper haut Klaubrüder, Klaubrüder sind böse.
(3) Kasper haut solche Klaubrüder, die böse sind.

Der durch (2) ausgedrückte Sinn von (1) wird an der folgenden syntaktischen Struktur des Terms "Klaubrüder, die böse sind" festgemacht.

Klaubruder, CNST
|
Klaubrüder, CN *pl*
|_____*die böse* sind, RS *pl*
Klaubrüder, die böse sind, CN *pl*
|
Klaubrüder, die böse sind, EN *pl*
|
Klaubrüder, die böse sind, NP *pl*

[41] Vgl. Smaby (1975) und (1976).

Hier modifiziert der Relativsatz das CN *pl*. Die Regel (3) für den Anschluß von restriktiven Relativsätzen wird gerade so gemacht, daß hier die
richtige Lesart herauskommt. Der explikative Sinn des Terms "Klaubrüder,
die böse sind", wird dagegen durch die Relativsatzregel (Rel 4) abgehandelt
werden. Ihr wird so in etwa die folgende syntaktische Struktur zugrundeliegen.

> *Klaubrüder,* CN *pl*
> *Klaubrüder,* EN *pl*
>   *die böse sind,* RS *pl*
> *Klaubrüder, die böse sind,* EN *pl*
> *Klaubrüder, die böse sind,* NP *pl*

Ich werde über artikellose Nominalphrasen im Plural in meinem Fragment aber nicht viel sagen, sondern verweise auf die vorzügliche Arbeit
von Carlson.[42] Diese Bemerkungen können vielleicht genügen, um die Einführung der folgenden Regel zu motivieren.

(N1) $\dfrac{\alpha \in CN \quad \text{gen}(a)\ \text{kas}(b)\ \text{fle}(c)}{\alpha \in EN \quad \text{gen}(a)\ \text{kas}(b)}$[43]

(N2)   *Quantoren*

$$\dfrac{\alpha \in Q\ \text{num}(a)\ \text{gen}(b)\ \text{kas}(c)\ \text{fle}(d)}{\beta \in CN\ \text{num}(a)\ \text{gen}(b)\ \text{kas}(c)\ \text{fle}(d)}$$

αβ ∈ NP num(a) *3.pers* typ(c)

6.3   QUANTOREN SIND ETWA:

1. *ein*   Q *sg mas nom strk*
2. *keines*   Q *sg neut geni strk*
3. *alle*   Q *pl mas nom schw*
4. *jede*   Q *sg fem akk schw*   etc.

---

[42] Cf. Carlson (1977).

[43] Semantisch ändert sich bei dieser Regel nichts.

Die Bedeutung der Quantoren kann man meines Erachtens nicht vernünftig beschreiben, ohne auf pragmatische Redeweisen zurückzugreifen. Ich will zumindest andeuten, warum das so ist. Wenn die Nominalphrase "ein Klaubruder" geäußert wird, dann muß man unterscheiden zwischen einem *spezifischen* und einem *unspezifischen Gebrauch*. Angenommen, wir reden in einer Situation c_0 über die Klaubrüder Tristan, Randi und Evi. Ferner verhaue Kasper gerade eines der Kinder. Wenn wir dann sagen, "Kasper verhaut einen Klaubruder", dann liegt es recht nahe, den Satz so zu interpretieren, daß damit ausgedrückt ist, daß Kasper Tristan, Randi oder Evi verhaut. Bei dieser Interpretation unterstellen wir eine spezifische Verwendung des Terms "einen Klaubruder". Er bedeutet also so etwa 'ein Klaubruder in c_0'. Es gibt aber auch eine andere Verwendung. Angenommen, Kasper ist in c_0 gar nicht zugegen. Ich frage dich: "Was Kasper jetzt wohl macht" und du antwortest: "Er verhaut einen Klaubruder". Dann ist damit sicher nicht ausgedrückt, daß er Tristan, Randi oder Evi verhaut, sondern daß er einen Klaubruder verhaut. Hier liegt unspezifischer Gebrauch vor. (Vgl. Gabbay und Kasher (1976) hierzu). Semantisch schlägt sich diese unterschiedliche Verwendung folgendermaßen nieder. Wird *ein Klaubruder* in c_0 geäußert, dann drückt dieser Term bei spezifischer Verwendung den Charakter χ_{spez}, bei unspezifischer Verwendung den Charakter χ_{unspez} aus. Dabei ist $\chi_{spez}(c) = \{\omega$: Es gibt ein a: a ist ein Klaubruder in c_0 und ω trifft auf a in c zu$\}$, $\chi_{unspez}(c) = \{\omega$: Es gibt ein a: a ist ein Klaubruder in c und ω trifft in c auf a zu$\}$, für eine beliebige Situation c. ω ist natürlich eine Eigenschaftsvariable.

Diese Erläuterungen motivieren hoffentlich die folgenden Bedeutungsfestlegungen. Seien ω_1, ω_2 Variablen für einstellige Eigenschaften, c stehe für einen beliebigen Umstand, a für ein Ding. (*einem*, Q) werde in c_0 spezifisch verwendet. Dann bezeichnet *einem* in c_0 diejenige Funktion ζ_{c_0}, so daß gilt: $\zeta_{c_0}(\omega_1)(c) = \{\omega_2$: Es gibt ein a: $\omega_1(a)(c_0) = 1$ und $\omega_2(a)(c)=1\}$. Wird *einem* in c_0 unspezifisch verwendet, dann bezeichnet *einem* diejenige Funktion ζ, so daß gilt: $\zeta(\omega_1)(c) = \{\omega_2$: Es gibt ein a: $\omega_1(a)(c) = 1$ und $\omega_2(a)(c) = 1\}$.

keines werde in c_0 spezifisch verwendet. Dann bezeichnet *keines* diejenige Funktion ζ_{c_0}, so daß gilt: $\zeta_{c_0}(\omega_1)(c) = \{\omega_2$: Es gibt kein a: $\omega_1(a)(c_0) = 1$ und $\omega_2(a)(c) = 1\}$. Wird *keines* in c_0 unspezifisch verwendet, so bezeichnet dies Wort diejenige Funktion ζ, so daß gilt: $\zeta(\omega_1)(c) = \{\omega_2$: Es gibt kein a: $\omega_1(a)(c) = 1$ und $\omega_2(a)(c) = 1\}$.

alle werde in c_0 spezifisch gebraucht. Dann bezeichnet *alle* diejenige Funktion ζ_{c_0}, so daß für einen beliebigen Gattungsbegriff ξ gilt: $\zeta_{c_0}(\xi)(c) = \{\omega_2$: ω_2 trifft in c_0 zu auf $\xi(c)\}$. Wird *alle* unspezifisch in c_0 verwendet, so bezeichnet *alle* diejenige Funktion ζ, so daß für einen beliebigen Gattungsbegriff ξ gilt:

$$\zeta(\xi)(c) = \{\omega_2: \omega_2(\xi(c))(c) = 1\}.$$

Man beachte, daß ξ (c) eine Menge ist. Mengen sind auch Dinge. ω_2 muß aber eine vernünftige Eigenschaft sein, die für Mengen erklärt ist.

jeder werde in c_0 spezifisch verwendet. Dann bezeichnet *jeder* in c_0 diejenige Funktion ζ_{c_0}, so daß $\zeta_{c_0}(\omega_1)(c) = \{\omega_2$: Für jedes a gilt: Wenn $\omega_1(a)(c_0) = 1$, so $\omega_2(a)(c) = 1\}$. Wird *jeder* in c_0 unspezifisch verwendet, so bezeichnet *jeder* in c_0 diejenige Funktion ζ, so daß $\zeta(\omega_1)(c) = \{\omega_2$: Für jedes a gilt: $\omega_1(a)(c) = 1 \Rightarrow \omega_2(a)(c) = 1\}$.

6.4 BEISPIEL

keines, Q sg neu geni strk (6.3.1) *Kindes, CN sg neu geni strk,* (M1)

keines Kindes, NP 3.pers sg geni, (N2) [44]

---

[44] Diese Kategorisierung wird in Sätzen wie "Kasper gedenkt keines Kindes" benötigt. Daneben muß "keines Kindes" noch als Q *extrastark* klassifiziert werden, um Konstruktionen wie "keines Kindes altem Vater" zu ermöglichen. Das Merkmal "extrastark" wird auf der nächsten Seite erläutert. Ich behandle diese veralteten Syntagmen aber nicht.

Eine Bemerkung zur Unterkategorie "fle". Sie war bisher in der Regel
(M1) noch nicht aufgetaucht. Die Regel muß in diesem Sinne ergänzt werden.
Die Lexikoneinträge für CN-Stämme müssen aussehen wie der folgende:

$$Frau \quad CN \quad fem \text{ fle(a),} \quad a = strk, schw.$$

In (M1) muß CNST und CN noch jeweils "fle(c)" hinzugefügt werden. Dies
sieht etwas künstlich aus. Die Unterkategorien sind aber nichts anderes
als ein technisches Verfahren, um rekursiv über die Regeln bestimmte morphologische und syntaktische Eigenschaften von Ausdrücken zu definieren.
Das rechtfertigt deren Einführung. fle($strk$) bei einem Q (und Det, wie
wir gleich sehen werden) besagt, daß die modifizierte CN-Gruppe nur starke
Adjektive bei sich haben darf. Bei der CN-Gruppe bedeutet fle($strk$), daß
nur starke Adjektive bei ihr sind bzw. sein können. Bei einem ADJ bedeutet
fle($strk$), daß es stark flektiert ist. Völlig Analoges gilt für die Unterkategorie fle($schw$).

Die Terminologie "stark" und "schwach" ist übrigens nicht ganz korrekt. "stark" ist hier das Adjektivparadigma, das von dem unbestimmten Artikel "ein" verlangt wird, "schwach" das zu "der" passende Paradigma. Diese
Klassifikation ist quer zur üblichen. Normalerweise würde man sagen, daß
in "ein alter Mann" das Adjektiv stark ist, in "einem alten Mann" dagegen
schwach. Hier werden beide Formen als stark klassifiziert. Dies verlangt
natürlich die Einführung einer dritten Flektionsklasse für artikellose
Konstruktionen wie z.B. "Gutem Wein spricht man gerne zu". Diese Klasse
könnte man "extrastark" nennen. Mir liegt wenig an den Bezeichnungen.
Allgemein gilt folgendes: man muß sich überlegen, ob man wenige Flektions-
klassen einführen möchte um den Preis komplizierter morphologischer Regeln
(so bei Wurzel) oder mehr Klassen, um dann die Regeln einfacher zu haben.
Ich habe schon an anderer Stelle gesagt, daß der morphologische Teil dieses Aufsatzes nicht ernsthaft ausgearbeitet ist.

Nach diesen Erläuterungen sind die folgenden beiden Regeln verständlich:

(N3)   *Definite Terme*

α ∈ DET num(a) gen(b) kas(c) fle(d)

β ∈ CN num(a) gen(b) kas(c) fle(d)

αβ ∈ EN num(a) gen(b) kas(c)[45]

(N4)   *Appellativgruppen*

α ∈ ADJ num(a) gen(b) kas(c) fle(d)

β ∈ CN num(a) gen(b) kas(c) fle(d)

αβ ∈ CN num(a) gen(b) kas(c) fle(d)[46]

Adjektive können auch Eigennamen modifizieren, z.B. in "der gute alte Kasper". In diesem Fall werden sie "explikativ" gedeutet. Ich behandle diese Konstruktion aber nicht.

Wieder Beispiele dazu:

6.5

1. *alten,* ADJ *sg mas akk schw*   2. *Mann,* CN *sg*
                                                    mas akk schw,

4. *den,* DET   3. *alten Mann,* CN *sg mas*   (wie 5.2.4)
   sg mas akk   *akk schw,* (N4)
   schw, (Lexikon)

5. *den alten Mann,* EN *sg mas akk,* (N3)

6. *den alten Mann,* NP *3.pers sg akk,* (N0)

---

[45] Die Semantik dieser Regel sieht analog aus wie die der Quantorenphrasen. Beispiel: Wird *der mann* in c_0 spezifisch verwendet, so wird damit der Mann in c_0 bezeichnet. Liegt unspezifische Verwendung vor, so wird für jedes c der Mann in c bezeichnet. *Die Männer* bezeichnet dementsprechend die Männer in c_0 oder die in c. *Diese Männer* bezeichnet stets die Männer in c_0.

[46] Für den Augenblick mag die Semantik dieser Regel einmal die funktionale Applikation der Bedeutung von α auf die von β sein.

Ich werde im folgenden die vorausgesetzten Lexikoneinträge meistens nicht mehr explizit einführen. Man kann sie den Beispielableitungen unmittelbar ablesen. So sieht man etwa anhand von 6.5, daß *den* ein DET *sg mas akk schw* ist. Weitere Determinatoren sind etwa die Formen des Demonstrativpronomens *dieser*. Wie man ferner sieht, zerlege ich die Ausdrücke hinfort auch nicht mehr morphologisch. Den Ausdruck *alten* gibt es nicht in meiner Theorie. Er entsteht nach Anwendung der morphographematischen Komponente aus *alt sg mas akk schw*.

Nun ein weiteres Beispiel:

6.6 SATZ

   einen alten Mann gehört zu NP *3.pers sg akk*

   Beweis:

   einen, Q, (6.3)   *alten Mann,* CN *sg mas akk strk*

       sg mas   (analog wie 6.5.3)

       akk strk

   einen alten Mann, NP *3.pers sg akk,* (N2)

Wie man sieht, ist dieser indefinite Term syntaktisch anders aufgebaut als die definite Nominalphrase *den alten Mann.* Von diesem Umstand werde ich einen wesentlichen Gebrauch machen, wenn es darum geht, die restriktiven von den explikativen Relativsätzen zu unterscheiden.

   (N5)   *Präpositionalobjekte* [47]

       α ∈ Präp   typ(a) erg(b)

       β ∈ NP   per(c) num(d) typ(b)

       ―――――――――――――――――――――――――

       αβ ∈ NP   per(c) num(d) typ(a)

---

[47] Die Bedeutung der NP αβ ist die Bedeutung von β, egal was α bedeutet.

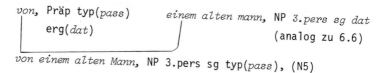

6.7 BEISPIEL

von, Präp typ(*pass*)   *einem alten mann,* NP *3.pers sg dat*

  erg(*dat*)   (analog zu 6.6)

von einem alten Mann, NP 3.pers sg typ(*pass*), (N5)

6.8 WEITERES BEISPIEL

durch, Präp typ(*pass*)   *einen alten Mann,* NP *3.pers sg akk*

  erg(*akk*)   (analog zu 6.6)

durch einen alten Mann, NP *3.pers sg pass,* (N5)

Ich benötige in meinem Fragment Präpositionalobjekte im wesentlichen zur Beschreibung von Passivkonstruktionen. Vielleicht ist natürlich *durch einen alten Mann* eher eine Präpositionalphrase. Letztere möchte ich aber als Adverbien ansehen. Und die Bedeutung von Adverbien sind keine Charaktere. Für mich war es praktischer, *durch einen alten Mann* als NP aufzuziehen.

7. KONSTRUKTIONEN MIT ENDSTELLUNG DES FINITUMS

Ich behandle nun Konstruktionen, wie sie daß-Sätzen und analogen Nebensätzen zugrundeliegen.

(V1) *Verbobjekte*

$$\alpha \in VP \ per(a) \ num(b) \ erg(c_1,\ldots,c_n) \ sgl(\gamma_1,\ldots,\gamma_m)$$
$$abtr(\delta) \ hptv(\varepsilon_1,\ldots,\varepsilon_1) \ stell(d)$$

$n > 1$, d = end, rels

$$\beta \in \begin{cases} NP \ num(b_1) \ gen(e) \ typ(c_n), \ \text{falls} \ c_n \in Kas \cup Präp \\ VINF \ erg(\textit{nom}) \ sgl(\zeta_1,\ldots,\zeta_r) \ art(c_n) \ diat(f) \\ \quad hptv(n_1,\ldots,n_p), \ \text{falls} \ c_n \in \{0\text{-Inf, zu-Inf}\} \\ S_{daß}, \ \text{falls} \ c_n = daß\text{-S.} \end{cases}$$

$\beta\alpha \in$ VP per(a) num(b) erg($c_1,\ldots,c_{n-1}$)

sgl($\beta,\gamma_1,\ldots,\gamma_m$) abtr($\beta\delta$) hptv($\varepsilon_1,\ldots,\varepsilon_1$) stell(d),

falls $c_n \in$ Kas $\cup$ Präp

$\alpha\beta \in$ VP per(a) num(b) erg($c_1,\ldots,c_{n-1}$)

sgl($\gamma_1,\ldots,\gamma_m\beta$) abtr($\delta\beta$) hptv($\varepsilon_1,\ldots,\varepsilon_1\beta$)

stell(d), falls $c_n \in$ {daß-S,   zu-Inf}

Syntaktisch ist diese Regel unübersichtlich, semantisch ist sie kompliziert.[48] Man hätte sie durch "Anhebung" des Infinitiv- und des Daß-Satzes zu Nominalphrasen einfacher gestalten können. Ich halte das aber nicht für ehrlich, denn diese Konstruktionen verhalten sich syntaktisch doch recht unterschiedlich zu "gewöhnlichen" Nominalphrasen.

[48] Ich benutze zur übersichtlicheren Darstellung der Semantik den metasprachlichen λ-Operator λ^*. Wenn ω eine n-stellige Eigenschaft ist, dann ist ($\lambda^*a\omega(a_1,\ldots,a_{n-1},a)$) diejenige einstellige Eigenschaft, die auf ein b zutrifft gdw. ω auf $a_1,\ldots,a_{n-1}$,b zutrifft. Wir müssen nun drei Fälle unterscheiden. 1. β bezeichnet einen Charakter, sagen wir χ,α eine n-stellige Eigenschaft, z.B. ω_n. Dann drückt $\beta\alpha$ diejenige (n-1)-stellige Eigenschaft ω_{n-1} aus, die auf $a_1,\ldots,a_{n-1}$ in c zutrifft gdw. ($\lambda^*a_n\omega_n(a_1,\ldots,a_n)$) $\in \chi$(c). 2. β ist ein Infinitiv, der die einstellige Eigenschaft ω_1 ausdrückt. Dann bezeichnet $\beta\alpha$ diejenige (n-1)-stellige Eigenschaft ω_{n-1}, die auf $a_1,\ldots,a_{n-1}$ in c zutrifft, wenn $\omega_n(a_1,\ldots,a_n,\omega_1)$(c) = 1. 3. β ist ein Daß-Satz. Es wird sich zeigen, daß β dann eine Proposition p ist. Dann drückt $\alpha\beta$ die Eigenschaft ω_{n-1} aus, die auf $a_1,\ldots,a_{n-1}$ in c zutrifft gdw. $\omega_n(a_1,\ldots,a_{n-1},p)$(c) = 1.

7.1 BEISPIEL

1. *einen Rettich,* NP
   3.pers sg akk
   (analog wie 6.6)

2. *anbietet,* VP *3.pers sg*
   (*nom, dat, akk*)
   sgl(+) abtr(*an*)
   hptv(*bietet*)
   end, (M2)

3. *einen Rettich anbietet,* VP *3.pers sg* (*nom, dat*)
   sgl (*einen Rettich,*+)
   abtr(*einen Rettich an*)
   hptv(*bietet*) end, (V1)

4. *Kasper,* NP *3.pers sg dat*
   (analog zu 6.1)

5. *Kasper einen Rettich anbietet,* VP *3.pers sg* (*nom*)
   sgl(*Kasper, einen Rettich,*+)
   abtr(*Kasper einen Rettich an*)
   hptv(*bietet*) end, (V1)

Das Kreuz in der Folge der Satzglieder markiert die Stellung des Hauptverbs. Bei Endstellung des Finitums sollte dieses eigentlich immer am Ende stehen, wie der Name nahelegt. Das ist aber nicht ganz richtig, weil daß-Sätze und Infinitivsätze hinter dem Finitum stehen. Deshalb ist auch der Name "Endstellung" nicht ganz korrekt.

Nun kommen die Regeln für abgeschlossene Nebensätze und für Daß-Sätze:

(S1) *Nebensätze mit Endstellung des Finitums* [49]

$\alpha \in$ VP per(a) num(b) erg(c_n) sgl(γ_1,...,γ_k)

abtr(δ) hptv(ε_1,...,ε_1) stell(end)

β wie bei (V1)

b_1 = b und a_1 = a, falls c_n = *nom*.

$\qquad$―――――――――――――――――――――――

$\beta\alpha \in S_{\text{end}}$

7.2   EIN BEISPIEL

1. *Hotzenplotz,* NP *sg nom 3.pers* (wie 6.2)

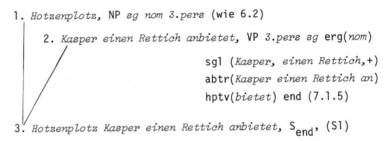

   2. *Kasper einen Rettich anbietet,* VP *3.pers sg* erg(*nom*)

      sgl (*Kasper, einen Rettich,*+)

      abtr(*Kasper einen Rettich an*)

      hptv(*bietet*) end (7.1.5)

3. *Hotzenplotz Kasper einen Rettich anbietet,* S_{end}, (S1)

[49] Die Semantik sieht folgendermaßen aus. α bezeichne die Eigenschaft ω.
Wie bei (V1) müssen wir hier wieder drei Fälle unterscheiden.
1. β bezeichne den Charakter χ. Dann drückt $\beta\alpha$ diejenige Proposition p
aus, so daß für ein beliebiges c gilt: $p(c) = 1 \Leftrightarrow \omega \in \chi(c)$.
2. β bezeichne die Eigenschaft ω_1. Dann ist $V(\beta\alpha)(c) = 1 \Leftrightarrow \omega(\omega_1)(c) = 1$.
3. $V(\beta)$ ist die Proposition q. Dann ist $V(\beta\alpha)(c) = 1 \Leftrightarrow \omega(q)(c) = 1$.

7.3 EIN WEITERES BEISPIEL

1. *erlaubt*, VP *3.pers sg*
       (*nom, dat, zu-Inf*)
       sgl(+) abtr(-)
       hptv(*erlaubt*)
       stell(end), (M2)

2. *zu rauchen*, VINF erg(*nom*)
       hptv(*zu rauchen*)
       sgl(+)
       art(zu-Inf)
       diat(akt) (M4$_1$)

3. *erlaubt zu rauchen*, VP *3.pers sg*
       (*nom, dat*) abtr(*zu rauchen*)
       sgl(+, *zu rauchen*)
       hptv(*erlaubt, zu rauchen*)
       stell(end), (V1)

4. *Hotzenplotz*, NP *3.pers sg dat*, (wie 6.2)

5. *Hotzenplotz erlaubt zu rauchen*, VP *3.pers sg nom*
       abtr(*Hotzenplotz zu rauchen*)
       sgl(*Hotzenplotz*,+,*zu rauchen*)
       hptv(*erlaubt, zu rauchen*)
       stell(end), (V1)

6. *Kasper*, NP *3.pers sg nom*, (6.1)

6. *Kasper Hotzenplotz erlaubt zu rauchen*, S$_{end}$, (S1)

Es empfiehlt sich, die Satzbildung für unpersönliche Verben separat abzuhandeln.

(S2) $\alpha \in$ VP *3.pers sg es* sgl(γ) abtr(δ) [50]
      hptv(a$_1$,...,a$_n$) stell(end)

---

    es $\alpha \in$ S$_{end}$

---

[50] Semantisch ändert sich hier nichts. Alle unpersönlichen Verben, denen nur noch das *es*-Subjekt fehlt, drücken Sachverhalte aus, d.h. Propositionen.

Diese Regel erlaubt zum Beispiel den Übergang von *tagt*, VP *3.pers sg* sgl(+) abtr(-) hptv(*tagt*) end zu *es tagt*, S_{end}. Man wird auch etwa dafür sorgen müssen, daß *gut ist daß Kasper raucht* zur Kategorie VP *3.pers sg* (*es*) sgl(*gut*,+,*daß Kasper raucht*) abtr(*gut daß Kasper raucht*) hptv(*ist*) end gehört. Davon kann man dann übergehen zu *es gut ist daß Kasper raucht*, S_{end}. Allerdings habe ich über derartige Konstruktionen noch nicht nachgedacht. Sätze mit suppletivem *es* werden durch (S2) nicht abgedeckt, also etwa *Es kommen Leute*. Das leistet die Regel (S4); vgl. Abschnitt 10.

Nun zu den daß-Sätzen. Die Regel für ihre Bildung ist sehr einfach.

(S3)   *Daß-Sätze* [51]

Wenn $\alpha \in S_{end}$, so *daß* $\alpha \in S$ daß.

7.4   BEISPIEL

1. *Hotzenplotz Kasper einen Rettich anbietet*, S_{end}, (7.3.3)

2. *daß Hotzenplotz Kasper einen Rettich anbietet*, S daß, (S3)

Nun können wir bereits recht komplizierte Nebensätze konstruieren, zum Beispiel gilt:

7.5   SATZ

er mir mitteilt daß Hotzenplotz Kasper einen Rettich anbietet $\in S_{end}$.

---

[51] Semantisch ändert sich durch Anwendung dieser Regel nichts.

Beweis

1. *mitteilt,* VP *3.pers sg*
   erg(*nom,dat,*daß-S) sgl(+)
   abtr(*mit*) hptv(*teilt*) end (M2)

2. *daß Hotzenplotz Kasper einen Rettich anbietet,* S-daß,
   (7.4.2)

3. *mitteilt daß Hotzenplotz Kasper einen Rettich anbietet,*
   VP *3.pers sg* (*nom,dat*)
   abtr(*mit daß Hotzenplotz Kasper einen Rettich anbietet*)
   hptv(*teilt, daß Hotzenplotz Kasper einen Rettich anbietet*)
   stell(end) sgl(+,*daß Hotzenplotz Kasper einen Rettich anbietet*)
   (V1)

4. *mir,* NP *1.pers sg dat,* (Lexikon)

5. *mir mitteilt daß Hotzenplotz Kasper einen Rettich anbietet,*
   VP *3.pers sg* (*nom*)
   abtr(*mir mit daß Hotzenplotz Kasper einen Rettich anbietet*)
   hptv(*teilt, daß Hotzenplotz Kasper einen Rettich anbietet*)
   sgl(*mir,+,daß Hotzenplotz Kasper einen Rettich anbietet*)
   stell(end), (V1)

6. *er,* NP *1.pers sg nom,* (Lexikon)

7. *er mir mitteilt daß Hotzenplotz Kasper einen Rettich anbietet,*
   S_{end}, (S1)

Ich überlasse es nun dem Leser zu beweisen, daß der folgende Ausdruck in unserem Fragment als Nebensatz klassifiziert wird, d.h. daß gilt:

7.5 BEHAUPTUNG

ich mir wünsche daß Kasper mir mitteilt daß Dimpfelmoser Hotzenplotz erlaubt daß er mir einen Rettich anbietet   gehört zu S_{end}.

Wir können allerdings noch nicht zeigen, daß *daß Dimpfelmoser Hotzenplotz erlaubt mir einen Rettich anzubieten* zu $S_{daß}$ gehört. Dazu müssen wir noch etwas an den Infinitivkonstruktionen tun.

8.   EINFACHE INFINITIVSÄTZE IM AKTIV

(I1) *Infinitivobjekte* [52]

α $\in$ VINF erg($c_1,\dots,c_n$) sgl($\gamma_1,\dots,\gamma_m$) art(g) diat(akt)
        hptv($\varepsilon_1,\dots,\varepsilon_1$)

$n > 1$

β wie bei (V1)

$\beta\alpha$ $\in$ VINF erg($c_1,\dots,c_{n-1}$) sgl($\beta,\gamma_1,\dots,\gamma_m$) hptv($\varepsilon_1,\dots,\varepsilon_1$)
        art(g) diat(akt),
        falls c_n $\in$ Kas $\cup$ Präp

$\alpha\beta$ $\in$ VINF erg($c_1,\dots,c_{n-1}$) sgl($\gamma_1,\dots,\gamma_m,\beta$)
        hptv($\varepsilon_1,\dots,\varepsilon_1,\beta$) art(g) diat(akt),
        falls c_n $\in$ {daß-S,   zu-Inf}

Wir können nun die zuvor genannte Konstruktion behandeln.

8.1 1. *anzubieten,* VINF erg(*nom,dat,akk*)
                sgl(+) art(zu-Inf) hptv(*anzubieten*)
                diat(akt), (M4$_1$)

                2. *einen Rettich,* NP 3.*pers sg akk,* (wie 6.6)

3. *einen Rettich anzubieten,* VINF (*nom,dat*)
                        sgl(*einen Rettich,*+) zu-Inf,
                        hptv(*anzubieten*) akt, (I1)

            4. *mir,* NP 1.*pers sg dat* (Lexikon)

5. *mir einen Rettich anzubieten,* VINF (*nom*)
                    sgl(*mir,einen Rettich,*+) zu-Inf,
                    hptv(*anzubieten*) akt, (I1)

            6. *erlaubt,* VP 3.*pers* ...
                    (vgl. 7.3.1)

[52] Die Semantik dieser Regel sieht genau so aus wie die von (V1).

7. *erlaubt mir einen Rettich anzubieten,*

        VP *3.pers sg* (*nom,dat*)

        abtr(*mir einen Rettich anzubieten*)

        sgl(+,*mir einen Rettich anzubieten*)

        hptv(*erlaubt,mir einen Rettich anzubieten*)

        stell(end), (V1)

    8. *Hotzenplotz,* NP *3.pers sg dat,* (wie 6.2)

9. *Hotzenplotz erlaubt mir einen Rettich anzubieten*

        VP *3.pers sg* (*nom*)

        abtr(*Hotzenplotz mir einen Rettich anzu-*
              bieten)

        sgl(*Hotzenplotz,*+,*mir einen Rettich an-*
              zubieten)

        hptv(*erlaubt,mir einen Rettich anzubieten*)

        stell(end), (V1)

   10. *Dimpfelmoser,* NP *3.pers sg nom,* (wie 6.2)

11. *Dimpfelmoser Hotzenplotz erlaubt mir einen Rettich anzubieten,*
        S_{end}, (S1)

12. *daß Dimpfelmoser Hotzenplotz erlaubt mir einen Rettich
    anzubieten,*   S daß, (S3)

Der Daß-Satz 8.1.12, den wir gerade erzeugt haben, soll aufgrund unserer semantischen Festlegungen die Proposition ausdrücken, daß Dimpfelmoser dem Hotzenplotz erlaubt, daß Hotzenplotz mir einen Rettich anbietet. Dagegen soll der Daß-Satz

    daß Dimpfelmoser Hotzenplotz verspricht
    mir einen Rettich anzubieten

die Proposition ausdrücken, daß Dimpfelmoser dem Hotzenplotz verspricht,

daß Dimpfelmoser mir einen Rettich anbietet. Im ersten Fall bezieht sich
also die durch den Infinitivsatz ausgedrückte Eigenschaft auf das Objekt,
im zweiten Fall auf das Subjekt. Diesem Umstand müssen wir in unseren
Bedeutungsregeln für "erlaubt" und "verspricht" Rechnung tragen. Sie
können ungefähr so aussehen:

erlaubt als VP erg(nom,dat,zu-Inf) drückt die dreistellige Eigenschaft ω
aus, die auf ein Individuum a, ein Individuum b und eine einstellige Eigenschaft ω_1 unter einem Umstand c genau dann zutrifft, wenn a dem b in c
ω_1(b) erlaubt.

verspricht als VP erg(nom,dat,zu-Inf) drückt dagegen die Eigenschaft ω aus,
die auf (a,b,ω_1) zutrifft, wenn a dem b ω_1(a) verspricht.

Ich überlasse es dem Leser, sich zu überlegen, daß bei diesen Festlegungen genau die erwarteten Propositionen ausgedrückt werden.

9. DIE UMSCHRIEBENE VERBKONJUGATION

(V2) *Finite Perfektform* [53]

$$
\begin{array}{l}
\beta\alpha \quad \in \text{VPPf } \text{erg}(a_1,\ldots,a_n) \text{ hiv}(b) \text{ hptv}(\delta_1,\ldots,\delta_k) \\
\qquad\qquad \text{sgl}(\varepsilon) \text{ diat}(e) \\[4pt]
\gamma \quad \in \text{HVP } \text{per}(c) \text{ num}(d) \text{ typ}(b) \\
\hline
\beta\alpha'\gamma \in \text{VP} \quad \text{erg}(a_1,\ldots,a_n) \text{ per}(c) \text{ num}(d) \text{ abtr}(\beta\alpha') \\
\qquad\qquad \text{sgl}(\varepsilon) \text{ hptv}(\delta_1,\ldots,\delta_k) \text{ stell}(end)
\end{array}
$$

$$
\alpha' = \left\{
\begin{array}{l}
\alpha'' \ \textit{inf,} \text{ falls } \alpha = \textit{part } \alpha'' \ \textit{part} \text{ mit} \\
\qquad \alpha'' = \textit{könn, müss, soll, dürf, lass, } \ldots \\
\qquad \text{und } (\delta_1,\ldots,\delta_k) = (\delta_1,\ldots,\delta_{k-1}, \textit{könn}),\ldots \\
\qquad \text{etc. mit } (\delta_1,\ldots,\delta_{k-1}) \neq \emptyset \\[4pt]
\alpha, \text{ sonst}
\end{array}
\right.
$$

[53] Zur Semantik dieser Regel sage ich genauso viel wie zu den übrigen
Temporalregeln, nämlich nichts.

Die Fallunterscheidung in dieser Regel dient dazu, etwa aus *wissen gekonnt* und *hat – wissen können hat* herzuleiten.

9.1 BEISPIEL

1. *verprügelt,* VPPf
   (*nom,akk*) *haben*
   hptv(*verprügelt*)
   sgl(+) diat(akt)
   (M5)

2. *hat,* HVP
   3.pers sg haben
   (M5)

3. *verprügelt hat,* VP (*nom,akk*)
   3.pers sg abtr(*verprügelt*)
   sgl(+) hptv(*verprügelt*)
   stell(end)
   (V2)

4. *Hotzenplotz,* NP
   3.pers sg akk
   (6.2)

5. *Hotzenplotz verprügelt hat,* VP (*nom*) *3.pers sg*
   abtr(*Hotzenplotz verprügelt*)
   sgl(*Hotzenplotz,*+)
   hptv(*verprügelt*)
   stell(end)
   (V1)

Ich überlasse es dem Leser zu überprüfen, daß wir nun etwa die folgende Behauptung zeigen können:

9.2   BEHAUPTUNG

daß Kasper mir mitgeteilt hat daß er Hotzenplotz verprügelt hat
∈ S daß.

(I2)   *Infinitiv Perfekt*

α ∈ VPPf erg(a_1,...,a_n) hiv(b) hptv(γ_1,...,γ_k)
         sgl(ε) diat(d)
β ∈ HINF typ(b) art(c)

$\alpha\beta$ ∈ VINF erg(a_1,...,a_n) sgl(+) hptv(γ_1,...,γ_k,β)
          art(c) diat(d)

9.2   BEISPIEL FÜR DIESE REGEL

1. *schwergefallen,*   2. *sein,* HINF *sein*
   | VPPf (*es,dat,*zu-Inf)   0-Inf
   | hptv(*schwergefallen*)   (M4$_0$)
   | *sein* sgl(+) akt
   | (5.10.2)

3. *schwergefallen sein,* VINF (*es,dat,*zu-Inf)
                          sgl(+) hptv(*schwergefallen sein*)
                          0-Inf akt
                          (I2)

Wir beschreiben jetzt sämtliche finiten Verbphrasen, die durch Um-
schreibung mit futurischem *werden* gebildet werden.

(V3)   *Futurische Tempora*

α ∈ VINF erg(a_1,...,a_n) sgl(ε_1,...,ε_k) hptv(γ_1,...,γ_1)
         diat(d) 0-Inf
β ∈ HVP per(b) num(c) typ(*fut*)

$\alpha\beta$ ∈ VP   per(b) num(c) erg(a_1,...,a_n) sgl(ε_1,...,ε_k)
          hptv(γ_1,...,γ_1) abtr(α) stell(end)

9.3   ANWENDUNG DIESER REGEL

1. *schwergefallen sein,*
   | VINF (*es,dat,*zu-Inf) sgl(+)
   | hptv(*schwergefallen sein*
   | 0-Inf, akt, (9.2.3)

2. *wird,*
   HVP *3.pers sg fut*
   (Lexikon)

3. *schwergefallen sein wird,*
   | VP *3.pers sg* (*es,dat,*zu-Inf)
   | sgl(+)
   | hptv(*schwergefallen,sein*)
   | abtr(*schwergefallen sein*)
   | end, (V3)

4. *mir einen Rettich anzu-*
   bieten,
   VINF (*nom*)
   sgl(+,*mir einen Rettich*
   anzubieten) zu-Inf,
   hptv(*anzubieten*) akt,
   (8.1.5)

5. *schwergefallen sein wird mir*
   einen Rettich anzubieten,
   | VP *3.pers sg* (*es,dat*)
   | abtr(*schwergefallen sein mir*
   | *einen Rettich anzubieten*)
   | sgl(+,*mir einen Rettich an-*
   | *zubieten*)
   | hptv(*schwergefallen sein,mir*
   | *einen Rettich anzubieten*)
   | end, (V1)

6. *Hotzenplotz,*
   NP *3.pers sg dat*
   (wie 6.2)

7. *Hotzenplotz schwergefallen sein wird mir einen Rettich*
   anzubieten,
   | VP *3.pers sg* (*es*)
   | abtr(*Hotzenplotz schwergefallen sein mir einen Rettich*
   | *anzubieten*)
   | sgl(*Hotzenplotz,*+,*mir einen Rettich anzubieten*)
   | hptv(*schwergefallen sein,mir einen Rettich anzubieten*)
   | end, (V1)

8. *es Hotzenplotz schwergefallen sein wird mir einen Rettich anzubieten,*

S_{end}, (S2)

9. *daß es Hotzenplotz schwergefallen sein wird mir einen Rettich anzubieten,*

S-daß (S3)

10   DIE HAUPTSATZSTELLUNGEN

Wir werden uns nun an die Hauptsatzstellungen wagen. Im Prinzip könnte man hier mit einem einzigen Regelschema auskommen. dessen Voraussetzungen im wesentlichen wie bei (S1), d.h. der Regel für die Nebensatzbildung aussehen. Die Stellungsmöglichkeiten für den Hauptsatz sind aber außerordentlich verzwickt, so daß ich es vorziehe, hier mehrere Regeln zu formulieren. Das wird dann übersichtlicher. Ein Satz wie

Kasper bietet Hotzenplotz einen Rettich an

wird ungefähr auf die folgende Weise konstruiert:

Hotzenplotz einen Rettich anbietet, VP (*nom*) end...

Kasper, NP_{nom} *bietet Hotzenplotz einen Rettich an,* VP (*nom*) zweit..

Kasper bietet Hotzenplotz einen Rettich an, S_{zweit}

Der letzte Ableitungsschritt geschieht mittels der Drachschen Regeln. Diese müssen sehr raffiniert sein, denn wir wollen etwa auch den folgenden Übergang haben:

dem Hotzenplotz versprechen wird ihm zu erlauben mir einen Rettich anzubieten, VP (nom) end

Dimpfelmoser, NP_{nom} *wird dem Hotzenplotz versprechen ihm zu erlauben mir einen Rettich anzubieten,* VP (nom) zweit

Dimpfelmoser wird dem Hotzenplotz versprechen ihm zu erlauben mir einen Rettich anzubieten

Auch wünschen wir uns, aus den Prämissen des letzten Ableitungs-
schrittes Hauptsätze wie die folgenden herleiten zu können.

(1) *Dem Hotzenplotz wird Dimpfelmoser versprechen ihm zu erlauben*
     mir einen Rettich anzubieten

(2) *Dem Hotzenplotz versprechen wird Dimpfelmoser ihm zu erlauben*
     mir einen Rettich anzubieten

(3) *Versprechen wird Dimpfelmoser dem Hotzenplotz ihm zu erlauben*
     mir einen Rettich anzubieten

(4) *Versprechen ihm zu erlauben mir einen Rettich anzubieten*
     wird Dimpfelmoser dem Hotzenplotz

Nicht zulassen wollen wir dagegen den Übergang zu

(5)+ *Versprechen ihm zu erlauben wird Dimpfelmoser dem Hotzenplotz*
     mir einen Rettich anzubieten

(6)+ *Ihm zu erlauben wird Dimpfelmoser dem Hotzenplotz versprechen*
     mir einen Rettich anzubieten

(7)+ *Mir einen Rettich anzubieten wird Dimpfelmoser dem Hotzenplotz*
     versprechen ihm zu erlauben

Ich will dabei nicht bestreiten, daß wir (5) bis (7) mit Mühe und
Kontext eventuell verstehen. Ganz blödsinnige Konstruktionen habe ich gar
nicht erst betrachtet. Der Punkt ist, daß (1) bis (4) dagegen völlig unproblematisch sind, wie auch die folgenden Sätze:

(8) *Es wird Dimpfelmoser dem Hotzenplotz versprechen ihm zu*
     erlauben mir einen Rettich anzubieten

(9) *Ihm zu erlauben mir einen Rettich anzubieten wird Dimpfelmoser*
     dem Hotzenplotz versprechen

Soweit ich es überschaue, scheinen den Konstruktionen mit Hilfsverb
an zweiter Stelle die folgenden kombinatorischen Prinzipien zugrundezu-
liegen. Vor Anwendung der Drachschen Regeln haben wir so etwa die folgende
Konfiguration:

$$SG_0 \quad HIV, \ SG_1, \ldots, SG_{m-1}, \ V, \ \left(\ H_1, \ldots, H_n, \ SG_m \ \right)$$

Dabei sind $H_1, \ldots, H_n$ Teile des Hauptverbkomplexes. (Sie müssen natürlich
nicht vorhanden sein. Das ist durch die Klammer angedeutet.) Diese haben
wir bisher noch nicht näher behandelt, ich möchte die Prinzipien aber
gleich allgemeiner erläutern.[54] SG_m ist immer ein Daß-Satz oder ein Infinitivsatz. (Auch SG_m kann selbstverständlich fehlen.) Die ersten beiden
Veränderungsmöglichkeiten sind simpel. Man schreibt entweder das supple-
tive *es* an die erste Stelle vor das Hilfsverb und setzt SG_0 direkt hinter
das Hilfsverb. Man erhält:

$$es, \ HIV, \ SG_0, \ SG_1, \ldots, SG_{m-1}, \ V, \ \left(\ H_1, \ldots, H_n, \ SG_m \ \right)$$

Die zweite Transformationsmöglichkeit ist das, was man Drachsche Regel
nennen kann. Man zieht aus $SG_0, SG_1, \ldots, SG_{m-1}, SG_m$ irgendein Satzglied an
die erste Stelle vor HIV. Alle anderen stehen in der genannten Reihenfolge an der alten Stelle. Falls $SG_i \neq SG_0$, muß SG_0 hinter das Finitum HIV.
Man erhält also eine der folgenden Konfigurationen:

$$SG_0, \quad HIV, \ SG_1, \ldots, SG_{m-1}, \ V, \ (H_1, \ldots, H_n, \ SG_m)$$
$$SG_i, \quad HIV, \ SG_0, \ldots, SG_{i-1}, \ SG_{i+1}, \ldots, \ V, \ (H_1, \ldots, H_n \ SG_m)$$
$$SG_m, \quad HIV, \ SG_0, \ldots, SG_{m-1}, \ V, \ (H_1, \ldots, H_n)$$

Die dritte Transformation ist die raffinierteste. Man bringt einen Komplex,
in dem sich auf jeden Fall das Hauptverb befindet, und der links beliebig
viel an Satzgliedern und rechts ebenfalls beliebig viel an den genannten
Ausdrücken einschließt, an den Anfang.

----

[54] Diese Darstellung hält sich ziemlich eng an Bierwisch (1973:36).

SG_o rückt an die erste Stelle hinter HIV. Wir erhalten dadurch die Konfiguration

$$SG_i, SG_{i+1}, \ldots, SG_{m-1}, V, H_1, \ldots, H_j, HIV$$
$$SG_o, \ldots, SG_{i-1}, H_{j+1}, \ldots, H_n, SG_m$$

Im Extremfall rückt der ganze Verbkomplex vor das Finitum, so daß man folgendes erhält:

$$SG_1, \ldots, SG_{m-1}, V (H_1, \ldots, H_n, SG_m), HIV, SG_o$$

Transformationen dieser dritten Art lagen etwa den Beispielsätzen (2), (3) und (4) zugrunde. In (5) wurde gegen die Transformation verstoßen, denn der rechts vom Finitum stehende Ausdruck *zu erlauben* ist kein Satzglied. Ähnliche Fehler lagen in (6) und (7) vor. Man sieht an diesen Beispielen übrigens, daß der Begriff 'Satzglied' kein absoluter ist: etwas ist ein Satzglied in einer Konstruktion.

Bevor ich die Regeln formuliere, möchte ich noch eine Folgerung aus diesen Beobachtungen ziehen. die skizzierten Stellungsprinzipien machen lediglich von der linearen Anordnung der Satzteile Gebrauch. Man benötigt hier keine hierarchischen Begriffe, wie etwa Konstituentenstruktur. Im Gegenteil, das stört hier nur. Das ist der Grund, weshalb ich etwa den Vorschlag von B. Partee, an jeder Stelle der Konstruktion die bisherige Konstituentenstruktur mitzuschleppen, nicht für günstig halte.[55] Es gibt dann denselben Ärger, den ich im Zusammenhang mit den Bierwischschen Regeln diskutiert habe: Umstellungsregeln lassen sich wohl kaum vermeiden. Und danach ist die Konstituentenstruktur zerstört.
Nun zu den Regeln.

[55] Vgl. Partee (1977), sowie Bach (1976).

(V4)   *Zweitstellung des Finitums*

$\alpha\beta\gamma \in$ VP per(a) num(b) erg(c) stell(end)
$\qquad$ abtr($\alpha\gamma$) sgl($\delta_1,\ldots,+,\ldots,\delta_n$) hptv($\varepsilon_1,\ldots,\varepsilon_k$)

$\beta\alpha\gamma \in$ VP per(a) num(b) erg(c) stell(zweit)
$\qquad$ abtr($\alpha\gamma$) sgl($+,\delta_1,\ldots,\delta_n$) hptv($\varepsilon_1,\ldots,\varepsilon_k$)

(Sowohl α als auch γ können natürlich leer sein.)

10.1 BEISPIEL

1. *Kasper einen Rettich anbietet,*
   VP *3.pers sg* (*nom*)
   sgl(*Kasper,einen Rettich,*+)
   abtr(*Kasper einen Rettich an*)
   hptv(*bietet*)
   end, (7.1.5)

2. *bietet Kasper einen Rettich an,*
   VP *3.pers sg* ... *zweit*
   sgl(+,*Kasper,einen Rettich*), (V4)

10.2 EIN WEITERES BEISPIEL

1. *Hotzenplotz schwergefallen sein wird mir einen Rettich anzubieten,*
   VP *3.pers sg* erg(*es*)
   abtr(*Hotzenplotz schwergefallen sein mir einen Rettich anzubieten*)
   sgl(*Hotzenplotz,*+,*mir einen Rettich anzubieten*)
   hptv(*schwergefallen,sein,mir einen Rettich anzubieten*)
   end, (9.3.6)

2. *wird Hotzenplotz schwergefallen sein mir einen Rettich
   anzubieten,*
> VP *3.pers sg (es)*
>
> abtr(*Hotzenplotz...anzubieten*)
>
> sgl(+,*Hotzenplotz,mir einen Rettich anzubieten*)
>
> hptv(*schwergefallen,sein,mir einen Rettich anzubieten*)
>
> zweit (V4)

10.3 NOCH EIN BEISPIEL

1. *Hotzenplotz verprügelt hat,*
> VP *3.pers sg*
>
> abtr(*Hotzenplotz verprügelt*)
>
> sgl(*Hotzenplotz,*+)
>
> hptv(*verprügelt*)
>
> stell(end), (9.1.8)

2. *hat Hotzenplotz verprügelt,*
> VP *3.pers sg*
>
> abtr(*Hotzenplotz verprügelt*)
>
> sgl(+,*Hotzenplotz*)
>
> hptv(*verprügelt*)
>
> stell(zweit), (V4)

Nun kommen die Regeln für die Hauptsatzstellung. Betrachten wir zuerst den Fall, wo das supplative *es* an den Anfang rückt.

(S4) *Es-Sätze* [56]

$$\alpha\beta_1\ldots\beta_{n-1}\ \gamma\beta_n \in \text{VP } 3.\textit{pers}\ \text{num(b) erg(c)}$$
$$\text{sgl}(\beta_1,\ldots,\beta_{n-1},+,\beta_n)$$
$$\text{hptv}(\delta_1,\ldots,\delta_k)\ \text{abtr}(\beta_1,\ldots,\beta_{n-1}\ \gamma\beta_n)$$
$$\text{stell(zweit)}$$

$$\zeta \in \left\{ \begin{array}{l} \text{NP } 3.\textit{pers}\ \text{num}(b_1)\ \text{typ(c), falls c} \in \text{Kas} \cup \text{Präp} \\ \quad \text{mit } b_1 = b,\ \text{falls c} = \textit{nom} \\ \text{VINF erg(nom) sgl}(\varepsilon_1,\ldots,\varepsilon_m)\ \text{art(c) dat(d)} \\ \quad \text{hptv}(\eta_1,\ldots,\eta_1),\ \text{falls c} \in \{\text{0-Inf,zu-Inf}\} \\ S_{\text{daß}},\ \text{falls c} = \text{daß-S.} \end{array} \right.$$

$$\zeta = \quad \emptyset,\ \text{falls c} = \textit{es}$$

$$\textit{es}\ \alpha\zeta\beta_1\ldots\beta_{n-1}\ \gamma\beta_n \in S_{\text{zweit}}$$

Die Beschränkung auf die dritte Person in den Voraussetzungen der Regel ist übrigens deshalb nötig, um Fälle wie die folgenden auszuschließen.

(10)+ Es komme ich.

(11)+ Es arbeitet ihr.

10.4 BEISPIEL

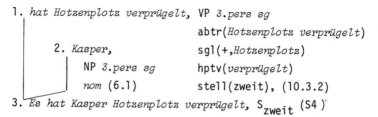

1. *hat Hotzenplotz verprügelt,* VP 3.*pers sg*

           abtr(*Hotzenplotz verprügelt*)

   2. *Kasper,*   sgl(+,*Hotzenplotz*)

    NP 3.*pers sg*   hptv(*verprügelt*)

    nom (6.1)   stell(zweit), (10.3.2)

3. *Es hat Kasper Hotzenplotz verprügelt,* S_{zweit} (S4)'

---

[56] Die Regel wird genau wie (V1) gedeutet.

10.5 NÄCHSTES BEISPIEL

1. *wird Hotzenplotz schwergefallen sein mit einen Rettich*
   anzubieten, VP $3.sg$ ... (10.2.2)
                 erg(*es*)

2. *Es wird Hotzenplotz schwergefallen sein mir einen Rettich*
   anzubieten, S_{zweit}, (S4)

Ich überlasse es dem Leser, darüber nachzudenken, wie Kopulasätze behandelt werden müssen, damit die Regel (S4) dazu paßt. Er vergleiche dazu:

(10) Daß Hotzenplotz wieder raucht, ist gut.

(11) Es ist gut, daß Hotzenplotz wieder raucht.

(12) Kasper zu gefallen, ist nicht leicht.

(13) Es ist nicht leicht, Kasper zu gefallen.

Das nächste Regelschema möchte ich Erich Drach widmen.

($S5_i$) *Die Drachschen Regeln* $i = 0, \ldots, n$ [57]

$$\alpha\beta_1 \cdots \beta_{n-1}\gamma\beta_n \in VP \; per(a) \; num(b) \; erg(c)$$
$$sgl(\beta_1, \ldots, \beta_{n-1}, +, \beta_n) \; hptv(\delta_1, \ldots, \delta_k)$$
$$abtr(\beta_1 \cdots \beta_{n-1}\gamma\beta_n) \; stell(zweit)$$

$\zeta \in \begin{cases} NP \; per(a_1) \; num(b_1) \; typ(c), \text{ falls } c \in Kas \cup \text{Präp} \\ \quad \text{mit } a_1 = a \text{ und } b_1 = b, \text{ falls } c = nom \\ VINF \; erg(nom) \; sgl(\varepsilon_1, \ldots, \varepsilon_m) \; art(c) \; diat(d) \\ \quad hptv(\eta_1, \ldots, \eta_l), \text{ falls } c = \{0\text{-Inf}, zu\text{-Inf}\} \\ Sda\beta, \text{ falls } c = da\beta\text{-}S \end{cases}$

$\zeta = es$, falls $c = es$

$\zeta\alpha\beta_1 \cdots \beta_{n-1}\gamma\beta_n \in S_{zweit}$, falls $i = 0$

$\beta_i \; \alpha\zeta'\beta_1 \cdots \beta_{i-1}\beta_{i+1} \cdots \beta_{n-1} \; \gamma\beta_n \in S_{zweit}$, falls $i > 0$.

[57] Die Semantik dieser Regeln sieht für den Augenblick so aus wie die von (S1). Allerdings tut sich hier bestimmt mehr. Das an den Anfang gestellte Glied wird thematisiert. Man kann bei Bedarf die Bedeutungsunterschiede an den verschiedenen Regeln des Schemas festmachen.

Für den zweiten Fall ist $\zeta' = \emptyset$, falls $\zeta = es$ und gewisse, näher zu untersuchende Bedingungen vorliegen.
Falls $\zeta \neq es$, ist $\zeta' = \zeta$.

Hier sind mehrere Bemerkungen angebracht. Die durch das Schema (S5)
beschriebenen Regeln hängen zusätzlich von einer bestimmten Stelle in einer Ableitung ab. Dies zu formulieren, erfordert begrifflichen Aufwand,
bringt nichts an Einsichten und stiftet Verwirrung. (Wie wahrscheinlich
schon diese Bemerkung.) Zweitens ist die Art und Weise, wie hier die Ein-
gabe- und Ausgabeausdrücke notiert werden, nicht besonders exakt. Ich werde
bei den Passivregeln einmal zeigen, wie eine genaue Formulierung aussieht.
Drittens sind die Bedingungen, unter denen nachgestelltes es getilgt werden muß, hier nicht formuliert. Zum Beispiel ist (14) grammatisch, (15)
dagegen nicht:

(14) Mir fällt es schwer zu arbeiten.

(15) +Zu arbeiten fällt es mir schwer.

Man kann sowohl (16) als auch (17) sagen, (19) und (21) sind aber ungrammatisch.

(16) Mich friert es.
(17) Mich friert.
(18) Den Teufel gibt es.
(19) +Den Teufel gibt
(20) Heute regnet es.
(21) +Heute regnet

Die Regeln ($S5_i$) sind also noch nicht vollständig. Sie dienen hier
nur dazu, eine Idee zu vermitteln, wie derartige Stellungsregeln prinzipiell aussehen können. Nun kommen wieder Beispiele:

10.6 BEISPIEL

1. *Hotzenplotz erlaubt mir einen Rettich anzubieten,*

    VP *3.pers sg (nom)* abtr(*Hotzenplotz mir einen Rettich anzubieten*)

    sgl(*Hotzenplotz,+,mir einen Rettich anzubieten*)

    hptv(*erlaubt,mir einen Rettich anzubieten*)

    end, (8.1.9)

2. *erlaubt Hotzenplotz mir einen Rettich anzubieten,*

    VP *3.pers sg* (nom) abtr(*Hotzenplotz ... anzubieten*)

    sgl(+,*Hotzenplotz, mir einen Rettich anzubieten*)

    zweit, (V4)

3. *Dimpfelmoser,* VP *3.pers nom sg*

    (wie 6.2)

4. *Dimpfelmoser erlaubt Hotzenplotz mir einen Rettich anzubieten,* S_{zweit}, $(S5_o)$

Die Anwendung von $(S5_1)$ auf (10.6.2) und (10.6.3) ergibt

Hotzenplotz erlaubt Dimpfelmoser mir einen Rettich anzubieten,

und zwar im Sinne von "dem Hotzenplotz". Die Anwendung von $(S5_2)$ liefert

mir einen Rettich anzubieten erlaubt Dimpfelmoser Hotzenplotz.

Wir können nicht herleiten:

+*Einen Rettich erlaubt Dimpfelmoser Hotzenplotz mir anzubieten,*

+*Mir erlaubt Dimpfelmoser Hotzenplotz einen Rettich anzubieten.*

Den letztgenannten Satz können wir allerdings auf andere Weise erzeugen, aber dann bedeutet er etwas anderes als (10.6.4). Wir müssen dazu $(S5_1)$ auf

erlaubt mir Hotzenplotz einen Rettich anzubieten und *Dimpfelmoser*

anwenden. Ich glaube, diese Ergebnisse werden dem Deutschen ziemlich gerecht. Das gibt mir Mut zu der bisher kompliziertesten Regel.

$(S6_{i,j})$ *Hauptverbvorstellung* [58]

i und j müssen den Bedingungen genügen, die gleich formuliert werden.

Sei α ein VP per(a) num(b) erg(c)

$sgl(+, \beta_1, \ldots, \beta_n)$
$hptv(\delta_1, \ldots, \delta_k)$
$abtr(\beta_1 \cdots \beta_{n-1} \delta_1 \cdots \delta_k \beta_n)$
$stell(zweit)$,

das sich als Verkettung der Folgen $\alpha_0, \ldots, \alpha_m$ darstellen läßt. $(\alpha_0, \ldots, \alpha_m)$ habe die Gestalt $(\alpha_0, \beta_1, \ldots, \beta_{n-1}, \delta_1, \ldots, \delta_k, \beta_n)$, falls $\delta_k \neq \beta_n$. Falls $\delta_k = \beta_n$, hat $(\alpha_0, \ldots, \alpha_m)$ die Form $(\alpha_0, \beta_1, \ldots \beta_{n-1}, \delta_1 \cdots, \delta_{k-1}, \beta_n)$. j sei größer oder gleich n, und höchstens so groß wie m. (D.h. i gibt eine Stelle in der Folge an, die in der Regel vor der Stelle ist, an der δ_1 vorkommt, j eine Stelle, die im allgemeinen hinter der Stelle liegt, an der δ_1 vorkommt.)

Sei ζ wie in (S5) beschrieben. Dann ist

$(\alpha_i, \ldots, \alpha_j)(\alpha_0, \zeta, \ldots, \alpha_{i-1}, \alpha_{j+1}, \ldots, \alpha_m) \in S_{zweit}$

Diese Regel wenden wir nun an.

---

[58] Die Semantik dieser Regel ist hier die Identität. Daß dies letztlich unzureichend ist, dürfte klar sein.

10.7 EIN BEISPIEL

1. *wird Hotzenplotz schwergefallen sein mir einen Rettich anzubieten,* VP *3.pers sg (es)*

   abtr(*Hotzenplotz ... anzubieten*)

   sgl(+,*Hotzenplotz,mir einen Rettich anzubieten*)

   hptv(*schwergefallen,sein,mir einen Rettich anzubieten*) zweit, (10.2.2)

2. *Hotzenplotz schwergefallen sein mir einen Rettich anzubieten wird es,* S_{zweit}, $(S6_{1,4})$

Daß diese Ableitung stimmt, wie auch die folgenden, macht man sich so kar:

10.7.1 läßt sich darstellen als Verkettung der Folgen

wird, Hotzenplotz, schwergefallen, sein, mir einen Rettich anzubieten.

Die Folge dieser Ausdrücke selbst hat im Sinne von (S6) die folgende Gestalt:

$$
\begin{array}{cccc}
\alpha_0 & \alpha_1 & \alpha_2 & \alpha_3 \\
(\textit{wird,} & \textit{Hotzenplotz,} & \textit{schwergefallen,} & \textit{sein,} \\
\alpha_0 & \beta_1 & \delta_1 & \delta_2
\end{array}
$$

$$\alpha_4$$

mir einen Rettich anzubieten)

$$\beta_2$$

Wenn man bedenkt, daß ζ für den Fall der Regelanwendung von $(S6_{1,4})$ gerade *es* sein muß, dann ist klar, daß wir das gewünschte Resultat erhalten.

Die Anwendung von ($S6_{2,2}$) liefert

Schwergefallen wird es Hotzenplotz sein mir einen Rettich anzubieten.

Durch ($S6_{2,3}$) bekommen wir

Schwergefallen sein wird es Hotzenplotz mir einen Rettich anzubieten.

($S6_{2,4}$) liefert

Schwergefallen sein mir einen Rettich anzubieten wird es Hotzenplotz.

Das sind alles gute deutsche Sätze. Unsinn kommt dagegen nicht heraus, soweit ich es übersehe.

11. DAS PASSIV

Die Passivregeln möchte ich aus methodischen Gründen einmal etwas genauer formulieren als die vorhergehenden Regeln. Nach ihrer Lektüre ist dann klar, wie man das Bisherige so präzise formulieren kann, daß auch der strengste Pedant nichts aussetzen kann. Der Punkt, um den es mir geht, ist folgender. Die Unterkategorie "erg" ist stets durch eine höchstens dreistellige Folge von Kasusmorphemen, Präpositionen oder Merkmalen (daß-S, O-Inf, zu-Inf) etc spezifiziert. Es geht darum, genau zu beschreiben, wie diese Folge durch eine Regel verändert wird. Das war bisher nur umschrieben worden, z.B. durch Notationen der folgenden Art:

$$a_1, \ldots, a_n \Rightarrow a_1, \ldots, a_{n-1},$$

die allerdings ziemlich anschaulich sind. Wir machen es nun noch genauer.

(Pass1) *Einfaches Passiv* [59]

$\alpha \in$ HVP per(a) num(b) typ(pass)

$\beta \in$ VPPf erg $(\gamma_0\gamma_1)$ hiv(c) hptv$(\delta_1,\ldots,\delta_k)$
    sgl$(\varepsilon_1,\ldots,\varepsilon_1)$ diat(akt)

b = *sg*, falls das letzte Glied von γ_0 *geni* oder *dat*
ist, γ_0 ist eine Folge von Kasus, d.h. von Elementen
aus {*nom, geni, dat, akt*}.

γ_1 ist leer oder *zu-Inf* oder *daß-S*.

$\beta\alpha \in$ VP per(a) num(b) erg(γ) sgl$(\varepsilon_1,\ldots,\varepsilon_1)$ abtr(β)
    hptv$(\delta_1,\ldots,\delta_k)$ stell(end)

wobei

$$\gamma = \begin{cases} \text{Subst } \dfrac{nom\ pass}{1\ \ 1(\gamma_0)} \ (\tilde{\gamma}_0\gamma_1), \text{ falls } 1(\gamma_0) > 1 \text{ und} \\ \qquad\qquad\qquad\qquad\qquad \text{das letzte Glied von } \gamma_0 = akk \\[2mm] \text{Subst } \dfrac{pass}{1(\gamma_0)} \quad (\tilde{\gamma}_0\gamma_1), \text{ falls } 1(\gamma_0) > 1 \text{ und} \\ \qquad\qquad\qquad\qquad\qquad \text{das letzte Glied von } \gamma_0 \neq akk \\[2mm] es, \text{ falls } 1(\gamma_0\gamma_1) = 1. \end{cases}$$

Die Semantik dieser Regel ist einfach die funktionale Applikation, d.h.
die Bedeutung des Hilfsverbs wird auf die Bedeutung des Partizips angewandt. Interessant ist nun natürlich, wie die Bedeutungen der passivischen Hilfsverben aussehen. Wenn wir von der temporalen Komponente
einmal absehen, dann läßt sich etwa die Bedeutung von *wird* von passivischen Typ folgendermaßen beschreiben:

V(*wird*, HVP$_{pass}$) $(\omega)(a_1,\ldots,a_n b)(c) = 1 \Longleftrightarrow \omega(a_n,a_{n-1},\ldots,a_1 b)(c) = 1$.
D.h., das Passiv ist im Wesentlichen die Konversenbildung. Die $a_1,\ldots,$
a_n entsprechen den Kasusergänzungen des Verbs. b steht für die Bedeutung des evtl. vorhandenen daß-Satzes oder Infinitivsatzes. Das b kann
fehlen.
Diese Definition betrifft allerdings nur Eigenschaften, die mindestens
zweistellig sind. Falls ω einstellig ist, so gilt: V(*wird*, HVP$_{pass}$)(ω)
ist die Proposition p, die in c wahr ist, wenn für ein a gilt:
$\omega(a)(c) = 1$. Diese Semantik für das unpersönliche Passiv ist allerdings zugegebenermaßen noch etwas ad hoc. Wichtig ist in diesem Zusammenhang vor allem, daß die beiden Passivkonstruktionen semantisch
verschieden behandelt werden.

Dabei ist $\widetilde{\gamma}$ das Spiegelbild der Folge γ. $1(\gamma)$ ist die Länge von γ, und

Subst $\dfrac{\beta_1}{m_1} \ldots \dfrac{\beta_n}{m_n}$ (α) bedeutet, daß die m_1-te ... m_n-te Stelle der Folge α

beziehungsweise durch $\beta_1, \ldots, \beta_n$ zu ersetzen ist.

Diese Regel ist ziemlich raffiniert, und wir wollen sie gleich anwenden.

11.1 BEISPIEL FÜR DAS PASSIV

1. *wird*, HVP   2. *gedacht*, VPPf

    | *3.pers sg*   erg(*nom,geni*) *haben*
    | typ(pass)   hptv(*gedacht*) sgl(+)
    | (Lexikon)   akt, (M5)

3. *gedacht wird*, VP

    | *3.pers sg*
    | erg(*geni,pass*) sgl(+)
    | abtr(*gedacht*)
    | hptv(*gedacht*)   4. *von uns*, NP
    | end, (Pass 1)   *1.pers pl*
                                            typ(pass), (N5)

5. *von uns gedacht wird*, VP

    | *3.pers sg*
    | erg(*geni*)
    | sgl(*von uns*,+)
    | abtr(*von uns gedacht*)
    | hptv(*gedacht*), end, (V1)

6. *wird von uns gedacht*, VP

    | *3.pers sg* (*geni*)
    | sgl(+, *von uns*)
    | abtr(*von uns gedacht*)
    | hptv(*gedacht*),   7. *Hotzenplotzens*, NP
    | zweit, (V4)   *3.pers sg geni* (wie 6.2)

8. *Hotzenplotzens* S_{zweit}, $(S5_0)$

        wird von uns gedacht,

Die Anwendung von (S4) auf (11.1.6) und (11.1.7) liefert *es wird von uns Hotzenplotzens gedacht,* durch (S5$_1$) bekommen wir *von uns wird Hotzenplotzens gedacht.* (S6$_{3,3}$) würde uns *gedacht wird Hotzenplotzens von uns* liefern, und durch (S6$_{2,3}$) erhalten wir *von uns gedacht wird Hotzenplotzens.*

Es ist klar, daß das passivische Präpositionalobjekt auch anders aussehen kann. (N5) erlaubt uns beispielsweise die Konstruktionen *durch uns.* Als weiteres passivisches Präpositionalobjekt käme *unsererseits* in Frage (wie dies genau gebildet wird, lasse ich hier einmal außer acht). Wir können also auch Sätze erzeugen wie *unsererseits wird Hotzenplotzens gedacht* oder *durch uns gedacht wird Hotzenplotzens.*

Ich möchte noch einen Augenblick den Übergang von (11.1.1) und (11.1.2) zu (11.1.3) betrachten. Die Eingabefolge dieser Regel ist $\gamma_0\gamma_1 = (nom, geni)$, wobei γ_1 leer ist. Das Spiegelbild von γ_0 ist $(geni, nom)$. Nun findet der zweite Fall der Bedingungen für γ Anwendung. Die Länge von γ_0 ist 2. Also muß man das zweite Glied durch *pass* ersetzen. Dadurch erhält man $(geni, pass)$. Das steht in der Tat bei der Unterkategorie "erg" von (11.1.3).

11.2 EIN WEITERES BEISPIEL

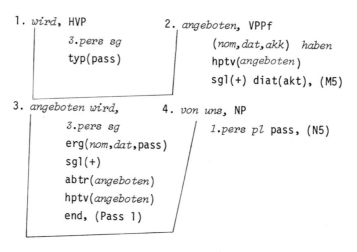

1. *wird,* HVP
   - 3.*pers sg*
   - typ(pass)

2. *angeboten,* VPPf
   - (*nom,dat,akk*) *haben*
   - hptv(*angeboten*)
   - sgl(+) diat(akt), (M5)

3. *angeboten wird,*
   - 3.*pers sg*
   - erg(*nom,dat,*pass)
   - sgl(+)
   - abtr(*angeboten*)
   - hptv(*angeboten*)
   - end, (Pass 1)

4. *von uns,* NP
   - 1.*pers pl* pass, (N5)

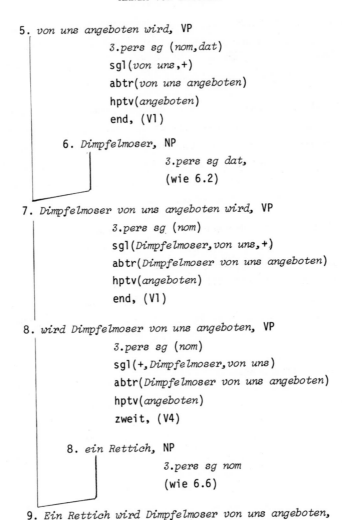

5. *von uns angeboten wird,* VP

        3.pers sg *(nom,dat)*

        sgl(*von uns*,+)

        abtr(*von uns angeboten*)

        hptv(*angeboten*)

        end, (Vl)

6. *Dimpfelmoser,* NP

        3.pers sg *dat,*

        (wie 6.2)

7. *Dimpfelmoser von uns angeboten wird,* VP

        3.pers sg *(nom)*

        sgl(*Dimpfelmoser,von uns*,+)

        abtr(*Dimpfelmoser von uns angeboten*)

        hptv(*angeboten*)

        end, (Vl)

8. *wird Dimpfelmoser von uns angeboten,* VP

        3.pers sg *(nom)*

        sgl(+,*Dimpfelmoser,von uns*)

        abtr(*Dimpfelmoser von uns angeboten*)

        hptv(*angeboten*)

        zweit, (V4)

8. *ein Rettich,* NP

        3.pers sg nom

        (wie 6.6)

9. *Ein Rettich wird Dimpfelmoser von uns angeboten,*

    S_{zweit}, $(S5_0)$

Ich möchte nun vorführen, wie die Passivregel arbeitet, wenn ein Verb passiviert wird, das einen Infinitivsatz als Ergänzung verlangt.

11.3 HIER IST SO EIN BEISPIEL

1. *wird*, HVP
    3.pers sg
    typ(pass)

2. *gestattet*, VPPf
    (*nom,dat*,zu-Inf)
    haben hptv(*gestattet*)
    sgl(+) diat(akt),(M5)

3. *gestattet wird*, VP
    3.pers sg
    (*dat,pass*,zu-Inf)
    sgl(+)
    abtr(*gestattet*)
    hptv(*gestattet*)
    end, (Pass 1)

4. *zu verreisen*, VINF (*nom*)
    hptv(*zu verreisen*)
    sgl(+)
    art(zu-Inf)
    diat(akt), (M4$_1$)

5. *gestattet wird zu verreisen*, VP *3.pers sg*
    (*dat,pass*)
    sgl(+,*zu verreisen*)
    abtr (*gestattet zu verreisen*)
    hptv (*gestattet,zu verreisen*)
    end, (V1)

6. *von uns*, NP
    1.pers pl pass
    (N5)

7. *von uns gestattet wird zu verreisen*, VP
    3.pers sg (*dat*)
    sgl(*von uns*,+,*zu verreisen*)
    abtr(*von uns gestattet zu verreisen*)
    hptv(*gestattet,zu verreisen*)
    end, (V1)

8. *wird von uns gestattet zu verreisen*, VP
    3.pers sg (dat)
    ...zweit, (V4)

           9. *dem Manne*, NP
               3.pers sg dat
               (N1)

10. *dem Manne wird von uns gestattet zu verreisen*,
    S_{zweit}, $(S5_0)$

Es folgt nun noch ein Beispiel für das unpersönliche Passiv.

11.4 EIN UNPERSÖNLICHES PASSIV

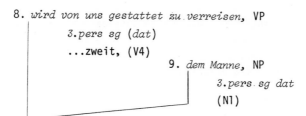

1. *wird*, HVP   2. *gestorben*, VPPf *(nom)*
    3.pers sg   *haben*
    typ(pass)   hptv(*gestorben*)
                      sgl(+) diat(akt), (M5)

3. *gestorben wird*, VP
    3.pers sg
    erg(*es*) sgl(+)
    abtr(*gestorben*)
    hptv(*gestorben*)
    end, (Pass 1)

4. *wird gestorben*, VP
    3.pers sg (es) sgl(+)
    hptv(*gestorben*)
    abtr(*gestorben*)
    zweit, (V4)

5. *es wird gestorben*,
    S_{zweit}, (S4)

Man könnte meinen, solche Sätze kämen nur bei Grammatikern vor. Das stimmt nicht. Der berühmte bairische Politiker F.J.S. soll nach der letzten, für seine Partei verlorene Wahl "Jetzt wird gestorben!" geäußert haben.

Im Zusammenhang mit unpersönlichen Passivkonstruktionen sieht man allerdings, daß die bisherige Analyse noch mangelhaft ist. Zum Beispiel ist (1) 'Von Hunden wird gebellt' ein guter Satz. Er läßt sich aber in meiner Syntax überhaupt nicht bilden; wir können nur (2) 'Es wird gebellt' herleiten. (1) bedeutet so etwas wie, daß sich die Tätigkeit des Bellens typischerweise durch Hunde verwirklicht. Diese Paraphrase legt eine gänzlich andere semantische Analyse des Passivs nahe als meine konservative Konversenbildung. Ich vertiefe dieses Problem hier aber nicht.

Bevor ich die restlichen Passivregeln behandle, möchte ich eine Zwischenbermerkung machen. Im Deutschen wird sehr oft das passivische Präpositionalobjekt weggelassen: (3) Kasper wird ein Lehrstuhl angeboten. Dies wird durch die folgende Regel ausgedrückt:

(V5) *Unterschlagung der passivischen Verbergänzung* [60]

$$\alpha \in VP \; per(a) \; num(b) \; erg(c_1,\ldots,c_n)$$
$$sgl(\beta_1,\ldots,\beta_k) \; hptv(\gamma_1,\ldots,\gamma_l) \; abtr(\delta) \; stell(end)$$
$$\underline{c_n \; = \; pass}$$

$$\alpha \in VP \; per(a) \; num(b) \; erg(c_1,\ldots,c_{n-1})$$
$$sgl(\beta_1,\ldots,\beta_k) \; hptv(\gamma_1,\ldots,\gamma_l) \; abtr(\delta) \; stell(end)$$

[60] Die Semantik sieht vielleicht so aus. $V(\alpha, VP_{(a_1,\ldots,a_n)})$ drücke die n-stellige Eigenschaft ω_n aus. Dann drückt $V(\alpha, VP_{(a_1,\ldots,a_{n-1})})$ diejenige (n-1)-stellige Eigenschaft ω_{n-1} aus, die auf $b_1,\ldots,b_{n-1}$ in c zutrifft gdw. es ein b_n gibt, so daß ω_n auf $b_1,\ldots,b_{n-1},b_n$ in c zutrifft.

Im Deutschen wird übrigens auch oft das Dativobjekt unterschlagen. Allerdings verändert man dann das Verb in der Regel morphologisch, etwa durch Präfigierung von *ver*. Vgl. etwa:

(4) Wir verschenken einen Rettich.

+(5) Wir schenken einen Rettich.

Ich behandle diese Fälle aber nicht. Sie sind auch nicht so schön regelmäßig, wie meine Bemerkung vielleicht nahelegt. Ein Beispiel für die Anwendung von (V5).

11.5 DIE PASSIVPHRASE WIRD UNTERSCHLAGEN

1. *angeboten wird*, VP
   - *3.pers sg (nom, dat,* pass)
   - sgl(+) abtr(*angeboten*)
   - end (11.2.1)

2. *angeboten wird*, VP
   - *3.pers sg (nom, dat)*
   - sgl(+) abtr(*angeboten*)
   - end, (V5)

3. *Kasper*, NP
   - *3.pers sg dat*
   - (wie 6.2)

4. *Kasper angeboten wird*, VP
   - *3.pers sg (nom)*
   - sgl(*Kasper*, +)
   - abtr(*Kasper angeboten*)
   - hptv(*angeboten*)
   - stell(end), (V1)

5. *wird Kasper angeboten*, VP
   - *3.pers sg (nom)*
   - sgl(+, *Kasper*)
   - abtr (*Kasper angeboten*)
   - stell(zweit), (V4)

6. *ein Lehrstuhl*, NP

   3.pers sg nom

   (wie 6.6)

7. *Kasper wird ein Lehrstuhl angeboten,*

   S_{zweit}, $(S5_1)$

Hat man sich einmal über die grundsätzliche Behandlung des Passivs Klarheit verschafft, so bieten die zusammengesetzten Passivformen keine Probleme mehr. Wir können die entsprechenden Regeln deshalb sofort hinschreiben.

(Pass 2) *Partizip Perfekt Passiv* [61]

$\alpha \in$ HPPf typ(pass)

$\beta \in$ VPPf erg$(\gamma_0\gamma_1)$ hiv(c) hptv$(\delta_1,\ldots,\delta_k)$ sgl$(\varepsilon_1,\ldots,\varepsilon_1)$

   diat(akt), $\gamma_0\gamma_1$ ist wie bei (Pass 1)

$\alpha\beta \in$ VPPf erg(γ) hiv(*sein*) hptv$(\delta_1,\ldots,\delta_k,\alpha)$

   sgl$(\varepsilon_1,\ldots,\varepsilon_1)$ diat(pass),

   wobei γ wie bei (Pass 1) ist.

11.6 BEISPIEL

1. *worden*, HPPf typ(pass), (M5)

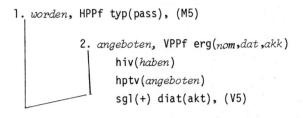

   2. *angeboten*, VPPf erg(*nom*,*dat*,*akk*)

     hiv(*haben*)

     hptv(*angeboten*)

     sgl(+) diat(akt), (V5)

[61] Die Semantik sieht genau wie für (Pass 1) aus.

3. *angeboten worden,* VPPf (*nom, dat,* pass)

    hiv(*sein*)

    hptv(*angeboten, worden*)

    sgl(+) diat(pass), (Pass 2)

            4. *ist,* HVP

                3.pers sg sein, (M2)

5. *angeboten worden ist,* VP

    erg(*nom, dat,* pass)

    3.pers sg

    abtr(*angeboten worden*)

    sgl(+)

    hptv(*angeboten, worden*)

    diat(pass), (V2)

            6. *von Franz Josef,* NP

                3.pers sg pass, (N5)

7. *von Franz Josef angeboten worden ist,* VP (*nom, dat*)

    3.pers sg

    abtr(*von Franz Josef angeboten worden*)

    sgl(*von Franz Josef,* +)

    hptv(*angeboten, worden*)

    end, (V1)

            8. *Kasper,* NP

                3.pers sg dat

                (wie 6.2)

9. *Kasper von Franz Josef angeboten worden ist,* VP (*nom*)

    3.pers sg

    abtr(*Kasper von Franz Josef angeboten worden*)

    sgl(*Kasper, von Franz Josef,* +)

    hptv(*angeboten, worden*) end, (V1)

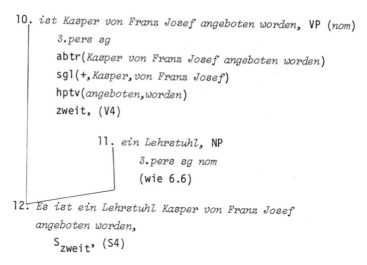

10. *ist Kasper von Franz Josef angeboten worden,* VP (*nom*)
    3.pers sg
    abtr(*Kasper von Franz Josef angeboten worden*)
    sgl(+,*Kasper,von Franz Josef*)
    hptv(*angeboten,worden*)
    zweit, (V4)

        11. *ein Lehrstuhl,* NP
            3.pers sg nom
            (wie 6.6)

12. *Es ist ein Lehrstuhl Kasper von Franz Josef*
    angeboten worden,
      S_{zweit}, (S4)

    Dieser Satz hört sich ein wenig wie ein Zitat aus der Weihnachts-
geschichte an. Man erhält etwas profanere Gebilde durch Anwendung der
Drachschen Regeln:

($S5_0$) liefert: *Ein Lehrstuhl ist Kasper von Franz Josef angeboten worden.*
($S5_1$) ergibt: *Kasper ist ein Lehrstuhl von Franz Josef angeboten worden.*
Durch ($S5_2$) erhalten wir: *Von Franz Josef ist ein Lehrstuhl Kasper ange-*
boten worden. ($S6_{3,3}$) gestattet, *Angeboten ist ein Lehrstuhl Kasper von*
Franz Josef worden abzuleiten. ($S6_{2,4}$) ergibt: *Von Franz Josef angeboten*
worden ist ein Lehrstuhl Kasper, usw. Diese Sätze sind übrigens zum Teil
etwas merkwürdig, vielleicht deshalb, weil *Kasper* ohne Artikel nicht
"schwer genug" ist, um am Ende stehen zu können. Es kann aber auch sein,
daß ich einige tiefere Regularitäten noch nicht erfaßt habe.

(Pass 3) *Infinitiv Passiv*

$\alpha \in$ VPPf erg($\gamma_0\gamma_1$) hiv(b) hptv($\delta_1,\ldots,\delta_k$) sgl($\epsilon_1,\ldots,\epsilon_1$)
diat(akt)

$\beta \in$ HINF typ(pass) art(a)

   $\gamma_0\gamma_1$ ist wie bei (Pass 1)

$\beta\alpha \in$ VINF erg(γ) hptv($\delta_1,\ldots,\delta_k,\alpha$) sgl($\epsilon_1,\ldots,\epsilon_1$) art(a)
diat(pass)

   γ ist wie in (Pass 1) beschrieben.

11.7 1. *verprügelt*, VPPf   2. *werden*, HINF
        (*nom,akk*)   typ(pass)
        haben   art(0-Inf)
        hptv(*verprügelt*)   (M5)
        sgl(+) Akt, (M5)

      3. *verprügelt werden*, VINF   4. *von Hotzenplotz*, NP
        (*nom*,pass)   *3.pers sg* pass
        hptv(*verprügelt,werden*)   (N5)
        sgl(+) art(0-Inf)
        diat(pass), (Pass 3)

      5. *von Hotzenplotz ver-*   10. *wird*, HVP
        prügelt werden, VINF   *3.pers sg fut*
        (*nom*)   (M2)
        hptv(*verprügelt,*
            werden)
        sgl(*von Hotzenplotz*,+)
        art(0-Inf) diat(pass)
        (I1)

11. *von Hotzenplotz verprügelt werden wird,* VP
     3.*pers sg* (*nom*)
     sgl(*von Hotzenplotz,+*)
     hptv(*verprügelt,werden*)
     abtr(*von Hotzenplotz verprügelt werden*)
     end, (V3)

12. *wird von Hotzenplotz verprügelt werden,* VP
     3.*pers sg* (*nom*)
     sgl(+,*von Hotzenplotz*)
     hptv(*verprügelt,werden*)
     abtr(*von Hotzenplotz verprügelt werden*)
     zweit, (V4)

          13. *Dimpfelmoser,* NP
               3.*pers sg nom*
               (wie 6.2)

14. *Dimpfelmoser wird von Hotzenplotz verprügelt werden,*
     S_{zweit}, (S5$_0$)

Auch bei Infinitivsätzen wird die passivische Ergänzung oft weggelassen. Wir führen deshalb eine Regel ein, die ganz analog wie (V5) arbeitet, nämlich:

(I3) *Unterschlagung der passivischen Ergänzung* [62]

$\alpha \in$ VINF erg($a_1,\ldots,a_n$) hptv($\delta_1,\ldots,\delta_k$) sgl($\varepsilon_1,\ldots,\varepsilon_1$)
          art(c) diat(a_n)

a_n = pass
_____

$\alpha \in$ VINF erg($a_1,\ldots,a_{n-1}$) hptv($\delta_1,\ldots,\delta_k$) sgl($\varepsilon_1,\ldots,\varepsilon_1$)
          art(c) diat(a_n)

[62] Die Semantik dieser Regel sieht genau wie die von (V5) aus.

11.8 WIEDER EIN BEISPIEL

1. *verprügelt*, VPPf   2. *worden*, HPPf
   (*nom, akk*) *haben*   pass, (M5)
   hptv(*verprügelt*)
   sgl(+) akt, (M5)

3. *verprügelt worden*, VPPf   4. *sein*, HINF
   (*nom*, pass)   typ(*sein*)
   hiv(*sein*)   art(0-Inf), (M4)
   hptv(*verprügelt, worden*)
   sgl(+) pass, (Pass 2)

5. *verprügelt worden sein*, VINF
   erg(*nom*, pass)
   sgl(+)
   hptv(*verprügelt, worden sein*)
   art(0-Inf) diat(pass), (I2)

6. *verprügelt worden sein*, VINF
   erg(*nom*)..., (I3)

                                  7. *wird*, HVP
                                     3.pers sg *fut*, (M2)

8. *verprügelt worden sein wird*, VP
   3.pers sg (*nom*)
   sgl(+)
   hptv(*verprügelt, worden, sein*)
   abtr(*verprügelt worden sein*)
   end, (V3)

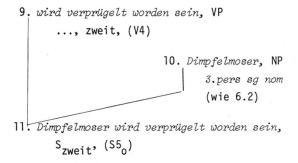

9. *wird verprügelt worden sein,* VP
   ..., zweit, (V4)

10. *Dimpfelmoser,* NP
    3.pers sg nom
    (wie 6.2)

11. *Dimpfelmoser wird verprügelt worden sein,*
    S_{zweit}, $(S5_0)$

$(S6_{1,1})$ würde *Verprügelt wird Dimpfelmoser worden sein* erbringen,
$(S6_{1,2})$ *Verprügelt worden wird Dimpfelmoser sein,* $(S6_{1,3})$ schließlich
Verprügelt worden sein wird Dimpfelmoser.

Das Passiv ist damit im Wesentlichen (d.h. im Rahmen meiner Ziel-
setzung) abgehandelt. Ich möchte deswegen zu etwas anderem übergehen,
nämlich zu den Relativsätzen.

12.　RELATIVSÄTZE

Relativsätze bieten zwei Probleme. Erstens muß man mit ihrer eigentümlichen Wortstellung fertig werden, und zweitens hat man zu erklären, worin der Unterschied zwischen explikativen und restriktiven Relativsätzen liegt. Befassen wir uns zunächst mit der Stellung

(Rel l_i) *Relativsatzstellung*, $i = 1,\ldots,n$ [63]

$\alpha \in$ VP per(a) num(b) erg($c_1,\ldots,c_n$) sgl($\beta_1,\ldots,\beta_k$)
hptv($\gamma_1,\ldots,\gamma_1$) abtr(δ) stell(end)

$\alpha \in$ VP per(a) num(b) erg(c_i,ζ) sgl($\beta_1,\ldots,\beta_k$)
hptv($\gamma_1,\ldots,\gamma_1$) abtr(δ) stell(rels)

Dabei entsteht ζ aus $c_1,\ldots,c_n$ durch Weglassen von c_i und $c_i \neq$ es.

In dieser Regel ist ausgedrückt, daß der Relativsatz im großen und ganzen genau wie ein Nebensatz gebaut ist mit dem einen Unterscheid, daß das relativierte Glied zuletzt an das Verb gefügt wird, und zwar als Relativpronomenphrase. Dabei kommt es dann zur Relativsatzbildung. Wie, das ist in der nächsten Regel beschrieben.

(Rel 2) *Relativsatzbildung* [64]

$\alpha \in$ VP per(a) num(b) erg(c) sgl($\beta_1,\ldots,\beta_k$)
hptv($\gamma_1,\ldots,\gamma_m$) abtr(δ) stell(rels)
$\beta \in$ RelP num(b_1) gen(d) typ(a_1)
a = *3.pers* und b_1 = b, falls c = *nom*

$\beta\alpha \in$ RS num(b_1) gen(d)

---

[63] Die Semantik: α drücke vor Anwendung der Regel (Rel l_i) die n-stellige Eigenschaft ω_n aus. Nach Anwendung von (Rel l_i) drückt α diejenige Eigenschaft ω_n^i aus, die auf ($a_1,\ldots,a_n$) in c genau dann zutrifft, wenn ω_n auf ($a_2,\ldots,a_i,a_1,a_{i+1},\ldots,a_n$) in c zutrifft.

[64] Die Semantik ist die funktionale Applikation, d.h. die Bedeutung der Relativpronomenphrase wird auf die Bedeutung der Verbalphrase angewandt.

12.1 BEISPIEL

1. *angeboten*, VPPf
     (*nom*, *dat*, *akk*)
     hptv(*angeboten*)
     sgl(+) diat(akt)
     hiv(*haben*), (M5)

2. *hat*, HVP
     3.pers sg
     haben, (M2)

3. *angeboten hat*, VP
     (*nom*, *dat*, *akk*)
     3.pers sg
     abtr(*angeboten*)
     sgl(+) hptv(*angeboten*)
     stell(end), (V2)

4. *angeboten hat*, VP
     (*dat*, *nom*, *akk*)
     3.pers sg
     abtr(*angeboten*) sgl(+)
     hptv(*angeboten*)
     stell(rels), (Rel 1$_2$)

5. *einen Lehrstuhl*, NP
     3.pers sg akk
     (wie 6.6.)

6. *einen Lehrstuhl angeboten hat*, VP
     (*dat*, *nom*) *3.pers sg*
     abtr(*einen Lehrstuhl angeboten*)
     sgl(*einen Lehrstuhl*, +)
     hptv(*angeboten*)
     stell(rels), (V1)

7. *Franz Josef*, NP
     3.pers sg nom
     (wie 6.2)

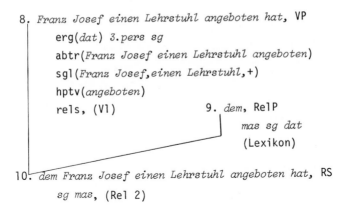

8. *Franz Josef einen Lehrstuhl angeboten hat,* VP
   erg(*dat*) *3.pers sg*
   abtr(*Franz Josef einen Lehrstuhl angeboten*)
   sgl(*Franz Josef,einen Lehrstuhl,+*)
   hptv(*angeboten*)
   rels, (Vl)   9. *dem,* RelP
                                          mas sg dat
                                        (Lexikon)

10. *dem Franz Josef einen Lehrstuhl angeboten hat,* RS
    sg mas, (Rel 2)

Wir sollten uns vielleicht überlegen, was dieser Relativsatz bedeutet. Dazu müssen wir lediglich die Bedeutung von *dem* kennen. Nun, V(*dem*,RelP) (ω) = ω für jedes einschlägige ω. (12.1.8) drückt offenbar die Eigenschaft ω_1 aus, die auf ein a zutrifft, wenn Franz Josef a einen Lehrstuhl angeboten hat. Die Anwendung der Bedeutung des Relativpronomens *dem* ändert nichts mehr daran. (12.1.10) drückt also die nämliche Eigenschaft aus.

Wir schauen nun, wie sich der Relativsatz mit Termen verbindet. Zunächst kommen die restriktiven Relativsätze dran. Hier modifiziert der Relativsatz einen Gattungsterm.

(Rel 3) *Restriktive Relativsätze* [65]
        α ∈ CN num(a) gen(b) cas(c) fle(d)
        β ∈ RS num(a) gen(b)
        ───────────────────────────────────
        αβ ∈ CN num(a) gen(b) cas(c) fle(d)

[65] Die Semantik dieser Regel muß unterscheiden, ob α ein singuläres oder ein plurales CN ist. Sei α ∈ CN *sg.* Dann trifft V(α) auf ein a zu, gdw. V(α) und V(β) auf a zutreffen. Falls α ∈ CN *pl* und α den Gattungsbegriff ξ bezeichnet, dann ist V(αβ) derjenige Gattungsbegriff ζ, so daß für eine beliebige Situation c gilt:
V(αβ)(c) = {a: a ∈ ξ(c) und V(β)(a)(c) = 1}.

12.2 EIN RESTRIKTIVER RELATIVSATZ

1. *Mann,* CN
   sg mas akk
   fle(*schw*), (N2)

2. *dem Franz Josef einen Lehr-*
   stuhl angeboten hat, RS
   sg nom
   (12.1.10)

3. *Mann dem Franz Josef einen Lehrstuhl*
   angeboten hat, CN
   sg mas akk schw
   (Rel 3)

4. *dem,* DET
   sg mas akk schw
   (Lexikon)

5. *den Mann dem Franz Josef einen Lehrstuhl angeboten hat,* EN
   sg mas akk
   (N3)

6. *den Mann dem Franz Josef einen Lehrstuhl angeboten hat,* NP
   3.pers sg akk
   (N1)

7. *verprügelt,* VP
   3.pers sg
   erg(*nom,akk*)
   sgl(+) abtr(-)
   hptv(*verprügelt*)
   end, (M2)

8. *den Mann dem Franz Josef einen Lehrstuhl angeboten hat*
   verprügelt, VP
   3.pers sg (nom)
   sgl(*den Mann dem Franz Josef einen Lehrstuhl ange-*
   boten hat,+)
   abtr(*den Mann dem Franz Josef einen Lehrstuhl ange-*
   boten hat)
   hptv(*verprügelt*)
   end, (V1)

9. *verprügelt den Mann dem Franz Josef einen Lehrstuhl ange-*
   boten hat, VP
   > 3.*pers sg (nom)*
   > sgl(+,*den Mann dem Franz Josef einen Lehrstuhl ange-*
   > *boten hat*)
   > hptv(*verprügelt*)
   > stell(end), (V4)   10. *Hotzenplotz,* NP
   > > 3.*pers sg nom*
   > > (wie 6.2)

11. *Den Mann dem Franz Josef einen Lehrstuhl angeboten hat*
    verprügelt Hotzenplotz
    S_{zweit}, (S5$_1$)

(12.2.11) drückt die Proposition aus, daß Hotzenplotz das Individuum, welches sowohl ein Mann ist als auch einen Lehrstuhl von Franz Josef angeboten bekommen hat, verprügelt. Hier ist also der restriktive Gebrauch des Relativsatzes rekonstruiert worden.

An dieser Stelle sollte ich etwas dazu sagen, wie Relativsätze bei Montague-Grammatikern sonst behandelt werden. Montague selbst hat die *Syntax* der Relativsätze überhaupt nicht ernsthaft in Angriff genommen, sondern sich mit Logikerenglisch begnügt. Satz 12.2.11 würde von ihm ungefähr so paraphrasiert werden:

> (1) Den Mann, *der ein solcher ist, daß Franz-Josef ihm einen Lehrstuhl angeboten hat,* verprügelt Hotzenplotz.
>
> (2) Hotzenplotz trounces the man *such that Franz-Josef has offered him a chair.*

Nun, so etwas kommt unter normalen Leuten weder im Deutschen noch im Englischen vor. Deswegen hat Rodman , (1976), die Syntax verbessert. Allerdings arbeitet er genau wie Montague mit indizierten Pronomina bzw.

mit Variablen. Übertragen auf meinen Ansatz, würden Rodmans Relativsatzregeln für das Deutsche ungefähr folgendermaßen aussehen.

Franz-Josef ihm$_{17}$ einen Lehrstuhl angeboten hat,
   | S$_{end}$

Franz-Josef d-ihm$_{17}$ einen Lehrstuhl, angeboten hat,
   | S$_{end}$, (Relativierung$_{17}$)

dem Franz-Josef einen Lehrstuhl angeboten hat, RS
   (d-Vorschiebung bei gleichzeitiger Umänderung von
   d-ihm$_{17}$ in *dem*)

Semantisch entspricht diesen Regeln bei Rodman ungefähr die folgende
Abfolge von "logischen" Formen:

((Ein,Lehrstuhl), λy[angeboten hat (F.-J.,x$_{17}$,y)])
   |
λx$_{17}$ ((Ein,Lehrstuhl), λy[angeboten-hat (F.-J.,x$_{17}$,y)])
   |
λx$_{17}$ ((Ein Lehrstuhl), λy[angeboten-hat (F.-J.,x$_{17}$,y)])

Mit anderen Worten, der Regel "Relativierung$_{17}$" entspricht in der
semantischen Darstellung die Bindung der Variable x$_{17}$ durch den λ-Operator.
Meine Relativsatzregeln kommen gänzlich ohne gebundene Variablen aus. Ich
halte das für einen Vorzug. Ansonsten ist meine Regel (Rel 1) relativ
verwandt mit der "d-Vorschiebung" (*wh-* Preposing) Rodmans.

Schauen wir nun einmal, wie man die explikative (oder appositive)
Relativsatzverwendung angehen könnte. Die folgende Regel beinhaltet einen
Vorschlag dazu.

(Rel 4) *Explikative Relativsätze* [66]

$$\alpha \in EN\ num(a)\ gen(b)\ cas(c)$$
$$\beta \in RS\ num(a)\ gen(b)$$
$$\overline{\alpha\beta \in EN\ num(a)\ gen(b)\ cas(c)}$$

Die explikative Lesart des eben diskutierten Beispielsatzes wird dann folgendermaßen rekonstruiert:

12.3 EIN EXPLIKATIVER RELATIVSATZ

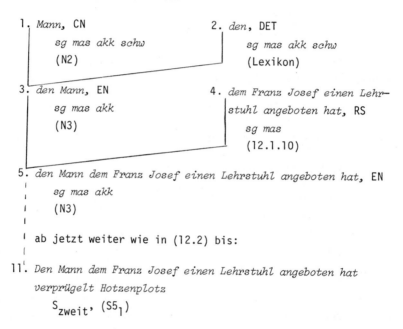

1. *Mann,* CN
   sg mas akk schw
   (N2)

2. *den,* DET
   sg mas akk schw
   (Lexikon)

3. *den Mann,* EN
   sg mas akk
   (N3)

4. *dem Franz Josef einen Lehrstuhl angeboten hat,* RS
   sg mas
   (12.1.10)

5. *den Mann dem Franz Josef einen Lehrstuhl angeboten hat,* EN
   sg mas akk
   (N3)

ab jetzt weiter wie in (12.2) bis:

11. *Den Mann dem Franz Josef einen Lehrstuhl angeboten hat
    verprügelt Hotzenplotz*
    S_{zweit}, $(S5_1)$

---

[66] Die Semantik kann ich wiederum sehr grob skizzieren, weil ich mich in diesem Aufsatz nicht ernsthaft mit Namenstheorie und Deixis beschäftigen kann. Für den Augenblick genügt folgendes: α bezeichne das Individuum a, β drücke die Eigenschaft ω aus. Dann bezeichnet αβ in c nur dann etwas, wenn a in c die Eigenschaft ω hat. Falls dies so ist, bezeichnet αβ in c a.

(12.3.11) drückt die Proposition p aus, die nur unter solchen Umständen c sinnvoll ist, unter denen das mit "der Mann" bezeichnete Individuum a die Eigenschaft hat, daß ihm Franz Josef einen Lehrstuhl angeboten hat. In jeder solchen Situation c ist p wahr gdw. Hotzenplotz a in c verprügelt.

Es sollte klar sein, daß die Sätze (12.2.11) und (12.3.11) verschiedene Wahrheitsbedingungen haben, und zwar gleichgültig, wie ich den bestimmten Artikel deute. In (12.2) ist es ein Teil der Kennzeichnung des Subjektes, daß es die Eigenschaft, ein Mann zu sein, dem Franz Josef einen Lehrstuhl angeboten hat, erfüllen muß. In (12.3) ist das nicht der Fall. Das Subjekt ist bereits durch den Term *der Mann* hinreichend gekennzeichnet. Daß das Subjekt unter anderem noch die Eigenschaft erfüllt, daß ihm von Franz Josef ein Lehrstuhl angeboten ist, wird von ihm vorausgesetzt (präsupponiert). Diese Information ist letztlich überflüssig. Es ist klar, daß sich dieser Unterschied nur in einer Präsuppositionstheorie formulieren läßt.[67]

Wenn man sich die beiden Ableitungen noch einmal anschaut, sieht man klar die Idee, wie die beiden Arten von Relativsätzen bereits syntaktisch unterschieden werden: ein restriktiver Relativsatz modifiziert ein CN, ein explikativer ein EN. Das erklärt auch, wieso ein genereller oder indefiniter Term mit Relativsatz nie explikativ verstanden werden kann und weshalb ein EN plus Relativsatz nie restriktiv verstanden werden kann. Vom syntaktischen Aufbau her sind diese Lesarten nicht möglich. Beispiele:

(3) Hotzenplotz verprügelt Kasper, dem Franz Josef einen Lehrstuhl angeboten hat.

(4) Kein Mensch, der Filbinger kennt, bezweifelt dessen ausgezeichnete juristische Fähigkeiten.

[67] Derartiges ist im Moment nicht en vogue. Ich halte eine solche Theorie aber für unverzichtbar. Vgl. dazu v. Stechow (1977).

In (3) kann das Objekt syntaktisch nur analysiert werden als

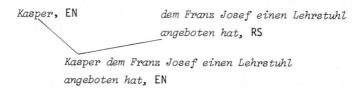

Kasper, EN   *dem Franz Josef einen Lehrstuhl*
                                          angeboten hat, RS

            Kasper dem Franz Josef einen Lehrstuhl
            angeboten hat, EN

Hier ist also nur die appositive Interpretation möglich. Das Subjekt von
(4) kann dagegen nur analysiert werden als

Mensch, CN   *der Filbinger kennt*, RS

            Mensch der Filbinger kennt, CN

Da kommt folglich nur die restriktive Interpretation in Frage. Nur definite Terme lassen beide Lesarten zu. Ich finde diese Erklärung eigentlich
sehr einfach und, für mich selbst, recht befriedigend.

    Wir wollen nun noch kurz die in Abschnitt 6 gestreiften Konstruktio-
nen mit pluralem CN ohne Artikel behandeln.

        (5) Kasper haut Klaubrüder die böse sind.

Hat das Objekt eine restriktive Lesart, so wird es folgendermaßen abge-
leitet:

12.4 1. *Klaubrüder,* CN *pl mas akk*
                          fle(*extrastark*), (M1)

                    2. *die böse sind,* RS *pl mas,* (Rel 2)

      3. *Klaubrüder die böse sind,* CN *pl mas akk*
                          extrastark, (Rel 3)

4. *Klaubrüder die böse sind*, EN *pl mas akk*, (N1)

5. *Klaubrüder die böse sind*, NP *3.pers pl akk*, (No)

Semantisch tut sich hier folgendes: V(*Klaubrüder*, CN *pl*) ist zunächst der Gattungsbegriff ξ, der jeder Situation c die Klaubrüder in c zuordnet. V(*die böse sind*) ist die Eigenschaft, böse zu sein. V(*Klaubrüder die böse sind*, $\begin{cases} \text{CN pl} \\ \text{EN pl} \end{cases}$) ist der Gattungsbegriff ξ_1, der jedem c diejenigen Klaubrüder in c zuordnet, die in c böse sind. V(*Klaubrüder die böse sind*, NP) ist der Charakter χ, so daß für ein beliebiges c, $\chi(c)$ = die Menge der Eigenschaften, die in c auf ξ_1 zutreffen. Wenn also etwa Kasper ξ_1 in c verprügelt, dann bedeutet das, daß er irgendwelche Exemplare aus $\xi_1(c)$ verprügelt, also Leute, die in c Klaubrüder und böse sind. Dies ist ganz klar die restriktive Lesart.

Nun zur explikativen Bedeutung. Diese wird folgendermaßen rekonstruiert:

12.5 1. *Klaubrüder*, CN *pl mas akk extrastark*, (M1)

2. *Klaubrüder*, EN *pl mas akk*, (N1)

3. *die böse sind*, RS *pl mas*, (Rel 2)

4. *Klaubrüder die böse sind*, EN *pl mas akk*, (Rel 4)

5. *Klaubrüder die böse sind*, NP *3.pers pl akk*, (No)

Hier bezeichnet "2. *Klaubrüder*, EN" den Gattungsbegriff ξ, der jedem c die Klaubrüder in c zuweist. "4. *Klaubrüder die böse sind*, EN" bzeichnet ebenfalls ξ, aber nur unter der Voraussetzung, daß ξ die Eigenschaft hat, böse zu sein. Was dies genau heißt, will ich im Moment einmal dahingestellt sein lassen. Vielleicht, daß sich ξ meistens in bösen Exemplaren manifestiert. Jedenfalls sollte plausibel sein, daß wir auf diese Weise eine explikative Lesart hinbekommen.

Ich möchte an dieser Stelle auf eine Schwierigkeit hinweisen, mit der meine Behandlung der Relativsätze behaftet ist. Ich habe hier nun syntaktisch zwischen definiten und den übrigen Termen unterschieden. Der Relativsatz verbindet sich dann mit beiden Arten von Termen verschieden. Das Problem ist nun, daß auch indefinite Terme mit Relativsätzen zuweilen explikativ verstanden werden können.

(6) Eine Studentin aus Amherst, die übrigens eine gute Freundin von mir ist, hat mich auf dieses Problem hingewiesen.

Daß der Term "eine Studentin aus Amherst, die übrigens eine gute Freundin von mir ist" definit verstanden werden muß, sieht man daran, daß er durch die Negation überhaupt nicht tangiert wird.

(7) Es stimmt nicht, daß mich eine Studentin aus Amherst, die übrigens eine gute Freundin von mir ist, auf dieses Problem hingewiesen hat.

So, wie die Syntax bisher angelegt wurde, müßte *eine* wohl zusätzlich als DET klassifiziert werden. Man könnte dann etwa folgendes sagen: Wird (*eine*,DET) in c_0 geäußert, so bezeichnet *eine* in c_1 nur dann etwas, wenn sich der Äußerer mit diesem Wort in c_0 genau auf ein Ding bezieht. Sei c_0 eine Situation, die diese Voraussetzung erfüllt, sei a das Ding, auf das sich der Äußerer von *eine* in c_0 mit diesem Wort bezieht. Dann bezeichnet *eine* diejenige Funktion ζ_{c_0}, so daß für eine beliebige Eigenschaft ω und eine beliebige Situation c gilt:

$\zeta_{c_0}(\omega)(c)$ ist nur definiert, wenn $\omega(a)(c) = 1$. Sei c so. Dann ist $\zeta_{c_0}(\omega)(c) = \{\omega_1 : \omega_1(a)(c) = 1\}$.

Im Grunde ist die Bedeutung von *eine* hier definiert wie die des bestimmten Artikels. Allerdings kommt ein subjektives Moment hinein: man weiß im allgemeinen nicht, worauf sich ein Äußerer mit der Äußerung von *eine* bezieht.

Eine andere Methode, explikative Relativsätze anzugehen, wäre, sie allgemein NP's modifizieren zu lassen. Man könnte dann die Einschränkung, daß es sich um ein definites NP handeln muß, semantisch formulieren. So etwas ist bei Rodman angedeutet, aber nicht ausgeführt. Man könnte dann auf die Sonderkategorien EN für definite Terme verzichten und würde "Kasper" analysieren als "der Kasper". Der bestimmte Artikel könnte *hier* wegfallen, in anderen Fällen aber nicht ("der gute alter Kasper"). Ich habe in einer früheren Arbeit eine derartige Analyse versucht (1975). Eigennamen verhalten sich aber syntaktisch und semantisch doch so verschieden von Gattungsnamen, daß sich die Einführung einer eigenen Kategorie vielleicht doch lohnt.

Ich möchte nun die Relativpronomenphrase noch ein wenig unter die Lupe nehmen. Betrachten wir dazu:

(7) Dimpfelmoser kennt die Frau, deren Tochter Hotzenplotz
    einen Rettich geschenkt hat.
(8) Dimpfelmoser kennt die Frau, deren neues Fahrrad von
    Hotzenplotz geklaut wurde.

In (7) ist *deren Tochter* eine Relativpronomenphrase, und zwar im Dativ. In (8) ist *deren Fahrrad* eine Relativpronomenphrase im Nominativ. Die syntaktische Analyse derartiger Konstruktionen ist mithilfe der folgenden Regel möglich.

(Rel 5) *Relativpronomenphrasen* [68]

$\alpha \in$ RelP num(a) gen(b) typ(*geni*)

$\beta \in$ CN num(a$_1$) gen(b$_1$) cas(c) fle(*extrastrk*)

$\alpha\beta \in$ RelP num(a) gen(b) typ(c)

Wir können nun unseren Beispielsatz analysieren. Ich will das allerdings nur für (8) durchführen.

12.6 EINE KOMPLEXE RELATIVPRONOMENPHRASE

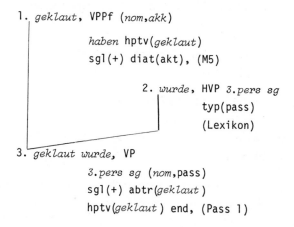

1. *geklaut*, VPPf (*nom,akk*)

    haben hptv(*geklaut*)
    sgl(+) diat(akt), (M5)

2. *wurde*, HVP *3.pers sg*
    typ(pass)
    (Lexikon)

3. *geklaut wurde*, VP

    3.pers sg (*nom*,pass)
    sgl(+) abtr(*geklaut*)
    hptv(*geklaut*) end, (Pass 1)

---

[68] Die Semantik muß hier unterscheiden, ob β eine einstellige oder eine zweistellige Eigenschaft ω ausdrückt. Generell gilt: Falls β die Eigenschaft ω ausdrückt, so drückt αβ diejenige Funktion f aus, so daß für eine beliebige einstellige Eigenschaft ω'gilt: f(ω') trifft auf a zu ⟺ ω' trifft auf *das ω von a* zu. Dabei ist für den Fall, daß ω einstellig ist, das ω *von a* das *b*, welches ω erfüllt und welches der *a* besitzt. Falls ω dagegen zweistellig ist, ist *das ω von a* das b, so daß ω(a,b) wahr ist.

4. *geklaut wurde,* VP
      *3.pers sg (nom,*pass)
      ...rels, (Rel 1_1)

         5. *von Hotzenplotz,* NP
             3.pers sg pass, (N5)

6. *von Hotzenplotz geklaut wurde,* VP
      3. pers sg (nom)
      sgl(von Hotzenplotz,+)
      abtr(*von Hotzenplotz geklaut wurde*)
      hptv(*geklaut*)
      rels, (V1)

      7. *deren,* RelP   8. *neues Fahrrad,* CN
         sg fem geni   *sg neut nom extrastrk.*
         (Lexikon)   (wie 6.5.3)

     8. *deren neues Fahrrad,* RelP
        sg fem nom
        (Rel 5)

9. *deren neues Fahrrad von Hotzenplotz geklaut wurde,* RS
      sg fem, (Rel 2)

      10. *Frau,* CN
         sg fem akk schw
         (M1)

11. *Frau deren neues Fahrrad von Hotzenplotz geklaut wurde,* CN
      sg fem akk schw
      (Rel 3)

Hier macht man dann ganz analog weiter wie ab (12.2.3). Das muß ich
wohl nicht mehr vormachen. Es ist klar, daß unsere Ableitung den restriktiven Gebrauch des Relativsatzes rekonstruiert. Will man den explikativen
Gebrauch, geht man wie in (12.3) vor.

Unsere Relativsatzregeln werden übrigens auch ohne weiteres mit passivischen Relativphrasen fertig. Allerdings müssen wir dazu letztere noch
aufbauen. Z.B. muß *von dem* als RelP *sg mas* typ(pass) erzeugt werden. Ich
will auf diese Regel hier verzichten. Setzt man diese Klassifizierung
aber einmal voraus, kann man leicht einen Satz wie den folgenden ableiten:

> (9) Dimpfelmoser sucht den Mann, von dem das neue
> Fahrrad geklaut wurde.

Die Ableitung dazu sieht so aus:

12.7 1. *geklaut wurde,* VP
         3.*pers sg* (*nom*,pass)
         sgl(+) abtr(*geklaut*)
         hptv(geklaut) end, (12.4.1)

      2. *geklaut wurde,* VP
         3.*pers sg* (pass,*nom*)
         ... rels, (Rel 1$_2$)

         3. *das neue Fahrrad,* NP
            3.*pers sg nom*
            (wie 6.5.6)

      4. *das neue Fahrrad geklaut wurde,* VP
         3.*pers sg* (pass)
         sgl(*das neue Fahrrad,*+)
         abtr(*das neue Fahrrad geklaut*)
         hptv(*geklaut*) rels, (V1)

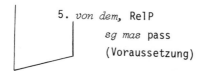

5. *von dem,* RelP

    sg mas pass

    (Voraussetzung)

6. *von dem das neue Fahrrad geklaut wurde,* RS *sg mas,* (Rel 2)

Es ist klar, wie es hier weitergeht. Aufgrund unserer semantischen Festlegungen (und der Annahme, daß die Phrase *von dem* so wie auch *dem* wieder als Identität gedeutet wird) drückt übrigens (12.5.6) die Eigenschaft aus, die auf ein a genau dann zutrifft, wenn das neue Fahrrad von a geklaut wurde. Das ist genau dieselbe Eigenschaft, wie sie der Relativsatz *der das neue Fahrrad klaute* ausdrückt. So muß es natürlich auch sein.

Bevor ich die Relativsätze verlasse, möchte ich noch eine Bemerkung zur Analyse von Relativpräpositionalphrasen machen. Vergleiche etwa den folgenden Satz:

(10) Dimpfelmoser besucht die Witwe Schlotterbeck, mit deren Geld Hotzenplotz nach Kreuth geflüchtet ist.

Die einfachste Methode wäre, *mit deren Geld* als eine Art Satzoperator zu analysieren, der aus einem Satz mit Endstellung des Finitums einen Relativsatz macht. Für Satz (10) hätten wir dann ungefähr die folgende Struktur:

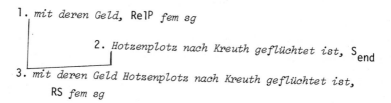

1. *mit deren Geld,* RelP *fem sg*

       2. *Hotzenplotz nach Kreuth geflüchtet ist,* S~end~

3. *mit deren Geld Hotzenplotz nach Kreuth geflüchtet ist,*

    RS *fem sg*

Man kriegt aber hier Ärger mit der Semantik. Die Präpositionalphrase
mit deren Geld modifiziert keinen Satz, sondern ein Prädikat. (Ich kann
das nicht beweisen. Man merkt das aber sofort, wenn man versucht, eine Bedeutungsregel zu formulieren.) Auch syntaktisch spricht alles dafür, daß
die Präpositionalphrasen Ad*verbien*, nicht aber Ad*sententiale* sind. Man
denke etwa an Sätze wie

> (11) Kasper hat sich eine neue Mütze
>   mit deren Geld gekauft.

Es ist sehr schwierig, Präpositionalphrasen in die Syntax einzubauen. Das
erfordert gründliche Überlegungen. Ich verweise dazu auf die Arbeit von
Renate Steinitz (1969) oder auch die von Renate Bartsch. Ich
habe diesen Komplex noch viel zu wenig durchdacht, als daß ich hier ernsthafte Vorschläge machen könnte. Die folgenden Regeln mögen daher als pro-
visorisch angesehen werden.

(PP1) *Präpositioneneinführung* [69]

$$\alpha \in \text{VP per}(a) \ \text{num}(b) \ \text{erg}(c) \ \text{sgl}(\gamma_1,\ldots,\gamma_k)$$
$$\text{abtr}(d) \ \text{hptv}(\varepsilon_1,\ldots,\varepsilon_1) \ \text{stell}(\text{end})$$
$$\beta \in \text{Präp typ}(\beta_1) \ \text{erg}(c_1)$$

$$\rule{10cm}{0.4pt}$$

$$\alpha \in \text{VP per}(a) \ \text{num}(b) \ \text{erg}(c,\beta_1) \ \text{sgl}(\gamma_1,\ldots,\gamma_k)$$
$$\text{abtr}(d) \ \text{hptv}(\varepsilon_1,\ldots,\varepsilon_1) \ \text{stell}(\text{end})$$

Die Aufgabe einer Präposition ist es also, die Stellenzahl des intransi-
tiven Verbs um eine Stelle zu erhöhen. So wird etwa aus einem *arbeiten* ein
arbeiten für und aus einem *fliehen* ein *fliehen mit*. Die Schwierigkeit bei
einem derartigen Vorgehen, das ich schon (1975) propagiert habe (vgl.
Egli (1974)),besteht darin, plausible Bedeutungen für die Präpositionen zu
finden.

---

[69] Die Semantik besteht in der funktionalen Aplikation von $V(\beta)$ auf $V(\alpha)$.

So wäre etwa:

$$V(\mathit{mit}, \text{Präp concom})(\omega)(a,b)(c) = 1:$$
$$\omega(a)(c) = 1 \text{ und } a \text{ ist in } c \text{ in Begleitung von } b$$

$$V(\mathit{mit}, \text{Präp instr.})(\omega)(a,b)(c) = 1:$$
$$\omega(a)(c) = 1 \text{ und } b \text{ bewirkt in } c \ \omega(a).$$

Dabei ist ω eine beliebige einstellige Eigenschaft. Das *mit* macht daraus eine zweistellige. Bei einem solchen Ansatz werden dann sämtliche Präpositionalphrasen zu reinen Präpositionalobjekten, d.h. wir können mit (N5) arbeiten und benötigen keine Extraregel mehr. Die Präpositionen sind Verboperatoren, nicht NP-Operatoren. Ob dies richtig ist, wird sich zeigen müssen. Immerhin legen einige Konstruktionen im Deutschen so einen Ansatz recht nahe, z.B. der folgende Satz:

(12) Ich fresse mich allmählich durch die Arbeit durch.

Hier liegt es nahe zu sagen, daß das zweite *durch* der Verbmodifikator ist, das erste *durch* ein Kongruenzphänomen zur Markierung der entsprechenden Ergänzung. Ich gebe aber zu, daß diese Konstruktionen so marginal sind, daß man nicht viel darauf begründen kann.

Zur Analyse unseres Satzes (10) benötigen wir noch die folgende Regel:

(Rel 6) *Relativpräpositionalphrasen* [70]

$$\alpha \in \text{Präp typ}(a) \ \text{erg}(b)$$
$$\underline{\beta \in \text{RelP num}(c) \ \text{gen}(d) \ \text{typ}(b)}$$
$$\alpha\beta \in \text{RelP num}(c) \ \text{gen}(d) \ \text{typ}(a)$$

---

[70] Semantisch tut sich hier nichts.

Man wird anhand der Beispiele sehen, daß sich diese Regel nicht
wiederholt anwenden läßt, derart, daß etwa *mit für deren Geld* ableitbar
wäre. Nun können wir (10) analysieren.

12.8 1. *nach Kreuth geflüchtet ist,* VP erg (*nom*)

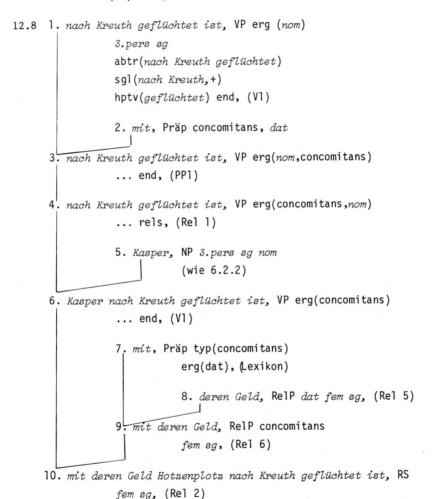

                3.pers sg

                abtr(*nach Kreuth geflüchtet*)

                sgl(*nach Kreuth,*+)

                hptv(*geflüchtet*) end, (V1)

                2. *mit,* Präp concomitans, *dat*

3. *nach Kreuth geflüchtet ist,* VP erg(*nom*,concomitans)

       ... end, (PP1)

4. *nach Kreuth geflüchtet ist,* VP erg(concomitans,*nom*)

       ... rels, (Rel 1)

                5. *Kasper,* NP *3.pers sg* nom

                    (wie 6.2.2)

6. *Kasper nach Kreuth geflüchtet ist,* VP erg(concomitans)

       ... end, (V1)

                7. *mit,* Präp typ(concomitans)

                    erg(dat), (Lexikon)

                       8. *deren Geld,* RelP *dat fem sg,* (Rel 5)

9. *mit deren Geld,* RelP concomitans

                fem sg, (Rel 6)

10. *mit deren Geld Hotzenplotz nach Kreuth geflüchtet ist,* RS
       fem sg, (Rel 2)

Schauen wir uns die Bedeutung des Relativsatzes einmal ein wenig näher an.

(12.8.1) drückt die Eigenschaft aus, nach Kreuth geflüchtet zu sein.
(12.8.3) bezeichnet die zweistellige Eigenschaft, die auf (a,b) zutrifft, wenn a nach Kreuth geflüchtet ist und a in Begleitung von b ist.
(12.8.4) trifft auf (a,b) zu, wenn b in Begleitung von a nach Kreuth geflüchtet ist.
(12.8.6) trifft auf a zu, wenn Kasper in Begleitung von a nach Kreuth geflüchtet ist.
Und (12.8.10) trifft auf a zu, wenn Kasper in Begleitung mit dem Geld von a nach Kreuth geflüchtet ist.

Die Semantik scheint also in den Grundzügen vernünftig zu sein. Damit möchte ich die Relativsätze verlassen, um mich den Modalverben zuzuwenden.

13.   MODALITÄT UND INTENSIONALITÄT

Mir geht es hier zunächst um Fälle wie die folgenden:

(1) Ich muß arbeiten.

(2) Es muß sterben gekonnt werden.
    (Zitat aus dem Werke "Didaktische Einheit Tod".)

(3) Wir müssen Hotzenplotz gestatten, Frau Schlotterbeck
    besuchen zu können.

(4) Dem Manne kann geholfen werden. (Schiller!)

(5) Von uns hat dem Manne gestattet zu werden
    zu rauchen. (v. Stechow!)

(6) Wir haben Hotzenplotz anbieten müssen,
    verreisen zu können.

Ich werde mich zunächst um die Syntax dieser Sätze kümmern. Erst wenn diese klar ist, werde ich einen Exkurs zu den einschlägigen semantischen
Problemen hinzufügen.

(Mod 1) *Modalisierte Finita*

$$\alpha \in \text{MVP per}(a) \text{ num}(b) \text{ erg}(c) \quad ^{71}$$
$$\beta \in \text{VINF erg}(c_1) \text{ sgl}(\beta_1, \ldots, \beta_n) \text{ hptv}(\gamma_1, \ldots, \gamma_k)$$
$$\text{art}(c) \text{ diat}(d)$$

$$\beta\alpha \in \text{VP erg}(c_1) \text{ per}(a) \text{ num}(b) \text{ sgl}(\beta_1, \ldots, \beta_n)$$
$$\text{hptv}(\gamma_1, \ldots, \gamma_k) \text{ abtr}(\beta) \text{ stell(end)}$$

---

[71] Die Semantik besteht in der funktionalen Applikation der MVP-Bedeutung
auf die VINF-Bedeutung.

13.1 EIN BEISPIEL DAZU

1. *muß,* MVP *1.pers* sg
    erg(0-Inf)
    (M2)

2. *arbeiten,* VINF erg(nom)
    sgl(+)
    hptv(*arbeiten*)
    art(0-Inf) diat(akt)
    (M4$_0$)

3. *arbeiten muß,* VP *1.pers sg* erg(*nom*)
    sgl(+) hptv(*arbeiten*)
    abtr(*arbeiten*) stell(*end*)
    (Mod 1)

4. *muß arbeiten,* VP ... stell(zweit), (V4)

5. *Ich,* NP *3.pers sg nom*
    (Lexikon)

6. *Ich muß arbeiten,* S$_{zweit}$, (S5$_0$)

Wir erinnern uns daran, daß die Bedeutung von *muß* im Anschluß an 5.5 bereits festgelegt worden ist. Demzufolge drückt (13.1.6) die Proposition, daß ich arbeiten muß, aus. 'arbeiten' drückt nämlich die Eigenschaft zu arbeiten aus. 'muß' darauf angewandt, ergibt die Eigenschaft arbeiten zu müssen. Diese gehört zu meinem Charakter, wenn ich arbeiten muß. (Tatsächlich gehört sie übrigens zu meinem Charakter.)

13.2 NÄCHSTES BEISPIEL

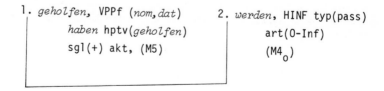

1. *geholfen,* VPPf (*nom,dat*)
    haben hptv(*geholfen*)
    sgl(+) akt, (M5)

2. *werden,* HINF typ(pass)
    art(0-Inf)
    (M4$_0$)

3. *geholfen werden,* VINF (*dat*,pass)

> hptv(*geholfen,werden*)
>
> sgl(+) art(0-Inf)
>
> diat(pass), (Pass 3)

4. *geholfen werden,* VINF (*dat*) ...., (I3)

> > 5. *kann,* MVP *3. pers sg*
> >
> > > erg(0-Inf), (M2)

6. *geholfen werden kann,* VP erg(*dat*) *3.pers sg*

> sgl(+) hptv(*geholfen,werden*)
>
> abtr(*geholfen werden*)
>
> stell(end), (Mod 1)

7. *kann geholfen werden,* VP ... stell(zweit), (V4)

> > 8. *dem Manne,* NP *3.pers sg dat*
> >
> > > (analog zu 6.5)

9. *Dem Manne kann geholfen werden,* S_{zweit}, $(S5_0)$

Man überlege sich, daß dieser Satz die Proposition ausdrückt, daß jemand dem Manne helfen kann.   Beispiel (5) stellt kein Problem dar. Der Leser leite diesen Satz einmal für sich her. Er kann sich dabei an (11.3) orientieren. Noch nicht erhalten wer dagegen (2). Dazu benötigen wir noch eine weitere Regel.

---

[72] Der Satz hat allerdings verschiedene Lesarten, je nachdem, ob *dem Mann* spezifisch oder attributiv verwendet wird. Ich komme darauf noch zu sprechen.

(Mod 2) *Modalisierte Partizipien Perfekti*

$$\alpha \in \text{VINF } erg(a_1,\ldots,a_n) \text{ hptv}(\gamma_1,\ldots,\gamma_k)^{[73]}$$
$$\text{sgl}(\delta_1,\ldots,\delta_1) \text{ art}(b) \text{ diat}(c)$$
$$\beta \in \text{MPPf } erg(b)$$

$$\beta\alpha \in \text{VPPf } erg(a_1,\ldots,a_n) \text{ hptv}(\gamma_1,\ldots,\gamma_k\cdot\beta)$$
$$\text{sgl}(\delta_1,\ldots,\delta_1) \text{ hiv}(\textit{haben}) \text{ diat}(c)$$

13.2 BEISPIEL

1. *sterben*, VINF erg(*nom*)
   hptv(*sterben*)
   sgl(+) art(O-Inf)
   diat(akt) (M4$_o$)

2. *gekonnt*, MPPf erg(O-Inf),
   (M5)

3. *sterben gekonnt*, VPPf erg(*nom*)
   hptv(*sterben,gekonnt*)
   sgl(+) hiv(*haben*) akt, (Mod 2)

4. *werden*, HINF typ(pass) art(O-Inf), (M4$_o$)

5. *sterben gekonnt werden*, VINF erg(*es*)
   hptv(*sterben,gekonnt,werden*)
   sgl(+) art(O-Inf)
   diat(pass), (Pass 3)

6. *muß*, MVP *3.pers sg* (O-Inf), (M2)

[73] Die Semantik besteht in der funktionalen Applikation der Bedeutung von β auf die von α.

7. *sterben gekonnt werden muß,* VP erg(*es*) *3.pers sg*
        sgl(+) hptv(*sterben,gekonnt,werden*)
        abtr(*sterben gekonnt werden*)
        stell(end), (Mod 1)

8. *muß sterben gekonnt werden,* VP erg(*es*) *3.pers sg*
        sgl(+) hptv(*sterben,gekonnt,werden*)
        abtr(*sterben gekonnt werden*)
        stell(zweit), (V4)

      9. *Es*

10. *Es muß sterben gekonnt werden,* S_{zweit}, $(S5_0)$

$(S6_{1,1})$ würde uns liefern: *Sterben muß gekonnt werden.* $(S6_{1,2})$ würde erbringen: *Sterben gekonnt muß werden,* und durch $(S6_{1,3})$ erhalten wir: *Sterben gekonnt werden muß.*
Wenn man sich die Deutung der Regeln übrigens einzeln anschaut, dann wird klar, daß (13.2) die Proposition ausdrückt, die in c wahr ist, wenn für ein a gilt, daß a in c die Eigenschaft hat, sterben können zu müssen.

Wir wollen nun noch eine Regel zur Verfügung stellen, die mit den Beispielsätzen (3) und (6) fertig wird.

(Mod 3) *Modalisierte Infinitive*

$$\alpha \in \text{VINF erg}(a) \text{ hptv}(\gamma_1,\ldots,\gamma_n) \text{ sgl}(\delta_1,\ldots,\delta_k)$$
$$\text{art}(b) \text{ diat}(c)$$
$$\underline{\beta \in \text{MINF erg}(b) \text{ art}(d)\hspace{4cm}}$$
$$\alpha\beta \in \text{VINF erg}(a) \text{ hptv}(\gamma_1,\ldots,\gamma_n,\beta) \text{ sgl}(\delta_1,\ldots,\delta_k)$$
$$\text{art}(d) \text{ diat}(c)$$

13.3 BEISPIEL

1. *anbieten,* VINF *(nom, dat,* zu-Inf)
      hptv(*anbieten*)
      sgl(+) art(O-Inf)   2. *gemußt,* MPPf erg(O-Inf)
      diat(akt), (M4$_0$)   (M5)

3. *anbieten gemußt,* VPPf erg(*nom, dat*)
      hptv(*anbieten, gemußt*)
      sgl(+) *haben* akt, (Mod 2)

      4. *haben,* HVP *1.pers pl, haben,* (M2)

5. *anbieten müssen haben,* VP *(nom, dat,* zu-Inf) *1.pers pl*
      hptv(*anbieten, müssen*) sgl(+)
      abtr(*anbieten müssen*) stell(end)
      art(O-Inf) akt, (V2)

      5. *verreisen,* VINF *(nom)* hptv(*verreisen*)
            sgl(+) art(O-Inf) akt, (M4$_0$)

      6. *zu können,* MINF erg(O-Inf) art(zu-Inf), (M4$_1$)

      7. *verreisen zu können,* VINF erg(*nom*) hptv(*verreisen*)
            sgl(+) art(zu-Inf) akt, (Mod 3)

8. *anbieten müssen haben verreisen zu können,* VP *1.pers pl*
      erg(*nom, dat*) sgl(+, *verreisen zu können*)
      abtr(*anbieten müssen verreisen zu können*)
      hptv(*anbieten, müssen, verreisen zu können*)
      stell(end)

      9. *Hotzenplotz,* NP *nom 3.pers sg,* (wie 6.2.2)

10. *Hotzenplotz anbieten müssen haben verreisen zu können,*
  VP *1.pers pl* erg(*nom*)
  sgl(*Hotzenplotz,+,verreisen zu können*)
  abtr(*Hotzenplotz anbieten müssen verreisen zu können*)
  hptv(*anbieten,müssen,verreisen zu können*)
  stell(end), (V1)

11. *haben Hotzenplotz anbieten müssen verreisen zu können,*
  VP *1.pers pl* (*nom*)
  sgl(+,*Hotzenplotz,verreisen zu können*)
  abtr(*Hotzenplotz anbieten müssen verreisen zu können*)
  hptv(*anbieten,müssen,verreisen zu können*)
  zweit, (V4)

   12. *Wir*, NP *1.pers pl nom*
    (Lexikon)

13. *Wir haben Hotzenplotz anbieten müssen verreisen zu können,*
  S_{zweit}, ($S5_0$)

($S5_1$) ergibt *Hotzenplotz haben wir anbieten müssen verreisen zu können,* ($S6_{3,3}$) liefert uns *Anbieten haben wir Hotzenplotz müssen verreisen zu können,* ($S6_{2,4}$) gibt uns *Hotzenplotz anbieten müssen haben wir verreisen zu können,* ($S6_{3,5}$) ergibt *Anbieten müssen verreisen zu können haben wir Hotzenplotz* und durch ($S6_{2,5}$) erhalten wir *Hotzenplotz anbieten müssen verreisen zu können haben wir.* Sätze wie der letzte sind allerdings so kopflastig, daß wir sie nicht erzeugen.

Dem Leser ist hoffentlich deutlich geworden, daß ich sehr perverse Konstruktionen betrachtet habe, um die Leistungsfähigkeit meiner Modalregeln zu demonstrieren. Mit "normalen" Fällen werden wir selbstverständlich erst recht fertig.

Ich möchte an dieser Stelle einige grundsätzliche Bemerkungen zu meiner Behandlung der Modalität machen. Ich kann die einschlägigen Probleme aber allenfalls an der Oberfläche streifen und verweisen an dieser Stelle auf die gründlichen Untersuchungen von Angelika Kratzer (1977), (1977a). Betrachten wir den folgenden Satz:

> (7) Der Präsident muß regieren.

Normalerweise sagt man, daß er zwei Lesarten hat, die man folgendermaßen wiedergeben kann:

> (8) Scheel muß regieren.
> (9) Es muß so sein, daß der jeweilige Präsident regiert.

Die erste Lesart bekommen wir gut hin, die zweite aber nicht. Das liegt an unserer Analyse von *muß* als Verboperator. Ich will dies eben einmal vormachen.

Wir setzen folgendes voraus. Wird *der Präsident* jetzt referentiell (spezifisch) verwendet, so bezeichnet dieser Term den Charakter x_{Scheel}. Dieser ist so definiert:

x_{Scheel} ist nur für solche Situationen c definiert, in denen Scheel existiert. Sei c so eine Situation. Dann ist $x_{Scheel}(c) = \{\omega: \omega(Scheel)(c) = 1\}$.

Wird *der Präsident* dagegen jetzt attributiv (unspezifisch) verwendet, so bezeichnet dieser Term den Charakter $x_{der\ Präsident}$. Dieser ist nur für solche c definiert, in denen es genau einen Präsidenten gibt. Sei c so eine Situation. Dann ist $x_{der\ Präsident}(c) = \{\omega: \omega(a)(c) = 1$, wobei a das Individuum ist, welches in c Präsident ist}.

Nun hat in unserer Syntax Satz (7) den folgenden Aufbau:

> (7a) ((*muß,regieren*), (*der,Präsident*))

V(*regieren*) ist natürlich die Eigenschaft zu regieren. Betrachten wir nun den Fall, daß *der Präsident* referentiell verwendet wird. Nach (S1) ist dann (7a) in einer Situation c wahr, wenn V(*muß,regieren*) $\in$ $\chi_{Scheel}(c)$. Dies ist genau dann der Fall, wenn V(*muß,regieren*) in c auf Scheel zutrifft. Nach unserer Festlegung der Bedeutung von *muß* (vgl. 5.5) ist dies der Fall, wenn Scheel in jeder Situation c' regiert, in der der Fall ist, was in c sein muß. Das ist die durch Satz (8) paraphrasierte Lesart, die der Modallogiker gemeinhin auch *de re* nennt. Erhalten wir nun, wenn wir vom attributiven Gebrauch des Terms *der Präsident* ausgehen, die durch (9) ausgedrückte Lesart? Nein. Dies wollen wir uns einmal näher anschauen. *der Präsident* werde also attributiv verwendet. Nach (S1) ist dann (7a) in c wahr gdw.

> V(*muß,regieren*) $\in$ $\chi_{der\ Präsident}(c)$.
> Dies ist genau dann der Fall, wenn V(*muß,regieren*)(a)(c) = 1,
> wobei a das Individuum ist, das in c Präsident ist. Dies ist
> genau dann wahr, wenn a in jeder Situation c' regiert, in der
> der Fall ist, was in c sein muß, wobei a der Präsident in c ist.

Der Unterschied zwischen dieser Lesart und der ersten ist subtil. Es handelt sich beidesmal um eine Modalität *de re*, allerdings handelt die erste Proposition von Scheel, die zweite zwar von dem Präsidenten, aber dieser ist nicht im Bereich des Modaloperators. Wie kann man diese Lesart plausibel eindeutig paraphrasieren? Vielleicht als

> (10) Wer immer Präsident ist, der muß regieren (und zwar
> egal, ob als Präsident oder als Diktator oder als König..)

Den Unterschied der beiden Lesarten von (7a) kann man sich auch so klarmachen:

Wird *der Präsident* referentiell verwendet, so impliziert (7a) nicht, daß es einen Präsidenten gibt. (7a) impliziert dann nur, daß Scheel existiert. Wird dagegen (7a) attributiv verwendet, so impliziert (7a) die Existenz eines Präsidenten.

Wie erhalten wir nun die durch die Paraphrase (9) intendierte Lesart von (7)? Offenbar muß hier *muß* so konstruiert werden, daß es ein Satzoperator ist. Ich habe über diese Konstruktionen noch nicht nachgedacht. Sie erfordern wahrscheinlich eine Revision meiner sämtlichen Regeln für die Modalverben und vielleicht auch für die Infinitivkonstruktionen. Ich versuche nicht, hier in diese Problematik weiter einzudringen. Für den Augenblick wollen wir *es muß so sein* einmal als unanalysierten Operator ansehen. Das gibt uns eine Idee, wie die de dicto-Lesarten aussehen. D.h. wir haben:

Es muß so sein $\in$ SA erg(Sdaß) typ(zweit), wobei

$V($*Es muß so sein*$)(p)(c) = 1 : \iff$

In jeder Situation c', in der der Fall ist, was in c sein muß, gilt: $p(c') = 1$.

Hinzu käme eine Syntaxregel, die, zugegebenermaßen gänzlich ad hoc ist:

(SA) *Ad hoc-Regel für "Satzadverbien"* [74]

$\alpha \in$ SA erg(a) typ(b)

$\underline{\beta \in S \text{ typ}(a)}$

$\alpha\beta \in S$ typ(b)

Mit dieser Regel können wir (9) herleiten:

---

[74] Die Semantik dieser Regel besteht natürlich in der funktionalen Applikation.

13.4   1. *Es muß so sein,* SA erg(SdaB) typ(zweit)

        2. *daß der Präsident regiert,* SdaB, (S3)

        3. *Es muß so sein daß der Präsident regiert,* S_{zweit}, (SA)

Wenn wir davon ausgehen, daß *es so sein muß,* ein SA erg(SdaB) typ(end)
ist, dann können wir mit dieser Regel auch ableiten *es so sein muß daß der
Präsident regiert.*

Nun, wie gesagt, das ist keine glorreiche Syntax. Aber die Semantik
stimmt. Betrachten wir nämlich etwa den Fall, daß *der Präsident* attributiv
verwendet wird. Dann drückt der daß-Satz die Proposition p aus, die in der
Situation c wahr ist, wenn der Präsident in c regiert.
(13.4.3) drückt dann die Proposition q aus, die in einer Situation c wahr
ist, wenn p in jeder Situation c' wahr ist, in der der Fall ist, was in c
sein muß. Mit anderen Worten: (13.4.3) ist in c wahr, wenn in jeder Situation c', in der der Fall ist, was in c der Fall sein muß, derjenige, der
in c' Präsident ist, in c' regiert. Das ist eine de dicto Lesart.

Wir erhalten nun auch die Lesart des Satzes

        (11) The mayor allowably presides necessarily,

die Cresswell (1973:150 f) diskutiert.   Er symbolisiert (11) folgendermaßen:

        (12) ((*the,mayor,* (λ,x,(*allowably,*(*presides,*x))))),*necessarily*)

Das Wichtige ist, daß der Bürgermeister hier wohl im Bereich des Notwen-
digkeitsoperators ist, nicht aber des Modalen Adverbs 'zurecht'. Cresswell
macht daraus ein Argument für die Notwendigkeit der Abstraktion in Kombi-
nation mit Nominalien.

Ein analoger Satz wäre der folgende:

(13) Es muß so sein daß der Präsident regieren kann.

Dieser wird folgendermaßen hergeleitet:

13.5 GESCHACHTELTE MODALITÄTEN

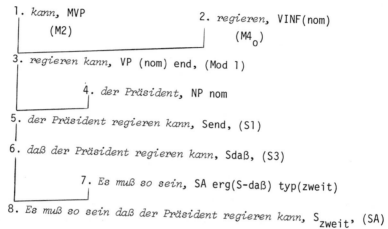

1. *kann*, MVP
   (M2)

2. *regieren*, VINF(nom)
   (M4$_0$)

3. *regieren kann*, VP (nom) end, (Mod 1)

4. *der Präsident*, NP nom

5. *der Präsident regieren kann*, Send, (S1)

6. *daß der Präsident regieren kann*, Sdaß, (S3)

7. *Es muß so sein*, SA erg(S-daß) typ(zweit)

8. *Es muß so sein daß der Präsident regieren kann*, S$_{zweit}$, (SA)

Nehmen wir einmal an, *der Präsident* werde attributiv verwendet. Dann drückt (13.5.6) die Proposition p aus, die in einer Situation c wahr ist, wenn es eine Situation c' gibt, in der der Fall ist, was in c der Fall sein kann, so daß gilt: der Präsident in c regiert in c'. (13.5.8) ist wahr in einer Situation c, wenn p in jeder Situation c' wahr ist, in der der Fall ist, was in c der Fall sein muß. Dies ist genau dann der Fall, wenn es für jede Situation c', in der Tatsache ist, was in c sein muß, eine Situation c" gibt, in der der Fall ist, was in c' sein kann, so daß gilt: derjenige, der Präsident in c' ist, regiert in c".
Das ist genau die Lesart, die Cresswell im Auge hat. Wir haben diese ganz ohne Abstraktion erhalten. Allerdings haben wir die notwendigen Information in die Verwendung des Terms *der Präsident* gesteckt, ferner in den syntaktischen Aufbau des Satzes.[75]

---

[75] Ich habe eine frühere Version dieses Abschnittes aufgrund einer Kritik von Irene Heim so umgearbeitet, daß diese Fälle erfaßt wurden.

Ich möchte nun noch eine Bemerkung zu den sogenannten "intensionalen"
Verben machen. Betrachte den folgenden Satz:

(14) Kasper sucht ein Einhorn.

In meinem Fragment wird er im großen und ganzen so analysiert:

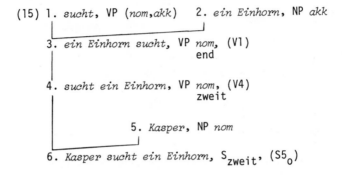

(15) 1. *sucht,* VP (*nom,akk*)   2. *ein Einhorn,* NP *akk*

   3. *ein Einhorn sucht,* VP *nom,* (V1)
                                    end

   4. *sucht ein Einhorn,* VP *nom,* (V4)
                                    zweit

               5. *Kasper,* NP *nom*

   6. *Kasper sucht ein Einhorn,* S_{zweit}, ($S5_0$)

Normalerweise analysiert man nun (14) so, daß er zwei Lesarten hat:
daß Kasper nach einem Einhorn sucht (ohne daß es eines zu geben braucht),
und daß es ein Einhorn gibt, welches Kasper sucht, ohne daß Kasper zu
wissen braucht, daß es ein Einhorn ist, was er sucht. Die erste Lesart
kann man die *unspezifische,* die zweite die *spezifische* nennen.

Wie kann man diesen Unterschied im Ausgedrückten rekonstruieren?
Wir wollen 'suchen' einmal beschreiben als 'danach streben zu finden'.
Um die Bedeutung angeben zu können, führen wir die folgende Eigenschaft
ein: ω_{findet} (a,b)(c) = 1 : $\Longleftrightarrow$ a findet b in c.
Dabei sind a und b Individuen. Die Eigenschaft zu finden ist extensional:
a und b existieren, wenn a den b findet. Bevor ich nun die Bedeutung von
sucht beschreibe, möchte ich darauf hinweisen, daß die von mir vorausgesetzte Semantik so reich ist, daß der Bereich der Dinge praktisch alles
umfaßt, also z.B. auch Charaktere.[76]

---

[76] Man muß aufpassen, daß diese Annahme nicht zu Widersprüchen führt. Vgl.
dazu etwa Cresswell (1973) oder v. Stechow (1977).

Die Bedeutungsregel für *sucht* sieht dann, grob gesprochen, folgendermaßen
aus:

$V(sucht,\ VP_{(nom,akk)})$ ist nur für solche Dinge a,b definiert, so
daß a ein Individuum und b ein Charakter ist. Falls diese Voraussetzung erfüllt ist, dann gilt für ein beliebiges c:
$V(sucht,\ VP_{(nom,akk)})(a,b)(c) = 1\ : \iff$ In jedem c', in dem der
Fall ist, was a in c erstrebt, gilt:
$\lambda^* b_1(\omega_{findet}(a,b_1)) \in b(c')$.

Gehen wir nun zunächst davon aus, daß der Term *ein Einhorn* in c_0
spezifisch verwendet wird. Dann wird damit der Charakter χ_{spez} bezeichnet.[77]

$\chi_{spez}(c) = \{\omega:$ Es gibt ein a: a ist ein Einhorn in c_0
und $\omega(a)(c) = 1\}$.
Bei diesem Gebrauch ist (15.6) in einer Situation c wahr, wenn
$\lambda^* b(V(sucht)(Kasper,b)) \in \chi_{spez}(c)$.

Und dies ist nach unseren Festlegungen genau dann der Fall, wenn es
ein a gibt: a ist ein Einhorn in c_0 und $V(sucht)(Kasper,a)(c) = 1$. Dies
wiederum besagt folgendes: Es gibt ein a: a ist ein Einhorn in c_0 und
jedem c', in dem der Fall ist, was Kasper in c erstrebt, gilt: Kasper
findet a in c'. Dies sieht recht gut nach der spezifischen Lesart aus.
Es werde nun der Term *ein Einhorn* in c_0 attributiv gebraucht. Dann bezeichnet er den Charakter χ_{unspez}:

$\chi_{unspez}(c) = \{\omega:$ Es gibt ein a: a ist ein Einhorn in c
und $\omega(a)(c) = 1\}$.
Bei diesem Gebrauch ist (15.6) wahr in einer Situation c, wenn
die Eigenschaft von Kasper gesucht zu werden zu $\chi_{unspez}(c)$ gehört.

---

[77] Vgl. die Ausführungen im Anschluß an 6.3. Die Semantik ist hier wahrscheinlich nicht ganz korrekt, läßt sich aber reparieren.

Dies ist genau dann der Fall, wenn es für jedes c', in dem der Fall
ist, was Kasper in c erstrebt, ein a gibt, so daß gilt: a ist ein Einhorn
in c' und Kasper findet a in c'. Das ist die unspezifische Lesart.
Bei beiden Lesarten wird hier nicht an Skopusunterschieden des Nominals.
"ein Einhorn" festgemacht, sondern am Gebrauch des unbestimmten Artikels.

Mit diesem Exkurs möchte ich auch diesen Abschnitt verlassen.

14.   BEMERKUNGEN ZU NEGATION UND KONJUNKTION

Zur Negation und Konjunktion möchte ich im Rahmen dieses Fragmentes
nicht viel sagen. Nur so wenig: ich stelle mir eine Behandlung der hier
einschlägigen Phänomene anders vor, als dies üblicherweise in der Literatur geschieht. Ich bin nicht der Ansicht, daß man nur Sätze negieren oder
konjugieren kann. Verneinen und verbinden kann man im Gegenteil so ziemlich alles, insbesondere Verben und Nominalphrasen. Man betrachte etwa die
folgenden Beispiele:

        (1) Nicht jeder himmelt einen Filmstar an.
        (2) Jeder himmelt nicht einen Filmstar an.
        (3) Jeder himmelt einen Filmstar nicht an.

Im ersten Satz wird meines Erachtens das Subjekt negiert, im zweiten
das Objekt und im dritten das Verb. Nirgendwo haben wir es dagegen mit
einer Satznegation zu tun, wie mir scheint, obwohl das üblicherweise wohl
für alle drei Fälle gesagt wird. Die Sätze (2) und (3) klingen übrigens
etwas merkwürdig und verlangen eine besondere Betonung. Satznegationen
sind sehr selten. Ich behandle sie nicht, weil jeder weiß, wie man das
macht. Untersuchen wir als erste die Negation der Nominalien. Dies wird
von der folgenden Regel ins Werk gesetzt:

(Neg 1) *Nominalnegation* [78]

$$\frac{\alpha \in NP \ per(a) \ num(b) \ typ(c)}{nicht \ \alpha \in NP \ per(a) \ num(b) \ typ(c)}$$

(1) läßt sich nun folgendermaßen analysieren:

14.1 NOMINALNEGATION

1. *anhimmelt*, VP *3.pers sg (nom,akk)*
                        sgl(+) hptv(*anhimmelt*)
                        abtr(*an*) stell(end), (M2)

                2. *einen Filmstar*, NP *3.pers sg akk*
                        (wie 6.4)

3. *einen Filmstar anhimmelt*, VP *3.pers sg (nom)*
                        sgl(*einen Filmstar*,+)
                        hptv(*anhimmelt*)
                        abtr(*einen Filmstar an*)
                        stell(end), (V1)

4. *himmelt einen Filmstar an*, VP *3.pers sg (nom)*
                        sgl(+,*einen Filmstar*)
                        hptv(*anhimmelt*)
                        abtr(*einen Filmstar an*)
                        stell(zweit), (V4)

---

[78] Die Semantik besteht in der Komplementbildung, d.h., wenn α den Charakter χ bezeichnet, dann bezeichnet *nicht* α den Charakter $\bar{\chi}$, so daß für ein beliebiges ω und c gilt: ω ∈ $\bar{\chi}$(c) = 1 ⟺ ω ∉ χ(c).

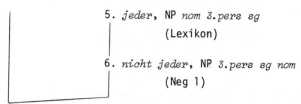

5. *jeder*, NP *nom 3.pers sg*

(Lexikon)

6. *nicht jeder*, NP *3.pers sg nom*

(Neg 1)

7. *Nicht jeder himmelt einen Filmstar an*, S_{zweit}, $(S5_0)$

Man kann sich leicht überlegen, daß dieser Satz die Proposition ausdrückt, daß mindestens einer einen Filmstar nicht anhimmelt. V(*jeder*) ist
nämlich die Menge der Eigenschaften, die jeder hat. V(*nicht jeder*) ist die
Menge der Eigenschaften, die nicht jeder hat. Also drückt (14.1.7) die Proposition aus, daß nicht jeder die Eigenschaft hat, einen Filmstar anzuhimmeln, und dies ist die eben genannte Proposition. Dabei lasse ich außer
acht, ob *jeder* spezifisch oder unspezifisch verwendet wird.

Nun zum zweiten Beispielsatz. Die Analyse lautet:

14.2   NOCH EINE NOMINALNEGATION

1. *anhimmelt*, NP (*nom,akk*) ...,

(wie 14.1.1)

2. *einen Filmstar*, NP *3.pers sg akk*

(wie bei 6.4)

3. *nicht einen Filmstar*, NP *3.pers sg akk*

(Neg 1)

4. *nicht einen Filmstar anhimmelt*, VP *3.pers sg* (*nom*)

sgl(*nicht einen Filmstar*,+)

hptv(*anhimmelt*)

abtr(*nicht einen Filmstar*)

stell(end), (Vl)

5. *himmelt nicht einen Filmstar an,* VP *(nom)* ...,
   stell(zweit), (V4)

6. *Jeder,* NP *nom 3.pers sg*
   (Lexikon)

7. *Jeder himmelt nicht einen Filmstar an,* S_{zweit}, $(S5_0)$

Dieser Satz drückt die Proposition aus, daß jeder nicht einmal einen einzigen Filmstar anhimmelt. Wir würden dieselbe allerdings natürlicher ausdrücken durch den Satz "Keiner himmelt einen Filmstar an". Gehen wir nun zur Analyse von (3) über. Dazu benötigen wir die folgende Regel. Die Verbnegationsregel ist nun so angelegt, daß es Negationsskopus gibt. Das werden die folgenden Beispiele gleich zeigen.

(Neg 2) *Verbnegation* [79]

$$\alpha \in VP \; per(a) \; num(b) \; erg(c_1,...,c_n) \; sgl(\beta_1,...,\beta_k)$$
$$hptv(\gamma_1,...,\gamma_1) \; abtr(\delta) \; stell(end)$$

---

nicht $\alpha \in VP \; per(a) \; num(b) \; erg(c_1,...,c_n) \; hptv(\gamma_1,...,\gamma_1)$
$sgl(\beta_1,...,\beta_k) \; abtr(nicht \; \delta) \; stell(end)$

Wir kommen nun zu unserem Beispiel (3).

14.3   1. *anhimmelt,* VP *(nom,akk) 3.pers sg* sgl(+)
          hptv(*anhimmelt*) abtr(*an*)
          stell(end), (wie 14.1.1)

[79] Die Negation bedeutet natürlich immer dasselbe. Also:
$V(nicht \; \alpha, VP_{(c_1,...,c_n)})(a_1,...,a_n)(c) = 1$

$\Longleftrightarrow V(\alpha, VP_{(c_1,...,c_n)})(a_1,...,a_n)(c) = 0.$

2. *nicht anhimmelt,* VP *3.pers sg* erg(*nom,akk*)

                sgl(+) hptv(*anhimmelt*)

                abtr(*an*) stell(end), (Neg 2)

                    3. *einen Filmstar,* NP *3.pers sg akk*

                       (14.1.2)

4. *einen Filmstar nicht anhimmelt,* VP *3.pers sg* erg(*nom*)

                sgl(+,*einen Filmstar*)

                hptv(*anhimmelt*)

                abtr(*an*) stell(end), (V1)

5. *himmelt einen Filmstar nicht an,* VP *3.pers sg ...* zweit

                (V4)

                    6. *Jeder,* NP *3.pers sg nom*

                      (Lexikon)

7. *Jeder himmelt einen Filmstar nicht an,* S_{zweit}, ($S5_0$)

Dieser Satz drückt die Proposition aus, daß Jeder die Eigenschaft hat, mindestens einen Filmstar nicht anzuhimmeln.[80] Das ist auch genau der Sinn, den wir uns wünschen. Anders sieht die Sache aus, wenn wir das Objekt *einen Filmstar* in den Skopus der Negation mit einbeziehen.

---

[80] Sei $\overline{\omega}_{\text{himmelt an}}$ die Eigenschaft, die auf (a,b) zutrifft gdw. a,b nicht anhimmelt. Dann drückt (14.3.7) die Proposition p aus, die in c wahr ist gdw. $\lambda^* a (\lambda^* b (\overline{\omega}_{\text{himmelt an}} a,b)) \in \chi_{\text{ein Filmstar}}(c)) \in \chi_{\text{Jeder}}(c)$.

14.4

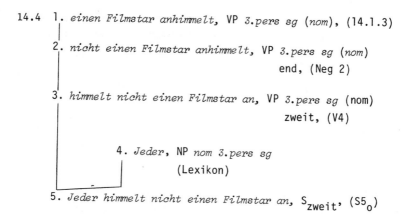

1. *einen Filmstar anhimmelt,* VP *3.pers sg* (*nom*), (14.1.3)

2. *nicht einen Filmstar anhimmelt,* VP *3.pers sg* (*nom*)
   end, (Neg 2)

3. *himmelt nicht einen Filmstar an,* VP *3.pers sg* (nom)
   zweit, (V4)

4. *Jeder,* NP *nom 3.pers sg*
   (Lexikon)

5. *Jeder himmelt nicht einen Filmstar an,* S_{zweit}, ($S5_0$)

(14.4.5) drückt die Proposition aus, daß jeder nicht einmal einen einzigen Filmstar anhimmelt.[81] Und auch das besagt dieser Satz in seinem intuitiven Verständnis. Dies ist natürlich genau derselbe Sinn, den auch (14.2.7) ausdrückt, und das muß auch so sein. Satz (3) kann übrigens auch als Satznegation verstanden werden. Ich habe aber schon gesagt, daß ich mich darum im Moment nicht kümmere, weil dazu nichts Neues zu sagen ist. Was ich festhalten möchte, ist folgendes: Wir können verschiedene Lesarten für Sätze erhalten, in denen das Negationswort an derselben Stelle vorkommt. Und dies alles ohne Abstraktion und gebundene Variablen.

---

[81] Sei $\overline{\omega}_{himmelt\ einen\ Filmstar\ an}$ die Eigenschaft, die auf ein a zutrifft gdw. $\lambda* a (\lambda* b\ (\omega_{anhimmelt}(a,b)) \in \chi_{einen\ Filmstar}(c))$ auf a nicht zutrifft. Dann drückt (14.4.5) die Proposition aus, die in c wahr ist gdw. $\lambda*\ (\overline{\omega}_{himmelt\ einen\ Filmstar\ an}(a)) \in \chi_{Jeder}(c)$. Dies ist genau dann wahr, wenn für jedes a gilt: (Wenn a eine Person in c ist, dann gilt: $\lambda* b$ $(\omega_{anhimmelt}(a,b)) \in \chi_{einen\ Filmstar}$). Und dies ist äquivalent mit: Für jedes a: Wenn a eine Person in c ist, dann gibt es kein b (b ist ein Filmstar in c und a himmelt b in c an).

Bevor ich diesen Abschnitt verlasse, möchte ich noch etwas zu *einem* Problem sagen, das in Zusammenhang mit Konjunktionen entsteht, nämlich zur Konjunktion von Verbalphrasen. Es geht mir um Fälle wie die folgenden:

(4) Kasper sucht ein Einhorn und säuft Bier.

Montague selber leitet diesen Satz ungefähr aus der folgenden Konstruktion her:

(5) *Kasper* λx (x *suchen ein Einhorn und* x *saufen Bier*)

Es gibt dann eine Regel, die das Nominal *Kasper* in das Abstrakt "hineinquantifiziert". Das heißt, es wird an die Stelle der ersten gebundenen Variablen x gesetzt. Die zweite Variable wird gestrichen und "das Hauptverb" des Abstrakts, also des Ausdrucks

λx(x *suchen ein Einhorn und* x *saufen Bier*)

wird in die 3. Person Singular gesetzt. Dabei kommt dann etwas Falsches heraus, denn *das* Hauptverb gibt es nicht in diesem Abstrakt. Bei Montague ist es (in "PTQ") die *erste* Verbform (siehe PTQ, S. 17). Das würde dann liefern

+*Kasper sucht ein Einhorn und saufen.*

Man kann hier herumdoktern, um die Quantifizierungsregeln richtig hinzukriegen. Für das Deutsche entsteht dabei aber ein zusätzliches Problem: Die Stellung der finiten Verben ist in den verschiedenen Satztypen verschieden. Man denke etwa an folgendes:

(6) Ich weiß, daß Kasper ein Einhorn sucht und Bier säuft.

Hier haben wir in beiden VP's Endstellung des Finitums. Oder:

(7) Suche ein Einhorn und saufe Bier, lieber Kasper!

Hier stehen die Finita zu Beginn. Selbstverständlich übertragen sich
diese Verhältnisse auf Verbphrasen von beliebiger Komplexität.

> (8) Kasper hat kein Einhorn finden können
>   und hat Milch getrunken.
>
> (9) Ich weiß, daß Kasper kein Einhorn finden können hat
>   und Milch getrunken hat.

In (8) haben wir Zweitstellung vorliegen, in (9) Endstellung. Eine
Quantifizierungsregel der skizzierten Art gerät hier in große Schwierigkeiten. In meinem Ansatz lösen sich diese Probleme durch die folgende Regel.

(Konj 1) *Verbkonjunktion* [82]

$$\alpha \in VP \ per(a) \ num(b) \ erg(c) \ sgl(\delta_1, \ldots, \delta_n)$$
$$hptv(\gamma_1, \ldots, \gamma_k) \ abtr(\beta) \ stell(d)$$

$$\beta \in VP \ per(a) \ num(b) \ erg(c) \ sgl(\varepsilon_1, \ldots, \varepsilon_1)$$
$$hptv(\zeta_1, \ldots, \zeta_m) \ abtr(\beta_1) \ stell(d)$$

$$\alpha \ und \ \beta \in VP \ per(a) \ num(b) \ erg(c) \ sgl(-)$$
$$hptv(-) \ abtr(-) \ stell(d)$$

In dieser Regel sind die Unterkategorienspezifizierungen für 'sgl',
'hptv' und 'abtr' getilgt worden, um eine Anwendung der Umstellungsregeln
für das Finitum zu blockieren. Schauen wir nun, was diese Regel leistet:

---

[82] Die Semantik besteht in der Konjunktion der durch α und β ausgedrückten
Eigenschaften, d.h. V(α *und* β) trifft zu auf a: $\Longleftrightarrow$
V(α) und V(β) treffen auf a zu. Ganz analog kann man auch eine Regel
für *oder* bilden, oder eine einzige, die diese beiden Fälle zusammenfaßt.

14.6 1. *hat kein Einhorn finden können,* VP *3.pers sg* (*nom*)
         sgl(+,*kein Einhorn finden können*)
         hptv(*finden,können*)
         abtr(*kein Einhorn finden können*)
         stell(zweit), (V4)

      2. *hat Milch getrunken,* VP *3.pers sg* (*nom*)
            sgl(+,*Milch*)
            hptv(*getrunken*)
            abtr(*Milch getrunken*)
            stell(zweit), (V4)

   3. *hat kein Einhorn finden können und hat Milch getrunken,*
         VP *3.pers sg* (*nom*)
         sgl(-) hptv(-) abtr(-)
         stell(zweit), (Konj 1)

      4. *Kasper,* NP *3.pers sg nom*
            (wie 6.2)

   5. *Kasper hat kein Einhorn finden können und hat Milch
      getrunken,* S$_{zweit}$, (S5$_0$)

14.7 1. *kein Einhorn finden können hat,* VP *3.pers sg* (*nom*)
            sgl(*kein Einhorn,*+)
            hptv(*finden*)
            abtr(*kein Einhorn finden können*)
            stell(end), (V2)

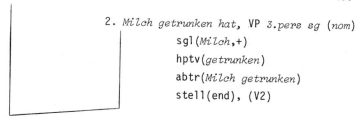

 2. *Milch getrunken hat,* VP *3.pers sg* (*nom*)
      sgl(*Milch*,+)
      hptv(*getrunken*)
      abtr(*Milch getrunken*)
      stell(end), (V2)

 3. *kein Einhorn finden können hat*
    und Milch getrunken hat, VP *3.pers sg* (*nom*)
      sgl(-) hptv(-) abtr(-)
      stell(end), (Konj 1)

Es ist deutlich, wie man hier weitermachen muß, um am Ende (9) zu
erhalten. Damit beschließe ich auch diesen Abschnitt.

15.   ZUR PROBLEMATIK VON "LASSEN"

    Das Verb "lassen" ist sicher eines der kompliziertesten des
Deutschen. Dies läßt sich in eindrucksvoller Weise in dem Aufsatz von Marga
Reis nachlesen.[83] Von den vielen Problemen, die die Autorin dort behandelt,
kann ich hier nicht alle aufgreifen, aber doch einige wichtige. Ich möchte
zu Beginn vorwegschicken, daß dieser Abschnitt mir der unfertigste des
ganzen Aufsatzes zu sein scheint. Die Materie ist auch schwierig genug.

    (1) Wir lassen Kasper Hotzenplotz verprügeln.
    (2) Wir lassen Kasper von Hotzenplotz verprügeln.

    Zunächst eine Bemerkung zur Bedeutung unseres Verbs. "Lassen" ist
echt mehrdeutig. (1) hat die Lesart, daß wir Kasper veranlassen, Hotzenplotz zu verprügeln, und daß wir zulassen, daß Kasper Hotzenplotz verprügelt. Der erste Sinn von "lassen" wird *faktitiv* genannt, der zweite

[83] Cf. Reis (1976).

permissiv. Allerdings wird der Verwendungskontext mal den einen, mal den anderen Sinn suggerieren.

Es liegt also nahe, *lassen* als ein VP (*nom,akk*,O-Inf) zu klassifizieren und die Bedeutung folgendermaßen festzulegen:

V(*lassen*, VP (*nom,akk*,O-Inf))(a,b,ω)(c) = 1
⟺ a veranlaßt in c ω(b) oder
   a läßt in c ω(b) zu.

Damit sind natürlich noch längst nicht alle Bedeutungsnuancen von *lassen* erfaßt; z.B. heißt

(3) Wir lassen das Buch liegen

hier, daß wir das Buch in einem bestimmten Zustand belassen, nämlich in einem liegenden.

Schauen wir zunächst einmal, ob wir mit der skizzierten Analyse von lassen ungefähr zurecht kommen. Betrachten wir Satz (1). Der läßt sich folgendermaßen ableiten:

15.1 ABLEITUNGSSKIZZE

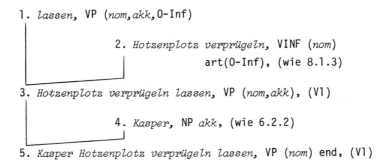

1. *lassen,* VP (*nom,akk*,O-Inf)

　　　　　　　　2. *Hotzenplotz verprügeln,* VINF (*nom*)
　　　　　　　　　　　　art(O-Inf), (wie 8.1.3)

3. *Hotzenplotz verprügeln lassen,* VP (*nom,akk*), (V1)

　　　　　　　　4. *Kasper,* NP *akk*, (wie 6.2.2)

5. *Kasper Hotzenplotz verprügeln lassen,* VP (*nom*) end, (V1)

6. *lassen Kasper Hotzenplotz verprügeln,* VP *(nom)*

zweit, (V4)

7. *wir,* NP nom, (Lexikon)

8. *Wir lassen Kasper Hotzenplotz verprügeln,* S_{zweit}, $(S5_0)$

Das sieht gut aus, und die Semantik macht auch keine weiteren Probleme.

Schauen wir uns nun einen Passivsatz an:

(4) Der Mann wurde von uns stehen gelassen.

Die Ableitung dazu sieht etwa so aus:

15.2 1. *gelassen,* VP *(nom,akk,0-Inf),* (M5)

2. *wurde,* HVP pass, (M2)

3. *gelassen wurde,* VP *(nom,*pass,0-Inf) end, (Pass 1)

4. *stehen,* VINF *(nom)* 0-Inf, $(M4_0)$

5. *stehen gelassen wurde,* VP *(nom,*pass) end, (V1)

6. *von uns,* NP pass, (N5)

7. *von uns stehen gelassen wurde,* VP *(nom)* end, (V1)

8. *wurde von uns stehen gelassen,* VP (nom) zweit, (V4)

9. *der Mann,* NP nom, (N1)

10. *Der Mann wurde von uns stehen gelassen,* S_{zweit}, $(S5_0)$

Die Semantik macht auch keinen Ärger. Die Passivregel ist so, daß das Richtige herauskommt.[84] Schwieriger ist die Behandlung von Satz (2). Hier hat der Infinitiv offenbar eine passivische Bedeutung, obwohl sich das nicht in seiner grammatischen Form niederschlägt.

In der früheren Version dieses Aufsatzes habe ich den Infinitivsatz aus einem eingebetteten Passivsatz transformationell hergeleitet. Ich hatte eine spezielle Regel formuliert, die den Übergang von etwa (5) zu (2) erbrachte:

(2) Wir lassen Kasper von Hotzenplotz verprügeln.

(5)+ Wir lassen Kasper von Hotzenplotz verprügelt werden.

Die Schwierigkeit ist nur, daß (5) überhaupt kein ordentlicher deutscher Satz ist. Eine Konstruktion wie (5) herzuleiten, widerspräche also der starken Wohlgeformtheitsbedingung, der wir uns unterworfen haben. Man könnte daran denken, ganz allgemein zuzulassen, daß aktivische Infinitivsätze passivische Bedeutung haben, etwa in denen man *von Hotzenplotz verprügeln* so herleitet:

---

[84] Die Passivregel ist sicher noch unzureichend. Aber einiges tut sie automatisch richtig, z.B. die Quantorenvertauschung. Chomsky hat einmal darauf hingewiesen, daß "Jeder spricht eine Sprache" und "Eine Sprache wird von jedem gesprochen" sich in der logischen Darstellung in der Quantorenreihenfolge $(\forall x)(\exists y)$ bzw. $(\exists y)(\forall x)$ unterscheiden. Der Leser überzeuge sich, daß dies korrekt herauskommt. "Eine Sprache wird von jedem gesprochen" hat ungefähr diese Wahrheitsbedingung: $\lambda^* a(\lambda^* b \, (V(\textit{wird gesprochen})(a,b)) \in V(\textit{jeder})(c)) \in V(\textit{eine Sprache})(c)$. Man rechnet leicht nach, daß dies äquivalent damit ist, daß es ein x gibt(x ist eine Sprache in c und für alle y gilt (wenn y eine Person in c ist, dann spricht y x in c)).

Das ist die Lesart, die Chomsky für das Passiv haben möchte. Vorläufig noch nicht schaffe ich allerdings zwei Lesarten für "Jedermann liebt jemanden". Hier kommt nur die schwache Lesart "$(\forall x)(\exists y)$" heraus. Eine entwickelte Pronominaltheorie wird mit der "Gewichtung" von Quantoren arbeiten müssen, die sich dann in der logischen Darstellung in unterschiedlichem Skopus niederschlägt.

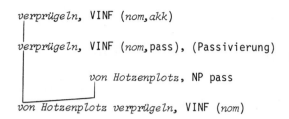

verprügeln, VINF (*nom,akk*)

verprügeln, VINF (*nom,*pass), (Passivierung)

von Hotzenplotz, NP pass

von Hotzenplotz verprügeln, VINF (*nom*)

Dies hat nur den Haken, daß derartige Konstruktionen nicht bei allen A.c.I.-Verben vorkommen können. Z.B. ist (6) nicht möglich; es muß wie in (7) lauten:

       (6)+ Wir sehen Kasper von Hotzenplotz verprügeln.

       (7) Wir sehen Kasper von Hotzenplotz verprügelt werden.

(7) wird man allerdings auch meistens vermeiden zugunsten von (8).

       (8) Wir sehen, daß (wie) Kasper von Hotzenplotz verprügelt wird.

Immerhin ist (7) noch einigermaßen akzeptabel, (6) dagegen keinesfalls. Was ist hier zu tun? Ich kann dazu keine fertigen Lösungen vorschlagen. Aber ein gangbarer Weg scheint mir der zu sein, die Verben feiner unterzuklassifizieren, als wir das bisher getan haben. Ich versuche das gar nicht erst, sondern setze voraus, daß sich für (2) eine Ableitung der eben skizzierten Art machen läßt, ohne daß an anderen Stellen Unsinn passiert.

D.h., (2) müßte etwa so analysiert werden:

15.3 SPEKULATION

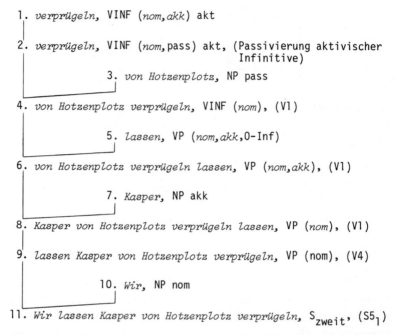

1. *verprügeln,* VINF (*nom,akk*) akt

2. *verprügeln,* VINF (*nom,*pass) akt, (Passivierung aktivischer
                                                Infinitive)

    3. *von Hotzenplotz,* NP pass

4. *von Hotzenplotz verprügeln,* VINF (*nom*), (V1)

        5. *lassen,* VP (*nom,akk,*0-Inf)

6. *von Hotzenplotz verprügeln lassen,* VP (*nom,akk*), (V1)

        7. *Kasper,* NP akk

8. *Kasper von Hotzenplotz verprügeln lassen,* VP (*nom*), (V1)

9. *lassen Kasper von Hotzenplotz verprügeln,* VP (nom), (V4)

            10. *Wir,* NP nom

11. *Wir lassen Kasper von Hotzenplotz verprügeln,* S_{zweit}, (S5$_1$)

Die Semantik der Regel "Passivierung aktivischer Infinitivsätze"
sieht genauso aus wie die der anderen Passivregeln auch. Man gebe sich
keiner Illusion hin: diese Ableitung sieht zwar schön aus, die semantische
Seite ist auch in Ordnung; aber es wird schwierig sein, das Syntagma "von
Hotzenplotz verprügeln" gerade so zu klassifizieren, daß es sich zwar mit
"lassen", nicht aber mit "sehen" verbindet. Bei derartigen Infinitivkonstruktionen muß noch eine weitere Spezialität bedacht werden: das Akkusa-
tivobjekt der A.c.L-Konstruktion wird zu einem Genitiv oder Dativ, falls
der passivische Infinitivsatz ein Subjekt in diesem Kasus verlangt.

(9) Wir lassen des Mannes von Kasper gedenken.

(10) Wir lassen dem Oberwachtmeister Dimpfelmoser durch Witwe Schlotterbeck helfen.

Ich lasse alle diese Probleme hier liegen, nachdem ich in dem Vorläufer dieses Aufsatzes Regeln dafür formuliert habe, die solche Ungetüme waren, daß ich sie hier nicht anzubieten wage.

Zum Schluß möchte ich noch etwas zum reflexivischen "lassen" sagen. Relativ unproblematisch ist die Behandlung von "läßt sich" in modaler Bedeutung. Der Satz

(11) Die Jungfrau läßt sich leicht besteigen

bedeutet etwa so viel wie

(12) Die Jungfrau kann leicht bestiegen werden.

"Läßt sich" kann also wie "kann" gedeutet werden. Allerdings wir die Infinitivergänzung wiederum passivisch verstanden.
Ein tieferes Problem bietet dagegen der Satz

(13) Kasper läßt Großmutter für sich arbeiten.

Hier kann sich *sich* einmal auf *Großmutter*, einmal auf *Kasper* beziehen. Wie man das behandeln könnte, darüber möchte ich nun noch ein wenig nachdenken. Dazu müssen wir zunächst das Reflexivpronomen einführen. Betrachten wir vorerst einen einfachen Fall von Reflexivierung.

(14) Irena himmelt sich an.

Das Reflexivpronomen wird gedeutet als ein Verboperator, der das letzte mit dem ersten Argument identifiziert. Nennen wir diesen Operator einmal "ref", dann haben wir $\text{ref}(\omega)(a_1,\ldots,a_n)(c) = 1 :\iff \omega(a_1,\ldots,a_{n-1}, a_1)(c) = 1$, wobei   eine n-stellige Eigenschaft ist.

Die Idee, das Reflexivpronomen so zu deuten, geht auf Quine zurück,
vgl (52). Sie ist unter Linguisten noch immer nicht sehr verbreitet. Vgl.
dagegen   (16) und (59), wo diese Regel schon benutzt wird.
Syntaktisch verhält sich nun das Reflexivpronomen wie ein NP. Deswegen
können wir es nicht ohne weiteres als ein Adverb auffassen; das heißt,
wir benötigen ein paar Tricks. Satz (14) wird etwa so analysiert werden:

15.4 SKIZZE

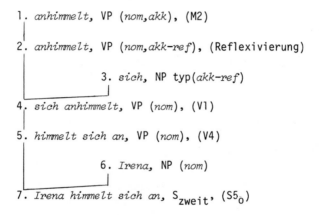

1. *anhimmelt*, VP (*nom,akk*), (M2)

2. *anhimmelt*, VP (*nom,akk-ref*), (Reflexivierung)

               3. *sich*, NP typ(*akk-ref*)

4. *sich anhimmelt*, VP (*nom*), (V1)

5. *himmelt sich an*, VP (*nom*), (V4)

               6. *Irena*, NP (*nom*)

7. *Irena himmelt sich an*, S_{zweit}, ($S5_0$)

Die für diese Konstruktion benutzten Regeln sehen folgendermaßen aus:

(Ref 1) *Reflexivierung*

$$\alpha \in VP\ 3.pers\ num(a)\ erg(b_1,\ldots,b_n)\ sgl(\beta_1,\ldots,\beta_k)$$
$$hptv(\gamma_1,\ldots,\gamma_e)\ abtr(\delta)\ stell(end)$$
$$b_n = dat,\ akk,\ benefaktiv,\ concomitans,\ \ldots$$

$$\alpha \in VP\ 3.pers\ num(a)\ erg(b_1,\ldots,b_{n-1},b_n\text{-}ref)$$
$$sgl(\beta_1,\ldots,\beta_k)\ hptv(\gamma_1,\ldots,\gamma_e)\ abtr(\delta)$$
$$stell(end)$$

Die Semantik besteht in der Anwendung des Reflexivoperators auf die Verbbedeutung. Das heißt:

$$V(\alpha, VP(b_1, \ldots, b_n\text{-ref}))(a_1, \ldots, a_n)(c) = 1$$
$$: \Longleftrightarrow V(\alpha, VP(b_1, \ldots, b_n))(a_1, \ldots, a_{n-1}, a_1)(c) = 1$$

Die Merkmalkombination *akk-ref*, *dat-ref*, benefaktiv-*ref*,... etc ist neu. Hier wird kodiert, daß an dieser Stelle der Verbergänzung eine Reflexivphrase zu stehen hat.

Auf eines möchte ich hinweisen: Der Reflexivoperator macht hier aus einer n-stelligen Eigenschaft wieder eine n-stellige Eigenschaft. Wenn man sich die Sache aber genau anschaut, dann sieht man, daß die neue Eigenschaft vom letzten Argument gar nicht mehr abhängt. Ein Beispiel: Die zweistellige Eigenschaft ref(zu lieben) trifft auf (a,b) genau dann zu, wenn die einstellige Eigenschaft λ*a (zu lieben(a,a)) auf a zutrifft. Der Reflexivoperator setzt also letztlich die Stellenzahl des Verbs um eins herab. Aus formalen Gründen wird die "leere" Stelle aber benötigt, nämlich dann, wenn die Reflexivphrase abgebaut wird.

Die Reflexivphrase *sich* erhält eine recht triviale Bedeutung:
$$V(\mathit{sich}, NP)(c) : = \{\omega: (\forall a)\omega(a)(c) = 1\} \text{ für jedes } c.$$

Wenn wir (15.4.7) auswerten, sehen wir, daß diese Bedeutung vernünftig gewählt ist:

$V(\mathit{anhimmelt}, VP(\mathit{nom}, \mathit{akk}))$ trifft auf (a,b) zu, wenn a b anhimmelt.
$V(\mathit{anhimmelt}, VP(\mathit{nom}, \mathit{akk\text{-}ref}))$ trifft nach der Semantik für die Regel (Ref 1) auf (a,b) zu, wenn a a anhimmelt.
$V(\mathit{sich\ anhimmelt})$ trifft auf a in c genau dann zu wenn λ*a(λ*b(V(*anhimmelt*, VP(*nom*,*akk-ref*))(a,b)) $\in$ V(*sich*)(c)) in c auf a zutrifft.
Diese Eigenschaft trifft auf Irena in c zu genau dann, wenn
λ*b(V(*anhimmelt*,VP(*nom*,*akk-ref*))(Irena,b)) $\in$ {ω: ($\forall a$) ω(a)(c) = 1}.
Und dies ist genau dann wahr, wenn
($\forall a$) (V(*anhimmelt*,VP(*nom*,akk-ref))(Irena,a)(c) = 1).

Nach unseren Festlegungen ist dies äquivalent damit, daß

(∀a) (V($anhimmelt$,VP(nom,akk)))(Irena,Irena)(c) = 1).

Den leerlaufenden Quantor können wir weglassen. Und wir haben so schließlich erhalten, daß (15.4.7) in c wahr ist genau dann, wenn Irena sich in c anhimmelt. Das wollten wir auch so haben.

Wir können uns nun allmählich an (13) wagen. Betrachten wir zuvor aber den etwas einfacheren Satz (15).

(15) Irena arbeitet für sich.

15.5   1. *arbeitet,* VP (*nom*) end, (M2)

2. *für,* Präp typ(benefaktiv) erg(*akk*)

3. *arbeitet,* VP (*nom,*benefaktiv) end, (PP1)*

4. *arbeitet,* VP (*nom,*benefaktiv-ref) end, (Ref 1)

5. *sich,* NP 3.*pers sg* typ(*akk-ref*))

6. *für,* Präp benefaktiv *akk*

7. *für sich,* NP 3.*pers sg* benefaktiv-ref, (Ref 2)

8. *für sich arbeitet,* VP (*nom*) end, (V1)

9. *arbeitet für sich,* VP (*nom*) zweit, (V4)

10. *Irena,* NP nom

11. *Irena arbeitet für sich,* S$_{zweit}$, (S5$_0$)

* Beim Durchlesen der Korrekturen fällt mir auf, daß es vielleicht konsequenter wäre, aus 1. und 2. zunächst *für arbeitet* abzuleiten und dieses *für* dann zu tilgen, wenn die Präpositionalphrase *für sich* an das Verb geklammert wird.

(Ref 2) ist eine ad hoc-Regel, die völlig parallel zu (N5), also der Regel für die Präpositionalergänzungen arbeitet. Wenn man die Syntax noch einmal durchgeht, wird man hier eine Vereinheitlichung schaffen können.

(Ref 2) *Reflexive Präpositionalobjekte*

$\alpha \in$ Präp typ(a) erg(b)

$\beta \in$ NP *3.pers* num(c) typ(b-*ref*)

$\alpha\beta \in$ NP *3.pers* num(c) typ(a-*ref*)

Die Bedeutung von $\alpha\beta$ ist, wie bei (N5), auch hier wieder die von β.

Man kann sich überlegen, daß (15.5.11) die richtige Bedeutung hat. V(*arbeitet*,VP(*nom,benefaktiv*)) ist die Eigenschaft, zugunsten von jemand zu arbeiten.

V(*arbeitet*,VP(*nom*,benefaktiv-*ref*) ist die Eigenschaft, zu seinen eigenen Gunsten zu arbeiten. Die Hinzufügung des reflexiven Präpositionalobjektes *für sich* ändert an dieser Eigenschaft nichts mehr. (15.5.11) drückt dementsprechend die Proposition aus, daß Irena zu ihren eigenen Gunsten arbeitet.

Wir sind nun in der Lage, uns an Satz (13) zu wagen, also an:

(13) Kasper läßt Großmutter für sich arbeiten.

Was wir hier benötigen ist eine Regel, die die Präpositionen auch für infinite Verben einführt.

(PP2) *Präpositioneneinführung für Infinitive* [85]

$\alpha \in$ VINF erg(a) hptv(δ_1,...,δ_k) sgl(a_1,...,a_e)
art(c) diat(b)

$\beta \in$ Präp typ(β_1) erg(a_1)

$\alpha \in$ VINF erg(a,β_1) hptv(δ_1,...,δ_k) sgl(a_1,...,a_e)
art(c) diat(b)

[85] Die Semantik sieht genau wie für die Regel (PP1) aus.

Wir wollen (13) auf zweierlei Weisen herleiten. Einmal soll das *sich*
den Infinitiv modifizieren und einmal das Finitum. Es ist zu hoffen, daß
dies die beiden oben erwähnten Lesarten erbringt.

15.6 ERSTE ABLEITUNG FÜR (13)

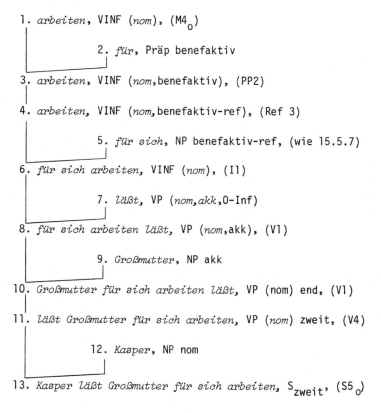

1. *arbeiten*, VINF (*nom*), (M4$_0$)

    2. *für*, Präp benefaktiv

3. *arbeiten*, VINF (*nom*,benefaktiv), (PP2)

4. *arbeiten*, VINF (*nom*,benefaktiv-ref), (Ref 3)

    5. *für sich*, NP benefaktiv-ref, (wie 15.5.7)

6. *für sich arbeiten*, VINF (*nom*), (I1)

    7. *läßt*, VP (*nom,akk*,0-Inf)

8. *für sich arbeiten läßt*, VP (*nom*,akk), (V1)

    9. *Großmutter*, NP akk

10. *Großmutter für sich arbeiten läßt*, VP (nom) end, (V1)

11. *läßt Großmutter für sich arbeiten*, VP (*nom*) zweit, (V4)

    12. *Kasper*, NP nom

13. *Kasper läßt Großmutter für sich arbeiten*, S$_{\text{zweit}}$, (S5$_0$)

Die in dieser Ableitung vorausgesetzte Regel (Ref 3) dient der Reflexivierung von Infinitiven. Sie wird völlig analog zu (Ref 1) formuliert, was ich dem Leser hier aber ersparen möchte.

Satz (15.6.13) drückt die Lesart aus, daß Kasper veranlaßt (erlaubt),
daß Großmutter zu ihren Gunsten arbeitet. Versuchen wir nun die zweite Ableitung für Satz (13).

15.7 VERSUCH DER ZWEITEN ABLEITUNG FÜR (13)

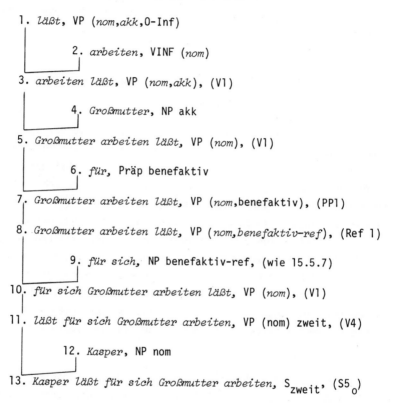

1. *läßt,* VP (*nom,akk,*O-Inf)

    2. *arbeiten,* VINF (*nom*)

3. *arbeiten läßt,* VP (*nom,akk*), (V1)

    4. *Großmutter,* NP akk

5. *Großmutter arbeiten läßt,* VP (*nom*), (V1)

    6. *für,* Präp benefaktiv

7. *Großmutter arbeiten läßt,* VP (*nom,*benefaktiv), (PP1)

8. *Großmutter arbeiten läßt,* VP (*nom,benefaktiv-ref*), (Ref 1)

    9. *für sich,* NP benefaktiv-ref, (wie 15.5.7)

10. *für sich Großmutter arbeiten läßt,* VP (*nom*), (V1)

11. *läßt für sich Großmutter arbeiten,* VP (nom) zweit, (V4)

    12. *Kasper,* NP nom

13. *Kasper läßt für sich Großmutter arbeiten,* S_{zweit}, ($S5_0$)

Hierzu ist zweierlei zu bemerken. Erstens ist (15.7.13) nicht der
Satz, den wir haben wollten. Die *für sich*-Phrase steht an der falschen
Stelle. Zweitens drückt dieser Satz nicht die Proposition aus, hinter der
wir her sind. (15.7.13) besagt nämlich, daß Kasper zu seinen Gunsten veranlaßt (gestattet), daß Großmutter arbeitet. Das ist durchaus eine ver-

nünftige Interpretation für den hergeleiteten Satz. Die Lesart, die wir
uns für (13) wünschen, lautet aber anders. Nämlich, daß Kasper veranlaßt
(gestattet), daß Großmutter zu *seinen Gunsten* arbeitet.

Ich sehe im Augenblick keine Möglichkeit, zu dieser Lesart zu kommen.
Das mag ein weiterer Anreiz sein, über die Syntax und Semantik von "lassen"
nachzudenken.

16.   ALTERNATIVE FORMULIERUNGEN DER SYNTAXREGELN:
      BACH, PARTEE, THOMASON

Ich möchte zum Schluß noch etwas zur Rolle sagen, welche die
Unterkategorien in diesem System spielen. Sie sehen zum Teil recht ad hoc
aus. Und es steht zu vermuten, daß noch weitere Unterkategorien hinzu-
kommen, wenn das Fragment erweitert wird. Das hat sich schon angedeutet,
als wir den ersten schüchternen Versuch gemacht haben, die Präpositionalphrasen mit in die Syntax einzubeziehen. Man könnte nun vermuten, daß es
zu einer Wucherung von Unterkategorien kommt, hier kein Ende abzusehen ist,
und man sie folglich irgendwie eliminieren sollte. Ich möchte gleich bemerken, daß ich an ein solches metastasierendes Krebswachstum nicht glaube.
Ich vermute, daß man mit einer Verfeinerung der "Innenstruktur" der Unterkategorien "sgl" und "hptv" ein gutes Stück weiterkommen wird. Trotzdem
möchte ich Möglichkeiten diskutieren, wie man die Regeln anders formulieren kann.

Als erstes ist zu bemerken, daß in den Unterkategorien zweierlei Art
von Information gespeichert wird: morphologische und syntaktische. Wenn
wir als Beispiel die Kategorie VP nehmen, so dienen die Unterkategorien
"per" und "num" der Aufnahme von morphologischer Information. Hier merkt
man sich einfach die Person und den Numerus des Hauptverbs der gesamten
Verbgruppe. Die Unterkategorien "erg", "sgl", "hptv", "abtr" und "stell"

beinhalten dagegen ganz klar syntaktische Information. Die morphologischen Unterkategorien lassen sich prinzipiell sehr einfach beseitigen, die syntaktischen nur mit großem Aufwand. Wie eine solche Elimination aussehen kann, will ich einmal für die morphologischen Unterkategorien der Kategorie CN vormachen.

Die Appellativgruppen werden mithilfe der Regeln (Ml$_a$) und (N4) aufgebaut. Dabei werden die komplexen Symbole

      CNST gen,

      CN   num gen cas fle   und

      ADJ num gen cas fle

benutzt.[86] Wenn ich die Unterkategorien beseitigen möchte, dann kann ich das so tun, daß ich hinfort nur noch mit den Kategoriensymbolen

      CNST, CN und ADJ

arbeite und simultan mit den Syntaxregeln die morphologischen *Eigenschaften* Numerus, Genus, Kasus und ein Adjektiv von starkem (oder schwachem) Flektionstyp bei sich zu haben rekursiv definiere. Das kann etwa folgendermaßen aussehen:

Induktionsanfang

1. Als Element der Kategorie CNST ist *Mann* ein Maskulinum.
2. Als Element der Kategorie CNST ist *Frau* ein Femininum.
3. Als Element der Kategorie CNST ist *Kind* ein Neutrum.
   etc. für die anderen 40.000 CN-Stämme des Deutschen.

[86] Die Relativsätze habe ich nicht mitberücksichtigt.

Induktionsschritte

Die Eigenschaften, ein Maskulinum, Femininum oder Neutrum zu sein, nenne ich *Genera*.

1. *Der Fall* (M_a) [87]

> Sei α ein CNST vom Genus a, β ein Element aus Kas und γ eines aus Num.
> Dann ist $\alpha\beta\gamma$ ein CN mit dem Genus a, dem Kasus
>
> Nominativ,   falls β = *nom*,
> Genitiv,   falls β = *geni*,
> Dativ,   falls β = *dat*,
> Akkusativ,   falls β = *akk*,
> und dem Numerus
> Singular,   falls γ = *sg*,
> Plural,   falls γ = *pl*.

2. *Der Fall* $(N4)$

> Sei α ein ADJ vom Genus a, dem Kasus b, dem Numerus c und von dem Flektionstyp d (d.h. stark oder schwach).
> Sei β ein CN vom Genus a, dem Kasus b, dem Numerus c.
> Ferner habe β die Eigenschaft, kein Adjektiv bei sich zu haben oder eines vom Flektionstyp d.
> Dann ist $\alpha\beta$ ein CN mit dem Genus a, dem Kasus b und dem Numerus c.
> Ferner hat $\alpha\beta$ die Eigenschaft, ein Adjektiv vom Flektionstyp d bei sich zu haben.

---

[87] Es ist klar, daß diese induktive Definition parallel zu den entsprechenden Syntaxregeln läuft. Deshalb diese Bezeichnungen.

Die morphologischen Eigenschaften für Adjektive müssen natürlich ganz
analog definiert werden wie die für Appellative.

Es ist klar, daß wir auf die vorgeführte Art und Weise sämtliche morphologischen Eigenschaften induktiv definieren können. Anstelle der in diesem Abschnitt diskutierten Symbole benötigt man dann nur noch CNST, CN,
ADJ etc. als Kategoriensymbole. Ein derartiges Vorgehen findet sich übrigens bei Bach (vgl. (5)). Bringt es irgendwelche Vorzüge gegenüber meiner
Art, die Regeln zu repräsentieren? Natürlich nicht. Beide Methoden laufen
der Sache nach genau auf dasselbe hinaus. An sich ist mir die zuletzt vorgeführte Betrachtungsweise von meiner Liebe für inhaltliche Redeweise her
lieber. Aber die Syntaxregeln und die sie begleitenden Definitionen werden
sehr lang und unübersichtlich.

Wesentlich schwieriger ist es, die syntaktischen Unterkategorien zu
eliminieren. Bei VP handelt es sich beispielsweise um "erg", "abtr", "sgl",
"hptv" und "stell". Die Beseitigung von "erg" bietet keine Schwierigkeiten.
Hier führt man einfach neue Hauptkategorien ein, die die entsprechenden
Ergänzungsmöglichkeiten widerspiegeln.[88] (Montague-Grammatiker benutzen im
Englischen oft die Kategorien IV (intransitives Verb), TV (transitives
Verb) und TTV (Verb mit zwei Objekten), aber das sind natürlich viel zu
wenige). Schwieriger ist es mit den Merkmalen "abtr", "sgl", "hptv" und
"stell". Nun, Satzglieder sind entweder NPs oder VINFs oder Nebensätze etc.
Das Hauptverb ist eine Verbalkonstruktion, und die Stellungskategorie re-
flektiert einfach die Stellung des Hauptverbkomplexes innerhalb einer syntaktischen Konstruktion. Es steht deshalb zu vermuten, daß man diese Unterkategorien los wird, wenn man auf die syntaktische Information zurück-
greift, die an jeder Stelle einer Ableitung vorhanden ist.

---

[88] Eine derartige Verbklassifizierung liegt bei Bierwisch vor.
Vgl. Bierwisch (1973).

Wie kommt man an diese Information heran? B. Partee meint, daß man für
die Formulierung von Syntaxregeln sich nicht die ganze Komplexität des jeweils Erreichten merken müsse. Es genüge,die Konstituentenstruktur mitzuschleppen.[89] Ich halte dieses Vorgehen nicht für praktisch. Im Zusammenhang mit Umstellungsregeln treten hier nämlich ganz genau dieselben Schwierigkeiten auf, die ich bei Bierwischs System diskutiert habe. Ich will das
kurz skizzieren. Wenn es um die Ableitung eines Satzes wie des folgenden
geht:

> (1) Einen Rettich vertrauten wir Kasper an,

dann sähe eine Ableitung in unserem System unter Benutzung des Vorschlages
von B. Partee folgendermaßen aus:

16.1 1. $(anvertrauten)_{VP_{(nom,dat,akk)}}$, (M2)

2. $((einen)_Q(Rettich)_{CN})_{NP}$, (N2)

3. $(((einen)_Q(Rettich)_{CN})_{NP}(anvertrauten)_{VP_{(nom,dat,akk)}})_{VP_{(nom,dat)}}$

4. $(Kasper)_{NP}$, (wie 6.2.2)

5. $((Kasper)_{NP}(((einen)_Q(Rettich)_{CN})_{NP}(anvertrauten)_{VP_{\substack{nom\\dat\\akk}}})_{VP_{\substack{nom\\dat}}})_{VP_{nom}}$

---

[89] Vgl. etwa Partee (1977).

Bevor ich etwas dazu sage, wie es hier weitergeht, ein Zwischenkommentar. Die etikettierten Klammern sind natürlich Bäume. Wie etikettierte Klammerausdrücke mengentheoretisch genau konstruiert werden, das will ich hier übergehen. Man lese einmal Abschnitt 3 durch und mache das dann für sich selbst. Syntaktische Regeln machen jetzt nicht mehr aus Zeichenketten neue Zeichenketten, sondern aus Konstituentenbäumen neue. Man sieht an (16.1) anschaulich ganz genau, was hier vor sich geht. Ich verzichte deshalb auf eine exakte Formulierung der Regeln. Technisch besteht hier kein Problem. Und diese Formulierung versetzt uns nun vielleicht tatsächlich in die Lage, die Unterkategorien loszuwerden. Wir müssen irgendwie rekursiv über die Verbregeln definieren, daß

$$(Kasper)_{NP}$$

und

$$((einen)_Q (Rettich)_{CN})_{NP}$$

Satzglieder von (16.1.5) sind, und daß

$$(anvertrauten)_{VP}{}_{(nom,dat,akk)}$$

das Hauptverb von (16.1.5) ist. Es ist vollkommen klar, daß man das machen kann. Allerdings werden derartige Definitionen sehr kompliziert, weil man den gesamten möglichen syntaktischen Aufbau von Verbalkonstruktionen berücksichtigen muß.

Ganz ähnlich wie bei den morphologischen Merkmalen wird auch hier die Rekursion alle einschlägigen Verbregeln parallelisieren müssen. Ich kann das leider hier nicht vorführen, weil ich wegen Platzüberschreitung ohnehin schon ein ganz schlechtes Gewissen gegenüber den Herausgebern des Sammelbandes habe, in dem dieser aus allen Nähten geplatzte Aufsatz erscheinen soll.

Hat man nun einmal die Unterkategorien "hptv" und analog auch "sgl"
und "stell" durch das Definieren von entsprechenden syntaktischen Eigenschaften eliminiert, dann kann man hoffen, auch die Unterkategorie "abtr"
loszuwerden. Die hier gespeicherte Information hängt vermutlich direkt von
den bereits genannten syntaktischen Eigenschaften ab.

So, angenommen, dies gelingt alles. Wie führt man dann die Ableitung
(16.1.5) weiter, um unseren Beispielsatz

(2) Einen Rettich vertrauten wir Kasper an

zu erhalten? Um dies zu wissen, müssen wir uns überlegen, wie die Konstituentenstruktur dieses Satzes aussieht. In Abschnitt 3 haben wir aber bereits gesehen, daß es keine plausible Konstituentenstruktur dafür gibt.
Noch weniger natürlich für den Satz:

(3) Vertrauten wir Kasper einen Rettich an?

Mit anderen Worten, B. Partee gerät hier in genau dieselben Schwierigkeiten, in die M. Bierwisch mit seinem transformationellen Ansatz gekommen
ist. Und die wollte ich gerade vermeiden.
Allerdings kann man Barbara Partees Idee vielleicht doch retten, wenn man
eine ärmere Struktur mitschleppt, als es die Konstituentenstruktur ist.
Diese Struktur müßte genau die Information enthalten, die bei mir in den
"syntaktischen" Unterkategorien steckt. So ein Vorgehen würde meine Unterkategorien entlasten, weil dann die Information eben woanders steht.

Konsequent ist das Vorgehen von R. Thomason, der die Syntaxregeln
prinzipiell an jeder Stelle der Ableitung auf die gesamten bisher vorhandenen Ableitungsbäume anwendet.[90] Als Resultat erhält man wieder einen
Ableitungsbaum. Das ist das brutalste syntaktische Vorgehen, das überhaupt
denkbar ist, und B. Partee möchte es mit ihrem Kunstgriff umgehen, weil
es ihr um Beschränkungen geht, deren Syntaxregeln einer natürlichen

---

[90] Vgl. Thomason (1976).

Sprache möglicherweise unterliegen. Trotzdem führt Thomasons Vorgehen nicht in die Schwierigkeiten, mit denen es jeder zu tun bekommt, der die Konstituentenstruktur partout retten möchte. Die Thomasonschen Regeln sind außerordentlich kompliziert zu formulieren, wenn man das ernsthaft tun wollte. Ich lasse es deswegen bei dieser Bemerkung bewenden, obwohl es mich reizen würde, dazu noch mehr zu sagen.

17.   ÜBERSICHT ÜBER DIE REGELN DES FRAGMENTES

Satz

Relativsatz

Passiv

Modale Hilfsverben

18.   LITERATUR

(1) Admoni, W.: *Der deutsche Sprachbau.* 3. Auflage, München 1970.

(2) Bach, E.: *The order of elements in a transformational grammar of German.* In: *Language,* Vol. 38, 1962, 263-269.

(3) Bach, E.: *Rezension von Bierwischs "Grammatik des deutschen Verbs".* In: *Language,* Vol. 40, 605-615.

(4) Bach, E.: *Montague   Grammar and Classical Transformational Grammar.* In: *Conference on Montague Grammar, Philosophy and Linguistics.* State University of New York, Albany, April 23-24, 1977.

(5) Bach, E.: *A Framework for Syntax and Semantics.* Mimeo, Amherst 1976(?)

(5a) Bartsch, R.: *Adverbialsemantik.* Frankfurt/M. 1972: Athenäum.

(6) Bäuerle, R.: *Tempus, Temporaladverb und temporale Frage.* Diss., Konstanz 1977.

(7) Bennett, M.R.: *Some Extensions of a Montague Fragment of English.* Diss., University of California, Los Angeles 1974.

(8) Bierwisch, M.: *Grammatik des deutschen Verbs.* Studia Grammatica II, 8. Aufl. 1973.

(9) Blatz, F.: *Neuhochdeutsche Grammatik.* Karlsruhe 1895; Nachdruck: Olms 1970.

(10) Boost, K.: *Neuere Untersuchungen zum Wesen und zur Struktur des deutschen Satzes.* Berlin 5. Auflage 1964.

(11) Brockhaus, K. und v. Stechow, A.: *On Formal Semantics: a New Approach.* In: *Linguistische Berichte 11,* 7-36, 1971.

(12) Carlson, G.N.: *Reference to kinds in English*. Diss., Amherst (Mass.), 1977.

(13) Chomsky, N. und Halle, M.: *The Sound Pattern of English*. New York - Evanston - London, 1968.

(14) Clément, D. und Thümmel, W.: *Grundzüge einer Syntax der deutschen Standardsprache*. Frankfurt 1975.

(15) Cooper, R. und Parsons, T.: *Montague Grammar, Generative Semantics and Interpretive Semantics*. In (48), 1976.

(16) Cresswell, M.J.: *Logics and Languages*. London 1973.

(17) Davidson, D. und Harman, G.: *Semantics of Natural Language*. Dordrecht 1972 (Reidel).

(18) Drach, E.: *Grundgedanken der deutschen Satzlehre*. Frankfurt/M., 3. Auflage 1940.

(19) Dudengrammatik, Mannheim 1973.

(20) Egli, U.: *Ansätze zur Integration der Semantik in der Grammatik*. Frankfurt/M. (Scriptor), 1974.

(21) Engel, U.: *Regeln zur Satzgliedfolge*. In: Hugo Moser u.a. (hrsg.), *Linguistische Studien I* (= Sprache der Gegenwart 19), Düsseldorf 1972, 17-75.

(22) Engelen, B.: *Der Relativsatz*. In: *Neue Beiträge zur deutschen Grammatik*. Duden Beiträge 37, Mannheim 1969.

(23) Engelen, B.: *Untersuchungen zu Satzbauplan und Wortfeld in der geschriebenen deutschen Sprache der Gegenwart*. Forschungsberichte des IDS, Band 3, 1973.

(24) Erben, J.: *Abriß der deutschen Grammatik*. Berlin 1964[7].

(25) Flämig, W.: *Grundformen der Gliedfolge im deutschen Satz und ihre sprachlichen Funktionen*. In: *Beiträge zur Geschichte der deutschen Sprache und Literatur*, Bd. 86, Halle/Saale 1960.

(26) Fourquet, J.: *Zur neuhochdeutschen Wortstellung*. In: *Das Ringen um eine neue deutsche Grammatik*. Darmstadt 1962.

(27) Gabbay, D.M. und Kasher, A.: *On the Semantics and Pragmatics of Specific and Non-Specific Indefinite Expressions*. in: *Theoretical Linguistics*, 1976(?)

(28) Ginsburg, S. und Partee, B.H.: *A Mathematical Model of Transformational Grammars*. In: *Information and Control 15*, 1969, 292-334.

(29) Glinz, H.: *Deutsche Grammatik I und II*. Frankfurt 1970.

(30) Groenendijk, J. und Stokhof, M.: *Epistemic Pragmatics: Outlines and two Applications*. Mimeo, Amsterdam 1977.

(31) Helbig, G. und Schenkel, W.: *Wörterbuch zur Valenz und Distribution deutscher Verben*. Leipzig 1969.

(32) Jørgensen, P.: *Tysk Grammatik*. 6. Auflage, København 1976.

(33) Kaiser, G.: *Zur Semantik polarer Adjektive*. In: Arbeitspapiere des SFB 99 "Linguistik", Konstanz 1978.

(34) Kaplan, D.: *Demonstratives. An Essay on the Semantics, Logics, Metaphysics and Epistemology of Demonstratives and Other Indexicals*. Mimeo, (UCLA), März 1977.

(35) Klein, W.: *Untersuchungen zu den Stellungsmöglichkeiten des Demon-
strativums "settig" im Oberbrienzer Dialekt der Axalp während der
Jahre 1976 und 1977*. In: *Supplementa zum Brienzer Idiotikon*.
Stähle-Hüggeler Verlag, Brienz 1978.

(36) Kratzer, A.: *Kontexttheorie*. In: Arbeitspapiere des SFB 99 "Linguistik", Konstanz 1977.

(37) Kratzer, A.: *Modale*. In: Arbeitspapiere des SFB 99 "Linguistik",
Konstanz 1977.

(38) Kratzer, A. und v. Stechow, A.: *Äußerungssituation und Bedeutung*.
In: *Zeitschrift für Linguistik und Literaturwissenschaft*, Heft 23/24,
1977.

(39) Kratzer, A. und Pause, E. und v. Stechow, A.: *Einführung in Theorie
und Anwendung der generativen Syntax*. Frankfurt 1974.

(40) Lakoff, G.: *Linguistics and Natural Logic*. 1972, in (17).

(41) Lewis, D.: *General Semantics*. 1972, in (17).

(42) Lewis, D.: *Adverbs of Quantification*. In: E. Keenan (ed.): *Formal
Semantics of Natural Language*, Cambridge 1975.

(43) Montague, R.: *English as a formal language*. In: Linguaggi 1969.

(44) Montague, R.: *The Proper Treatment of Quantification in Ordinary
English*. In: Hintikka & Moravcsik & Suppes (Hrsg.): *Approaches to
Natural Language*, 1973.

(45) Montague, R.: *Formal Philosophy*. (hrsg. von R.M. Thomason, New Haven
and London, Yale University Press, 1974.

(46) Partee, B.: *Montague Grammar and Transformational Grammar*. In: *Linguistic Inquiry*, Vol. VI, 1975.

(47) Partee, B.: *Montague Grammar and the Well-Formedness Constraint*. L.A.U.T., No. 45, 1977.

(48) Partee, B.: *Montague Grammar*. New York - San Francisco - London (Academic Press), 1976.

(49) Pause, E.: *Zur Theorie transformationeller Syntaxen*. Athenaion, Frankfurt/M. 1976.

(50) Peters, P.St. und Ritchie, R.W.: *On the Generative Power of Transformational Grammars*. In: *Information Sciences 6*, 1973, 49-83.

(51) Pütz, H.: *Über die Syntax der Pronominalform 'es' im modernen Deutsch*. Paris (DRLAV), 1973.

(52) Quine, W.V.O.: *Variables explained away*. In: *Proceedings of the American Philosophical Society 104*, 1960, 343-347.

(53) Reis, M.: *Reflexivierung in deutschen A.c.I.-Konstruktionen. Ein transformationsgrammatisches Dilemma*. In: *Papiere zur Linguistik*, Vol. 8, Frankfurt 1976 (Scriptor).

(54) Rodman, R.: *"Scope Phenomena, "Movement Transformation" and Relative Clauses"*. in (48).

(55) Ruttenberg, J.: *Some difficulties with Cresswell's Semantics and the method of shallow structure*. In: u/mass *Occasional papers in linguistics*, Vol. II, 1976.

(56) Schpak-Dolt, N.: *Zur Semantik von Tempus und Aspekt des Russischen im Rahmen einer λ-kategorialen Sprache*. Diss., Konstanz 1977.

(57) Smaby, R.: *Ambiguity of Pronouns; A Simple Case*. University of
Pennsylvania, October 1975, Mimeo.

(58) Smaby, R.: *Ambiguous Coreference with Quantifiers*. Mimeo: University
of Pennsylvania, Juni 1976.

(59) von Stechow, A.: *Zur formalen Syntax und Semantik des Deutschen*. In:
Arbeitspapiere des SFB 99 "Linguistik", Konstanz 1975.

(60) von Stechow, A.: *Deutsche Wortstellung und λ-kategoriale Sprachen*.
Mimeo, Konstanz 1976.

(61) von Stechow, A.: *Semantische Präsuppositionen*. In: Arbeitspapiere
des SFB 99 "Linguistik", Konstanz 1977.

(62) von Stechow, A.: *Occurrence-Interpretation and Context-Theory*.
In: Arbeitspapiere des SFB 99 "Linguistik", Konstanz 1977.

(63) Steinitz, R.: *Adverbialsyntax*. Studia Grammatica X, Berlin 1969.

(64) Thomason, Richmond H.: *Some Extensions of Montague Grammar*. in (48).

(65) Wurzel, W.U.: *Studien zur deutschen Lautstruktur*. Berlin (DDR) 1970;
Studia Grammatica VIII.

INDEX OF SUBJECTS

Please note that the items appearing in Arnim von Stechow's paper
are in italics.

REFERENCES

Admoni, W. 1970. *Der deutsche Sprachbau*. 3rd. ed. Munich: Beck.

Akmajian, A., and F. Heny. 1976. *An Introduction to the Principles of Transformational Syntax*. Cambridge/Mass.: MIT Press.

Anderson, J. M. 1971. *The Grammar of Case: Towards a Localistic Theory*. London: Cambridge University Press.

-----. 1976. *On Serialization in English Syntax*. Ludwigsburg: Ludwigsburg Studies in Language and Linguistics 1.

-----. 1977. *On Case Grammar*. London: Cromm Helm.

Anderson, J., and C. Jones (eds.). 1974. *Historical Linguistics*. 2 vols. Amsterdam: North-Holland Publ. Co.

Anderson, S. R., and P. Kiparsky (eds.). 1973. *A Festschrift for Morris Halle*. New York: Holt, Rinehart & Winston.

Antinucci, F. 1977. *Fondamenti di une teoria tipologica del linguaggio*. Bologna: Il Mulino.

Bach, E. 1962. "The Order of Elements in a Transformational Grammar of German". *Language* 38: 263-269.

-----. 1964. Review of M. Bierwisch, *Grammatik des deutschen Verbs* (1964). *Language* 40: 605-615.

-----. 1965. "On Some Recurrent Types of Transformations." *Georgetown University Monograph Series on Language and Linguistics* 18: 3-18.

-----. 1968. "Two Proposals Concerning the Simplicity Metric in Phonology". *Glossa* 2: 128-149.

-----. 1970. "Is Amharic an SOV Language?" *Journal of Ethiopian Studies* 8: 9-20.

-----. 1975. "Order in Base Structure." In: C. N. Li (ed.) 1975: 307-343.

-----. 1976. *A Framework for Syntax and Semantics*. Mimeo. Amherst, Mass.

-----. 1977. "Montague Grammar and Classical Transformational Grammar", In: *Conference on Montague Grammar, Philosophy and Linguistics*. State University of New York, Albany, April 23-24, 1977.

Bach, E., and R. T. Harms (eds.). 1968. *Universals in Linguistic Theory.* New York: Holt, Rinehart & Winston.

Bartsch, R. 1972. *Adverbialsemantik.* Frankfurt/Main: Athenäum.

Bartsch, R., and T. Vennemann. 1972. *Semantic Structures.* Frankfurt/M.: Athenäum.

Bäuerle, R. 1977. *Tempus, Temporaladverb und temporale Frage.* Doctoral Diss., Univ. of Konstanz.

Bennett, M. R. 1974. *Some Extensions of a Montague Fragment of English.* Ph.D. Diss. University of California, Los Angeles.

Berman, A. 1973. "A Constraint on Tough-movement", *CLS* 9: 34-43.

-----. 1974. "On the VSO Hypothesis". *Linguistic Inquiry* 5: 1-38.

Bierwisch, M. 1963. *Grammatik des deutschen Verbs.* Berlin.

Bierwisch, M., and K. Heidolph. 1970. *Progress in Linguistics.* The Hague: Mouton.

Blatz, F. 1895. *Neuhochdeutsche Grammatik.* Karlsruhe. (Repr., Hildesheim: Olms, 1970.)

Boas, H. U. 1975. *Syntactic Generalizations and Linear Order in Generative Transformational Grammar.* Tübingen: TBL-Verlag Gunter Narr.

Bolinger, D. 1972. "Accent Is Predictable (If You're a Mind-reader)". *Language* 48: 633-644.

Boost, K. 1964. *Neuere Untersuchungen zum Wesen und zur Struktur des deutschen Satzes.* 5th ed. Berlin: Akad. Verlag.

Brainerd, B. 1976. "On the Markov Nature of Text". *Linguistics* 176: 5-30.

Brame, M. K. 1976. *Conjectures and Refutations in Syntax and Semantics.* Amsterdam: North-Holland, Publ. Co.

Bresnan, J. 1970. "On Complementizers: Toward a Syntactic Theory of Complement Types". *Foundations of Language* 6: 297-321.

-----. 1971. "Sentence Stress and Syntactic Transformations". *Language* 47: 257-281.

-----. 1972. "Sentence Stress and Syntactic Transformations". *Language* 48: 326-342.

-----. 1975. "Transformations and Categories in Syntax". In: Butts and Hintikka (eds.) 1975: 261-282.

Brockhaus, K., and v. Stechow, A. 1971. "On Formal Semantics: A New Approach". *Linguistische Berichte* 11: 7-36.

Burt, M. K. 1971. *From Deep to Surface Structure: An Introduction to Transformational Syntax.* New York & London: Harper & Row.

Butts, R. E. and J. Hintikka (eds.). 1975. *Logic, Methodology and Philosophy of Science.* Dordrecht: Reidel.

REFERENCES

Byarushengo, E. R. and S. Tanenbaum. 1976. "Agreement and Word-Order: A Case for Pragmatics in Haya". *BLS* 2: 89-99.

Carlson, G. N. 1977, *Reference to Kinds in English*. Diss. Amherst/Mass.

Chafe, W. L. 1970. *Meaning and the Structure of Language*. Chicago & London: University of Chicago Press.

Chomsky, N. 1956. "Three Models for the Description of Language". *I.R.E. Transactions on Information Theory. Vol. IT-2*. Proceedings of the Symposium on Information Theory: 113-124.

-----. 1957. *Syntactic Structures*. The Hague: Mouton.

-----. 1964. *Current Issues in Linguistic Theory*. The Hague: Mouton.

-----. 1965. *Aspects of the Theory of Syntax*. Cambridge/Mass.: MIT Press.

-----. 1968. *Language and Mind*. New York: Harcourt, Brace & World.

-----. 1973. "Conditions on Transformations". In: S. R. Anderson and P. Kiparsky (eds.) 1973: 232-286.

-----. 1975. *Reflections on Language*. New York: Pantheon Books.

-----. 1976. "Conditions on Rules of Grammar". *Linguistic Analysis* 2: 303-351.

-----. 1977. "On Wh-movement". In: P. Culicover, T. Wasow and A. Akmajian (eds.) 1977: 71-132.

-----, and M. Halle. 1968. *The Sound Pattern of English*. New York & London: Harper & Row.

Clément, D., and W. Thümmel. 1975. *Grundzüge einer Syntax der deutschen Standardsprache*. Wiesbaden: Athenaion.

Cole, P. and J. Sadock (eds.) 1977. *Syntax and Semantics*. Vol. 8: *Grammatical Relations*. New York & London: Academic Press.

Contreras, H. 1976. *A Theory of Word Order with Special Reference to Spanish*. Amsterdam: North-Holland. Publ. Co.

Cooper, R., and T. Parsons. 1976. "Montague Grammar, Generative Semantics and Interpretive Semantics". In: B. Partee. 1976: 311-362.

Corum, C. T., Smith-Stark, T. C. and Weiser, A. (eds.) 1973. *You take the High Node and I'll Take the Low Node*. Chicago: Chicago Linguistic Society.

Cresswell, M. J. 1973. *Logics and Languages*. London: Methuen.

Culicover, P., Wasow, T., and A. Akmajian (eds.) 1977. *Formal Syntax*. New York & London: Academic Press.

Dahl, Ö. 1976. "What Is New Information?" In: N. Enkvist and V. Kohonen (eds.) 1976: 38-50.

Davidson, D., and G. Harman. 1972. *Semantics of Natural Language*. Dordrecht: Reidel.

Derbyshire, D. 1977. "Word Order Universals and the Existence of OVS Languages". *Linguistic Inquiry* 8: 590-599.

de Rijk, R. P. G. 1974. "A Note on Prelexical Predicate-Raising". In: P. A. M. Seuren 1974: 43-74.

Dickinson, L. and R. Mackin. 1969. *Varieties of Spoken English: Workbook.* London: Oxford University Press.

Dik, S. C. 1968. *Co-ordination.* Amsterdam: North-Holland Publ. Co.

Dixon, R. M. W. 1972. *The Dyirbal Language of North Queensland.* London: Cambridge University Press.

Drach, E. 1940. *Grundgedanken der deutschen Satzlehre.* 3rd ed. Frankfurt/M.

Dudengrammatik. 1973. 3rd. rev. ed. Mannheim: Duden Verlag.

Egli, E. 1974. *Ansätze zur Integration der Semantik in der Grammatik.* Frankfurt/M.: Scriptor.

Emonds, J. E. 1970, *Root and Structure Preserving Transformations.* Bloomington: Indiana University Linguistics Club.

-----. 1976. *A Transformational Approach to English Syntax.* New York & London: Academic Press.

Engel, U. 1972. "Regeln zur Satzgliedfolge". In: H. Moser et al. (eds.) 1972. *Linguistische Studien I* (= Sprache der Gegenwart, 19.) Düsseldorf: Schwann: 17-75.

Engelen, B. 1969. "Der Relativsatz". *Neue Beiträge zur deutschen Grammatik.* Duden Beiträge 37. Mannheim: Duden-Verlag.

-----. 1973. *Untersuchungen zu Satzbauplan und Wortfeld in der geschriebenen deutschen Sprache der Gegenwart.* Mannheim.

Enkvist, N. 1976. "Prolegomena to a Symposium on 'The Interaction of Parameters Affecting Word Order'". In: N. Enkvist and V. Kohonen (eds.) 1976: 5-13.

-----., and V. Kohonen (eds.) 1976. *Reports on Text Linguistics: Approaches to Word Order.* Åbo: Publications of the Research Institute of the Åbo Akademi Foundation 8.

Erben, J. 1964. *Abriß der deutschen Grammatik.* 7th ed. Berlin: Akad.-Vlg.

Fillmore, Ch. 1965. *Indirect Object Constructions in English and the Ordering of Transformations.* The Hague: Mouton.

-----. 1966. "Towards a Modern Theory of Case". *POLA* 13: 1-24. Columbus: Ohio State University.

-----. 1968. "The Case for Case". In: E. Bach and R. T. Harms (eds.) 1968: 1-88.

-----. 1977. "The Case for Case Reopened". In: P. Cole and J. Sadock (eds.) 1977: 59-81.

Flämig, W. 1960. "Grundformen der Gliedfolge im deutschen Satz und ihre
    sprachlichen Funktionen". *Beiträge zur Geschichte der deutschen Sprache
    und Literatur* 86. Halle/Saale.

Fourquet, J. 1962. "Zur neuhochdeutschen Wortstellung". *Das Ringen um
    eine neue deutsche Grammatik*. Darmstadt: Wissensch. Buchgesellschaft.

Gabbay, D. M., and A. Kasher. 1976. "On the Semantics and Pragmatics of
    Specific and Non-specific Indefinite Expressions". *Theoretical
    Linguistics*.

Ginsburg, S., and B. H. Partee. 1969. "A Mathematical Model of Transfor-
    mational Grammars". *Information and Control* 15: 292-334.

Glinz, H. 1970. *Deutsche Grammatik I und II*. Frankfurt/M.: Athenäum
    Verlag.

Green, J. 1976. "How Free Is Word Order in Spanish?". In: M. B. Harris
    (ed.) 1976: 7-32.

Greenberg, J. H. 1963a. "Some Universals of Grammar with Particular Re-
    ference to the Order of Meaningful Elements". In: J. H. Greenberg 1963b:
    73-113.

-----. 1963b. *Universals of Language*. 2nd ed. Cambridge/Mass.: MIT Press.

Groendijk, J., and M. Strokhof. 1977. *Epistemic Pragmatics: Outline and
    Two Applications*. Amsterdam. Mimeo.

Gruber, J. 1976. *Lexical Structures in Syntax and Semantics*. Amsterdam:
    North-Holland Publ. Co.

Gundel, J. 1975. "Left-Dislocation and the Role of Topic-Comment Structure
    in Linguistic Theory". *Ohio State University Working Papers in Ling-
    uistics* 18: 72-131.

Hall, B. 1964. Review of Saumjan & Soboleva (1963). *Language* 40: 397-410.

-----, and R. M. R. Hall and L. P. Sheerin. 1973. "NP Climbing in Classical
    Greek". Paper read at the LSA Winter Meeting.

-----, and R. M. R. Hall. 1978. Dinka, Mabaan, and the Penthouse Principle.
    Ms.

Halliday, M., and R. Hasan. 1976. *Cohesion in English*. London: Longman.

Halmos, P. R. 1960. *Naive Set Theory*. New York: Van Nostrand Co.

Hankamer, J. 1974. "On the Non-Cyclic Nature of WH-Clefting". *CLS* 10: 221-233.

Harris, M. B. (ed.) 1976. *Romance Syntax: Synchronic and Diachronic Per-
    spectives*. Salford: Salford Univ.

Harris, Z. S. 1952. "Discourse Analysis". *Language* 28: 474-494.

-----. 1957. "Co-Occurrence and Transformation in Linguistic Structure".
    Language 33: 283-340.

Helbig, G., and W. Schenkel. 1969. *Wörterbuch zur Valenz und Distribution
    deutscher Verben*. Leipzig: Verlag Enzyklopädie.

Hetzron, R. 1975. "The Presentative Movement, or Why the Ideal Word Order
    Is V.S.O.P.". In: C. N. Li (ed.) 1975: 346-388.

Higgins, F. R. 1976. *The Pseudo-Cleft Construction in English.* I.U.L.C.

Hintikka, J., Moravcsik, J. M. E., and P. Suppes (eds.). 1973. *Approaches to Natural Language.* Dordrecht: Reidel.

Hockett, C. F. 1954. "Two Models of Grammatical Description". *Word* 10: 210-321.

-----. 1958. *A Course in Modern Linguistics.* New York: Macmillan.

Horn, G. 1972. "Generalizing the Sentential Subject Constraint". Paper delivered at the New England Linguistic Society. Amherst/Mass.

Horn, W. (ed.). 1924. *Beiträge zur germanischen Sprachwissenschaft. (Festschrift für Otto Behaghel).* Heidelberg: Carl Winter.

Horvath, J. 1976. "Focus in Hungarian and the X Notation". *Linguistic Analysis* 2: 175-197.

Householder, F. W. (ed.). 1971. *Syntactic Theory 1.* Harmondsworth: Penguin.

Huddleston, R. 1976. *An Introduction to English Transformational Syntax.* London: Longman.

Hudson, G. 1972. "Why Is Amharic Not a VSO Language?". *Studies in African Linguistics* 3: 127-165.

-----. 1975. *Suppletion in the Representation of Alternations.* UCLA PhD Dissertation. Ann Arbor: University Microfilms.

Hudson, R. A. 1976. *Arguments for a Non-Transformational Grammar.* Chicago & London: Chicago University Press.

Hyman, L. M. 1975. "On the Change from SOV to SVO: Evidence from Niger-Congo". In: C.N. Li (ed.). 1975: 113-147.

Jackendorff, R., and P. Culicover. 1971. "A Reconsideration of Dative Movements". *Foundations of Language* 3: 397-412.

-----. 1972. *Semantic Interpretation in Generative Grammar.* Cambridge/Mass.: MIT Press.

-----. 1975. "Tough and the Trace Theory of Movement Rules". *Linguistic Inquiry* 6: 437-447.

-----. 1977. $\overline{X}$ *-Syntax.* (Linguistic Inquiry Monograph Series 2.) Cambridge/Mass.: MIT Press.

Jespersen, Otto. 1909-1949. *A Modern English Grammar.* London: George Allen & Unwin.

Johnson, D. 1977. "On Relational Constraints in Grammars". In: P. Cole and J. M. Sadock (eds.). 1977: 151-178.

Jørgensen, P. 1976. *Tysk Grammatik.* 6th ed. Copenhagen.

Kaiser, G. 1978. "Zur Semantik polarer Adjektive". *Arbeitspapiere des SFB 99 "Linguistik".* Konstanz: Univ. of Konstanz.

Kaplan, D. 1977. *Demonstratives: An Essay on the Semantics, Logics, Metaphysics and Epistemology of Demonstratives and Other Indexicals.* Univ. of California, Los Angeles. Mimeo.

Keenan, E. (ed.). 1975. *Formal Semantics of Natural Language.* Cambridge: Cambridge University Press.

Keenan, E. and B. Comrie. 1976. "Towards a Universal Definition of 'Subject'". In: C. N. Li (ed.). 1976: 303-333.

-----. 1972. "Noun Phrase Accessibility and Universal Grammar". *Linguistic Inquiry* 8 (1977): 63-99.

Kinchin-Smith, F. 1948. *Teach Yourself Latin*. London: Hodder & Stoughton.

Klein, W. 1978. "Untersuchungen zu den Stellungsmöglichkeiten des Demonstrativums 'setting' im Oberbrienzer Dialekt der Axalp während der Jahre 1976 und 1977". In: *Supplementa zum Brienzer Idiotikon*. Brienz: Stähle-Hüggeler Verlag.

Koutsoudas, A. 1971. "Gapping, Conjunction Reduction, and Coordinate Deletion". *Foundations of Language* 3: 337-386.

-----. 1972. "The Strict Order Fallacy". *Language* 48: 88-96.

Kratzer, A. 1977. "Kontexttheorie". In: *Arbeitspapiere des SFB 99 'Linguistik'*. Konstanz: Univ. of Konstanz.

-----. 1977. "Modale". In: *Arbeitspapiere des SFB 99 'Linguistik'*. Ibid.

----- und v. Stechow, A. 1977. "Äußerungssituation und Bedeutung". *Zeitschrift für Literaturwissenschaft und Linguistik* 22/23.

-----, E. Pause und A. v. Stechow. 1974. *Einführung in Theorie und Anwendung der generativen Syntax*. Frankfurt/M.: Athenäum.

Kuno, S. 1974. "The Position of Relative Clauses and Conjunctions". *Linguistic Inquiry* 5: 117-136.

-----. 1973. *The Structure of the Japanese Language*. Cambridge/Mass.: MIT Press.

Lakoff, G. 1970. *Irregularity in Syntax*. New York: Holt, Rinehart & Winston.

-----. 1971. "On Generative Semantics". In: D. Steinberg and L. Jakobovits (eds.). 1971: 232-296.

-----. 1972. "Linguistics and Natural Logic". In: D. Davidson and G. Harman 1972: 545-665.

Langacker, R. W. 1969. "Mirror Image Rules". *Language* 45: 575-598 and 844-862.

-----. 1972. Review of Chafe (1970). *Language* 48: 134-161.

-----. 1974. "Movement Rules in Functional Perspective". *Language* 50: 630-634.

-----. 1976. "Semantic Representations and the Linguistic Relativity Hypothesis". *Foundations of Language* 14: 307-357.

Lasnik, H. and Fiengo, R. 1974. "Complement Object Deletion". *Linguistic Inquiry* 5: 535-572.

Lawler, J. 1977. "A Agrees with B in Achenese: A Problem for Relational Grammar". In: P. Cole and J. M. Sadock (eds.) 1977: 219-248.

Lehmann, T. 1972. "Some Arguments against Ordered Rules". *Language* 48: 541-550.

Lehmann, W. P. 1973. "A Structural Principle of Language and Its Implications". *Language* 49: 47-66.

-----. 1974. *Proto-Indo-European Syntax*. Austin: University of Texas Press.

Leslau, W. 1968. *An Amharic Reference Grammar*. UCLA. Mimeo.

Levine, A. 1971. *Penguin English Reader*. Harmondsworth: Penguin.

Lewis, D. 1972. "General Semantics". In: Davidson & Harman 1972: 169-218.

-----. 1975. "Adverbs of Quantification". In: Keenan 1975.

Li, C. N. (ed.) 1975. *Word Order and Word Order Change*. Austin: University of Texas Press.

-----. (ed.) 1976. *Subject and Topic*. New York and London: Academic Press.

----- and S. Thompson. 1976. "Subject and Topic: A New Typology of Language". In: C. N. Li (ed.) 1976: 457-489.

Lyons, J. 1977. *Semantics 1 and 2*. London: Cambridge University Press.

Macdonell, A. A. 1927. *Sanskritt Grammar*. 3rd. ed. Oxford: Oxford UP.

Maling, J. 1972. "On Gapping and the Order of Constituents". *Linguistic Inquiry* 3: 101-108.

Marouzeau, J. 1948. "Quelques vues sur l'ordre des mots en latin". *Lingua* 1: 155-161.

Matthews, G. H. 1967. "Le Cas échéant". Institute of Technology, Cambridge/Mass.: Unpublished mimeo, Massachusetts.

Matthews, P. H. 1972. *Inflectional Morphology*. London: Cambridge University Press.

Maurer, F. 1924. "Zur Anfangsstellung des Verbs im Deutschen". In: W. Horn (ed.) 1924.

-----. 1926. *Untersuchungen über die deutsche Verbstellung in ihrer geschichtlichen Entwicklung*. Heidelberg: Carl Winter.

McCawley, J. D. 1970. "English as a VSO Language". *Language* 46: 286-299.

-----. 1973. *Grammar and Meaning*. Tokyo: Taishukan.

Meillet, A. 1912. "L'évolution des formes grammaticales". In: A. Meillet 1926: 130-148.

-----. 1926. *Linguistique historique et linguistique générale*. Paris: Champion.

Montague, R. 1969. "English as a Formal Language". *Linguaggi nella soc.*: 189-223.

Montague, R. 1973. "The Proper Treatment of Quantification in Ordinary English". In: J. Hintikka, J. M. E. Moravcsik and P. Suppes (eds.) 1973: 221-242.

-----. 1974. *Formal Philosophy*. New Haven & London: Yale University Press.

Newmeyer, F. J. 1976. "The Precyclic Nature of Predicate Raising". In: M. Shibatani 1976: 131-163.

Olsvanger, I. 1947. *Röyte Pomerantsen*. New York: Schocken Books.

Palmer, F. 1964. "'Sequence' and 'Order'". In F. Householder (ed.) 1971: 140-147.

Parisi, D. and F. Antinucci 1976. *Essentials of Grammar*. New York and London: Academic Press (English Translation of D. Parisi and F. Antinucci 1973. *Elementi di grammatica*. Turin: Boringhieri.)

Partee, B. H. 1975. "Montague Grammar and Transformational Grammar". *Linguistic Inquiry* 6: 203-300.

-----. (ed.) 1976. *Montague Grammar*. New York and London: Academic Press.

-----. 1977. "Montague Grammar and the Well-Formedness Constraint". Trier: L.A.U.T. Mimeo.

Pause, E. 1976. *Zur Theorie transformationeller Syntaxen*. Frankfurt/M.: Athenaion.

Peters, St. 1970. "Why There Are Many 'Universal' Bases". *Papers in Linguistics* 2: 27-43.

----- and R. W. Ritchie 1973. "On the Generative Power of Transformational Grammars". *Information Sciences* 6: 49-83.

Peterson, T. H. 1971. "Multi-Ordered Base Structures in Generative Grammar". *CLS* 7: 181-192.

-----. 1973. "Conjunction Reduction in Tagalog: A Global Rule or Case Grammar?" Unpublished Paper.

-----. 1974. "Auxiliaries". *Language Sciences* 30: 1-12.

-----. 1977. "On Constraining Grammars through Proper Generalization". *Theoretical Linguistics* 4: 75-127.

Postal, P. M. 1968. "The Cross-Over Principle". Duplicated prelim. version.

-----. 1969. "Anaphoric Islands". *CLS* 5: 205-239.

-----. 1971. *Cross-over Phenomena*. New York: Holt, Rinehart & Winston.

-----. 1972. "On Some Rules that Are Not Succesive Cyclic". *Linguistic Inquiry* 3: 211-222.

-----. 1972. "A Global Constraint on Pronominalization". *Linguistic Inquiry* 3: 35-59.

-----. 1974. *On Raising*. Cambridge/Mass.: MIT Press.

-----, and J. R. Ross 1971. "Tough Movement, Si, Tough Deletion, No". *Linguistic Inquiry* 2: 544-546.

Pütz, H. 1973. *Über die Syntax der Pronominalform 'es' im modernen Deutsch*. Paris: DRLAV.

Praetorius, F. 1879. *Die amharische Sprache*. Halle/S.

Presch, G. 1977. *Syntaktische Diskontinuität*. Hildesheim: Georg Olms.

Pullum, G. K. 1976. "The Duke of York Gambit". *Journal of Linguistics* 12: 83-102.

-----. 1977. "Word Order Universals and Grammatical Relations". In: P. Cole and J. M. Sadock (eds.) 1977: 249-277.

Quine, W. V. O. 1960. "Variables Explained away." *Proceedings of the American Philosophical Society* 104: 343-347.

Quirk, R., and S. Greenbaum 1973. *A University Grammar of English*. London: Longman.

Radford, A. R. 1977. *Italian Syntax: Transformational and Relational Grammar*. Cambridge University Press.

Reid, A. A. et al. 1968. *Totonac: From Clause to Discourse*. Oklahoma: Summer Institute of Linguistics of the Univ. of Oklahoma.

Reis, M. 1976. "Reflexivierung in deutschen A.c.I.-Konstruktionen: Ein transformationsgrammatisches Dilemma". In: *Papiere zur Linguistik* 8. Frankfurt/M.: Scriptor.

Robinson, J. J. 1969. "Case, Category and Configuration". *Journal of Linguistics* 6: 57-80.

-----. 1970. "Dependency Structures and Transformational Rules". *Language* 46: 259-285.

Rodman, R. "Scope Phenomena, 'Movement Transformation' and Relative Clause". In: B. Partee (ed.) 1976: 165-176.

Rosenbaum, P. 1967. *The Grammar of English Predicate Complement Constructions*. Cambridge/Mass.: MIT Press.

-----. 1977. "Zapotec Gapping as Counterevidence to Some Universal Proposals". *Linguistic Inquiry* 8: 379-395.

Ross, J. R. 1967a. "Gapping and the Order of Constituents". In: M. Bierwisch and K. E. Heidolph (eds.) 1970: 249-259.

-----. 1967b. *Constraints on Variables in Syntax*. MIT doctoral diss. (Mimeographed, Bloomington: Indiana Univ. Linguistics Club, 1968.)

-----. 1969. "Auxiliaries as Main Verbs". *Journal of Philosophical Linguistics* 1: 71-162.

-----. 1973. "The Penthouse Principle and the Order of Constituents". In: C. T. Corum, T. C. Smith-Stark and A. Weiser (eds.) 1973: 397-422.

Ruttenberg, J. 1976. "Some Difficulties with Cresswell's Semantics and the Method of Shallow Structure". In: *University of Massachusetts Ocasional Papers in Linguistics*. Vol. II. Amherst, Mass.

Sadock, J. M. 1970. "Whimperatives". In: J. M. Sadock and A. L. Vanek 1970: 223-238.

-----. 1971. "Queclaratives". *CLS* 223-231.

-----, and A. L. Vanek. 1970. *Studies presented to R. B. Less by His Students*. Edmonton, Alberta: Linguistic Research Inc.

Sampson, G. R. 1975. "One Fact Needs One Explanation". *Lingua* 36: 231-239.

Sanders, G. A. 1967. *Some General Grammatical Processes in English*. Indiana University doctoral dissertation.

-----. 1968. Mimeographed version of Sanders 1967. Bloomington: Indiana University Linguistics Club.

-----. 1969a. "Invariant Ordering". Univ. of Texas at Austin. Mimeo.

-----. 1969b. "On the Equational Nature of Grammar". Austin, Tex.: University of Texas at Austin. Mimeo.

-----. 1970. *Invariant Ordering*. Mimeographed version of Sanders 1969a. Bloomington: Indiana University Linguistics Club.

-----. 1972. *Equational Grammar*. (Rev. version of Sanders 1969b.) The Hague: Mouton.

-----. 1975a. *Invariant Ordering*. (Rev. version of Sanders 1969a.) The Hague: Mouton.

-----. 1975b. "On the Explanation of Constituent Order Universals". In: C. N. Li (ed.) 1975: 389-436.

-----, and J. H.-Y. Tai. 1969. "Immediate Dominance and Identity Deletion in Mandarin Chinese". Paper presented at the Winter Meeting of the Linguistic Society of America, December 29, 1969.

-----. 1972. "Immediate Dominance and Identity Deletion in Mandarin Chinese". (Rev. version of Sanders and Tai 1969.) *Foundations of Language* 6: 161-198.

Saumjan, S. K., and P. A. Soboleva. 1963. *Applikativnaja poroždajuščaja model i isčislenie transformacij v russkom jazyke*. Moscow: Izd. Akademii Nauk SSSR.

Schachter, P. 1977. "Reference and Role-Related Properties of Subjects". In: P. Cole and J. Sadock (eds.) 1977: 279-306.

Schmerling, S. F. 1976. *Aspects of English Sentence Stress*. Austin: Univ. of Texas Press.

Schpak-Dolt, N. 1977. *Zur Semantik von Tempus und Aspekt des Russischen im Rahmen einer λ-kategorialen Sprache*. Doct. Diss., University of Konstanz.

Schwartz, Arthur. 1972. "Constraints on Movement Transformations". *Journal fo Linguistics* 8: 35-86.

Seuren, P. A. M. 1974. *Semantic Syntax*. London: Oxford University Press.

Shibatani, M. (ed.) 1976. *Syntax and Semantics. Vol. 6: The Grammar of Causative Constructions*. New York & London: Academic Press.

Smaby, R. 1975. *Ambiguity of Pronouns: A Simple Case*. University of Pennsylvania. Mimeo.

-----. 1976. *Ambiguous Coreference with Quantifiers*. University of Pennsylvania. Mimeo.

Staal, J. F. 1967. *Word Order in Sanskrit and Universal Grammar*. Dordrecht: Reidel.

von Stechow, A. 1975. "Zur formalen Syntax und Semantik des Deutschen". In: *Arbeitspapiere des SFB 99 'Linguistik'*. Konstanz: Univ. of Konstanz.

-----. 1976. *Deutsche Wortstellung und λ-kategoriale Sprachen*. Konstanz: Univ. of Konstanz. Mimeo.

-----. 1977. "Semantische Präsuppositionen". In: *Arbeitspapiere des SFB 99 'Linguistik'*. Konstanz: University of Konstanz.

Steinberg. D. D., and L. Jakobovits. (eds.). 1971. *Semantics: An Interdisciplinary Reader in Philosophy, Linguistics and Psychology*. Cambridge: Cambridge University Press.

Steinitz, R. 1969. *Adverbial Syntax. Studia Grammatica* 10. Berlin: Akad.-Verlag.

Stockwell, R., P. Schachter and B. H. Partee. 1973. *The Major Syntactic Structures of English*. New York: Holt, Rinehart & Winston.

Tai, J. H.-Y. 1969. *Coordination Reduction*. Ph.D. dissertation. Bloomington: Indiana University. Mimeo.

-----. 1973. "Chinese as an SOV Language". In: *Papers from the Ninth Regional Meeting of the Chicago Linguistic Society:* 659-671.

Tesnière, L. 1965. *Eléments de syntaxe structurale*. Paris: Klincksieck.

Thomason, R. H. 1976. "Some Extensions of Montague Grammar". In: B. Partee 1977: 77-118.

Tic Douloureux. 1971. "A Note on One's Privates". In: A. Zwicky et al. 1977: 45-51.

van Dijk, T. A. 1972. *Some Aspects of Text Grammars*. The Hague: Mouton.

-----. 1977. *Text and Context: Explorations in the Semantics and Pragmatics of Discourse*. London: Longman.

Vennemann, T. 1971. "Natural Generative Phonology". Paper read at the 1971 meeting of the Linguistic Society of America, St. Louis.

-----. 1972. "Phonological Uniqueness in Natural Generative Grammar". *Glossa* 6: 105-116.

-----. 1974. "Topics, Subjects and Word Order: from SXV to SVX via TVX". In: J. Anderson and C. Jones (eds.) 1974: 339-376.

-----. 1976. Unpublished talk given at the University of Lancaster, May 1976.

Vincent, N. 1976. "Perceptual Factors and Word Order Change in Latin".
    In: M. B. Harris (ed.) 1976: 54-68.

-----. 1978. "Some Issues in the Theory of Word Order". *York Papers in
    Linguistics* 8.

-----. forthcoming. Review of P. Cole and M. Sadock (1977). To appear
    in *Journal of Literary Semantics*.

Wackernagel, J. 1891. "Über ein Gesetz der indogermanischen Wortstellung".
    Indogermanische Forschungen 1: 333-436.

Werth, P. N. 1976. "On the Semantic Representation of Relative Clauses in
    English". Unpublished Ph.D. thesis, University of London.

-----. 1977. "Focus-Pocus". *Pragmatics Microfiche,* Fiche 2.3, F. 3.

-----. forthcoming. *Focus and Grammar.*

Wilkins, W. 1976. "On Elimination of Variables in Syntax". Unpublished
    paper, Univ. of California, Los Angeles.

Williams, E. S. 1977. "Discourse and Logical Form". *Linguistic Inquiry* 8:
    101-139.

Woodbury, A. C. 1977. "Greenlandic Eskimo, Ergativity, and Relational
    Grammar". In: P. Cole and J. M. Sadock 1977: 307-336.

Wurzel, W. U. 1970. *Studien zur deutschen Lautstruktur.* (Studia Gramma-
    tica, 8.) Berlin: Akademie-Verlag.

Zwicky, A. et al. 1971. *Studies out in Left Field.* Edmonton, Alberta:
    Linguistic Research Inc.